IT'S A
HELL OF A LIFE
BUT NOT
A BAD LIVING

IT'S A
HELL OF A LIFE
BUT NOT
A BAD LIVING

Edward Dmytryk

NYT
Times
BOOKS

Published by TIMES BOOKS, a division
of Quadrangle/The New York Times Book Co., Inc.
Three Park Avenue, New York, N. Y. 10016

Published simultaneously in Canada by
Fitzhenry & Whiteside, Ltd., Toronto

Library of Congress Cataloging in Publication Data

Dmytryk, Edward.
   It's a hell of a life but not a bad living.

   Filmography: p. 299
   Includes index.
   1. Dmytryk, Edward.   2. Moving-picture
producers and directors—United States—Biography.
I. Title.
PN1998.A3D5854   791.43'0233   78–58166
ISBN 0–8129–0785–X

Manufactured in the United States of America

For Jean –
My Only Love

". . . the most extraordinary thing about my life
was the people in it."

—EDNA ST. VINCENT MILLAY

CONTENTS

 1. Flowers for Miss Gish   3
 2. If the Projectionist Likes It, It's a Hit   7
 3. The Movies Talk—and Talk—and Talk   10
 4. The Gold Rush to Sound   14
 5. Low Wages, High Hopes   18
 6. "Butchers" and Geniuses   21
 7. Down and Out in Hollywood   26
 8. Cheating Is an Art   30
 9. Renaissance in Tinseltown   34
10. Free and Easy   40
11. "Use It": Directing the Bs   45
12. Another Ill Wind   51
13. How to Ruin a Tenor   57
14. The Cold War and the Duke   63
15. The Party's Over   69
16. New Dreams   73
17. A Very Good Year   79
18. "Mr. RKO"   88
19. The Hottest Act in Town   93
20. "This Is War!"   99
21. Whistling in the Dark   104
22. A Dog's Life   110
23. Christ in Concrete   115
24. There's Madness in the Method   119
25. The Fighting Is Over   125
26. Building Time   132
27. The Big Decision   138

28. Out of the Party and in the Red   144
29. A New Deal   165
30. *The Caine Mutiny*   171
31. A Turn with the Greatest   179
32. Hollywood, International   187
33. Bogey   194
34. "Read the Lyrics, Kid"   198
35. Monty   208
36. *The Young Lions*   219
37. The Fastest Gun in the West   231
38. Fits and Starts   238
39. Before *The Flying Nun*   248
40. Hollywood on Hollywood: *The Carpetbaggers*   256
41. Time Out   263
42. Bayou Country   270
43. Never Say No to An Admiral   274
44. And Never Mess with a Myth   280
45. Liz, Dick, and a Dash of Paprika   286
46. A High-Risk Life   296
    Filmography of Edward Dmytryk   299
    Index   301

IT'S A
HELL OF A LIFE
BUT NOT
A BAD LIVING

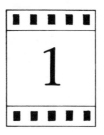

1

FLOWERS FOR MISS GISH

My life has been one long roller-coaster ride. I've had more ups and downs than a two-bit whore in a lumber camp. And I've learned one thing. Every time fate beckons with her middle finger, it's a complete surprise. Misfortune doesn't take off her coat, put up her dukes, and say, "Come on, let's fight." She creeps up on you when you're not looking, clobbers you, then keeps hitting you while you're down.

I was fourteen when I realized that the beatings I was getting at home were counterproductive. So I split, a sweater on my back and thirty-five cents in my pocket. For some unremembered reason, I headed for Chicago. But the high Mojave can be miserably cold in January, and two days of riding in open gondolas and two nights of freezing in the open desert brought me to my senses. I turned back to Hollywood, but not to home.

After an enlightening experience with the juvenile authorities, who finally conceded I might be safer on my own than in the bosom of my family, I settled down to work my way through high school. That was no new experience—I had been carrying my weight with the family budget since I was six years old. I had peddled papers on street corners, delivered them morning and evening, caddied at the Los Angeles Country Club (where I learned that the richer the player, the smaller the tip), but now none of these jobs was steady enough. And in the Hollywood of that day, work meant agriculture or movies—corn or Corn.

Fortunately, I had a great, good friend. Harry C. James was the head of a boys' organization I had belonged to, the Woodcraft Rangers. A friend of Harry's, Victor Clark, was one of the heads of the Famous Players–Lasky Hollywood studio, soon to be known as Paramount Pictures. He charitably "made" a job for me as a messenger and handy boy in the studio's sample-copy room. The pay was $6 a week. On March 23, 1923, I reported for work.

I had been placed with a private family where I got breakfast, dinner, the use of the bathroom, and a bed on the sleeping porch. All this cost me six dollars a week.

$6 − 6 = 0$. And there was the matter of lunch, clothes, and transportation. Transportation was no problem—I had a workable thumb. Lunch was easy—I served in the school cafeteria. Clothes, also easy—I joined ROTC. Questions of war and peace aside, I have always had a soft spot in my heart for ROTC. Through the last three years of high school, most of my wardrobe, complete with rolled leggings, came to me through the courtesy of the U.S. Army. I looked a little silly wearing my uniform on those occasional days when the corps was allowed to wear "civvies," but my fellow students were understanding, and I was too broke, busy, and bashful to have any dates, so it all worked out fine. It wasn't until many years later, in a Florabelle Muir column rationalizing my membership in the Communist Party, that I learned I had had a deprived childhood. If it hadn't been for Florabelle I never would have known.

In 1923 Famous Players–Lasky consisted of four stages, some offices, projection rooms, etc., on one square block bounded by Sunset and Vine, Selma and Argyle. The studio's back lot was across Argyle to the east, where a new laboratory was being built. Three of the stages were merely huge floors with no walls or ceilings. The fourth, the envy of Hollywood, was not only walled, but had a roof of clear glass. Though klieg lights were common, a good deal of the lighting was still provided by that same energy-saving sun that had attracted filmmakers to Southern California in the first place. Sets were usually three-walled and built side by side. Noise was no problem except infrequently, when the harmonium music from one set interfered with that from another a few yards down the line.

Vine Street was a half-paved, pepper-tree-lined country road. Sunset Boulevard, two lanes bordered by palm trees and rose bushes, was not much bigger. And cars were still driven primarily by the well-to-do. So actors could work in relative peace and quiet, reacting only to the offstage reed organ and the beseeching voice of the director begging for more of this or less of that.

Those were the days when, even in America, no well-brought-up lady would be caught dead carrying a package in public. And that's how I got to meet my first star. A hurry-up call from the main entrance, across the lot on Vine Street, told me I was needed. It turned out that Lillian Gish had been given a large box of flowers, and her car was parked some distance away. I lifted the box in both arms and followed her down the road. She was perceptive enough not to offer me a tip.

In spite of Miss Gish, the studio held no glamour for me, and I gave no thought to making films my life work. But I did have to get through high school, and, since my job was not essential, I knew I would have to make myself indispensable to last out the next three years as a part-time worker. So, like any good butcher's apprentice, I started to learn the trade.

The sample-copy room. That is now an archaic phrase, but then it was where a great deal happened. Our setup probably was not typical. Several young women and a couple of men worked in the room assembling the rushes of the previous day's shooting. At a height of about seven feet, a balcony circled the room and on the balcony were a number of workbenches and Moviolas. Here the film editors, working in close proximity, went about their daily tasks of "saving the picture." When a cutter had clipped together enough scenes and titles to fill a reel, she would lean over the railing and drop it down to be caught by someone on the floor below. It would then be handed over to one of the girls at a splicing bench where the film would be patched together. The girls couldn't catch as well as I could, and I had myself a job. Next, I learned how to splice. Hand splicing is a lost art now, but the Paramount sample-copy room had no splicing machines. We would see them in operation for the first time when the new lab was opened.

Hand splicing was a skill, though a minor one. Splicers had to learn just how much of a frame to cut, how to lick the overlapping bit of film with just enough spit to soften the emulsion that had to be removed, how to scrape it off with an Eveready razor blade without weakening the celluloid base underneath, how to apply the right amount of cement and then fit the pieces together so precisely that the doubled film would ride smoothly through the sprockets of the projection machine.

Hollywood unions were still some years in the future, so none of the girls complained that I was muscling in on her job. On the contrary, the splicers seemed to enjoy a bit of extra time for a smoke, and I felt useful. But the projection rooms intrigued me even more.

Most people have a complete misconception of the silents because, without special equipment, it is impossible to duplicate the conditions under which they were originally made and shown. I can remember no black-and-white silent pictures at Paramount, for example. All positive film stock was tinted and camera slates always indicated the color for each shot. An outdoor day scene would be printed on "straw" (pale yellow) stock, an outdoor night scene on "blue," an artificially lit interior on "amber," a fire scene on "red," and so on. No color today can catch the feeling of desert heat like sepiatone.

When sound track was placed on film, the "state of the art" made it difficult to get proper sound against the background of different colors. So all sound pictures, until the general use of color began in the fifties, were printed in black and white and the manufacture of tinted stock was discontinued. Whenever new prints of old silent films were needed, only black-and-white stock was available.

The term "flickers" is based on another misconception. I would have been fired for operating a projection machine so badly that the images flickered or moved too quickly. Silents were shot at a speed of sixty feet per minute. When projected at a similar speed, movement was completely normal. For technical reasons which any hi-fi buff can understand, sound speed was standardized at ninety feet per minute. Variable speed controls, standard on silent projectors, were removed from sound machines in an effort to keep the running speed smooth and steady. Consequently, when old silent prints are run on sound machines, all movement is half again as fast as when originally shown. That's why a couple of generations of movie viewers consider all old silent films "funny."

I spent every minute I could in the machine booths, and I soon got the hang of manipulating the seven knobs it took to keep the carbon crater properly centered in the lamp-house. In a short time the projectionists as well as the splicers were getting extra smoking time. I was settling in.

IF THE PROJECTIONIST
LIKES IT, IT'S A HIT

I n 1924 we moved into our new quarters in the lab across the street. The cutters now had individual rooms and the latest equipment. There were new splicing machines and the new projectors used Mazda bulbs as light sources so there were no more knobs to turn, no odor of burning carbon, and no jumping hot-spot to keep in constant focus.

No challenge. I could thread a reel, start the machine, sit down in my director's chair (even then), and for ten or twelve minutes study my homework by the spill-light from the lamp-house. Once in a great while, I became too engrossed in my books and there was an occasional fire, but over the years every projectionist has his fires. I guess the boss figured I was just chalking up my share.

Famous Players—Lasky was in the process of buying and setting up a new studio, complete with enclosed stages, at Bronson and Marathon, on the southern edge of Hollywood, but shooting continued at the Vine Street lot. The directors and supervisors still saw their rushes and cut reels in our viewing rooms—among them, James Cruze (still carrying prestige from *The Covered Wagon*), Raoul Walsh, Frank Melford, George Brennan, Alan Crosland (who married that loveliest of stars, Billie Dove), Buchowetski, "Wild Bill" Wellman, and, of course, C. B. De Mille. They took in stride the presence of a teen-aged projectionist in army khakis, and were generally friendly and kind.

At every opportunity I sneaked out on the lot to watch the shooting. One of the films I watched being made was the original *Ten Commandments*. I still remember Theodore Roberts standing on a rocky eminence built on one of the stage floors and shrouded in tarpaulin, receiving God's Commandments while lightning, created by electricians wielding scissor arcs, crashed around him.

("C.B., why do you make so many religious films?" asked Charles Laughton.

"It makes me feel—well—closer to God," answered De Mille.

7

"How cozy," said Laughton.)

A short time later, I looked in on Roy Pomeroy in his little workshop and watched him create the parting of the Red Sea in a little spillway built on a workbench no larger than a snooker table. The shot must have cost a few hundred dollars. A few decades later, for the remake of *The Ten Commandments*, C.B. spent several million dollars to create an effect that looked not one dime better. What was once created by imagination is now bought with dollars, and, like a cold-storage tomato, it doesn't taste quite the same. It is my firm belief that affluence in art is debilitating and leads to the erosion of creativity. In the scratching days, imaginative men and women created startling effects with light, shade, a cutout, a shadow. Josef von Sternberg put together a reel (*The Extra*) at a cost of $28.50 and won his chance to direct.

Now if you need five thousand bodies to fill a hall you hire five thousand bodies to fill a hall.

There is a relevant De Mille story, purely apocryphal I'm sure, which I first heard many years ago. C.B. was a guest of Adolph Ochs, who was now showing De Mille some of his fine old paintings. The old man gestured toward a large canvas at the other end of the room.

"How many people do you see on that canvas?" he asked. De Mille scanned it carefully.

"Over a hundred, I should say," he finally ventured. Ochs beckoned him across the room. Close up, only a few figures were explicit; the rest, suggested.

"That," said Ochs, "is Art."

I, too, think that making 500 look like 5,000 is a lot more creative than using 5,000. In other words, if you want to remain creative, stay poor—at all costs.

My boss had gotten tired of chasing me out of the projection booths back to the sample-copy room, and after a few months, I was allowed to spend my full working time as a projectionist. I was now able to watch the films progress from daily form through the various "cuts" to final completion—the "answer print." I ran occasional photographic tests of promising beginners for the executives, among them those of Dick Arlen and Gary Cooper, not to mention Betty Bronson and Mary Brian for *Peter Pan*.

I paid little conscious attention to these aspects of filmmaking, but I was aware of some of the more flamboyant side of studio life. Pola Negri uttered a couple of "damns" one day while viewing rushes. It was the first time I'd heard a woman swear. I was almost as impressed that the same Negri owned a different Rolls-Royce to match each of her fur coats.

Then there was the momentous occasion when I ran the first cut of *The Wedding March* for its director, the famous Erich von Stroheim. It was 126 reels long (that's 21 hours of film) and it took several days to run to its completion. I still remember certain portions vividly—one in particular of von Stroheim, playing the poverty-stricken but arrogant nobleman and cavalry officer, sitting his horse along the parade route of the Emperor Franz-Josef, and flirting with Fay Wray, a peasant girl, while her companion, a vulgar butcher (played by Matthew Betz), bit huge chunks out of a monstrous salami. Four reels (40 minutes) of bold looks from von Stroheim, shy glances from Fay Wray, and chewing and spitting from Betz taught me that good drama should mimic life in details, but never, never *in detail*.

For some months, von Stroheim labored to shorten the picture but couldn't get it under 60 reels. So the studio took it away from him and called in Paul Weatherwax for the final editing. If memory serves, Paul finally got the film down to 26 reels, enough for two full-length films. And that is exactly what F.P.–L. did—made two features out of it. The first, called *The Wedding March*, was released and died a miserable death at the box office, so the second was conveniently buried in the film vaults. What a shame! Because the picture, as a whole, was a dramatic and photographic work of art, at least to my immature mind. And wasn't I, after all, a projectionist?

Because they deal with so many intangibles, show people are generally a superstitious lot. For many years, directors, producers, and executives viewed the projectionist as a perfect example of the public norm; if the operator liked it, so would John Q. I often argued that if the projectionists (at the time I was making about 25 cents an hour) were that omniscient, they should be running Hollywood. Alas, superstition will get you only so far.

During the last few years of the silents, I also had the opportunity to man the booth for composers (or, rather, arrangers). It was the practice to write complete scores for some of the specials, or hard-ticket films, and send them to the first-run theaters along with the prints. Three such pictures were *The Wanderer of the Wasteland, Old Ironsides*, and *Abie's Irish Rose*. The routine was interesting, but at the same time very tedious.

First, the musicians (usually a composer and a pianist) would view the picture as a whole and then in pieces. At their request, I would run a small portion of the film, generally a sequence which might measure from fifty to four or five hundred feet. Then the house lights would go on while they rummaged through the reams of music they had brought into the viewing room, experimented with this strain or that, called for another look, tried another strain, ad infinitum. The music was usually a mixture of classical, sentimental, and pop. Nothing original was written, except for the bridges. All the musicians I ran for were night people, and the sessions lasted till dawn, six nights a week for several months. Now, I am a day person, and during the last of these jobs, in 1927, when I was living at a fraternity house at Cal Tech, in Pasadena, there were many mornings when my eyes would snap open at the Colorado Street bridge and I would try, without the least success, to remember how I had tooled my old Model T roadster around the many curves through Eagle Rock. I must have had an angel on my shoulder then. Where was he when I needed him in 1947?

THE MOVIES TALK—
AND TALK—AND TALK

S ometime during my last year in high school, I was called into the office of Hector Turnbull, a brother-in-law of Jesse Lasky and a supervisor at the studio. He had often viewed rushes in my projection room, and on occasion I had run films at his home on the studio's portable machines. We had never exchanged more than the ordinary few moments of small talk, but for some reason he had interested himself in me and had checked into my school record. He offered to pay my way through any college or university I wanted to enter. There was an opportunity for a scholarship at Stanford, but since I had shown some originality in mathematics, I now decided the only place to go—if I could get in—was the world's greatest school of pure science, the California Institute of Technology, now more intimately known to anybody who follows our space program as Cal Tech.

Without any fuss, Turnbull handed me a check for $1,000. He made no conditions, asked for no reports—his only stipulation was that my record would be reviewed before arrangements were made for my sophomore year.

I was so high, I nearly blew it. I bought some new clothes and a Model T roadster (full price $15) which was to keep me mobile for the next three years. But I settled down in time to start school in the fall of 1926. For the first time in my life, I was able to indulge my passion for sports. I won my numeral in all the major sports and wrestling. I even made the Gnome Club, Frank Capra's old fraternity. In between, I worked at my studies and did relief duty at the studio during the Christmas and Easter holidays. I could always use the extra money, and, since all the students went home for the holidays, time could hang heavy in Pasadena.

Though I enjoyed the year at Cal Tech as something completely out of my world, now and then small second thoughts nickered at the back of my brain. I had been too young, too busy, and too shy to live the "Hollywood life"; still, some of the "knowingness" and extremely wide field of interests of the people among whom and for whom I worked had infiltrated my consciousness. I now found most of my fellow students— and even some of my teachers—unsophisticated, very bright but scholastically and socially narrow-minded. Before the splitting of the atom there wasn't much for a mathematical physicist to do but teach, and the ivory tower loomed as a prison rather than a retreat.

I realize now I was just looking for an excuse. I found the most convincing was my football knee, which I had acquired in frosh football. Since there were no cartilage operations then, I knew a football career, even at Cal Tech, was doubtful. Thus are life-changing decisions made—no football, no school. Film was to be my work from then on, and in the late summer, I reported my decision to Mr. Turnbull. He showed no surprise, no regret for his wasted $1,000, and offered no help or advice. A rare man.

Times were a-changing now. During the early twenties, a couple of interesting new developments had sneaked into the studios. I say "sneaked" because the film business has been by long odds the most reactionary in the world when it comes to research. The original movie tycoons believed they had caught on to a fad, something like the miniature golf courses of the thirties, a craze that would one day run its course, and they didn't want to get stuck with too much money invested in plant and inventory. Today's cameras are basically the same as those of sixty years ago; new lighting systems are only now coming into general use and these were developed for TV. The introduction of sound was an almost accidental by-product of the Bell Company's research to improve the telephone system. Sound refinements have come almost exclusively from radio and TV. There is the Academy, of course, founded by the studios to promote research; but so far its main accomplishments have been the awarding of some scholarships, the establishment of a first-class film library, and the Academy Awards.

The two developments were back projection, generally called "process," and the projection printer. Previously, separate background was married to foreground action through the medium of front projection, which was both time-consuming and only partly effective. (A much-improved form of front projection has surfaced again in the last few years and has proved very useful.) Back projection demonstrated its superiority and rapidly became an indispensable tool of the filmmakers.

The projection printer made it possible to change the image after it had been fixed on the negative. It could be enlarged to any size (limited only by the grain of the film), it could be run backward or forward at will, distorted, and each frame could be exposed at a different light intensity. The result was an almost infinite number of photographic effects, the most useful of which was the dissolve. Previously, all dissolves were made in the camera and remained immune to cutting or changing.

Now the director and cutter were free to time the dissolves as they wished, and to change the outgoing or incoming scene at will. Overnight, camera dissolves were out, and as fast as new effects were created, they were thrown on the screen: lap dissolves, barn-door wipes, flips, spirals, and dozens of others. Eventually, sanity and taste returned, and now most of these effects are reserved for commercials, some TV shows, and the occasional young director who is still more impressed by form than by substance.

Apparently, at the time, the Germans were too poor to invest in the new printers, so some of their pictures were released without any dissolves at all—nothing but straight cuts from scene to scene regardless of the lapse of time involved. A Warner executive saw one of these films, thought it was a cracking new technique, and ordered all dissolves eliminated from Warner films, a practice which continued for a number of years. Much later, some TV director saw one of these early Warner films, thought the straight cutting was a new technique, and it soon swept the field. It is still in considerable use, though the more conventional lap dissolve has made a remarkable comeback.

During my year at Cal Tech, the studio's major operations had shifted to the Marathon lot. There were new faces and new bosses, but few new jobs. After several weeks of unemployment, I pocketed my pride and called Hector Turnbull for help. He responded by arranging an appointment with the new studio boss, B. P. Schulberg. Now, who goes to the top for a fifty-cent-an-hour job? But, palms sweating, I arrived at Schulberg's plush offices, announced myself, and waited. And waited.

Two hours later I got up and left. I made my way to Turnbull's office where I angrily relieved myself of two hours of frustration. My chief beef was that bane of all loners, nepotism. Turnbull listened patiently, then gave me an answer that has kept me from losing my perspective ever since.

"You're picking a sandlot baseball team," he said, "and for your ninth man, you're down to one of two choices. Now, one of the two is a friend, and you know he can play at least a little baseball. The other is a stranger—he may be a potential Babe Ruth, but at this point you have no way of knowing if he can play at all. Whom would you choose?"

I have often thought that Turnbull staged the whole thing. Considering what he had already done for me, that was not beyond the realm of possibility. He had taught me a couple of lessons (though I didn't appreciate that until I was working again), and he offered me no further help. Now I was really on my own. And for a nineteen-year-old who had never asked for a job in his life, it was a little scary.

I had moved back with the family I had lived with during high school—well, actually another family had rented the house, but I came with it. Now I couldn't pay my board and room, and they couldn't afford to maintain a freeloader. They didn't kick me out, but they urged me repeatedly to go out and find a job. So each morning I left the house, walked ten to fifteen miles of pavement, and returned home late in the afternoon with a negative report. Until finally, one day on Hollywood Boulevard, who should step out of a shop door but my old friend and fellow projectionist, Ted Egan, who told me there was an opening at Paramount. While my guardian angel preened his wings in self-satisfaction, I hurried down to the studio. Sure enough, the job was waiting.

The studio was new, but the old sample-copy-room gang and the old cutters were still there, as were the old operators. It took me about two hours to feel at home. Back in the saddle again, but this time, which way to ride?

THE GOLD RUSH TO SOUND

The new gold rush was in full swing. Sound was in! Midnight supper was the busiest meal of the day.

But not all at once. It probably took the better part of a year, perhaps more. With the notable exception of Charlie Chaplin, all Hollywood was getting on the bandwagon. There were as yet no true sound stages, so heavy drapes were hung from ceiling to floor, creating the stuffiest enclosures imaginable but not ameliorating the noise problem very much. Most of the filming was done at night, when there was relatively little traffic on the nearby streets. There weren't any 100 percent "talkies" either, but every studio converted at least some of each film to sound to meet the competition at the box office.

Paramount had beaten its rivals to the punch with a combination of sound *and* "big screen" in *Wings*, William Wellman's salute to America's World War I air force. The Biltmore Theater, a legitimate house, was turned into a cinema for the hard-ticket presentation.

The first half of the picture was standard silent-film fare; then, after the intermission, came the thrill of a lifetime. As the curtain opened, the sound of revving airplane motors literally filled the house. Simultaneously, the visual image expanded past its normal proportions into a "big screen" (70 mm.) shot of a field of fighter planes warming up for the dawn patrol. The thunderous applause from the audience almost drowned out the sound of the airplane engines, and no one could fail to realize that the silent era was at an end. If memory serves, there was no dialogue—only sound effects—but that was enough. After this, almost anything could happen—and almost everything did.

During that time I had been fired for laziness and insubordination, and had spent part of my enforced hiatus in the warehouse of the American Can Company (my older brother was then the chief factory clerk), loading five-gallon gasoline cans into boxcars and piling packed crates into twelve-foot-high stacks. No fork-lifts then, only muscle power. After a few weeks, I quit and ate up what little principal I had through the following weeks of unemployment. By the time Paramount called me back to work, I had regressed to my early high school poverty level, and was spending my nights on a sleeping porch again, this time in a house just off Sunset and Gower. At least I could walk to the studio, not much more than a mile away.

The chief projectionist, a very decent fellow, assumed I had learned my lesson. I was eager to prove him right, and, incidentally, to feather my bare nest a little. I asked for all the overtime available, and I got it! Within three months, at sixty cents an hour, straight time, I had a new wardrobe, new living quarters, and a down payment on a brand-new apple-green Model A Ford coupe. Things were looking up, but I had a small problem—I had very little ambition. I had a great deal of competitiveness (I'm a lousy loser), a strong desire to excel, a fair amount of drive—but no goal at all. So I just let the swelling tide carry me along.

Work went on around the clock. One of my jobs was manning a portable projection machine on the set so the director, cameraman, and actors could see the previously shot silent scenes and match the new dialogue scenes—usually just the close-ups—to them. In one such stint, I spent three days and three nights on the set without going home. But so did nearly everyone else in the company. For most of us there was no such thing as overtime, but the extra meals were free. Midnight was a madhouse, with long lines of workers, technicians, and actors queuing up for their Swiss steaks cafeteria-style.

And most of us loved it. Every day, every hour, presented new problems, with no precedents to help point the way to solutions. And, of course, there were casualties—mostly artists, for it was the art form that was changing the most. Many actors were not at home with the spoken word; some had voices that grated on the ear. Some directors had no ear for dialogue, or for staging scenes under the new restrictive technical conditions. There was, as yet, no public input to rely on, and in many cases the executives overreacted, setting narrower limits than usual in their estimates of public taste. Just as their image of the ideal leading man was usually that of the "collar-ad" type, so the only acceptable male voice was a full, rounded baritone. It has become Hollywood gospel that John Gilbert's career was cut short by an effeminate voice. Not true. There is enough footage of Gilbert talking to give the lie to that belief, but who wants to scotch a good story? What is probably nearer the truth is that the MGM officials *thought* Gilbert's voice ranged the wrong octave; two decades later, they would not have given the "problem" a second thought.

The most obvious solution to the problems sound presented was to borrow from the "live" theater, where the spoken word had reigned from time immemorial. Players and directors were imported in droves, bringing new problems with them. What looked good behind the proscenium did not always look good on the screen. The movement, acting, and sound level aimed at the balconies was too much for the sound cameras, the readings were often mannered, the diction (I once heard "Wild Bill" Wellman describe it as "Kansas City British") was acceptable to the Broadway elite, but hardly to the Bible Belt.

For the actors, the solution was not too difficult. Some "naturalistic" acting had already made inroads into the theater, and these artists were gradually wooed to Hollywood, though it wasn't always easy. Many stars of the stage still regarded the movies as an illegitimate activity, and not an art form at all. But most of those who came found the transition not too difficult. A few, like Spencer Tracy, became the ideal film actors and the models for all aspiring cinematic thespians to follow. Then, happily, the industry discovered that a surprising number of silent-film stars—William Powell, Myrna Loy, Wallace Beery, Mary Astor, and Greta Garbo, to name a few—had the gift, for gift it certainly is, and soon, in this area, there was no void at all.

Directors faced a more difficult problem, one of confidence. Film directors were felt to be insecure with dialogue, and stage directors were definitely insecure with the camera. Most of them felt uncomfortable in a medium where a look or a gesture could mean more than a spoken phrase, where "upstage" and "downstage" were replaced by "camera left" and "camera right," and where the depth of a set was limited only by the number of arc lights available.

How to solve the problem? Why, by using codirectors, of course, and for a time the screen bore such titles as "Directed by Edward Sutherland and John Cromwell" or "Cyril Gardener and George Cukor," and other unholy combinations. The theory was simple: The film man placed the cameras and staged the scene physically; the stage man was in charge of the playing of the scene and the dialogue. There was one slight snag.

Definition: To direct—to regulate the activities or course of; to instruct authoritatively.

By nature, good directors are strong-minded men who consider sharing of control an invalid concept. In any efficient army, a strong general can take advice and delegate responsibility, but he will never delegate command. Still, somehow things turned out all right. A number of directors proved able to handle the new medium on their own. Oddly enough, most of the survivors, with a few exceptions, were film men; and the trend has continued in that line to the present day, with some modification taking place in the last few years.

In principle, photography changed little—actually, it suffered a good deal and for a very long time. At first, cameras (usually at least three: long shot, medium shot, close shot) were placed in soundproof boxes. Since these "coops" had to be small enough to be easily moved around the set between setups and not take up too much of the playing space, the equipment and three operators crammed them to the limit. A commonplace sight was three men reeling out of an oxygen-starved booth at the end of a long take, gasping for life and breath.

Using several cameras simultaneously (a common practice in live TV filming) may save time, but it is impossible to use one set of lights for a long shot, a medium shot, and a close-up, and still achieve optimum quality in each shot. So quality suffered. Wide-angle lenses were a definite no-no. The setting of the lights was circumscribed by the placing of the microphone. Sound mixer and cameraman became natural enemies and some glorious scraps resulted. In the first few years, the mixer almost always won; his comeuppance was delivered by Orson Welles.

At first, microphones were either tied off overhead or camouflaged in convenient locations such as telephones or vases of flowers. Since the recording range was small, actors had to stand directly under or by the mike to be properly heard. If the scene required moving from one part of the set to another, the actors would cross in silence until they reached the vicinity of the next microphone. This procedure generally resulted in static scenes and bad staging.

In a comparatively short while, two of these problems were minimized. Each camera acquired a "blimp" of its own which kept it relatively silent while allowing a considerable amount of movement. The mike-boom permitted the mike-man to follow the actors and keep the mike in position for continuous recording. But the problem of lighting around the boom and microphone remained as troublesome as ever and continued to inhibit cameramen until Orson Welles, fresh from radio, ingeniously severed the shackles of sound, and photography became once more as effective as it had been in the last days of the silents.

The cutting rooms, too, underwent a qualitative and quantitative change. The addition of recorded sound presented many technical problems. Some of the women, intimidated by the new complexities, voluntarily retired. Others were replaced by department heads who felt that the ladies just couldn't cope; the fact that at least some of these ladies remained top editors right through the transition had little effect on their prejudices. Beyond this, the problems of working with a doubled amount of film, of keeping picture and sound track "in sync," of organizing the "trims" properly for possible later use, necessitated the establishment of a new working classification—the assistant cutter. There had always been apprentices, but the assistant cutter was a rarity before sound. Now there was a stream of personnel flowing into the cutting department, and because of the real and imagined difficulties involved in cutting sound, that stream was almost exclusively male. Fortunately, I was a man.

LOW WAGES, HIGH HOPES

T he projection department was an arm of the cutting department so there was an affinity between editors and operators, and in those changing, growing, nonunion days many young men entered the cutting rooms via the projection booths.

For some years I had been watching directors' rushes and the work of editors through the projection booth porthole. Working overtime also had its advantages: Occasionally a director with a knowledge of cutting would enter the cutting room to run a problem sequence through the Moviola. I would take up a position at the usually open door and listen to the experts' discussions.

On one such evening, Josef von Sternberg and Marlene Dietrich came in after dinner. He was running some cut film through the Moviola while she watched intently over his shoulder. At one point she winced and tapped him on the arm.

"Why that particular cut?" she asked. "It looks like a bad jump." (She was as smart as she was beautiful.)

"I want it to jump," said von Sternberg. "I want people to know there was a cutter on the film—me."

I felt there was something wrong with that answer, and years of experience have strengthened my opinions on that subject, but I'll discuss them in a later chapter.

When I finally decided to break into the cutting department, it was still early in the game, and there was only one man ahead of me on the waiting list—another projectionist. But when a job opened up, he had second thoughts. An assistant's pay was $40 a week, and he probably made $10 to $20 more as an operator. He was a good deal older than I, and a family man. The cut was more than he felt he could afford, and since a few bucks a week meant little to me, the job was mine.

I soon found that cutting had its own built-in incentives. I was doing those very things which had helped drive me from the sample-copy room—carrying piles of film cans and splicing miles of celluloid. Though weightlifting had been for years my chief form of exercise, voluntary and obligatory heavy labor are two very different things. I quickly made up my mind to abandon this work, but in looking around for an avenue of escape, I found the only way out was up.

However, in the interim there were compensations. My first picture as an apprentice cutter was *Burlesque*, later titled *The Dance of Life*. It starred Hal Skelley (who had created the leading role on Broadway) and Nancy Carroll. The directors were Edward Sutherland (movies) and John Cromwell (stage). The editor was George Nichols, Jr., a new man at the studio, and considered one of the two or three best cutters in the industry. Jane Loring, later a supervising editor at RKO, was cutting the film under Nichols' supervision, and I was her assistant.

Nichols was the son of George Nichols, Sr., a character actor of some reputation. His latest—and last—picture had been *The Wedding March*, for Erich von Stroheim. That film contained a bachelor-party sequence—a wild Austro-Hungarian orgy—and von Stroheim had saved it for the end of his schedule. He filled a stage at Paramount with actors playing dissolute aristocrats and gay women of all ages, shapes, and colors, and shot for a number of days. After the last "cut," those who wanted to leave were paid off and excused (few did), the doors of the stage were locked, and for the next few days the orgy continued in earnest. Nichols, Sr., who had played von Stroheim's father-in-law, was one of the guests who stayed. He had a reputation as a rather heavy imbiber, which he was now at some pains to uphold. His death from overdrinking spoiled the party. The younger Nichols never forgave von Stroheim, which seemed to me somewhat unfair. But he did have one kind thing to say about him. He noted that no matter how "unimportant" you were, von Stroheim always looked directly into your eyes when he talked to you, which was quite true, and rare enough in a town of overinflated egos to be worthy of comment.

Sound-cutting techniques were at a very primitive stage, and this alone made my job interesting. There were no sound Moviolas—at least not in our cutting department—so we learned to read lips, and, to some extent, sound modulations as recorded on the sound track. Lip-reading was not too difficult—reading sound track was another matter. But most of us learned to distinguish the different categories of sound, such as dialogue, music, or crowd noise (called "walla-walla" in the cutting rooms), and to pick out certain spoken consonants, of which the terminal "s" was the easiest to identify.

My familiarity with projection equipment, added to my scientific bent, made it possible for me to develop methods for circumventing or diminishing a number of the early difficulties. Each day brought a new problem to be solved, and I was soon doing such chores for most of the other cutters, as well as working on my own picture. Many of the techniques I initiated became standard practice, to be refined and improved by others as new equipment became available. Eventually, the introduction of magnetic tape made the whole thing obsolete, but the thrill of solving even small problems creatively stayed with me and helped shape my career in the ensuing years.

I had been an assistant for six or seven months when I suddenly got a chance to be a full cutter simply because I could speak Spanish. Sound looping and dubbing were still beyond our capabilities, and foreign-language films were in demand. It was the general practice to shoot a "foreign version" take of every scene. These scenes were later cut together by an assistant cutter. Since the art of lip-syncing had not yet been developed, the trick was to play the dialogue over the back of the character speaking, so the lack of proper sync would not be noticed. But it's pretty hard to fool those foreign devils, and the Spanish-speaking market, at least, was deemed profitable enough for straight shooting.

I cut two or three of these films in short order; then it was found that the babel of accents (in our ignorance, we had mixed Spaniards, Mexicans, Cubans, Argentinians, etc., with a fine disregard for the nationalistic ear) made no Spanish-speaking country happy, and another promising enterprise went down the drain.

But during this period I had developed a good working relationship with the director, Cyril Gardener, himself a former editor, and when he was assigned as codirector on a regular English-language film, *Only Saps Work*, I went along as editor. Subsequently, Gardener was assigned as codirector, with George Cukor, on *The Royal Family of Broadway*, a screen version of Ferber and Kaufman's Broadway hit *The Royal Family*. It had a topflight cast, headed by Ina Claire and Frederick March, and was to be shot at Paramount's Astoria studio on Long Island. And, happy day, I was assigned to cut it!

"BUTCHERS" AND GENIUSES

Them Big Apple! For a young man who had been born to
Ukrainian immigrant parents in the wilds of British Columbia, and outside of a sketchily remembered trip back to the
"old country" in the steerage of a stinking liner, had spent
his entire life on the West Coast, New York was—well—New York—
full of fresh surprises and drab disappointments.

It was 1930—the depth of the Depression. Apples were a nickel
apiece on almost any street corner. One French restaurant I frequented
served a really fine five-course dinner for a dollar. My single room at the
Barbizon Plaza, whose top floors were still unfinished, cost me $18 a
week with Continental breakfast. My expense allowance was $75 a
week, the equivalent of my salary. I lived like a king.

Still, even in those days New York could be a disappointment. The
streets were filthy, crosstown traffic was impossible, the theater was
largely mediocre, and the residents shockingly rude. It was in New
York that I learned one of life's axioms: The livability of any large city is
directly proportional to the quality of one's friends, and to the degree
that one confines oneself within the circle of those friends. So, after a few
of New York's rude residents became generous friends, life went on
pretty much as it does in any town. And I had a picture to cut.

On the first day of production I was introduced to the film's star, Ina
Claire.

"So you're the cutter," she smiled. "I suppose I'll have to be particularly nice to you." And that was about the last thing she said to me
during the entire production.

This brief anecdote illustrates two points: Cutting is recognized as an
important part of filmmaking, and, generally speaking, no one has to be
nice to anyone else to ensure proper consideration in the making of a
film. If I seem to accentuate the role of film editing throughout this
book, it is for two reasons. First, it was in the cutting rooms that I
learned the rudiments of filmmaking. Second, a consideration rarely, if

ever, remarked on: Cutting is the only film craft that is entirely indigenous to the cinema. As such, it has some bearing on every other facet of the art.

Sometime in the middle thirties a Baron Rothschild was touring the studio. He was brought into my cutting room for a rundown on the "art" of film editing. After twenty or thirty minutes, I ran out of breath. He politely concealed a smile.

"If I understand you correctly," he said, "this is where films are *really* made."

Well, sometimes. It might be argued that cutting *is* Motion Pictures. Certainly, before the development of cutting, films were merely photographed stage plays, employing only full shots, with the players favoring the camera—much as they do today in most live TV shows. As the cutters' skills developed, so did the opportunities for more wide-ranging use of camera setups and dramatic effects.

Not that this made everybody happy. It was George Jean Nathan, I believe, probably history's first Hollywood-baiter, who deplored the screen because people's legs were frequently cut off. Sometimes, when I'm confronted with one of the huge super-close-ups spawned by the electronic medium, I'm inclined to agree with old George Jean.

It is the "in" thing today to admire the skill, the strength, the "art" of the early movies. Trends and movements are discerned and analyzed, psychological motivations and effects are discovered in almost every frame of film. Directors once considered near-idiots are hailed as geniuses. And almost every surviving filmmaker of the "good old days" is enjoying the laugh of his life.

In the Hollywood I grew up in, a Director of Photography was a cameraman, an Art Director was a set designer, a Script Supervisor was a script girl (or boy), and "Art" was a dirty word. Empiricism was the watchword of the day, though probably not one film worker in twenty had heard the word and not one in a hundred could define it. So I hope the American Society of Film Editors will forgive me for using the words "cutter" and "cutting" more frequently than the more dignified terms, "Film Editor" and "Film Editing." In what I know is a losing battle, I enjoy resisting the intellectualization of the movies or, as some would say, The Cinema.

Long before I started my career, cutting had been developed to a remarkably high degree with an almost Renaissance–like speed. It is probable that the Italians, the first masters of the movie camera, originated the "close-up." It is certain that D. W. Griffith (or someone working with him) created the technique of intercutting, which made true suspense possible. The viewer could now see each of two trains speeding blindly toward a head-on crash, see them separately and from different points of view in succeeding moments of time. He could see the cavalry riding hell-bent to the rescue of the besieged wagon train and worry whether the soldiers would get there in time. And by the proper alignment and timing of the cuts, a good cutter could inflame that concern, build it up to near-trauma, then let it explode with relief at the inevitable rescue. For the magic of the movies is that, when properly cut, the "payoff" never *seems* inevitable, no matter how often a similar sequence has been seen.

In silents it was possible to make decided changes in a picture through the manipulation of titles. Roy Stone, who had cut for Thomas Ince, once told me that Ince would occasionally stow a rough cut in the vaults if he felt the time was not quite ripe for its release. On taking it out again, he might decide that the story line needed changing. If in the original cut an actor and actress had been brother and sister, an explanatory title could easily make them lovers. Or if it were decided to eliminate one of the characters partway through the picture, a title could easily send him on a long trip to China or to his grave.

Sound rendered such drastic changes impossible without extensive reshooting, nor were they often considered necessary. But emphasis and tempo are something else. By the use of overlapping cutting, the pace of a scene can be increased considerably. The opposite effect, that of slowing up the tempo, is also frequently used. For instance, a statement is made by a player, followed by a cut to the listener. The length of the listener's reaction can be stretched out at will, often accentuating the effect of the statement. This artificial delay of an actor's response has been one small tool in a good cutter's kit for as long as I can remember— at least a full generation before Marlon Brando popularized it as standard acting technique and made the *shortening* of the actor's reaction an absolutely necessary part of the cutter's craft.

"It was saved in the cutting room" is a phrase often heard in Hollywood, and once in a while that's true. But I have also seen pictures destroyed by unskilled cutters, or as we call them, "butchers." A little bit of saving or a litle bit of butchering can be found in most pictures.

One of the odd but interesting facts about any art form is that during the act of creation no one sees it as it actually is—not the artist himself, nor any other interim viewer. The author writes a scene and finds unanticipated possibilities. A director starts working with the script and discovers more penetrating motivations and different facets of character not noted in the script but inherently there. A creative actor will make discoveries about his screen character that neither the writer nor the director was aware of. And whoever does the editing will sometimes put the existing scenes together in ways that were not planned for when these scenes were shot. A part of the magic of show business is that when the project is a superior one, such continuing discoveries ring true and bring increased interest and clarity to the film.

Deletion can be as important and useful as intensification, and is much more common. A frequently encountered fault in all scripts, good and bad, is overwriting. The cure is obvious: surgery.

"The face on the cutting-room floor" is a phrase widely known even outside the industry. And many aspiring actors and actresses have blamed all kinds of selfish or vengeful interests for their lack of presence in a film they worked in. The truth is that scenes are eliminated because they are found to be extraneous to the story. Sometimes they merely hold up the action; sometimes they actually weaken the film.

I have known only one instance of ego-based deletion. The film starred Mae West, who wrote most of her own material. Her contract gave her final editing approval. At our first preview, the picture was well received, but the biggest howl of the evening was in response to a line delivered by the leading man. Nothing was said that night after the showing, but she was waiting when I arrived at the studio the following morning. The line had to go! In vain I argued that she had written the line herself and should be proud of its success, that the laugh was good for the picture and anything that was good for the picture was good for her (an old ploy). Still, the line had to go. And it went. But once in a lifetime isn't bad, is it?

Another form of deletion is more in the nature of a face-lift: correcting some actors' mannerisms. It is quite common for stars to be mannered—a particular manner is often the basis for a star's popularity. But a mannerism can become a crutch, an affectation, ultimately self-defeating.

Example: *Ruggles of Red Gap*, directed by Leo McCarey in 1934, and starring, among others, Charles Laughton. Laughton had a "rubber" face, and, though certainly a very fine actor, was occasionally given to severe attacks of mugging. Throughout the film I had to carefully cut around much of his face-making, particularly in his close-ups. But one sequence proved to be a dilly. The scene is played in a saloon in a Western town. Laughton, an English butler to Charlie Ruggles, has accompanied his boss to the bar. At one point, Charlie Ruggles wants to quote from Lincoln's Gettysburg Address, but can't remember it. He calls on others in his party, the bartender, anybody, with no results. Suddenly their attention is arrested by Laughton, who, in a very low voice, starts to recite the speech. All are amazed that an Englishman should know the Address, and give him their rapt attention. Encouraged, he goes on, delivering the entire speech to the delight of his listeners, on screen and off.

Shooting the scene was hell. Laughton was highly emotional and extremely nervous. Getting his shots alone took a day and a half. McCarey, a very patient director, started the scene some forty or fifty times—rarely did he get a complete take, and never a perfect one. Finally Laughton was literally on his knees, begging for mercy. I suggested that by using the best parts of a number of takes, I could patch together a complete sound track and present it for McCarey's approval. He agreed and went on with the rest of the shooting. I cut together pieces of eighteen or twenty takes and got a complete speech that pleased Leo. But fitting the picture to the track brought chaos, since each sound cut needed a matching picture. Only one solution presented itself. After a shot of Laughton starting the speech, I stayed with the reactions of the others in the scene—first, Charlie Ruggles and his companions, then other onlookers as, one by one, they gradually left their seats and walked over for a closer look and listen. Offstage, Laughton's voice gradually strengthened with his confidence, and the speech ended triumphantly to the applause of the crowd and the shy discomfiture of Laughton himself.

Logic says that a great portion of the speech should be played on the speaker, but every time I looked at the matching film of Laughton, his rather generous lips were blubbering, his eyes were turning backward in their sockets, and huge tears (real) were running down his cheeks. I'm sure this was caused by his emotion and nervousness—he didn't have the faintest idea of what his face looked like at the time. Yet there it was. So, except for a short cut or two, the speech was played entirely over the shots of the onlookers.

For a very brief period, Ernst Lubitsch was head of Paramount Studio. Why such an outstanding director should want to play studio boss no one could understand, but there he was at our executive running, and his only suggestion was that I put in a few more cuts of Laughton during the delivery of the Gettysburg Address. McCarey went along, and I was outgunned. I picked a pair of the least offensive cuts available and put them in for the preview.

Ruggles of Red Gap turned out to be one of the top films of the year. At the preview, it played beautifully—up to the Gettysburg Address. The scene started, players on the screen reacted, everything still fine. Then came a cut of Laughton speaking, tears pouring down his cheeks. Our audience burst into immediate laughter, which continued to build throughout the rest of the now-inaudible speech. Each new cut of Laughton fueled the fire and by the end of the scene, there wasn't a dry seat in the house. It wasn't exactly the kind of reaction we were looking for. The following morning the extra cuts of Laughton were deleted, and the next preview confirmed the good judgment of that decision. The scene became famous in its own right and, until the end of Laughton's life, hardly a Lincoln's Birthday passed without some national radio network inviting that fine actor to deliver Abe's most famous speech. He almost always accepted. So, you see, a cutter can make something out of nothing—or, when necessary, nothing out of something.

But I was hardly aware of these things, and many more, when I finished *The Royal Family of Broadway* and headed back to Hollywood. I had a great deal to learn about cutting, and much of it was to be learned the hard way.

DOWN AND OUT
IN HOLLYWOOD

New Year's Day—1931. I had the flu, the finest case of delirium since my bout with scarlet fever, and a train ticket to Hollywood, dated January 2. I had to make it. The blue skies of Southern California were calling—no, screaming. I was sick of the cold, I was sick of sloshy streets, I was sick of getting cinders in my eyes. I was sick. D.T.'s on a train, I figured, could be no worse than D.T.'s in a lonely hotel room. I made it.

Four days later I arrived in Los Angeles. The skies were unbelievably blue, the air was clean, sweet, and warm. I'll never be cold again, I thought, as I kissed the ground. But I was. The very next day when I got to the studio.

What a difference a day makes, runs the old saw, and I had been away for six months. It was a new studio, with a new policy and a new head cutter. There had been a top to bottom shake-up, and I was shaken out—finished. Barely twenty-two and a failure.

It seemed that every time Paramount changed its administration I was out on my tuckus. But what hurt most was that it now seemed to make sense. George Arthur had taken over the cutting department at one of those fortunate times in local history. First National had sold out to Warner Brothers, there were some first-class people looking for a new place to nest, and Arthur took advantage of the situation. He hired probably the finest group of cutters ever gathered together in one studio, including Stu Heisler and Hugh Bennet, Leroy Stone and Doane Harrison, Otho Lovering and Billie Shea. With new blood coming in, the old blood had to go, and, with one or two well-entrenched exceptions, we went.

Now I really got to know the Depression from the inside, an experience I would just as soon have missed. Seven months without work, and no welfare or unemployment insurance. A man could starve to death—and some did. I signed up with an already overloaded employment agency, and for several weeks I worked as a janitor at the Avon Apartments, around the corner from Columbia Pictures. It was an honest living but I found it difficult to dodge some of the tenants whom I knew and who were still working at the studio. Face is as important in Hollywood as in the Orient. After one near-miss, I quit. I knew a couple of car-less people and now and then got a tankful of gas for chauffeuring them around. And there was always Schwab's.

The Schwab brothers (I think there were three) had just one drugstore then, and they ran it themselves. You could go on the tab and never get any pressure. I don't know how many struggling young actors and technicians they carried through those years—it must have been hundreds, even thousands. But what a decent way to make a lot of friends.

There were bad things and there were good things. Meeting the girl who was to become my first wife—that was bad. Borrowing money from Eddie Knopf—that was bad, but interesting in a way. I had worked for Knopf as a cutter at Paramount, and he was now preparing a script at Universal. It had been months since I had made a dollar and I owed every tradesman I knew. I didn't mind asking for credit, but asking for hard cash was like asking for work—nearly impossible. However, it had to be done, so I screwed up my courage, called on Eddie and asked for $300. I only had to sweat a little before he agreed to lend it to me.

A very short time later he and Willie Wyler chartered a sixty-five-foot schooner for a week's cruise to Ensenada with their wives. Eddie decided the trip would be good for my morale, which was at rock bottom, and invited me to go along.

Ensenada was a beautiful, sleepy village then. But it did have a couple of small gambling salons, and there my hosts betook themselves and quickly got rid of all their ready cash. A telegram to Hollywood soon brought several thousand dollars more, which shortly disappeared down the same drain. The effect on me was considerable. A few days before I had had to nearly get down on my knees to borrow $300, and here was my benefactor, throwing thousands away. It was enough to drive a man to socialism. I've never gambled seriously since then. At least, not for money.

But, some of the best things in life *are* free. A friend of mine played piano at the College Inn, down below street level at the Roosevelt Hotel on Hollywood Boulevard. A cup of coffee cost a nickel and, since the place was rarely crowded on week nights, no one minded my spending a couple of hours listening to the music. Musicals were coming in, the leading lights of Tin Pan Alley were all on the Coast, and the College Inn was one of their hangouts. Doug Fairbanks and Charlie Chaplin dropped in often, as did many scarcely lesser personalities.

John Carradine walked the Boulevard, threadbare overcoat thrown capelike over his long, thin bones, his Barrymore hat perched jauntily on his hollow-cheeked head. He often came down to the College Inn, ordered a cup of coffee, and sat quietly until the bellboy, previously primed with a two-bit piece, came bouncing down the steps. "Mr. John Carradine—calling Mr. John Carradine!" With a sweeping wave of the arm and his most Barrymoreish enunciation, Carradine would get the boy's attention. "Here, boy!" He would rise, pick up his walking stick, and stalk grandly up the stairs to disappear until the next time he had two bits to spare. I never saw Fairbanks or Chaplin pay the slightest bit of attention, and indeed it was some years before Carradine began to get the notice and the work he so richly deserved.

Another colorful watering place was Henri's Restaurant. During the long period of our all-night stints, George Nichols, a couple of his other assistants, and I would drop in between 5:00 and 7:00 A.M. for a bowl of graveyard stew. There was a double entryway with a cashier's counter in between. Immediately in front of the cashier's counter was a brick floor, measuring perhaps 10 by 12 feet, then a long, relatively narrow passage whose center was occupied by a delicatessen counter. This finally opened into a large, well-lit dining room where Hollywood's best food was served twenty-four hours a day. Our time of the morning was showtime at Henri's.

Just across from the cashier's counter sat a piano, complete with player—usually a volunteer. The smooth brick floor was an almost perfect place for dancing, and on entering or leaving, we would usually take a few seconds to watch the "rolls" and "breaks" of some tap dancer showing off his wares.

The small hours of Saturday morning were special. The renowned Madame Frances would sit at a large table accompanied by five or six of her newest girls. Where better to display fresh goods to her clientele?

I certainly wasn't eating at Henri's now. Simon's cafeteria on the Boulevard was more my style, but sometimes fate lets you up as suddenly as she knocks you down. George Arthur called me in to talk about a job. I made the studio in record time, but the talk was a shock. I could come back to work at my old salary, but as an assistant. I was too stunned to speak or get up to leave, so Arthur had a chance to explain. He was inaugurating a new and unique system at Paramount—a cutter would stay on the set during the shooting to help the director if and when he could. An assistant—really a second cutter—would put together the rough cut under the first cutter's supervision, after which the first cutter could take over the final editing of the film or continue in a purely supervisory capacity.

Arthur promised me early consideration for promotion, the salary was good, and I had no choice. I took the job.

8

CHEATING IS AN ART

I t is no original observation that fortune works in screwy ways. A number of potentially fine artists have been ruined in Hollywood because they made it too fast, particularly in recent years. They push too hard and take off too soon. The resulting crashes are messy—even the infinitely talented Orson Welles couldn't keep himself on track. A young director who gets an early break will usually make his first picture with the freely given support of every member of an experienced crew, particularly the cameraman and the cutter. If the neophyte's first film is a success, his head inflates and off he floats even though he isn't fully feathered yet. As a rule, he begins to consider advice a threat to his authority, so little is offered. Failure is assured.

You still learn your trade on the field of battle. Not only does each film present its own problems, but many of the more profound aspects of characterization and character interaction are beyond the range of youthful experience. Contrivance, action, flashy technique—yes. Substance—well, rarely.

"Changing with the generation" once meant that an artist dealing in ideas could coast along for twenty or thirty years on his store of awareness. Now an ideological generation rarely lasts ten years. Most "old-timers" fall by the wayside because they can't accommodate the new attitudes which arrive with each new decade. And some kids become "old-timers" in a hell of a hurry. Good groundwork, a solid base, is priceless, but it does take time.

Against my will, I was given the time. Working without pressure, since Roy Stone was there to rescue me if I got into trouble, I began to find out a few things about myself. I thought I knew so much, but I really knew so damned little.

Stone was a taciturn, almost inarticulate man, thoughtful and unselfish. Knowing my previous position, he never once put scissors to film, but let me handle all the actual cutting from the first day's rushes to the final print. This not only salved my injured pride, but gave me greater opportunities to experiment. His advice, when offered, was invaluable.

He was soft in criticism and free, though subtle, with his praise. I was finally learning how to cut a picture, but I was learning even more about people.

Cutters generally have a tendency to act tough. Ask one how the rushes looked that day, and he'll say, "Okay," and very little more. He is the supercritic, examining every facet of a scene with microscopic eye. He will overlook the clever staging or effective acting to nitpick at some bit of mismatched action. Perfection he takes for granted.

I had made a very bad impression on George Cukor during the shooting of *The Royal Family of Broadway* because I was so intent on playing the cutter. I usually saw the rushes in the afternoon, then would go down to the set. Naturally, Cukor and Gardener would enquire about the rushes. My terse answers would turn Cukor off immediately. Gardener, who had been a cutter, understood my attitude and knew he had only to wait and draw me out a little, and I'd soon be telling him everything he wanted to know. It was years before I realized that no one, no matter how exalted he may seem, is so secure that he doesn't welcome a reassuring word about his work. If there is one single thing that separates art from mere craftsmanship, it is the uncertainty of knowing whether what you're doing is worth a damn.

The first picture I cut under Stone's supervision was directed by George Cukor. He did a double take when I walked on the set and stared in stony silence when Roy told him I was on the picture. I knew I was in trouble, but Roy soothed his feelings. By the end of the production, we were good friends, and it was partly because of the work I later did for Cukor as a full cutter that I got my chance to direct.

Working with Stone, I cut films like *If I Had a Million*, *Duck Soup*, *Six of a Kind*, and several others. *The Phantom President* was special. It was a musical, and it gave me the chance to experiment with some unusual techniques. And it starred George M. Cohan. Cohan was already a legend—a difficult man to touch, a difficult man to know. He was all theater, and I was impressed by his strict observance of one of the theater's oldest traditions: He never passed a beggar without dropping a silver dollar into the outstretched palm. Word got around, and for the duration of the film there was a bevy of beggars waiting for him at the Paramount gate every evening. He never failed them. After all, the actor's code says, "There but for the grace of God . . ." Not that every actor observes the code. But that's another story.

I was getting to know the directors, too. There was Cukor, of course, and Leo McCarey, Henry Hathaway, and Norman Taurog. Cukor was—and is—a perfectionist with dialogue. McCarey, in my opinion, was the best comedy-drama director in Hollywood. Hathaway is still known as a master of action. And Taurog—well, Taurog knew his way around the set and around people. And that was something I had to learn. I'd been a loner too long, and if I was to get anywhere, I had to let people know I could play a little baseball, just in case they were looking for a ninth man for the team.

It took nearly three years, but all things come to an end, and so did my apprenticeship. B pictures were coming in, which meant more pictures made and more cutters needed—and you just couldn't ask an A cutter to edit a B film. So Arthur kept his word, and I found myself cutting a Hathaway Western. Working with Hathaway was not considered a reward for work well done, but I was cutting again—all on my own—and any risk seemed worth taking.

Hathaway was not just a director, he was an experience—like a case of smallpox. If you get it you either die or get over it. Once over it, you're immune forever. People hated him and quit, or grew to love him. He took a little understanding. Hathaway had gone the distance. Starting out as a prop man, he had become an assistant director, then one of the few assistants who made it to the director's chair. He could do every job on the set and went wild if he thought a chore was being done incorrectly. I've seen him stop a carpenter to show him how to carry a plank.

There are probably more anecdotes about Hathaway than any other director, with the possible exception of John Ford. Most of them are true.

Henry demanded quiet while rehearsing—absolute quiet. One day on location a driver pulled his truck into a parking area just over the hill from where Henry was running his players through their lines. The hill masked out most of the sound of the truck, but not quite enough. Henry screamed for his assistant and demanded that the keys to all the vehicles be gathered up and given into his keeping. On a distant location that can mean a lot of keys, but Hank was adamant and refused to go on with the scene until the keys were gathered up in a hat and presented to him. For the rest of the day, the work went smoothly. Then the light grew yellow, and it was time to head for home and mother. But all the keys were company keys, and all looked pretty much the same. The end of a long working day is no time to start checking thirty keys in thirty locks. But that was now the order of the day, and it was only justice that Henry's limousine was one of the last cars identified.

Story number two: Hathaway was probably Hollywood's premier location director, and on this particular day he was shooting in Wall Street. The windows of the enclosing skyscrapers were filled with office workers craning down on the scene in the street below. For some time

Henry fought to control himself, but, as usual, it was a losing battle. Finally, throwing down his hat, he leaped from his chair, turned his face up toward the windows, and screamed, "God damn it, I don't look over your shoulders when *you* work!" Ulcers were Henry's occupational disorder.

I learned a lot of "don'ts" from Hathaway, but I also learned one "do"—how to cheat. Location in the summer calls for an early start indeed, generally between 7:30 and 8:00 A.M. With breakfast, traveling time, etc., that means the crew is up around 4:00 A.M., and so are the actors or actresses who have to be made up for the first shot. Henry was always an early riser, and each succeeding day he would start earlier and earlier. It usually took a strike threat to make him quit. Now, shooting with the sun is a tricky business. Some sequences take hours, or even days, to shoot. There's no modern-day Joshua to make the sun stand still—so the shadows move. And when they move too much, the shots don't match. That's where cheating comes in. To be able to cheat properly is one of the most useful (though noncritical) bits of technical knowledge in a director's bag. First, you must be willing to take a chance. Henry was fearless.

To lick a moving shadow, you have to move your players so the shadows on their faces stay relatively constant. But you can't move your scenery, so the background changes every time you move your people. If you're a background watcher (all sorts of kooks go to the movies), you'll notice the cheat. But if the scene is well played and holds your interest, you won't have the foggiest. The trouble is the director and the cutter know the cheating is there, and it takes an iron nerve to work on the film in the cutting room without becoming spooked by the various backgrounds of supposedly matching shots. You must have faith—and charismatic actors.

There are also many ways the technique can be used in interior shots. In a long shot, say the general tone is that of the deep red wallpaper. The close-up of one of the players, however, is framed by a doorway which opens onto a brightly lit set whose color is basically white. The doorway is not particularly noticeable in the long shot because it is only a small part of the total background, but, in the close-up, it fills the frame. Such a cut would be unpleasantly startling. So we move the player against a background more compatible with the long shot.

I use a variation of this in shots with background crowds. As I move in closer with my camera, I remove an increasing number of people from the background, until, in a fairly large close-up, there may be no one there at all. The technique is quite ancient. Some silent directors shot their close-ups against cloth backgrounds to get a portrait effect. What I learned from Hathaway is that nobody in the house will know.

After a couple of Westerns, I got a break. McCarey was starting *Ruggles of Red Gap*, and Roy Stone, his usual cutter, was on another picture. Roy recommended me, and Leo decided to take a chance. I was cutting As—again.

RENAISSANCE IN TINSELTOWN

N o one has ever satisfactorily explained the renaissance phenomenon, that recurring period in history when unusual numbers of supremely gifted men and women suddenly appear, and with a sunburst of activity, briefly illuminate the bleak atmosphere of human existence. (I'm not sure anyone has tried.) Films had such a period throughout the world from the middle teens to the middle thirties.

Genius surfaced simultaneously in many countries of the West— Russia, Germany, France, Scandinavia, England. Some of its names, like Dupont, flickered only briefly. Others, like Murnau, Lang, Renoir, Pabst, Lubitsch, and Eisenstein, burned with a flame that was extinguished only by death. Hollywood had more than its share—Griffith, Chaplin, Vidor, Ford, Capra, Wyler, Stevens—the names run on as long as memory lasts.

Leo McCarey was a book by himself. His father, Tom McCarey, had been a fight promotor at Vernon, an L.A. suburb, in the four-round limit days, and though Leo passed the bar, and even bailed a few prostitutes out of jail, he knew too many of his father's friends. Men like Mizner, Wagner, Fowler, and Geraghty can make a life at law seem very dull. Besides, he was a lousy lawyer.

But he was great material for the movies. He served a very brief appenticeship with Lord-knows-who, and was soon directing Laurel and Hardy two-reelers. He is generally credited with establishing the format which elevated those two comedians to fame.

When I went with McCarey on *Ruggles*, he was just reaching the top, but one would hardly know it. Insecurity was his middle name. He often told this story on himself: Leo had a habit of looking around at the crew after the completion of a good take to gather assurance from their joint reaction before committing himself to print it. Early on in the shooting, his eyes lit on one hefty electrician who stood with arms folded over a barrel chest. When he saw he had Leo's attention, the juicer, keeping a dead pan, slowly closed one eye in a leaden wink. From that moment on, no matter how he tried to prevent it, Leo's gaze would search out the electrician before he could okay a print. He always got the same response: the slow, knowing wink. "I thought, 'He's on to me!'" McCarey said. And slowly his confidence began to ebb. After a few days, he had the juicer transferred to another picture.

More to his liking was the grip who shouted, "That's a lily!" after every good take, saving Leo the trouble of having to look around. Comedy is a fragile thing, and what will bring down one house will leave another cold. There is a new jury at every performance. That's why most comedians (and singers, too) usually travel with an entourage—a peripatetic claque. They need the constant reassurance just to stay even with the world.

Paramount's practice of keeping the editor on the set was a wonderful source of education for the cutter, but it wasn't always a happy experience. Some directors considered the cutters a threat to their authority, and wouldn't be caught dead talking to one for fear some of the crew would draw the conclusion that they were asking for advice or listening to a suggestion. However, one condition worked in the cutter's favor and made a useful relationship possible in a large number of cases.

The director usually has no real assistant—not in the creative sense. The A.D. (Assistant Director) is an invaluable man, of course, but he is the foreman, the whip hand who, with the help of the production manager, keeps the company operating smoothly. He sees that the right actors are called for the right times, that the sets and locations are ready, the necessary extras are on hand (and often supervises their action), and has other duties too numerous to mention. He is probably the hardest-working man in the company. But, in a large percentage of cases, the assistant is really the production department's watchdog, helping but not really working with the director at all. At most studios, an assistant with a reputation as a "director's man" will have trouble getting employment. I suspect that a high vocational test score for an A.D.

would not at all match that of an equally high score for a director. Actually, until the advent of TV series, assistants became directors very infrequently, being promoted instead into the production department or even, on occasion, into producing.

So, if a director needs a "bouncing board" he looks to someone else. It might be the dialogue director (who does *not* direct dialogue), if such a person is used. In some cases, it might be the sketch artist. At times, if the production can afford his salary, the writer of the script may be on the set, but this can sometimes lead to more trouble than good. The cutter, on the other hand, drops into the slot nicely. To the production department, he is always a "director's man." His filmic concerns are those of the director, he has plenty of time on his hands, and he is usually a good listener. He can certainly help solve some simple problems like "Do we need a close-up here?" with some authority. And, if he is creative, he may even pop up with a clever solution to a more perplexing puzzle now and then.

One of my chief duties with Leo was keeping him on track. He had an amazingly fertile mind, and he worked in a somewhat unusual way. To most good directors, the script is a rough blueprint. All consider themselves writers, of sorts, though some will admit that, as Fred Allen put it, they write best on dirty paper. However, some will work the final drafts with the writer until they have the script exactly the way they want it and will then shoot it pretty much as finally written. Others, like McCarey, are incapable of rewriting until they actually start working on the scenes with the cast. Most are somewhere in between.

McCarey's films bore little relation to his starting scripts. Once on the set, he would gather his players and start chatting. He might tell a couple of funny stories (I gradually realized they usually had a subtle bearing on the scene), then start throwing tentative lines or bits of action at the players. They would try them on for size, pin them up a little here or there, and toss them back to McCarey. Sometimes he'd throw the whole mess out and start all over again. Or he might change the cut, sharpen the style, and toss it back to the cast. Eventually they would arrive at something all were happy with (though Leo was always the final and absolute judge) and McCarey would turn to the journeyman writer he always kept at his side and say, "Take it up and write it." While he and the cast ran through the scene for movement, the writer put the scene down on paper. Later, copies would be distributed to the concerned parties and, while the players went to their dressing rooms to memorize their lines, the cameraman and crew would begin to light the set. That's when my work with Leo would start.

The longer the scene stayed on his mind, the more convinced he was that it wasn't funny. And I would have to do my best to convince him that it was. I won more often than not—but they were tough battles to fight. Keeping a proper perspective on a scene after you've been over it a number of times takes tremendous discipline. Even Disneyland seems dull after you've been there a dozen times. A scene—particularly a comedy scene, which usually depends so much on surprise—can feel very flat after you've worked it out on paper and then rehearsed it with a cast. Try it yourself some time in the privacy of your own home. Tell the funniest story you know to your captive guests ten times running. Check the laugh meter after the final repetition. It won't even be close to a laugh—it will be a whimper.

My own recipe for minimizing the dulling effects of repetition is to hang on to the memory of my very first reaction. If I considered it superior when I first read it or worked it out, it must have had some impact—at least on me—and at that stage that's all that counts.

Leo had tremendous comedic inventiveness coupled with superior recall. He remembered every funny thing that had ever been said or done in his presence. And he was always pulling something out of his mental attic to see if it fit. He knew that some things which were not funny in past attempts might be extremely funny under new circumstances, and he never minded stealing from himself. The hilarious hat routine performed by Cary Grant in *The Awful Truth* was taken bodily from one of Leo's early Laurel and Hardy films.

Leo had made a picture at Paramount quite early in his career. The executive in charge of production was B. P. Schulberg, never notorious for his sense of humor. As the production progressed, the front-office reaction grew chillier and chillier. On the final day of shooting, an accountant stood by and handed Leo his closing check as he said, "Print it" on his last take. Leo took his coat off the back of the chair, went through the stage doors, and straight out of the studio. He didn't return until a new administration had taken over. But that wasn't enough.

"I'm a great hater," he told me. "It takes a lot to salve my pride. Every picture I make for Paramount costs them a half-million more than it should."

He meant it. The costliest item on the average film is time, and no one can waste it like a director with a beef.

Leo kept a piano on the set. He would start noodling while the set was being lit and appear to be lost in thought. When all was ready, the A.D. would approach the piano, trying to catch Leo's eye. No way! After five or ten minutes, the A.D. would essay a cough. Still no reaction. Eventually a quiet "Leo, we're ready." Nothing. After about half an hour, the A.D.'s fifth or sixth "Leo, we're ready" would bring a sudden shake of the head, a focusing of the eyes.

"Did you want me?"

"Yes, Leo. We're ready on the set."

"Well, why didn't you call me?"

"I did, Leo."

"Oh, sorry. I didn't hear you."

He'd tap his ear. Leo's hearing was not perfect, but you didn't dare say anything derogatory within a hundred yards. Of course the assistant, a close friend of McCarey's, knew what was going on. But the act was carefully played out over and over again. Everyone understood— and quietly approved. It was not a unique situation. I hesitate guessing how many millions of dollars have been unknowingly paid out by studios to help ease the pain of indignities they have inflicted.

A few years later, I cut *Love Affair* for Leo at RKO. A great deal of the film had already been shot when a hurry-up call came to Paramount requesting me to take over the cutting. I was free, it meant a substantial increase in salary, so Arthur kindly consented to let me go. The problem was a cutter who was a working alcoholic. The picture was a shambles. I could make so little sense out of the stuff already cut that I ordered up a complete set of rushes from day one. To my surprise, I saw a number of scenes for a sequence that was nowhere to be found. I asked Leo about it, and he told me that the cut sequence had been such a disappointment that he had ordered it destroyed. I got his permission to put it together again from scratch. Played completely in pantomime, it turned out to be one of the funniest routines in the film. It was no big deal—any sober cutter could have done it. I mention it only to show how cutting can help make a film. Alcohol never does.

Leo was no slouch with the bottle himself. Through the final cutting of *Love Affair*, Leo kept saying, "Eddie, we're going to have a real sneak on this one—just you and me. Okay?"

Okay? That's the kind of preview every cutter dreams about but almost never realizes. This preview was no exception.

I rode to a theater in San Bernardino, some sixty miles east of Los Angeles, in a car containing the film, the studio head cutter, and a sound technician who would check the theater's sound system. Situation normal—so far. Eventually, Leo drove up in his new Lincoln Zephyr, with his wife, the writer of the film, Delmer Daves, and Mrs. Daves. Leo was feeling no pain, which is not a bad way to approach a preview. There goes our "real sneak," I thought.

The others went into the auditorium while Leo stayed outside with me. It's the usual procedure. We like to case the joint, size up the members of the jury as they come into the theater. Then another limousine pulled up—no mistaking a studio car. Out stepped our producer with his latest girlfriend, a famous star, followed by his assistant and the assistant's wife. Leo cast a baleful glance at the leading couple.

"I'm a pretty good rabbit myself," was his rather oblique remark.

The studio's supervising editor, whom Leo couldn't tolerate within fifty yards, also turned up—God knows why. The glass was dropping fast.

The picture started, but Leo showed no desire to move, so I excused myself and entered the theater. About ten minutes into the film, the head cutter touched my elbow.

"Leo wants to see you," he said.

"Where?"

"The men's room," he said.

I found Leo standing at the urinal—steaming.

"I need a drink," he said, which wasn't true. "Let's get out of here." And we did.

We climbed into the Zephyr and headed for Mother Massetti's, an excellent Italian restaurant on the outskirts of town. He took off like Juan Fangio, made a sharp turn, and flew west. Everything was fine, except that we were riding straight down the Santa Fe Railroad tracks. I tried to remember if the Super Chief was a night train, and when it came through San Bernardino. After four or five blocks, I finally coaxed him out into the street. We made Mother Massetti's without further adventure, and the long evening began. He sat at the piano, noodling with one hand and manipulating his whiskey with the other. I nursed my tall ginger ale and wondered how the preview was going.

About half after midnight and about fifteen minutes before closing time—for Leo, that is—Mother Massetti called me to the phone. I knew the preview had been over for two hours, and it was about time that our friends tracked us down. Sure enough, it was Delmer Daves, and they were stuck at a closed theater with no transportation. Leo was going to drive them up the mountain to his Lake Arrowhead lodge that night. I begged Delmer to hang in, hung up, and slowly made my way back to the piano. How to keep a loaded Fangio from driving up that precipitous road that night?

I told Leo his wife and the Daveses were waiting at the theater. The wife part seemed to shake him up a bit. (It always did.) I also told him I had always dreamed of driving a Zephyr—which was true—and could I please drive the car on our way back to the theater. To my surprise, he consented. By the time we picked up his wife and his guests, he was sound asleep in the seat beside me. I made the big hill with a song in my heart.

The next week, we had another sneak preview—just the two of us. The film played beautifully.

FREE AND EASY

The decade of the thirties was perhaps the most equable period of my life. A representative graph would have shown relatively straight lines. My career line moved steadily upward—assistant cutter, cutter, director. The line representing my personal life moved inexorably downward.

In 1932 I had married out of sheer loneliness. Not an unusual reason for marriage, but not a very good one. It lasted for sixteen years—the first twelve of them spent together—with not one truly happy moment to remember. Why suffer for that length of time? Who knows? I am inclined to believe that one really fights to save the dreams, not the reality.

Everyone is aware of the burgeoning of sexually oriented films, but few remember how unacceptable such films were barely a decade ago. Censorship or removal of censorship had little to do with it—the censors never led, they merely reflected the common attitudes of the day. This was vividly illustrated by a film I cut at Paramount in 1938.

The studio had decided to remake an old silent, *Zaza*—an adaptation of a well-known French play. The script was written by Zoe Akins; the film was directed by George Cukor. Its cast included Claudette Colbert, Herbert Marshall, and Bert Lahr. Very briefly, it was the story of a young soubrette who falls in love with an upper-class Parisian. She gives up any prospect of a career and settles down in a village outside Paris, accepting her lover's occasional visits as a happy enough kind of life. Then she is told that her lover is married, confirms it, tries to accept it, but can't. At the final fade-out, they have decided to go their separate ways. Obviously, it was what was then beginning to be called an "adult" picture.

The studio brass thought the film one of Paramount's best in many years. Louella Parsons viewed the film and flipped—as did reviewers for several national magazines. With great confidence we traveled to the Bay area for a double preview, in Oakland and San Francisco, on succeeding nights. The showings seemed an empty formality.

First night—Oakland. The film played beautifully for the first three-quarters of its length. Then all hell broke loose. Colbert has gone to Paris, confirmed the fact of her lover's marriage, has returned home, and is now awaiting his imminent arrival. (He, of course, knows nothing of her discovery.) She has, or so she hopes, convinced herself that all will be the same as before—nothing has really changed. There is a knock on the door. She opens it and Marshall, her lover, enters, preceded by a huge bouquet of white roses. And here our world fell apart. The audience began to hiss. Not Friday-night students-at-the-flicks kind of hissing, but the real thing. Though one of the film's best scenes now unrolled on the screen, no one heard it. The audience's angry reaction continued right through to the bitter end.

Naturally we were shocked. The next morning, we made a few emergency cuts, hoping to minimize the impact, and told ourselves that the more sophisticated San Francisco audience would find the situation more acceptable. How wrong we were. The reaction was a duplicate of the one of the night before. The return trip to Hollywood was a nightmare of despair. One of the odd things about the world of the theater is the intensity of our commitment. Everything we deal with is pretense—"tinsel," our more envious critics like to call it—but our involvement is often—no, usually—greater than that in our real lives. Your wife can be walking out of your life forever, but you can only throw her a quick good-bye because you're having a hell of a time straightening out your heroine's life in the script.

The previews seemed to indicate that the audience could accept a premarital involvement, but couldn't forgive our hero for having deceived our heroine, making a "loose woman" out of her. There was evidence that a person watching the film in solitude accepted it with no adverse reaction to its moral aspects, but had a puritanical "mob" reaction when surrounded by other people, even though they were strangers.

Parts of the ending were reshot, but nothing helped. Whether tested in the city or in the Orange Belt, the reactions were remarkably similar. The picture was quietly launched and it just as quietly sank. Nothing like it could possibly happen today.

Some time in the middle thirties, my graph would show two tiny blips. I directed my first picture, and the Film Editors Guild was organized. I'll take them in inverse order of their importance.

A friend approached me with a Western script—*The Hawk*. He had $5,000 with which to produce it, furnished by a family friend of the proposed leading lady, an amateur actress from Long Beach. Today we'd say, "It's a challenge." Then we said, "What the hell—why not?"

I took a leave of absence from Paramount and set about preparing.

Our leading man, Yancey Lane, had been one of twelve winners of a Paramount male beauty contest. There was a police dog and one professional actor, a minor child star who could act rings around anyone else in the cast, Dickie Jones. We also had a lead horse who overstepped himself when he ran, injuring his forelegs, so we couldn't use him in the running shots, and who was too high-strung to stand still, so we doubled him in the close shots. These two small handicaps aside, he was a magnificent animal.

The cameraman charged us $90 for the five days' work, and furnished his own camera—free. It was Glen Glenn's first sound job; they probably did it for nothing. We shot four days on location and one day on a sound stage at Monogram. I rolled up about 130 setups that day. During the last couple of weeks, my personal funds ran out. We lived on milk-bottle returns and the tag-end receipts of a 25-cent chain-letter scheme.

The film's financiers made a 100 percent profit immediately, selling it to Herb Aller for $10,000. A good many years later, Herb resold the negative to a southern distributor for $20,000. I wish I'd a piece.

After the passage of the Wagner Labor Relations Act, there was a flurry of organizational activity in Hollywood. The studios had decided that it would be dangerous if the workers organized on their own, so they beat us to the punch. Picking their men with care, they started their campaigns. I became the Paramount representative quite by accident, replacing Roy Stone at his request. Eventually I became the Guild's first secretary and the holder of card number 4. It was decided that we would hold an annual dinner-dance and not bother the studios too much, but after a few years, as I had predicted, the cutters started to make noises like bona fide union members. The rest is history, in some of which I played a small part.

As a junior member of an exceptionally fine cutting department, I was bouncing back and forth on pictures, sometimes doing an A with a McCarey or a Cukor, more often a B with God-knows-who. One learns more from Bs. There is less to work with—less time, less film, and less artistry—so more ingenuity is needed to arrive at something passable. One of the inequities of the Oscar awards is demonstrated here. A fine director with a top cast, shooting from a superior script, hands the cutter a quantity of superbly photographed film. Is an award-winning job such a difficult achievement? The poor clod who takes hack material, ineptly staged, inexpertly played, unimaginatively shot, and puts it together with sufficient skill to ensure its later playing as a "Movie of the Week" on a major television network—he's the genius.

Cutting a *Bulldog Drummond* was memorable—if only because John

Barrymore played the inspector. He was near the end of his great career, and, like the hero of *The Fool of Venus*, the once-great troubador was reduced to playing the clown and kissing the donkey's ass. But flashes still remained. To pass the time, John Howard, Barrymore, Colin Clive, John Sutton, and I would play the spelling game. Adding to either end was permissible, and any word included in Webster's Unabridged was allowed (we kept a twenty-pound copy handy). Barrymore, who couldn't repeat a single word of a scene unless it was written on a blackboard, would dredge up the most obscure words from what must have been a truly amazing vocabulary. He was never wrong. He never bathed either, which sometimes made it dicey on a hot stage, but it was worth it.

He played the fool on Kay Kaiser's radio show at that time, and he was usually bagged. But on those occasions when some "heavy" actor was guesting on the show, and a Shakespearean "spot" was mandatory, Barrymore was something else again. His drunken diction disappeared, and Shakespeare's words became sheer magic once more. He made Orson and the others, good as they were, seem the mere mouthers that Willie so abhorred. Then the scene would end, and Jack was once again the fool.

Lou King was Henry King's younger brother, and as decent a man and as good a B director as I've known. He allowed me to stage and shoot a couple of sequences on the pretext that he had to get away for an early appointment. The next day at rushes, he pointed out a couple of simple errors I'd made—not noticeable enough to require reshooting, but bad enough to warrant my avoiding them in the future.

Kurt Neuman made *Hold 'em, Navy!* starring Lew Ayres, a fine actor and a good friend. The climactic sequence was, as the title indicates, a football game. Kurt was German, and the nuances of American football were somewhat beyond him, so I was given the opportunity of supervising the shooting of the football scenes. I also wrote the material and shot the action involving the play-by-play radio commentator.

George Cukor, a whiz with dialogue, was never quite at home with the camera. During the shooting of *Zaza*, he would rehearse and stage a scene, then allow me to work out the camera setups. All these experiences, added together, made the final step possible.

It was very early in 1939, and I was restless. I didn't know where I was going and I didn't really care much, but some move was indicated. The studio was considering the creation of a special position, that of a script editor. The concept was one of those that seem right but are doomed to failure. All scripts were to be analyzed in the hope of reducing the amount of wasteful shooting that often took place. I was tentatively approached about the position and was considering it when something new developed. Harold Hurley, Paramount's top B-picture executive, had hired a director on a two-picture deal. The first one had been completed and was considered a disappointment. So what else was new? Rather than pay the director off on his second film, they decided to let him direct it, but with help. I was assigned to the project as a codirector, but with no authority whatever. The weakness of the setup was obvious to everyone but the front office. The final result was inevitable.

It was an impossible situation, and the director reacted accordingly. Our verbal exchanges were perfunctory. He went to great lengths to make it clear that I had no influence on him or the picture. At the same time, his equivocal position sadly weakened his self-confidence. No matter how good his work might have been, the executives were looking for incompetence. Naturally, they found it. The director struggled on for about a week before the ax fell. No other director would take on the picture without a few days' hiatus for familiarization. It was felt that the cost of such a shutdown was prohibitive for a B. Since I had been with the project from its inception, I was asked if I felt competent to take over. Who ever heard of a thirty-year-old who felt incompetent? With no time for butterflies, I found myself in the director's chair.

The film was *Million Dollar Legs*. Not the broad comedy made some years earlier, but a light college musical starring Betty Grable, Donald O'Connor, Jackie Coogan, and a host of pleasant but undistinguished youngsters. I finished on schedule. The film was probably no worse— and certainly no better—than if the original director had finished it. But the front office felt vindicated. And I started to wonder about my next cutting assignment. Instead, I was offered a contract to direct, at $250 a week. I take my breaks where I find them. What the hell—why not?

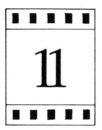

"USE IT":
DIRECTING THE Bs

What can be said for B pictures? To the young and hopeful, they were a school, a laboratory, a stepping-stone—and they were a living. To the older and more tired, they were soul-eroding tripe, dreams turned to nightmares—and they were a living. To the studios, they were grist for their mills; they helped pay the overhead, furnished steady work for the crews, and occasionally served as a proving ground for young writers, directors, and especially players.

The movie theaters had their captive audiences then just as the networks do now. And the studios had the theaters—or vice versa. If a film were made at a certain cost, which varied in direct proportion to a studio's guaranteed outlet, it was sure of a profit. Paramount had a lot of theaters. Our B schedule was eighteen days.

1939 was a good year for me—particularly in June. I signed my new contract, and I became a United States citizen. My cup was certainly running over, some of it dribbling all over me, though I wasn't aware of it for years. Almost immediately, I started work on my first picture, a film called, oddly enough, *Television Spy*. It starred William Collier, Sr., Bill Henry (not the newspaper columnist), and a number of other actors whose names I can't remember. One of the very small bits in the film was played by a young man named Anthony Quinn.

I was as nervous as a child bride. The first day I shot a party scene. I've always disliked crowds, and that dislike slopped over into my work. There's an old actor's phrase that is very valuable: "Use it." Simply interpreted, it means if something is difficult, unpleasant, or bother-some, don't waste energy fighting it. Absorb it, use it as an impetus for your performance. I do that with crowd scenes. I don't enjoy them, but I work twice as hard with them.

If my first day was a trial, my second was purgatory. We were on location at a ranch in the San Fernando Valley. Lou King had been assigned to hang around—just in case. Obviously, that didn't do much

45

for my ego—or my nerves. And I knew the studio executives would be looking at rushes before lunch. About 11:30, Lou was called to the phone at the nearby farmhouse. I had a ball of lead in my stomach. In a few minutes he came back, his face expressionless.

"Hurley wants to talk to you," he said.

I walked the last mile to the farmhouse. The phone weighed a hundred pounds. Hurley's voice came through loud and clear.

"Congratulations," he said. "The dailies looked great. I just told Lou to come home."

I floated back to the set. Lou was getting into a studio car, wearing a grin a mile wide. Suddenly, I loved him.

"Stay for lunch," I shouted.

"I hate box lunches," he said. "Good luck."

And he left, taking my lead ball with him.

The *Daily Variety* review of October 6, 1939 was less than enthusiastic:

> Equipped with story material that should have built it into strong supporting feature, *Television Spy* slumps into filler division because of inability of Director Edward Dmytryk to draw convincing characterizations from his players . . . piloting hand drops confident grip with resultant slow down in pacing.

No one ever started directing Bs in the expectation of making it overnight. I hoped to start developing some techniques, to learn how to deal with actors, to get a feel of the medium, and to impress the front office. The last was easy, but the first three—Lord!

Impressing the front office was no big deal. Few executives can look at rushes and really see just how well it will all add up. So they look for technique—and you give them technique—armpit shots, crotch shots, shots through odd foreground pieces, low setups, high setups, ad infinitum—almost. We had no illusions; we knew what we were doing, and why. Among ourselves we called these angles "gruesomes." But they did the trick. When you have no substance, you accentuate the form. It pays to have a few "gruesomes" in your arsenal.

Impressing the brass in rushes is one thing—the finished film is something else. There the brass is more resistant to deception. So you go on to the next film, and the next, hoping that you'll find a sound story, a simple story, with economy of movement, so that you can spend more time with your players than you do changing sets, and maybe you'll wind up with a sleeper. Sooner or later lightning does strike, but I didn't have to seek shelter for quite a while.

My second film was *Emergency Squad*, which I remember chiefly for two things—I ran into my first "method actor," and a small bit in the film was played by Anthony Quinn. Young actors often learn bad habits in the theater, which they bring with them into films. One of them is upstaging. That's really difficult to do on the screen since there is no upstage or downstage on the set. The camera—hypothetically our audience—can move in a complete circle. Except when you're in a hurry.

Boys will be eager, and Quinn was one of the eagerest. In one short scene with a fine character actor, which I was trying to get in a "two-shot" to save time, Tony kept sliding away from the camera, forcing the older actor to turn his back to the lens. A "two-shot" is quite simply a frame, from full figure to close up, in which two people appear in which neither actor is especially favored. I cut the scene two or three times, mentioned the problem nicely to Tony, but he had the bit in his teeth. What to do? I called for an apple box, turned it upside-down and positioned it on the spot I wanted Tony to hold, then put him in it. It worked. I've used Tony in a couple of much better films since then because I think he's one of the best around, but I've never had to resort to the apple box again.

The method actor was something else. He played one of the villains who has planted a bomb in a mine tunnel our good guys are inspecting. But the other bad guys take the elevator, leaving him down there to share the good guys' fate. He gets a little frantic and plays one of those "I'm too young to die" scenes. We rehearsed, then lit the set. The actor asked me to give him a couple of minutes before I started the scene. In those days, that kind of request was an eyebrow raiser, and I wondered a bit, but agreed. When the set was ready, I asked for silence, put the crew on standby, and gave the actor the nod. He circled a couple of times; then, grabbing a six-by-six upright which supported the tunnel's ceiling, he banged his skull against it two or three times just as hard as he could. I'd thought he'd split his head like an overripe watermelon, but he merely staggered a little and nodded his head in my general direction. I started the camera, and we shot the scene. Thank God we were able to print the first take.

Press preview time arrived, and I dreaded it. I begged my producer to cancel the showing, citing my roasting after *Television Spy*. He laughed.

"Did you take out an ad before the showing?" he asked.

"I couldn't afford it," I said.

"Can you afford bad reviews?"

I could see his logic, but I couldn't believe his cynicism.

"Tell you what," he said. "You write your own review. I'll bet you ten it will be printed."

I was reluctant, so he wrote a review on the spot. Artfully done, not overboard, it was a good review to have on one's record. *Variety* ran it, word for word. Later, I learned the paper had nothing to do with either review. The reviewer's chief source of income was selling ads. So much for naïveté. I paid the producer his ten bucks—it was a lot cheaper than buying an ad.

My third effort was called *Golden Gloves*, a rather nice little film about the amateur fight racket. It featured Richard Denning, Robert Page, Jeanne Cagney, and J. Carrol Naish, and it was Robert Ryan's first film. The studio's casting director had caught him in a play at the Pasadena Community Playhouse (the alma mater of William Holden, Robert Preston, and many others), had liked his style, and had recommended him for the lead. I made a film test. We decided he wasn't quite ready for us. (Later I wondered if we had been ready for him.) Since he had been Intercollegiate Heavyweight Champion while at Dartmouth, I thought he might do well in the part of a "ringer" brought into the Golden Gloves tournament by the heavies. He was 6'4", weighed 198 pounds, boxed beautifully, and hit like a mule. He did well. He tapped Denning in the ribs during their fight, and Dick made three trips to the hospital for X rays. To this day he insists his ribs were broken, though the pictures showed nary a crack. Paramount signed Ryan to a contract but let him go after six months. Eventually he came back.

I had to do a few days in a boxing arena. I had hoped to get the Hollywood Legion Stadium and 3,000 extras; I got an empty stage and 300. I was in trouble. I looked at earlier fight films. *Kid Galahad* had used bodies painted on backdrops behind the first three rows of live extras. Not good enough. Others were no better. Go to the source—I started to study the real thing and noticed the house lights were turned on only between rounds; while the fighters were at work the ring was brightly lit and the house lights were dimmed. This, coupled with the heavy haze of cigar and cigarette smoke, made it impossible to see anything beyond the ring. There was my solution: Play long shots of the stadium only while a fight was in progress. That served two purposes: our audience's attention would be on the ring, and the stadium would be in relative darkness. My art director, my assistant, and I went to work.

Setting aside twenty or thirty extras, we placed the rest in the shape of a triangle, with the apex at the camera and the base at the ring. The sides of the triangle just overlapped the sides of the frame—we couldn't afford to waste a body. When we were ready to shoot, the lights were bright over the ring, backlighting the spectators between the ring and the camera. Grips ran through the crowd with bee-smokers, filling the set with a hazy smoke.

But the clincher lay behind the ring in the darkness. We had hung black drapes from ceiling to floor and from wall to wall of the stage. In front of the drapes, rostrums of varying heights had been placed at odd distances from each other across the entire stage. On each of these we placed two or three extras from the group we had originally set aside, each armed with a number of flare matches. During the scene they would from time to time, at random, light their flare matches. The effect on the screen was of a couple of thousand fight fans, invisible in the darkness behind the ring, except when occasional smokers lit their cigarettes.

Bill LeBaron, then the production head of Paramount, and a rabid fight fan, sent me a note congratulating the crew on the "most realistic fight scenes" he had ever seen in a film. He was quite right.

My next film, *Mystery Sea Raider*, was a step up—a B-plus. I had that fine actor Henry Wilcoxon, Carole Landis, a first-rate supporting cast, and a 24-day schedule. I felt like D. W. Griffith. It was 1940, Europe was at war, and we were with it. The story concerned a group of Americans imprisoned on a German sea raider after their ship had been torpedoed by a U-boat in the Caribbean. The film was a lark—except for one thing. For the first time, I ran into a problem every director faces time and again during his career—the test of strength.

The lead heavy was a Pasadena Playhouse character actor—a bit pompous, as older actors who are still playing little theater are sometimes inclined to be—but a very good actor nevertheless. He wanted due credit and respect for his greater experience. His sparring technique was new to me, though I've run into it on a number of occasions since. It is effectively irritating.

Arriving on the set early, the actor would pull his chair up beside mine, open his script, and start punching. Every line of the day's scene, he would maintain, was just a little off, and he would suggest his changes. If his line were "good-bye," he'd want to say "so long"; if it were "so long," he'd insist that he could feel comfortable only with "good-bye." And so it went, each objection putting me to the test—would I resist and defend the writer's words, would I try a compromise, or would I fold up completely? I was behind the eight ball.

This went on for three or four days, until I dreaded his appearance on the set. Then I decided to "use it." One morning as he entered the stage, I called to him. He wasn't expecting that and was a little surprised. I had the prop man put his chair beside mine, and my script was open by the time he sat down.

"I studied this scene very carefully last night," I said, "and I think some of your lines need a little work."

"Oh?" he said.

"Yes. Here, for instance, where you say 'excuse me,' wouldn't you feel more comfortable with 'I beg your pardon'?"

"Well, I don't really —"

"And here, where you say 'thank you,' how about 'much obliged'?"

"No," he said. "I really think I can be quite at ease with —"

I continued through the scene. By the time I finished, the lines were set, exactly as they had been written. As long as he could force me into making repeated defenses or decisions, he had the upper hand. When I put the responsibility onto his shoulders, he backed away. I never had a moment's trouble with him again, not even when I had some real changes to suggest.

But my step up turned out to be my way out. There was another housecleaning. Hurley had walked out or been fired—I never knew which. Sol Siegel took over as king of the Bs, and he wanted a free hand and a clean slate. He got both. Every one of the writers, directors, and producers who had been working under Hurley was dropped as soon as his contract expired. Kurt Neuman and Lou King were the first to go. I envied James Hogan; he had about two years left of a no-option contract. I had about three weeks. I was ready to accept any decent offer.

12

ANOTHER ILL WIND

Every artist must have an agent—for two reasons: to find jobs and to make deals. For an established star, director or writer, by far the more important of the two is deal making. At the upper levels, the demand generally exceeds the supply, and job getting is really job selection—picking the most promising project of the lot. Then the wheeling and dealing starts, and it involves a great deal more than money. In fact, the question of salary is often the least difficult aspect of contract negotiations. An established artist has an established salary, though that can be modified by his current rating at the box office. To a player, the most important item under discussion is usually screen credit.

Actors have been known to give up money for improved position on the main title. That's not as silly as it sounds. Improved screen credit can bring increased recognition which can bring more money in the future.

When there are two or more stars of equal stature in the same film, turn off the fan before it's too late. Now the producer or personnel executive earns every penny he gets. After the shouting, begging, demanding, threatening, and screaming finally stop, the impasse is usually resolved by compromise. For example, player A will get first billing on the title while player B gets first billing on all advertising. Three stars create a problem equaled only by the three-body problem in astronomy; it is hardly solvable. What makes it worse is that these battles are usually ego trips, and discussion of merit without personal insult is extremely difficult.

The director's contract is not such a problem. There is one director on a picture, and his credit has been set for years by guild agreement with all the studios; it occupies the last card on the main title, immediately before the start of the actual film. Of course, if he is a director of stature, there are other (ego-inflating) credits—John Doe's Production, A John Doe Film, etc. These, however, are fairly routine, though not to the

Writers Guild. The conflict of opinion about whose film it really is—the writer's, the director's, or the producer's—never stops. At the moment, the directors have an edge in the battle.

Aside from his salary, which, as with the players, is usually established, the most important demands a director makes concern rights and conditions. He usually wants control of the material, on the set and in the cutting room. Once he takes over, it is "his" film. With name directors, all this is usually understood, and in the old days not too much was made of it. Today it had better be all down on paper, and even then it often doesn't mean much.

Contracts in all fields of endeavor have gradually come to mean less and less. In Hollywood's heyday, a man's word was really his bond. An executive like Harry Cohn, for example, might have an unsavory personal reputation, but if he said, "You have a deal," you had a deal. If, for some reason or other, the film didn't materialize, he might try to switch the deal to another time or another film. He might even try to get you to take half, but if you didn't agree, you were paid in full. Today the phrase is "So sue us," and most, if not all, of the studios are involved in breach-of-contract suits worth many millions of dollars. Until the last ten years, I have never signed a contract until well after completion of production. By then the papers were a mere formality, important only for the studio files. Today the money has to be in escrow before one is willing to even reread the script.

Soon after I started directing, I had been flattered by Bert Allenberg's request to represent me. The Berg-Allenberg Agency was one of the best in town. However, when Paramount let me go, I found there was a slight problem. Berg-Allenberg was an important agency—I was an unimportant director. It was not an ideal mating. The big agents played gin only with the big executives, and they hardly knew I existed. Nor were they involved in the kind of films I was equipped to handle. After a time of no work and much worry, I got an agent more my size. Hallam (Hal) Cooley had been a second-line comic on the silent screen. Now he was a second-line agent. But he dogged the second-line producers, and that was where my immediate future lay.

In the meantime, I directed a $50,000, two-week musical for Ike Chadwick, an independent quickie producer. It was notable chiefly for the presence of Alan Ladd in the role of the second male lead. Ladd had briefly been a studio grip and was now trying to establish himself as an actor. He drove his agent, Sue Carrol (later Mrs. Ladd) on her rounds of the studios. She stopped at my little office next to Columbia and plugged Alan. He looked good, sounded very masculine, his price was right, but did he have a tuxedo? Sue assured me that he did. (Next day she purged herself by renting him one.) I decided to take a chance. Sometime later it paid off.

The picture created no stir on film row, but a year or so later, Alan made *This Gun for Hire* and a bright new star was born. Chadwick rereleased our film, with Ladd's name now prominent in the advertising and on the main title, and cashed in on Ladd's skyrocketing popularity. I had a small piece of the film and now received more from my percentage than I had gotten up front. Particularly notable was the fact that Chadwick was the only producer in my experience to pay me my share without pressure or threat of suit.

Just before what turned out to be a Merry Christmas, Columbia hired me to make a Boris Karloff feature, *The Devil Commands*. It had a two-week schedule (Columbia had fewer theaters than Paramount). But it also had Karloff, an extremely thoughtful and unselfish person who made the whole effort worthwhile. A man of moderate height and kindly mien, he is the only actor I ever knew who could actually "play it big"—physically, I mean—and scare you to death in the bargain. Like most of his films, this was a story of horror and suspense, and it gave me an opportunity to experiment with lighting and photographic effects. I also learned something about audiences.

Hollywood liked to think it made each film to please everybody, which is nonsense. But it wasn't something I concerned myself with at the time. We sneaked *The Devil Commands* before a packed house in Inglewood. When the main title, announcing a Karloff film, flashed on the screen, fully half the audience got up and walked out. It was a shock—until I realized that there were a lot of people who just didn't want to see a Karloff film, no matter how painstakingly it had been made. For pictures, too, there are horses for courses.

Columbia liked my work, and in the next eighteen months I did a number of films for them—a couple of *Lone Wolfs*, a *Boston Blackie*, and a few others I find it easy to forget. My only solace was that my films were being received pretty straight by the Pantages Theater Friday-night crowd, who delighted in hissing and booing the average B. Still, I began to feel the learning process was being overdone—with sufficient practice one can easily learn to be a hack. So I delivered an ultimatum: no more Bs. Columbia couldn't have cared less. They did call me once in a while for more quick ones, but I was adamant—for six months. Then my money ran out. At about that time, Irving Briskin (Columbia's top B executive) personally dropped by my home with a script for a B musical to feature Ozzie and Harriet Nelson and Ruby Keeler. The combination of Briskin's personal visit and an empty bank account was hard to resist. I returned to Columbia and low-budget films.

By the time I had finished *Sweetheart of the Campus*, my agent had gotten me an interview at RKO. The result was a commitment to make *Seven Miles from Alcatraz*, with James Craig and Bonita Granville. Nazi shenanigans in a lighthouse. Good for experimenting with techniques, and I was getting damned sick of it. But at least I was in new territory.

Robert Ryan was back in Hollywood—this time under contract to RKO. He had signed to play the lead in Pare Lorentz's film, *Name, Age and Occupation*. Lorentz was a fine critic, a top maker of documentaries, but completely lost in straight drama. After 90 days of shooting, he was 87 days behind schedule. RKO decided to take the loss and call it a day.

Not long before this, they had made the same decision on Orson Welles' latest and last project for them. It was intended to be a trilogy. The third story was a documentary on the birth of the samba at the carnival in Rio de Janeiro, which he was in the process of shooting when RKO pulled the plug.

About three years later I was told an interesting story in Buenos Aires. Welles had come down from Rio for a brief visit. The city officials had given him the full VIP treatment and in the process had taken him down the broad steps leading from the city hall to the river's edge. Dipping his hand in the rust-colored brackish water, Orson scooped up a palmful, brought it to his lips, sipped a bit, then turned to the officials and, in his most sonorous voice, declaimed, "Now I understand Buenos Aires." The city fathers laughed and were quite flattered, even though they recognized an equivoke when they heard one.

The ability to use flattery at just the right time was only one of Orson's many talents. Some years later I was in New York with the president of RKO, N. Peter Rathvon. He spotted Welles cross the lobby of the St. Regis Hotel, excused himself, and walked over to speak to him. When he returned a few minutes later, a broad smile lit up his face.

"He's just cost us a few million," he said, "but he's such a charming bastard, with a little push I'd sign him again tomorrow."

Trying to make a spot for myself at RKO, I attempted to salvage the scrubbed projects. I was even able to talk the studio into laying out a few bucks for a writer, Charles (Blackie) O'Neal, a fine artist in his own right, now known chiefly as Tatum's granddad. We looked at all the material of both films, found some documentary scenes of the TVA dams that looked interesting, and worked out a treatment for a new *Name, Age and Occupation*. Then we learned that both Lorentz and Welles were suing RKO, and the material would be tied up in litigation into eternity. Another waste of good film and another good scheme down the drain. The old black hole was opening up again. And then, once more, the ill wind.

A friend of mine, Irving Riis, had prepared and actually started shooting a film called *Hitler's Children*, an exploitation B. Irving was rather headstrong and somewhat touchy—a bad combination in Hollywood. After a few days, he got into a fight with producer Doc Golden. Getting his back up, he quit the film, expecting, so he told me later, to win a quick apology and a free hand. Instead, the studio said, "As you wish," and asked me to take over the direction. Following guild procedure, I talked it over with Irving before making my decision. He gave me his blessing, asking only that his name be completely removed from the film's credits. The studio was willing and I went to work. I finished on schedule, cut and dubbed it, and turned it over to the distribution department. None of us at the studio was sure of what we had.

I took a short side trip to Universal for *Captive Wild Woman*, with John Carradine, no longer spending quarters to be paged, and Acquanetta, the Venezuelan hot-pot. The title of the film tells everything about it worth knowing. I learned one thing. Actors rarely mind playing ugly roles, actresses almost always do. I returned to RKO for *The Falcon Strikes Back*. After that—pennies from heaven.

Hitler's Children had been released and was making minor film history. It starred Tim Holt and Bonita Granville. Taken from a novel titled *Education for Death*, its story concerned the treatment of youthful nonconformists in Nazi Germany. A title with the word "Hitler" in it was considered certain box-office poison, and the exhibitors asked Doc Golden and RKO to change ours. Doc was stubborn—and he was right. The film cost a little over $100,000, and, running only in England and the Western Hemisphere (exclusive of pro-Axis Argentina) grossed, by some accounts, $7,500,000.

I had my sleeper. My salary for the film had been exactly $500; now I was given a bonus of ten times that much and a fat contract offer. I was on my way—but not quite yet.

A new agency popped into the scene. Famous Artists was one of the "name" offices in town, and they wanted to represent me. But I already had an agent.

"Talk to Hal Cooley," I said. "What he says goes."

Imagine my surprise when he told me he was selling my contract (for well up in five figures) to Famous Artists. I felt rejected. I had been self-righteously proud of being loyal to my "little" agent when I was on the brink of real success, and he was selling me up the river.

"Look at it this way," said Hal. "My contract with you has a year to run—what can I make? Five, ten thousand dollars? At the end of that time, you'll have big ideas—I've seen it happen a hundred times—and you'll think I'm holding you back. You'll switch to an important agency, and when you do, I won't get a dime. This way I get a little money in the bank."

He was probably right, but it still hurt a little way down deep.

Before I reached the As, I had to make another exploitation film—this time, naturally, about the other end of the Axis, Japan. Emmet Lavery, who had written the script of *Hitler's Children*, and I contrived this one together. We bought a book for its title—*Behind the Rising Sun*—not an unusual practice in Hollywood. Then we concocted a story based largely on incidents as they had been reported from the Orient before Pearl Harbor. For example: The slapping of American women, the dispersal of opium to Chinese to keep them docile, etc. On a not very original plot, we strung ten or twelve incidents calculated to increase the flow of patriotic juices. It worked. This one was a little more expensive—$250,000 (fake eyelids don't come cheap)—and the film returned some $5,000,000. No *Hitler's Children*, but still a tidy profit.

One of the more stimulating sequences in the film was a fight between Bob Ryan, playing an American boxing coach in Tokyo, and a huge Japanese judo expert, played by the wrestler, Mike Mazurki. Based on an actual prewar incident, in which the boxer won, it was a beautifully choreographed battle between two superior athletes. Even the pro-Axis Argentines cut the fight out of the film and ran it as a special short. Both *Hitler's Children* and *Behind the Rising Sun* had long runs across the bay in Montevideo. The Argentines organized overnight boat excursions to Uruguay, which included a ticket to the film. They did a land-office business.

Now the studio asked me to do another propaganda film—this time about the home front. But what a different kettle of fish. *Tender Comrade* had a script by Dalton Trumbo, one of the best writers in town, and starred Ginger Rogers, fresh from her Oscar win for *Kitty Foyle*. Ginger Rogers—oh, boy!

Now I knew I had it made.

HOW TO RUIN A TENOR

Directing one's first A film is like taking one's first solo flight: nerve racking, sick-making, and thrilling—particularly after a safe landing.

Ginger Rogers was a very big star, and I was a bit in awe of her. The major studio publicity departments did such a superlative job of blowing up the stars into larger-than-life figures that every one sooner or later succumbed to the snow job—the public, the stars themselves, the front office, the studio workers, and finally even those who had started the whole thing—the publicity departments. All this gave the stars great power within the studios, which, on the whole, was used most circumspectly.

Robert Alan Aurthur once told me of an incident which is quite to the point. Billy Wilder was making a film with Marilyn Monroe. This unhappy, frighteningly insecure woman had been the source of unbelievable slowdowns and other problems too numerous to mention. Finally, losing his last shred of patience, Wilder picked up the phone and called the producer. Having reached his man, he launched into a long list of completely justified complaints, ending with a strongly felt "Either she goes or I go!" He listened for a moment, hung up the phone, and turned to his cohorts. "He says *I* go," he wailed.

Though Ginger was a thoroughly conscientious professional, she had that kind of power, and during the first few days of production there was hardly a moment when I wasn't aware of it. To make matters a touch more difficult, I had brought my cameraman, Russ Metty, up from the Bs with me. Quality of photography is of primary interest to nearly all actresses—in some instances, it is the *only* interest—but Miss Rogers decided she might as well go for broke and said okay. Sure enough, the first day's rushes were pictorially spotty. Ginger, Russ, and I had a tense conference. Russ thought he could solve the problems, and Ginger decided to give him another day or two. The succeeding rushes showed Ginger to her best advantage. I breathed easier and so did Russ. He has never looked back.

Tender Comrade was a somewhat maudlin film, which did moderately well at the box office. It concerned itself with the problems of four working war wives who decide to pool resources while their husbands are at the front. They share a house, a housekeeper, a car, and their fears, hopes, triumphs, and disappointments. Their motto is "Share and share alike," which sounded quite innocently democratic when we made the film, but which turned up to haunt me a few years later when I was instructed that the real motto of a democracy is "Get what you can while you can and the devil take the hindmost."

Adrian Scott, a former writer newly turned producer in his search for something different, had turned up a story which RKO already owned and had filmed only a few years before. It was a Raymond Chandler mystery titled *Farewell, My Lovely.* Chandler was still decades away from cult status. He was considered no better than any number of pulp mystery writers, and this particular story had been bought cheaply, gutted in typical Hollywood fashion, and transformed into one of the *Falcon* series. Scott saw the virtues of the original novel, and, since most of them had been jettisoned in the *Falcon* film, decided it could be remade immediately and nobody would be the wiser. The price was right and he had no trouble convincing the studio. He and John Paxton, the writer, put together a first-rate script. The film had to be made at a price—around $400,000—and Scott came to me as a hopeful choice. I was fresh enough out of the Bs to be able to make it relatively quickly and inexpensively, but at the same time I now had the pleasant aura of a successful, "in demand" A director. I decided to do the film.

In those days, every script was written for Clark Gable or Cary Grant. Once down to earth, you started looking. Scott and I put together our list of male stars suitable for the part of Philip Marlowe, then went in to ask Charlie Koerner for his advice and approval.

When Koerner had taken over the production reins of RKO a couple of years before, it was in receivership. Before he died of acute leukemia a short while later, he had, with great skill and daring, put RKO up among the four leading studios of Hollywood. He was the best executive I have ever known. He made decisions quickly and firmly, he could be convinced, and he had the one truly great executive talent—once he delegated authority, he never interfered. Also, like all truly competent executives I have known, he always seemed to have plenty of time. Whenever I called his secretary with a request to see Koerner, the answer was either "Come right up" or "He's got someone with him— can you come up in fifteen minutes." How rare that is.

Koerner also knew how to deal with a trust betrayed. One producer on the lot had an unimpeachable upper-class background, the goodwill of a number of top stars, and an ironclad contract. He also had a fat head. I made a film for him and found myself keeping most appointments at Lucey's, where it was his custom to drink a long lunch. Koerner tried to straighten him out diplomatically, but to no avail. "I'm getting tired of being hit on the head with a silver spoon," he said, but the studio could not afford to buy the producer out. Koerner studied the contract carefully, then wrote a letter. It said, in effect, that the producer would have to be in his office by 9:00 A.M. each day, leave the lot for no more than a one-hour lunch period, and remain in his office until at least 6:00 P.M. in the evening. As I have mentioned before, "face" is very important in Hollywood; the producer had no choice but to resign.

Under Koerner's direction, the studio was in the process of rebuilding its entire program policy. He believed that musicals were due for a comeback and was trying to put together a stable of singing stars. Now, he listened to our suggestions politely, then had one of his own.

"Could you use Dick Powell in the role?" he asked.

Dick who? Scott and I looked at each other. Powell had been the singing star of many of the great Warner musicals of the thirties. When they fell on hard times, so did he, not financially, but professionally. He had done nothing worthwhile for several years, and even now, when musicals were making a small comeback, he insisted he wanted only to play hard guys. He had seen our script and liked it. But the idea of the man who had sung *Tiptoe through the Tulips* playing a tough private eye was beyond our imaginations. Koerner explained that he wanted to put Powell under a multi-picture contract, hoping to star him in musicals, but Powell would not sign unless he could make *Farewell, My Lovely* as his first picture of the deal. Koerner would leave the final decision to us, but he would be grateful if we could do him a favor. . .

Adrian and I sat on a bench in the little RKO park and tried to recover from the shock. "What do you think?" Scott finally asked me.

"It's a challenge," I finally said. (In 1944 that was almost an original remark.)

And that was how we had to think of it. The next day, we called Koerner and told him to go ahead with Powell's contract. We got an excellent cast together: Claire Trevor, Anne Shirley, Otto Kruger, Miles Mander, and Mike Mazurki, the wrestler, to play Moose Malloy. He was supposed to tower above Marlowe, but Dick was 6'2", while Mike was 6'4½". So Dick walked in the gutter while Mike walked up on the curb, or Dick stood in his stocking feet while Mike stood on a box. But it came out right in the end. I had sent the script to an actor I wanted for a supporting role. He apparently considered it beneath him and sent the script back with a three-word message: "Opened by mistake." I never tried to cast him again, nor did anyone else, to my knowledge. He disappeared from Hollywood; arrogance is supportable only *after* success, and then just barely.

I felt Powell was quite nervous at the start of photography, and I used some of the tricks I had been developing to bring him into the character and increase his self-confidence. One was to involve him in the technical aspects of the film, some of which were unique. I would ask him to look through the camera while it followed Dick's stand-in through the movements of the scene. After humoring me a few times, he finally pulled me aside and said, "Eddie, just tell me what to do, and I'll do it." Well, you live and learn.

There are a number of different types of actors in films and the theater, and Powell was a perfect example of one. He was not "creative," but he did what was needed competently and effortlessly, with never a sign of an ego problem. Philip Marlowe has been played by some of the best actors in films—Bogart, Montgomery, Mitchum—but I still believe Powell came closer to the essence of the character than any of them. Bogart and Mitchum were too tough, Montgomery too sophisticated. I wanted Marlowe played as I believed Chandler visualized him—really an Eagle Scout, a do-gooder, with the patina of toughness only skin deep. This good-guy characterization is implicit in many of the things Chandler has him say, and that is the way Powell played him. Not because that was what I wanted, but because that's what he was: an Arkansas farmboy who got into show business because his voice was too sweet for calling hogs, and who never quite got all the hay out of his hair.

For one of the few times in my life, my small scientific background proved useful. The first meeting between Marlowe and Moose Malloy (who starts off the chain of events that make the film) takes place in Marlowe's office. It is late, Marlowe is tired, the office lights are off, and the room is sketchily lit by the light of the shop signs streaming through the window. The strongest of these flashes on and off. When it is off, the window becomes a partial mirror reflecting the interior of the office. During one of these brief off periods, Marlowe, out of the corner of his eye, sees a flash of a reflection in the window. As the sign lights up again and the image vanishes, Marlowe remains immobile, waiting for the light to go off again so he can confirm what he thinks he saw. Sure enough, after a few seconds, the light goes off and the window reflects the big, ugly, menacing face of a towering figure standing in front of the desk. Now Marlowe turns slowly and looks up at Moose.

We staged and shot it normally, but when we looked at the rushes the next day, the effect was not there—the image was not in the least menacing. I spent some time analyzing it. As anyone knows, an object's relative size depends on its distance from the point of view—the eye or the camera. The farther away one is, the smaller one looks. I realized the cumulative distance of Moose from the camera was much greater than that of Marlowe, therefore his image was much smaller than Marlowe's and consequently less menacing.

Both men had to be in the same shot to create an effective contrast—but what to do? The only way to make Moose look larger than Marlowe was to have his reflected image much closer to the camera. But I couldn't move the window—so we put in an invisible one. The next day I reshot the scene, placing a large piece of plate glass (about 8' by 8') between the desk and the camera. All light was carefully screened from it so that it was invisible when viewed through the camera. Moose stood off screen beside the camera. When the neon light flashed off outside the window, a strong spot simultaneously lit up his face. This was reflected in the plate glass in front of the camera, but since the plate glass is clear, the reflection seems to be in the window in the background. However, the cumulative distance from Moose to the camera lens was now much shorter than the distance to Marlowe, and his image appeared much larger. The effect of size and menace was more than we had hoped for. I never heard from anyone who felt cheated.

Later in the film, we had occasion to use the plate glass again. In the final moments of the picture, Miles Mander shoots at Moose. In an effort to stop the killing, Marlowe dives for the gun. It goes off immediately in front of his eyes, inflicting powder burns on his eyeballs and temporarily blinding him. Obviously, we couldn't risk Powell's diving into a gun (even blanks cause powder burns) or a stuntman either, so we put Powell on the far side of the glass, and Mander's hand, holding the gun, on the camera side. The positions had to be carefully calculated so that Marlowe would appear to be diving directly through the line of fire, which was actually only the reflection. Mander had to hold the pistol in his left hand because of the mirror image. The shot worked to perfection. Not only was Powell several feet away from the gun, but the intervening plate glass gave him double safety.

Another interesting technical effect was used in the film. After Marlowe is hit on the head (for the second or third time in the picture), he wakes up in a private sanitarium still quite heavily drugged. Between these two scenes we used a series of unrelated shots (called a montage) dramatizing the effect of drug-caused D.T.'s. A repeated cut in the series showed Marlowe falling away from the camera into nothingness. The technique for filming this effect is standard and always results in the falling figure dropping at a constant speed. The effect is really that of soaring rather than of falling. As any high school student knows (but soon forgets), a falling body *accelerates* at the rate of 32 feet per second per second. Viewed from above, it is this rapid and constant increase in the speed of falling that gives a dropping object its frightening aspect. We were able to achieve this effect beautifully by incorporating an extra step in the process. We projected the standard falling shot on a screen and reshot it with a camera moving away at an ever-increasing speed.

For the first time, I was also able to use forced perspective in a number of scenes. For example, one set was built with a slanting ceiling. This was not obvious to the camera, but a player walking from the high side of the room toward the low side appeared to grow disproportionately large in a short distance and space of time, creating an unusually menacing effect. To the best of my knowledge, this technique was first used by Franz Murnau, the great German director, particularly in *Sunrise*. Orson Welles adapted it much later in *The Magnificent Ambersons*. It is most frequently used to cut down on set size and expense. In *So Well Remembered*, I had to shoot a scene on the terrace of the House of Commons. We were not allowed to use the real thing, so we had built it on the stage. Not only would the set have been very expensive if we had built an actual duplicate of the long terrace, but the number of extras needed to fill it would have been prohibitive. We built only about a thirty-foot length with normal proportions. The rest quickly came together in a forced perspective. The rear part of the set was probably only a quarter as long as the real thing, but seen through the camera, it stretched on and on. For extras, we used increasingly smaller people, finally getting down to midgets—and even these were scaled from tall to short. Still, no one ever suspected the set wasn't real. Against a pint-sized set, a pint-sized human being looks completely normal.

Farewell, My Lovely was a success with the front office and with the critics, but when it was first released somewhere in New England, it did miserably at the box office. We quickly discovered that the public thought a film called *Farewell, My Lovely*, starring Dick Powell, had to be a musical, and they wanted no part of it. The studio recalled the film, changed the title to *Murder, My Sweet*, and rushed it out again. It was one of the very few instances where a change of title had a positive effect. *Murder, My Sweet* was an unqualified success. Dick Powell never had to sing another note again.

THE COLD WAR
AND THE DUKE

From a neat, concise and satisfying film, I moved on to a loose, disorganized, and aggravating one. *Back to Bataan* was a story of Philippine resistance behind the Japanese lines. There were a couple of built-in problems: The original script showed white Americans as responsible for all the heroics, and, even while we were shooting, the situation in the Pacific was changing from day to day.

Relatively early in the war, I had tried to anticipate my eventual participation in it. I brushed up on my math and the science of navigation, sold my home in Sherman Oaks to Richard Arlen, and bought an income-producing apartment house in Beverly Hills, meant to keep my wife and eighteen-month-old son, Michael, in relative comfort while I was in the service. About this time, I heard that Colonel Frank Capra was putting together a Signal Corps film unit. I visited his temporary offices at the old Western Avenue Fox studio, and volunteered my services as a cutter, or in any other useful capacity. My offer was warmly accepted. I was told to go home and wait for the word. It never came. Some years later, I was to learn that the Signal Corps had turned me down as a security risk; I had been a premature antifascist.

This queer concept was one of the leading loyalty check guidelines used during the war. Anyone who was against Fascist Spain or Italy, or Nazi Germany *after* Pearl Harbor was okay—obviously. But anyone who was against the fascists *before* Pearl Harbor had to have strong leftist leanings because only the Communist countries of the world officially resisted the spread of fascism at that time. Besides, what American was well informed enough to take such a stand unless he was being supplied information from a non-American source? American foreign policy then, for many decades previously, and up to the present day, has consistently supported the extreme right—or reactionary—forces in almost every instance: South Korea, South Vietnam, Spain, Chile, Brazil, and any number of other dictatorial Latin American regimes. Our one "mistake" was backing Castro against the corrupt Batista in

Cuba, and our government has been wearing a hair shirt and reciting its *mea culpa*s for that dreadful error ever since.

In 1944 I held no strong political views. I had voted for Roosevelt in 1940, I was antifascist on humanitarian rather than political grounds, and I was beginning a leftward lean. The People's Educational Center was starting to function in several private homes in the community, and I was occasionally invited to lecture on cutting or direction. Later the school got money enough to move into an office building at Hollywood and Vine, and I accepted—at no salary, as was customary—the chairmanship of an orientation course in film directing. Our guest lecturers included Lewis Milestone, George Cukor, William Cameron Menzies, James Wong Howe, and a few other film figures of that caliber. Under the auspices of a number of leading writers, the Writers' Mobilization seminars were organized to inform people about the political background and causes of the war. Sometime later I learned that both of these groups had been organized by Communist members of the community.

I considered that the work of the labor school was irreplaceable—few universities of the time had motion picture courses, and these were crude and unsatisfactory. The Writers' Mobilization was the only group that really concerned itself with the causes and purposes of the war against fascism. At the same time, study groups were organized to help young war wives fill their time while they waited for their husbands' possible return. The Hollywood Committee for the Arts, Sciences and Professions was also very active in its support of the war effort. As usual, the Democrats and the Republicans were taking no special action to mobilize American youth, so I decided the Communists were the only ones who cared. When I was approached (sometime in late 1944 or early 1945), I was ready to be had.

I was invited to a gathering of some twenty-odd people at the home of a prominent Hollywood director. Some of those attending were Communists; some, like myself, were there to learn what it was all about. Alvah Bessie had been an active member of the Lincoln Brigade in the Spanish civil war and was now a bit of a celebrity in local leftist circles. We were all quite impressed by his story of the Communist effort in that war. When, during the ensuing discussion, we were warned that the discipline of the Communist party was difficult and rigid, it made us only the more eager to prove our mettle. At the end of the evening, we were given small membership blanks to fill out. All in all, it was very similar to an evening I recalled when I was twelve. That evening ended in my joining the Boy Scouts of America. This evening ended in my joining the Communist Party of America. The honeymoon was short, but disillusionment was slow in developing. As I mentioned earlier, dreams die hard.

Back to Bataan featured John Wayne, Beulah Bondi, and a young actor named Anthony Quinn, no longer a prisoner of the Bs. Tony played a young Philippine aristocrat who is won over to the cause of the guerrillas and leads them to eventual victory. Ben Barzman worked with me to try to bring the film in line with at least a modicum of reality and to try to keep up with developments as they were actually occurring. For instance, while we were shooting, MacArthur returned to the Philippines. The prisoners were released from Cabanatuan, the infamous prison camp, and started returning to the States. These incidents, obviously, had to be incorporated into our film.

Our technical adviser was a Colonel Clark of the U.S. Army. He had served most of his career in the Philippines and had been one of the few who, as serious casualties, had been evacuated from Corregidor just before its surrender to the Japanese. His accounts of the war in the islands were fascinating, his loyalty to and love for the Philippine troops and citizens was touching, his hatred for MacArthur was unending.

One day, while looking for locations, we stopped in San Bernardino for lunch (Mother Massetti's, naturally). The colonel disappeared. As we were leaving the restaurant to get under way again, up he popped, explaining that it was his custom to watch the signs at the entrance to every town. If he noted that the Lions, or Rotary, or whatnot, were having their weekly or monthly lunch that day, he would show up and introduce himself. He was invariably asked to speak to the gathering, and, for a small fee, he always obliged. His speech consisted of a narration of the heroics of the natives and the villainies of MacArthur. One of his most bitter stories concerned the general's departure from Corregidor by submarine, accompanied by another sub full of his personal furniture rather than fighting men. Because of his wounds, Clark was one of the few exceptions.

Aside from Wayne, whose faith in MacArthur was unshakable, we in the company were puzzled by the colonel's attitude, not really knowing what to believe. However, as some of the Americans who had fought with the guerrillas behind the lines started coming home, we heard their stories, too, and our sympathies shifted in Colonel Clark's favor. One such story, told by a U.S. Navy chief petty officer who had spent the war in the mountains of Luzon, was typical. From time to time they had been in radio contact with American submarines. Their most pressing need was armaments and ammunition. Finally they got the word that a supply submarine would rendezvous with them on a particular night. The meeting went off without incident, and the rubber rafts and other makeshift craft ferried ashore a number of crates. The first crate was torn open in great anticipation, but it contained no guns, no bullets—nothing but cartons of cigarettes. Each carton was emblazoned with the words: "I shall return—Douglas MacArthur." Crate after crate contained the same cargo. At first they were so shocked and angry that, if they had had the equipment, they would have tried to blow the sub out of the water. Then they just sat down and cried.

We heard a number of such stories at first hand, none of which we could incorporate into our film, designed, as it was, to keep the home front inspired and at their lathes until victory was won. I fully agreed with this purpose. Now, when I occasionally see bits of it on late TV, I am a touch embarrassed at its blatant chauvinism. The bugle blowing and flag waving that is so necessary to keep a people on course during the progress of a "just" war seems a bit too much during these times of peace, when mutual respect and consideration necessitate less self-congratulatory trumpeting and more awareness of the potential good inherent in all members of the human race.

But I am still proud that, at a time when Errol Flynn and many other English-speaking heroes almost single-handedly won battles in which they were not only heavily outnumbered by the enemy, but somewhat handicapped by the presence of nonwhite allies, our film presented the Duke primarily in the role of adviser and contact man, while the Filipinos themselves, led by Quinn (playing a Filipino) did most of the fighting and occasional dying. In our version, Wayne left the islands by sub and returned the same way, bringing with him not cigarettes, but the guns and ammunition so desperately needed by the guerrillas.

I had one battle myself during the shooting. Makeup and prop men were dirtying up the clothes worn by our guerrillas when Colonel Clark suddenly blew his top. His beloved Filipinos, he maintained, were the world's cleanest people—their clothes were never allowed to get dirty. I pointed out the conditions under which the guerrillas operated, but the colonel would have none of it—the guerrillas had to be clean. But I was still the boss, and, though I hated to be put on the colonel's MacArthur list, I insisted on even more dirt on the costumes. (Dirt, like wetness or rain, photographs with difficulty, particularly in black and white. For a realistic appearance, a great deal more must be applied than seems normal to the naked eye.) The colonel stomped off the set to phone Washington, but the brass decided to keep out of what was strictly a parochial affair. Not long after, newsreels of liberated guerrillas started coming back from Leyte. Without exception they showed the fighters wearing almost indescribably dirty and threadbare clothes—far more so than anything we had shown in the film. I showed some of these newsreel shots to the colonel, but he never saw the dirt—only the light in the eyes of his beloved brown battlers.

During the filming, I had occasion to ask Colonel Clark to give us a list of the sort of small toys or game equipment a native boy might carry in his pockets. The colonel assured me that, aside from baseball, the Philippine children played no games. Doubtful, I went to the source, some of the two or three hundred Philippine extras and bit players we had with us throughout the production. They immediately reeled off a number of games—one, for example, played with pigs' knucklebones. The yoyo, I found, was a Philippine invention. But the colonel had seen none of this in twenty years of occupation. What native boy would be caught dead playing a child's game when the great conqueror was in the neighborhood?

The same circumstances explained his convictions concerning cleanliness. The Filipinos are no more and no less clean than most people but, as the colonel himself told me, his native orderly kept his uniforms so clean and starched that his collar tabs would ping like a bell when struck with a snapped thumbnail (they had better!). And obviously, whenever he visited a native town or compound, the residents dressed in their Sunday best.

Our motley extras were a jovial group to be with. I learned their bamboo dances and kickball games and we spent our lunch hours in friendly competition. Those, and gambling. Almost all Orientals are great and compulsive gamblers. I've seen two Filipinos stretch out their hands and bet on which one a fly will light first. We had a running game of "Chinese poker" going. Wayne and Tony Quinn played a great deal, since time was often heavy on their hands. I played at odd times, when my conscience allowed.

One day a crowd leader came to me and warned that a new extra hired that day was a cardsharp. To avoid trouble, he recommended that none of the non-Filipinos be allowed to play. Though fully aware of the situation, Quinn couldn't resist the temptation. Early in the afternoon I had Tony called to the set for rehearsal. He had lost several hundred dollars, and was steaming. I reminded him that he had been told the dealer was a ringer.

"I know," he said. "But I'm going to beat the sonofabitch if it takes all week!"

I made sure the sonofabitch was not on the next day's call.

This film was my only experience with John Wayne—truly an amazing man—in some ways. He threw his 6'4½", 245-pound body around like a lightweight gymnast. Wayne lived life with gusto. He was already beginning to consider himself some kind of political thinker, but we all make mistakes. Once, in a charitable mood, he told me that though our methods were different, he considered our political aims were really the same—an interesting comment in light of later events. At that time, due to the network set up by the Hollywood Alliance for the Preservation of American Ideals (sic), he knew things about me I had no idea he knew. But we got along well during the shooting. We even attended a number of the same affairs thrown by our mutual business manager. The office handled Johnny Weismuller, among other notables, who also came to the parties. Both big men drank well, if not wisely. The business manager's nephew, Charlie Trezona, a bespectacled pixie when slightly under the influence, would wait patiently until both Johnny and the Duke were loaded (he was never disappointed) and then try to goad them into battle. It would truly have been the fight of the century, but it never took place. Neither of them ever got so boxed that he lost respect for the other's prowess. But it was always worth a try.

One hundred-thirty days of shooting produced a picture which did well in the United States and sensationally in the Philippines. But long before I was through with the postproduction of *Back to Bataan*, I was working on the preparation of another film with my now very good friend, Dick Powell. The film was *Cornered.*

THE PARTY'S OVER

Villiam Dozier had become the new story head at RKO. Either because he considered it a good property, or because he wanted to make his presence immediately felt (Adrian Scott, again the producer, assumed the latter), he had purchased a twenty-page treatment of a tough suspense mystery written by Ben Hecht. Or was it? It was such poor stuff that we were inclined to guess that Hecht had simply put his name to someone else's material and shared in the payoff, which was a fat $50,000. I do not mean to malign Ben Hecht, as delightful a person as I've ever known. He took pleasure in outwitting the establishment. Once, with great glee and some pride, he told me of a caper he masterminded.

Ben Hecht and Charles MacArthur had written and produced a series of films for Paramount. The first two were films of some quality. Then deterioration set in—the last two were unreleasable. Paramount wanted out, and an amicable divorce agreement was finally reached. Then, just before signing, Ben suddenly remembered that they had spent months writing a script which would now be a total loss. After much discussion, Paramount agreed to buy the story for $50,000, a good price at the time. Of course, the studio wanted immediate possession. Leaving the lot, MacArthur turned to Hecht and asked, "How are we going to turn over a script we haven't got?"

"We're going to write it," said Hecht. And in the space of a very few days, they did. It stayed in Paramount's files for years until George Arthur, the head of the cutting department, became a producer. He dusted it off and filmed it. It was a great mistake; he never got the chance to make another film.

Cornered was more of the same. But Bill Dozier was a friend—he couldn't be thrown to the wolves on his first executive decision. Scott and I decided to use the title and contrive a new story, but first there was a hurdle to surmount. For some reason which was never quite clear to me (probably contractual), the studio insisted on our using a well-known mystery writer. Adrian (who, I now learned, was also a Communist) had strong private objections on purely political grounds: the writer was a leading member of Hollywood's right wing.

"Never mind," said Adrian. "I'll handle it."

And he did. He waited a few days until the writer had turned in his first sequence. Then, without even bothering to read the stuff, he hurried off to Dozier and declared the material to be so poor as to be unusable. The writer was off the project and John Wexley was on. Wexley, the author of *The Last Mile*, was a man of extreme leftist leanings. He had been Scott's choice from the beginning. His screen credits weren't all that impressive, but. . .

One day Scott and I were walking across the lot and I happened to mention that I was reading an extremely interesting book.

"Which book?" asked Adrian.

"Koestler's *Darkness at Noon*," I replied.

Adrian stopped in his tracks, turned to me, and spoke in a hushed voice. "Good God," he said, "don't ever mention that to anyone in the group."

I was honestly puzzled. "Why not?" I asked.

"It's on the list," replied Scott. "Koestler is an *ex*-Communist. Everything he writes is corrupt, and no member of the party is allowed to read him."

That was the end of the honeymoon for me, but by no means the end of the marriage. That would be brought about by further events related to *Cornered*.

Long before Wexley had finished his version of the script, even Scott realized we were in trouble. The plot was simple: A Canadian war pilot is looking for the present hideout of an S.S. officer who had been responsible for the brutal murder of the pilot's young French bride. He traces him to Buenos Aires, finally runs him to earth, and beats him to death. Simple and straightforward, no? Not to Wexley. At every turn he inserted long speeches loaded with Communist propaganda thinly disguised as antifascist rhetoric—manifestoes by the dozen, but little real drama. Major surgery was in order. Wexley was allowed to finish the script, politely thanked, and dismissed. Good old reliable, nonpolitical John Paxton was called in. The script was rewritten quite extensively, retaining a strong antifascist bias (after all, that was basically what the picture was all about) but nothing that any good American citizen, short of C. B. De Mille, could disapprove of.

In the meantime, I flew to Buenos Aires to research the town. We were to shoot the film in Hollywood, but I wanted to make no ridiculous mistakes. The trip by DC–3, flying only in the daytime and stopping every few hundred miles to refuel, took about eight days.

Just after my arrival in Buenos Aires, Franklin Roosevelt's death was announced. Though Argentina was officially pro-Axis, I have never seen such a mass demonstration of sorrow. The great Square of the Obelisk was packed with thousands upon thousands of people, no one dry-eyed. My pride in my country has never been greater.

I learned a number of things in Buenos Aires: Evita Peron had confiscated what little negative was available in Argentina for her own film, the city has a subway (a fact I subsequently used to advantage in the film), the people are extremely friendly, the hotels are great, they bake better croissants than one can find in Paris, and the common nickname for an American is "Borracho," which means "drunk." Think about that. They also eat more than anyone I've ever known, with the possible exception of their neighbors across the bay in Uruguay.

In time the script of *Cornered* was completed, and a cast was assembled. Besides Dick Powell in the lead role, we had Walter Slezak and Luther Adler (both superb actors) as heavies and Micheline Cheirel as the leading lady. My script girl, Ellen Corby, played a tiny bit in the film. Like most contrived pictures, it was not completely satisfactory, though the last reel and a half is a first-class example of what suspense ought to be and nearly makes the whole effort worthwhile. Though not in the same class as *Murder, My Sweet*, the film grossed more money because the exhibitors were now completely aware of Dick Powell's new image and had all climbed on the bandwagon. This follow-up phenomenon is by no means unique in film annals. But before the picture was released, Scott and I went through a series of events that precipitated our break with the party. Unfortunately, it came too late.

Cornered had been cut, dubbed, and was ready for release printing when Adrian and I received a summons from John Howard Lawson. We were to meet with him and John Wexley at Wexley's request. Thinking it was some complaint about credits, we readily agreed.

We were shocked to find ourselves facing a committee of the party to hear Wexley's complaint. He claimed we had completely emasculated his work to the extent that, far from being the antifascist film he had intended, it was now definitely slanted to the other side. He demanded that we recall the film and reshoot his propaganda scenes which we had eliminated. The situation was unbelievable. To begin with, neither Scott nor I could recall the film for reshooting at this point without the permission of the front office. We could not get that permission without a complete disclosure of our reasons, which was impossible. Everyone at the meeting knew this. Beyond that, neither Scott nor I would have agreed to reshoot the eliminated scenes even if we had been able to do so. However, knowing party procedure much better than I did, Scott asked for another meeting during which we could explore the situation in greater depth.

The second meeting took place at my apartment a few days later. My wife and I had separated, and she was living in New York. I had the place to myself. We met in the basement rumpus room—what could be more appropriate? There were, to the best of my recollection, four men (all Hollywood writers) on Wexley's side of the room and four on ours—all members of the party, of course. Scott had rallied Albert Maltz to our side. He was as shocked by this threat to the freedom of creative activity as we were. After a long and Kafkaesque meeting, nothing had changed. Wexley took his lumps, none too graciously. Everyone left, and Adrian and I accompanied John Howard Lawson to his car.

"If this is the way things are going to go," I finally ventured, "I think I want out." Scott agreed with me.

"I think you're quite right," said Lawson. "For the time being, consider yourselves adrift. When you decide that you can accept party discipline, we'll explore the situation again." Wearing his typical humorless smile, he left. I stood there feeling like a child in a ridiculous world. Adrian and I looked at each other, then turned and went our separate ways. But our relationship was far from ended.

Albert Maltz was incensed at the whole purpose of the meeting. He wrote a carefully considered, clearly reasoned essay on the necessity for creative freedom in the arts, which was published in *The New Masses*. Later, a rebuttal by one of the party hierarchy appeared in, I believe, *The Daily Worker*. It maintained that artists were obliged to cleave to the party line and severely criticized Maltz for his remarks. This was, in effect, an official chastisement. Albert capitulated, and, in a later issue of the periodical, confessed his error. The same thing happened some years later when Maltz wrote a glowing review of *Doctor Zhivago*. When the Moscow regime changed and Pasternak fell into disfavor, Maltz felt constrained to re-review the novel. He found that it had been a bad book all along.

For thirty years there has been much talk of the Hollywood Ten's fight for freedom of thought and speech. The incidents I have just mentioned, plus others to come, may put the whole question in a somewhat different light. I do not expect to change anyone's mind—but I was there. The same cannot be said for most of those now writing their versions of the events.

A great weight was off my back. Two marriages—one to the Party—were finished, or nearly so. The next two years were to be the most carefree and happy years of my life. It was with a light heart that I approached my next assignment, *They Dream of Home*.

NEW DREAMS

At its inception, *They Dream of Home*, adapted from Niven Busch's study of returning veterans, was largely an exercise in subterfuge. Dore Schary, the producer, had come to RKO from Selznick. I believe some sort of professional relationship still existed there, but I'm not certain. RKO and Selznick frequently made deals with each other, often as secret as Kissinger's foreign policy machinations. Selznick "owned" some of the biggest stars in Hollywood, but made very few pictures; RKO made the usual major studio's quota of films, but had very few stars. A trade-off was mutually advantageous. Selznick often collected ten times as much for a star as he was paying out in salary. Val Lewton once told me that while he was story editor for Selznick, it was obligatory for the department to stay in the black. Of the stories and scripts bought during the course of any year, a number had to be resold at prices high enough to enable Lewton to show a profit.

Such practices sometimes had their seamier sides. An agent I knew very well—in fact, I worked for him incognito during the lean years—developed a cute racket. He bought scripts from writers, had somebody do a little work on them for a little money, then resold them to studios at a very handsome profit. Very enterprising, but the writers he bought from were his own clients whose work he was supposed to sell directly to the studio, which made the practice highly unethical. In time, the Writers Guild stepped in and stopped it, but not until a good deal of money had passed into the wrong hands.

They Dream of Home was the title of Busch's novel. Toward the end of the war, theme songs became hot-selling items; a good one could add hundreds of thousands of dollars to a film's gross. Eventually, long after our production had gotten under way, it was decided to change its title to *Till the End of Time*, the name of the extremely popular slick version of Chopin's "Polonaise."

The only star set for the film was Dorothy McGuire, a Selznick contractee. Now we started a search for a leading man. I must have tested more than a dozen. Some of them were very good, but all were unsatisfactory to Schary. Eventually we tested Guy Madison. The test was dreadful—I was sick—but he got the part.

Henry Hathaway tells a priceless story about the casting of one of his films at 20th Century–Fox. Over a period of time, all the major parts were cast except that of the leading lady. Henry came up wth dozens of suggestions, but none pleased Zanuck. He was looking for someone very special. At last, the starting day was upon them. Hathaway, ready to explode, went to Zanuck's office for a showdown. Darryl sweet-talked him while his assistant paced the office floor, thinking. Finally, slapping his forehead, he turned to Zanuck.

"Darryl, how stupid we've been! I've got it!" he shouted. Darryl looked at him innocently. (Some of our finest acting takes place off-stage.)

"Got what, Lou?"

"The girl! We've been blind! She's been here all the time, right under our eyes! The perfect casting!" Hathaway's heart sank.

"Who, Lou?" pleaded Zanuck. "For God's sake, tell me who."

Lou took a pregnant pause. "Bella Darvi!" he said. Bella was Darryl's current amour, and Henry had been trying to avoid her like the plague. But he knew when he was licked.

"Of course," agreed Zanuck, "the perfect choice. Why couldn't we think of her before?"

Some time after that, Marlon Brando was signed to play *The Egyptian*. Darvi was the feminine lead. One day he was asked to come in for a reading. He lounged in, sat down, and listened to Bella read a few lines. Slowly he rose from his chair.

"Excuse me," he said. "I have to go to the toilet."

A week later, they ran him down in New York, the farthest anyone has ever gone to take a leak, though Spencer Tracy once went there for a drink. Marlon refused to make the picture, and one day I benefited from that decision. But that's another story.

Guy Madison's saga is one of Hollywood's miracles. Originally a young telephone lineman from Bakersfield, California, he was spotted by an agent while in Hollywood on leave from the navy. The agent took him to Selznick and persuaded David to let Guy play a three-minute bit in *Since You Went Away*, which he did during a week's leave. The reaction was sensational. He was an extremely good-looking boy, and his pictures hit all the fan magazines. Even before the film was re-leased, his popularity rating was higher than that of Dick Powell, Bob Mitchum, Robert Young—in fact, all but a few top stars. Selznick thought he had a gold mine and could hardly wait for Guy to get out of the service. When he did, we were looking for a young leading man.

"David, he's been here all the time. Right under our noses!" Even Dorothy said she thought he would be very appealing, but I thought her arm looked a little out of joint.

Shirley Temple was also borrowed from Selznick to play the role of the girl next door—the one who had always loved our boy but was destined to lose him. She suddenly decided to marry John Agar, so we started the search again, testing every girl in Hollywood who could play a teen-ager—but none was quite right. I was due to start location shooting at the Marine boot camp in San Diego, and we still had no girl-next-door.

Finally Dore had a brainstorm. "There's a girl at MGM," he said (at least it wasn't Selznick's!), "who always comes through when it gets down to the nitty-gritty. Her name is Jean Porter."

I had never heard of her.

"She's been doing leads and second leads at Metro," he said, "and there's a lot of film on her. I'll have them send some over." And he did.

What I saw looked promising enough for a closer look. Fortunately, she was not working at the moment, and Metro's casting director agreed to send her over. She bounced into the office, all five beautifully proportioned feet of her, dark brown eyes flashing. On her cheek was a small Band-aid. I couldn't keep my eyes off her while Dore made the introduction.

"Every week Dore does something especially nice for me," I said. "This week you're it." I wasn't being charming—it's against my nature.

Later Jean told me that she had misheard my name (not unusual with a monicker that Ray McCarey once said looked like some of the alphabet thrown at random onto the screen) and had thought the studio had wanted her to see Dieterle. He had interviewed her once, and she had never forgotten it (Teutonic directors can be very trying). She had used every trick in the book to avoid the appointment, but a casting director can be very persistent when he sees a good chance of making a little money on an investment. Her relief at seeing a stranger instead of the man she feared was almost overwhelming. She was licked before she knew it. She agreed to play the part and headed for home. I left for San Diego.

Joining the cast were Bob Mitchum and Bill Williams, playing Guy's Marine buddies. Mitchum is an unusual man, tough and taciturn on the outside, soft and sentimental on the inside, and very insecure. He is an exceptional actor, but I've often thought that if he could let himself go, he could be the best there is—or he could once have been. During the San Diego shooting, we spent our evenings at the Del Mar Hotel, shooting pool. Mitchum's caricatures and impersonations kept us in stitches, and he was playing to pros. His mastery of all dialects was exceptional—greater, even, than that of Marlon Brando's. His knowledge and use of the English language was extraordinary. But as soon as the camera turned over, his face would grow tight, his eyes would half-close, and what came out, good as it was, was only a part of what it might have been. I made several films with him, but I was never able to break him down.

While we were shooting in San Diego, I ran into a problem. A certain sequence seemed to me unduly prolix. Since both Schary (who had won an Oscar for coscripting *Boys' Town*) and Allen Rivkin, our writer, were visiting us on location, I called a conference on my problem. They agreed that the scene could stand a little work, and they went into a huddle. The next day Dore gave me the result. What had been an overlong five- or six-page scene was now a fat ten pages. I read it and realized that if I asked for further cutting, I might find myself with a fifteen-page short subject. So I praised their work and kept my own counsel. I shot the scene in such a way as to permit extensive pruning in the cutting room, and, indeed, that's where it took place.

My own experience has been that I prune the script until I think it is right for shooting. When we rehearse and film each scene, further cuts are almost always in order. Later, in the cutting room, I find I can slice still more. If I see the picture again months later, I kick myself for leaving some scenes too long.

One of John Ford's associates once told me of Ford's editing habits. His favorite writer in his great years was Dudley Nichols, at that time generally conceded to be Hollywood's best screenwriter. Volumes of his scripts were published in book form. Each sequence he wrote was submitted to Ford who, grabbing his blue pencil, would start slashing mercilessly. What had been a ten-page scene might come down to five or six pages—or even three. Then he would hand it back to Nichols to remove the surgical scars.

Nichols finally directed two scripts of his own. They were disasters, and he directed no more. It is possible that he was just a bad director who murdered his own scripts; but, having seen the films, I think it was simply that the wordiness of his scenes buried the good that was in his words. This is a major pitfall for filmmakers who direct their own material. Many writers and directors have done fine work when kept under firm control by a producer of Selznick's caliber, only to fail badly when their growing reputations finally won them the right to edit themselves. Selznick himself, an intelligent if ruthless editor of other people's material, never made a good or successful film once he started collaborating as a writer on his own productions.

It seems to be the nature of a storyteller to think that what he has to say is so important that it must be said at length, and so profound that it must be repeated in various guises to ensure complete understanding. This is sheer nonsense. Though the "common man" may use a smaller vocabulary and a simplified grammatic structure, there's not too much he isn't aware of or doesn't understand, particularly in this period of constant dramatic exposure. I have always found that I have to move fast to stay even with the average moviegoer's capacity to understand. The better filmmakers, of course, have ways of keeping their audiences' interest and attention. Allowing their characters to run off at the mouth isn't one of them.

We finished shooting in San Diego and arrived back at the studio—to face a picket line. The "painters' strike" was in progress. Most of us decided not to walk through the lines, so we stood chatting with the pickets until they dispersed for lunch. Then we went inside. I checked out my set. All was in readiness, but the crew was in the commissary, so I headed in that direction. It was a madhouse. The waitresses had arrived late, seen the picket line, and gone home again. Now the counter was being manned—or womaned—by volunteers. I made my way to the counter to pick up a sandwich and found myself face to face with the world's prettiest waitress, all made up and dressed to look just like the girl next door. I fell in love with her instantly. Only over the years have I discovered the myriad reasons that made my snap decision so very sound.

Jean had to learn to ice-skate for the film, and we spent many happy evenings at the rink near the studio. She was a dancer, and the figures came easily. She also had to rehearse a jitterbug number with Guy. That did not come easily. Guy had two left feet and a tin ear. Our dance director, Charlie O'Curran, finally hit on a happy solution. He recorded a piano track of "Anchors Aweigh" in the required tempo, and that did the trick.

For me no easy solution was possible. It certainly wasn't Guy's fault—he was completely without experience, professional or amateur—but he simply couldn't act. It didn't seem to bother him any. Where many a more accomplished player would have worried himself sick, Guy, after a ridiculous rehearsal, would go to his dressing room and conk off until the assistant called him back to the set. It was probably just as well. A bad actor was trouble enough—a bad and frightened actor might have made things impossible.

I would talk him through a scene, telling him where to look, when to speak, when to walk, when to pause. I felt very Germanic but not very comfortable.

Dorothy McGuire made things no easier. She is an extremely fine actress and a lovely woman, though she didn't always think so. She told me once that when she was an aspiring young actress seeking work in New York, she would visit the producers' offices only when it was raining, because the rain excused an unattractive or sloppy appearance. How's that for insecurity? She also had slightly discolored teeth and a silly pride that wouldn't allow her to go to one of the fine dentists in Southern California who for years had specialized in eradicating such problems.

I never knew whether Dorothy was upset by Guy's ineptitude (she was extraordinarily patient with him), whether she had no confidence in me, or whether she was ticked off because I spent so much time with the second leading lady (under ordinary circumstances a practice to be strictly avoided), but she gave me nothing but trouble. If I planned a sitting scene, she wanted to walk; if I wanted her to move, she insisted on sitting down. Adopting a risky strategy, I always suggested the opposite of what I really wanted her to do. If she had gone along with me, I would have been up a tree, but fortunately she was consistent.

William Wyler was also making a picture about the veterans' homecoming and seemed to be concerned that our stories might conflict. He needn't have worried. *The Best Years of Our Lives* and Willie were Oscar winners. *Till the End of Time* went out quietly, made a little profit, and disappeared from view. The only thing that made it the best year of my life was the presence of Jean Porter—one day to be Jean Porter Dmytryk.

A VERY GOOD YEAR

1946 was a vintage year. I was RKO's fair-haired boy. I was deeply in love with a girl who was bringing me out of myself for the first time in my life and who had just bought me a Chrysler Town and Country convertible (they don't make cars like that anymore); and my wife, who was still in New York, was considering a property settlement preparatory to a divorce.

Irving Riis made another critical decision.

He had been working with Adrian Scott and John Paxton on a film version of James Hilton's novel, *So Well Remembered*. A joint venture of RKO and J. Arthur Rank, it was to be shot in England. Now Riis decided he didn't want to leave the States. Adrian asked me to take over.

Leaving the States was no problem for me—leaving Jean was. However, we decided that the advantages outweighed the disadvantages, and I took the assignment.

I had not been to Europe since before World War I, and never to England. We traveled by air, still a tedious journey at this time. From the plane, the green fields and small villages looked very inviting. Except for the prevalence of airstrips, there was no sign that a great war had so recently been fought here. But this impression was changed when we arrived at London's Heathrow airport. There were no permanent buildings—only Quonset huts—to serve one of the world's busiest fields. But in all this mad scramble, the patience, politeness, and good nature of the airport personnel stood out like a skyscraper. And not a single gun visible on a single policeman!

The drive into town led me to wonder how such a densely populated country could have so much green space. I soon found out. In spite of its pockmarked, bombed-out visage, London was packed to the limit. Hotel space was unavailable. The half dozen members of our party were separated and placed in odd, dirty, completely unequipped rooms, in odd, dirty little rooming houses. Even for a guy who hadn't seen an inside toilet until he was eight years old, the conditions were unbearable. Fortunately, the next day we were able to make arrangements that, while by no means luxurious, were at least considerably more comfortable.

Within a couple of weeks, we were all in residence at Savay Farm, a three- or four-hundred-year-old manor house within short walking distance of the studio in Denham, a charming small town some twenty-five miles west of London. We each had a separate room, and arrangements had been made for breakfast and dinner at the house. The farm had belonged to the Mosley family before the war, but was now the property of an ironmonger (which, I learned, meant hardware dealer) and his alcoholic wife. During the course of our stay, there were some moments of high adventure when she occasionally slipped over the edge and ran screaming from the house in the buff, pursued by an embarrassed and anxious husband. Once or twice we were called on to help corral the escapee. One evening, while walking down one of the house's dimly lit hallways, I was startled by two eyes peering at me from a tiny cubbyhole under the stairway. When I had collected myself, I recognized them as belonging to our landlady, but I didn't take the time to discover how she had stuffed herself into that small space. Once I had learned how to lie on an even keel in a bed which rested on a sharply sloping four-hundred-year-old floor, things were not too uncomfortable.

To our astonishment, the English were by no means distant or aloof. On the contrary, they were extremely friendly and hospitable. True, certain formalities had to be observed, but once this was done, friendships developed quickly and lasted a long time. A case in point: At one of our studio conferences, I had met Sir Edward Villiers, a gentleman who shared a number of my interests, one of which was fishing. The very next day he brought me a beautiful split-bamboo trout rod, pressing it on me in spite of my remonstrances. Some days later, he invited me for lunch at a restaurant. A few days after that, I was invited to dine at his club. After some weeks, he asked me to his home. When I felt I knew him well enough, I questioned the procedure. He explained, "It's just that we want to make sure of you before we trust you with our families."

Now honestly, isn't that better than meeting some guy on a plane or in a bar, slapping him on the back and telling him you'd like him to meet the little woman, and then, when he shows up at your house for a boring—or embarrassing—four or five hours, wishing to God you'd kept your mouth shut?

Our meeting with J. Arthur Rank and his associates held to the pattern. The great industrialist and revitalizer of the British motion-picture industry was a very down-to-earth man. Though he had been to the United States several times since the war and could have outfitted himself completely, he still wore the shirts with frayed collars and cuffs and the frayed ties that adorned the other Britishers who had still to practice austerity at home.

At that time, the British way of doing businesss was quite different from ours, and it took some getting used to. Paul Jarrico, who was writing the script of *The White Tower*, which I was to produce and direct for RKO, had flown to England with us. When my preliminaries were settled in London, he and I were going on to the French Alps to scout possible locations. He had obtained a transit visa only for England, but certain problems on *So Well Remembered* had taken longer than scheduled, and it was necessary for him to get an extension. We called on the appropriate official and made our request. He glanced at Paul's papers. "Impossible," he said. "Quite impossible." And he seemed to mean it. But I was prepared. I started talking about something in the news that I thought might interest him. I hit on the right subject, and soon the three of us were deep in conversation. After about twenty minutes, he suddenly turned to Paul and said, "Let me see your passport." Flipping the pages, he found an empty one, reached for a rubber stamp, and, as simply as that, Paul had his extension.

The country around Denham was Constable country, ideal for cycling. England was on double-daylight-saving time, and night fell very reluctantly—as late as 11:30 in the summer. Since union quitting hours were very rigid—5:15 on two "short days" a week and 5:45 on the three long days, with a half day on Saturday, my "creative" assistant, Bill Watts, and I found we could make ten or fifteen miles after our work day ended and still have time to shower and change before dinner.

One of our trips led to a most unusual experience. One Sunday we decided to cycle to Oxford, a trip of some eighty miles. We were still inexperienced enough to start out without a prepared lunch. In England, each year is either the wettest on record or the driest on record. 1946 was the wettest. Our trip out was almost entirely in the rain. Every inn along the way was closed. By the time we reached Oxford, we were tired, hungry, and exceedingly wet. We went from hotel to hotel trying to get a room for just an hour to dry off and rest. For the first time since we had arrived in England, we met with hostility. Though slow to anger, Bill finally had enough and pedaled off with such great speed that he left me some distance behind. When I finally caught up with him, he was pulled up at a curb and loudly berating a placid-looking young bobby for all of the day's woes.

The policeman let Bill vent his anger, then quietly said, "I quite agree with you. Oxford is the most inhospitable town in all of Great Britain. But your GIs did stir up a bit of trouble on occasion." We had seen some of this kind of thing firsthand in France, so we began to understand the situation. However, we were still wet and miserable. The bobby, who came from Scotland, pulled out his pad and pencil and jotted down an address. He handed it to Bill and pointed down the street.

"It's just a few hundred yards," he said, "and I'm sure they will put you up for a bit and let you have a fire to dry your clothes."

We thanked him and pedaled off. We found the small gray house in a typical lower-class neighborhood, where wall meets wall in permanent embrace. A young woman with a baby in her arms answered the door. When Bill explained our needs, she invited us in. It was a very poor place, but friendly and warm. An elderly couple—her mother and father—greeted us politely with a few words about the weather. Then we climbed a narrow flight of stairs. On the second floor was a biggish room with eight cots in it. The woman explained that during the war they had taken in GIs, given them a bed for the night, breakfast in the morning, and sent them on their way. Now the cots were empty. She picked up a couple of tattered gray robes and led us into a small sitting room, where a fire was burning in the typical tiny grate. After she left us, we took off our wet clothes and spread them in front of the fire to dry. The cheap robes felt luxuriously warm. Soon the woman returned with hot tea and the ubiquitous pound cake. Rarely had anything tasted so good.

In about an hour, our clothes were relatively dry, and it was time to leave for home. We had barely changed when there was the sound of footsteps on the stairs, then a knock on the door. The man who entered was the bobby. I was completely surprised. This was his home; the young woman and the baby were his wife and child. On a salary of £4 or £5 a week—about $15 or $16 at the current exchange—he and his wife had been hosting and feeding American soldiers throughout the latter years of the war. We tried to get them to accept some payment, but they refused. Before we left, we managed to stuff a £10 note into a chair where it would be easily found. Then we pedaled our way out of the most inhospitable town in all of Great Britain.

After a few weeks of brussels sprouts, boiled marrow (merely soggy squash, whatever you call it) and watercress sandwiches, Paris was a culinary paradise. Of course, England had suffered over five years of brutal and expensive war and was now trying to pull itself up by its bootstraps, with as little help as possible from Uncle Sam. France, on the other hand, was comparatively unscarred, and may even have profited a bit from the Occupation. The food was good and plentiful, the town was vibrating with postwar excitement, and Americans were not yet the enemy.

The exhilaration in the city, a full year after the war, could be tangibly felt. Every night was New Year's Eve on the Champs-Élysées; excitement gusted out of hotel lobbies with every turn of the revolving doors. We were still rescuing civilization in those days and it was a heady sensation. Now the accent is not on saving the world but on finding one's self. How our expectations have diminished.

Paul Jarrico, Bill Watts, and I were on our way to Chamonix, but we were spending the night in Paris. We were in the company of a couple of British reporters who, since RKO was footing the bill, were seeing to it that we ate and drank at only the finest places. One nightclub stands out in my memory. Green champagne was obligatory (you didn't have to drink it, you just had to pay for it). The room was drafty, and there was a scrawny girl singing named Edith Piaf. I had never heard of her—nobody had outside of Paris—and at first I thought her style awkward and her voice quite ordinary. Then, somewhere about the third song, she raised that stiff right arm and pointed in our general direction, and for the rest of the evening I was mesmerized.

Sometime in the small hours of the morning, we found ourselves in the room of one of the reporters at the Hotel Scribe. We had been joined by an American girlfriend of theirs, a buyer for some Manhattan store. The reporters were Communists; the girl, like me, an ex-Communist. Naturally, the talk had swung around to the future of the Communist party in Western Europe.

Paul, like most Hollywood leftists, was the scion of an upper-middle-class family. He had never known a day's hunger or spent a night in the cold. His anger arose out of a sense of guilt, not out of need.

Now he was engaged in a popular intellectual pastime, rhapsodizing about the innate goodness of the "salt of the earth," the common man. Finally, the girl could stand it no longer.

"That's a lot of shit," she said. "I've known a lot of common men, and I've known some uncommon ones, and believe me—I've seen a lot of stupidity and senseless cruelty down among the salt of the earth."

Well, so have I. I know all about the extenuating circumstances, but I've still seen more brutality in Boyle Heights in a year than in Beverly Hills in a lifetime. My point, I think, is that glorification and senti-mental oversimplification solve nothing at all.

Chamonix and the French Alps remain in my memory because of

their breathtaking beauty, a wonderful twenty-mile hike through deep snow and ice from the top of the Aguille de Midi, to the foot of the Mer de Glace glacier, and for the finest non-Chinese meal I have ever had in my life. It was laid on for us by our local guide, and cooked and served by two gentle ladies who owned and ran a tiny pension on the outskirts of town. And it beat anything I ever had in Paris by a country mile.

We had left London about the middle of June when it was still spring. When we returned two weeks later, summer had gone. Rain set in and hardly left us. We scoured the Midlands looking for the right locations—Birmingham, Leeds, Manchester. Finally our search led us to Macclesfield, a leading mill town of England. In order to save time, we pulled up beside the first bobby we saw.

"We're looking for a slum section," I said, after some introductory remarks.

He looked at me with a very small smile on his face. "I don't think you'll find anything else in Macclesfield," he said. So much for civic pride.

But he was right; it was our town. A short time later, we were out of our cars and making our way through some open ground alongside a massive four- or five-story brick building. There must have been seven or eight in our party—all men. Suddenly I was aware of loud, banging noises. I looked up. The windows of the building were crowded with women of all ages peering out at us through the dirty panes and pounding loudly for our attention. Once they had gotten it, there were smiles, whistles, suggestive remarks. I turned to our guide.

"What's that, a prison?" I asked.

"Oh no," he answered, "it's just one of our mills."

I guess it's a matter of definition.

We started shooting our picture in Macclesfield. Hollywood-style, we had scheduled our locations first. The English crew was aghast; in England it was never done that way. The inside work was finished first; then the crew traveled to location and waited—sometimes for months—for a few days of just the right weather. They always had to have that soft English sun which gave British Technicolor such a fine reputation for pastel shades. But we decided to take a chance. We had two solidly packed weeks of location work on our schedule, and not a single member of the crew thought we could make it. But they were a good group, led by cameraman Freddie Young and art director Bill Williams, and they were certainly willing to try.

We organized a crash unit—everything essential in one station wagon. We often shot at three different locations on the same day, moving from one to another, then back again as the weather changed.

One location was shot in sunlight. When it started to rain, we quickly threw the gear into the station wagon and headed for our rain location. When it stopped raining, but before the sun came out again, we had a third—our overcast location. But the water glistening from the slate roofs gave us all the contrast we needed. Then back to one of the other locations as the weather commanded.

Near the end of the Macclesfield shooting, we were almost caught short. We had started a sequence in the rain, but now the sun had come out and we had no place else to go. The Macclesfield Fire Department came to our rescue. Pointing their spouting hoses high in the air, they rained in the whole of the main town square. We finished our locations on schedule.

Something I found extraordinary was the unfailing good nature of the townspeople we used as extras. None was a professional, but they all worked with a will under circumstances that would have sent the average Hollywood extra screaming to the Screen Extras Guild for adjustment—for danger money, rain money, bonus money—money. When the hoses were turned on our people, it was a lark, even though some of them were wheeling prams with their babies inside. And now I found out why, in our eyes, so many English women looked dowdy. The rain was a fact of their lives, something they had to live with. They walked in it, sat in it, met and talked in it. And if that's a little hard on the hairdo, so what? There are more important things.

The cast of our film included John Mills, Martha Scott, Trevor Howard, Patricia Rock, and Richard Carlson. John and Trevor were the first English actors I had ever worked with, at least on their home grounds. Still carrying some of my stereotyped notions with me, I was not quite sure how things would develop. On one of our very first days in the Midlands, we were playing pool in our hotel in Buxton. I sank an impossible shot.

"Why, you lucky sonofabitch!" screamed Mills, with typical British understatement. I knew we were going to get along just fine. I have since done a few other films with John. I will never work with a finer actor or a better man.

Martha Scott was another superb performer, but she had a problem. She was supposed to be English, but she was a girl from the Corn Belt. It's interesting that good British actors can do most British dialects well, but find neutral American nearly impossible. At best, they usually affect a broad, nasal Middle Western speech. Americans, with the possible exception of Danny Kaye and Bob Mitchum, experience the same difficulty with most English dialects. For weeks before start of photography, Martha had been studying with a dialogue coach. Now we were shooting our first scene, and naturally, she was anxious. As I said, "Cut!" on our first good take, she turned toward her coach and asked his opinion.

"Take ten!" I said, and called the coach aside.

A film crew is a small city in itself. Some forty-five or fifty crafts are represented, and as many different kinds of activity take place. The crew must be closely organized; if the organization falls apart, it invariably increases the cost of production by hundreds of thousands, even millions of dollars. The hand on the tiller can be gentle (indeed, I believe it should be) but it should always be firm—and undivided.

The dialogue coach continued to work with Martha in her dressing room, but he never again came on the set. Martha looked only to me for approval and argued only with me if she thought I was wrong. After a few days of coolness, the coach and I became good friends and the organization stayed more or less intact.

For an American, working in England was a touchy business. To begin with, what the workers lacked in wages they made up for with strict union rules. The system in Hollywood is basically simple: Work them as long as you want, but if you go past mealtime or quitting time, you pay them overtime. Since the rate of overtime increases geometrically, breaking the rules too much can become very expensive. An American workman can finish at 1:30 in the morning, get in his car, and go home. Most British workers ride the trains, or they did then. Since the trains keep to exact schedules, so must the workers' starting and quitting times. Five minutes late means another hour of waiting. Instead of "golden hours," the English worker's main weapon is the strike. And, like an American policeman's pistol, his weapon is always at hand.

We had been at Denham only a few days when Rank welcomed his nationwide exhibitors to a studio convention. He spent a couple of months' worth of ration stamps to lay out a few sandwiches for a cocktail party on one of the stages. Adrian and I had seen the spread and thought it rather sad, though we were in sympathy with England's austerity program. A couple of shop stewards had also visited the stage, however, and a short while later, a two-day strike was called. The workers, the union, Rank, and even Britain had lost far more than the few sandwiches were worth, but some sort of strange sense of order had been satisfied.

The English crew was split roughly down the middle in their attitudes toward Hollywood. There were those who truly admired Yankee ingenuity and accepted with appreciation every new technique. But the English character is also strong in tradition, which often means protection of the status quo. To the other half of the crew, the mere mention of Hollywood was a red flag, and the phrase "This is how we do it in Hollywood" was a call to arms. A somewhat undiplomatic American director who preceded us had used this phrase neither wisely nor too well. He was sabotaged to kingdom come.

I walked a tightrope, but there were times I had to take a chance. We were doing a "process" shot of Johnny and Trevor in a car. A process shot is one in which actors perform in front of a transparent screen on which a suitable background is projected. The background showed a road winding through a narrow valley. My first setup was over the actors' shoulders, showing the road ahead through the windshield. Obviously, as the car turned through the curves, the driver had to turn the steering wheel. I had paid no attention to the installation of the car, but when I got behind the camera for a rehearsal, I noticed that the driver was sliding his hands over a stationary wheel as the car took the curves. When I questioned him, he pointed out the wheel was immobilized. I got down to see for myself and noticed that the front wheels had been chained off tight. In answer to my question, the grip in charge said, "That's the way we always do it."

I called on art director Bill Williams and explained that a more effective way was to free the front wheels and raise them slightly off the platform so that the driver could actually turn the wheels. (That's the way it's done in Hollywood, but I didn't have to use the phrase—not even to Bill.) He, in turn, talked to the head grip and it was done. The shot worked fine. Then I had the car turned around for a front view of the two passengers. The background film now showed the road as it twisted away behind the car. When I came back to rehearse the scene I couldn't believe my eyes. The front wheels were tied off tight again, and this time the driver couldn't even slide his hands around the wheel because he couldn't see what the road was doing behind him. I had to do the job all over again, this time with a difference. For this, the more usual setup for a driving shot, a two-by-four is usualy clamped on to one of the front wheels, and a grip watches the screen around the side of the car and moves the wheel in one direction or the other to match the road's curves. The driver need only hold onto the wheel as it responds to the front wheels' action, and his hands are carried with it. We finally worked it out.

Bill Williams subsequently headed a research team which developed the finest process techniques and equipment in the world. Unfortunately, it all went down the drain with Rank's production dreams.

We finished in good time and good shape. The "hands across the ocean" were still friendly as we boarded the *Queen Elizabeth* for New

York. If I've said nice things about England, it's purely hindsight here. In spite of the bicycle rides, the Alps, the lovely countryside, John Mills, Bill Williams, and many other friends I had made, I hated England for every minute I had been away from Jean. Letters just aren't enough, and in 1946 the long-distance phone was an instrument of torture. But at last I was on my way home—so slowly.

Sailing on the *Queen* was exactly like being locked up in a luxury hotel for five days. The same walks, the same meals, the same routine. The only item of interest on the trip was the Duke of Windsor. We took our walks around the deck at the same time of day, though in opposite directions, which gave me the opportunity to note that he, like Erich von Stroheim, never avoided a gaze but looked you squarely in the eye as he passed by. Now why can't some of our Hollywood nobility learn how to do that? We also had the same schedule in the steam room, where he was always accompanied by his equerry. They spoke of nothing but the restaurants they had frequented and the chefs they had known. A kingdom is a sometime thing, but a good meal is forever.

"MR. RKO"

*C*rossfire was by no means the greatest picture ever made, but it was a very, very good one which set important precedents and probably won a greater variety of awards than any other film in RKO's history. It was also perhaps the best-planned film project of all time.

Crossfire was a milestone in my career. As I look back, I'm puzzled. I was definitely the number-one man at the studio. I was invited to attend and speak at the national sales conventions. All the exhibitors were more than complimentary—some called me Mr. RKO—I was basking in the limelight. But why? I'd made a couple of sleepers, one better-than-average mystery suspense film, a few other pictures of no particular note. I'd won a couple of awards, like the Mystery Writers of America award for *Murder, My Sweet*, and all of my films had made money—some even a lot of money. But there wasn't really an outstanding picture in the lot. It certainly didn't bother me then. I was riding the crest of a beautiful wave. I didn't know it was going to turn out to be a sand-buster.

Adrian Scott had optioned Richard Brooks' novel, *The Brick Foxhole*, almost a year before. It was a loose, rambling story of the frustrations of stateside soldiers at the end of the war. The book had a number of subplots, one of which concerned the murder of a homosexual by a sadistic bigot. Adrian had an inspiration: What if the murder and its aftermath were the whole spine of the story, and what if the victim were a heterosexual Jew? We could then do at least a partial study of bigotry—particularly as it relates to anti-Semitism—and nothing like that had ever been done in Hollywood before. Adrian discussed it with our friend Dore Schary, and Schary advised him against it.

Adrian decided to persevere. John Paxton had come with us to England to finish work on *So Well Remembered*, and at odd times, when that film's problems were not too pressing, we discussed and worked on *The Brick Foxhole*. By the time we were back in Hollywood, around the beginning of 1947, John had a full treatment, but not yet a complete script. Now our option was running out, and the studio planned to drop it. N. Peter Rathvon was the interim head of production, so we hurried to his office. After some minutes of fervent sales talk, Rathvon said, "I'll gamble a thousand dollars on your enthusiasm." A thousand dollars! Good Lord!

Now we went to work in earnest. *The Brick Foxhole* became *Crossfire*, a change for the better. Neither Scott, nor Paxton, nor I was Jewish. We realized that could be an advantage, since no one could accuse us of selfish interest or religious bias, but it was also a disadvantage. We had a lot to learn about anti-Semitism and the techniques for combatting bigotry. How does one dramatize that Wasps—rather than Jews—are in control of the financial structure of the United States? How does one get across the fact that Jews *don't* control the film industry? The percentage of Jewish workers in the studios was no greater than their percentage of the national population.

Since we considered the picture a risky experiment, we decided it had to be made at a price, and $500,000 seemed a reasonable figure. Even if the film were a bust, it would probably get back its cost and the chances for making experimental pictures in the future would not be hurt too

badly. To strengthen its box-office potential and ensure quality performances, we decided to make the budget top-heavy on the talent side.
That meant B-picture expenditure below the line, and a very short
schedule—eventually fixed at 22 days. The above-the-line cost (story
and talent) turned out to be double the below-the-line cost (sets,
materials, and labor), just the reverse of the average film.

Not long before we were ready to take off, Schary became the studio
production boss. By this time his doubts—if not all his fears—had
disappeared, and he facilitated our start greatly with his influence and
support. He postponed a couple of B pictures which were about to start
and okayed our using some of their sets and stages, which helped a good
deal to keep our budget in line. He was also helpful in the assembling of
a first-rate cast. Robert Young, Robert Mitchum, and Robert Ryan
were supported by Sam Levene, Gloria Graham, Paul Kelly, and half of
RKO's stock department.

J. Roy Hunt, the cameraman, deserves a chapter to himself, but a
paragraph or two is all I can afford. In 1947 he was almost seventy. He
had gotten into pictures about Year One by building his own camera,
and he had never stopped inventing. Half the improvements on RKO's
special sound camera—the best in the business at that time—were of
his design. I don't think he ever made a penny from them. During the
war, he had built his own electric car and a bus which ran on charcoal
gas. But, best of all, he was one hell of a photographer—and one of the
sweetest men ever created. I made two films with him and saw him
angry only once. That was during my Kirk Douglas film and Kirk could
crack the patience of Job. Roy was a specialist in low-key lighting,
which is what I wanted for *Crossfire*, and he was very fast.

"Low-key lighting" is a misnomer; what it really means is high
contrast. This is the generally accepted style of lighting mystery,
suspense, and heavy mood films. An added advantage is that the lighting can be accomplished much more quickly, since the broad strokes of
light and shade are more important than details of the set, which can
take a long time to light and add little dramatic value to the scene.

In keeping with our aim of getting as much talent as possible "on the
screen," I shot only 140 setups, averaging 7 setups a day—about
normal for a schedule three times as long as ours. It meant playing long
scenes, which was not my usual style. I still wanted action and movement, posing some difficult problems for Hunt and our camera grip.
Once, when I had set up a complex moving shot, Roy asked if I could
hold off until the following day. I could and I did. The next morning,
the setup was ready when I walked in. Roy had spent the entire night in
the studio machine shop building an extension of his own design for our

crab dolly, which made it possible to get what I wanted with a minimum of time and effort. Because of Roy's speed in lighting, we were also able to reverse the usual statistics on time of preparing versus time of shooting. On the average short-schedule film, setting up and lighting take five to ten times as long as the actual shooting. On *Crossfire*, my actors and I were in action at least twice as long as Hunt and his crew.

Too often a director's prestige is related to the length of his schedules. I knew one man who, once he became famous, never asked, "How good is the story?" but "How big is the budget and how long is the schedule?" Although it's true that one can rarely get too much time, it's also true that very often time is badly used.

Another top director—one of the best in the long history of Hollywood—was also one of the greatest time wasters. Apparently, he couldn't visualize the final result, so he would shoot even a simple scene from every possible angle, perhaps ten or twelve setups in all, sometimes taking two or three days to complete. In the final cut, the scene often played in an uninterrupted two-shot—probably set up and filmed in a couple of hours. The rest of the time went into the waste bin with the unused scenes. The man was not only cheating the studio, he was cheating himself.

Actually, working too long is a very mixed blessing. Creative work is constant and fatiguing, and when the brain is tired, mistakes of judgment occur much more frequently. This is a daily danger. And when there is a long schedule, after a certain period, each day brings increasing tension. People who have worked in harmony now start to annoy one another. Long before the final day of shooting, paranoia reigns. The end-of-the-picture party is more than a formal celebration, it gives members of the crew a chance to stop barking and start talking to each other again.

Neither of these problems existed on *Crossfire*. Our schedule was short, and I never worked more than a six-and-a-half-hour day. It was the start of a system I've used since then whenever possible. I found that if I quit shooting about 4:30 and rehearsed the next day's work, which might take fifteen minutes to half an hour—rarely more—everybody benefited. The actors went home knowing what to expect from me and from each other. If there were problems in the scene or with the lines, they could be discussed and rewritten overnight, if necessary. The cameraman and crew knew what the next day's demands were, and since they had to remain on the set until 5:30 or 6:00, they usually started lighting the next morning's first setup. And I could go home with a much easier mind because I knew what tomorrow would bring. The system worked so well I finished *Crossfire* in 20 days, two days ahead of schedule. I wouldn't have done anything differently if I'd had a schedule four times as long.

The film cut together easily and smoothly; there was no footage problem. One tiny change was made. In speaking of the history of bigotry in America, Robert Young had said at one point, "You may not learn it in schools, but it's good American history just the same." Dore was afraid that the public might misconstrue the use of the word "good" as meaning we favored the lynching of minorities (in this case the Irish in the 1840s). So we had Young redub the line to read, "it's *real* American history," etc. A small thing, of no consequence, really, but what a large problem it points to—the continued underestimation of the public's ability to understand.

And yet, I could be wrong. After our rough-cut showing to the sound and music department, one of the young assistant sound cutters, an Argentine, complimented me on the picture.

"It's such a fine suspense story," he said. "Why did you have to bring in that stuff about anti-Semitism?"

"That was our chief reason for making the film," I answered.

"But there is no anti-Semitism in the United States," he protested. "If there were, why is all the money in America controlled by Jewish bankers?" I stared at him in astonishment.

"That's why we made the film" was all I could think of to say.

Our previews were great. Scott and I were walking on air. But Dore is Jewish, and "once bitten, twice shy"; his feet were on the ground. He was still unsure about the public's reception of the film. He had "private runnings" for every possible kind of group—priests, rabbis, Germans, Irish, young, old. In general, the verdict was, "Get it out—fast." There were occasional dissenting opinions. Two or three of my ex-comrades came to see me—all critical of the film. It was too subtle, they said, too susceptible to misinterpretation. Except that they had no creative input in the film at all, this was almost *Cornered* all over again. It seemed the gnat had to be squashed with a sledgehammer. It always surprises me that so many of those who claim to love the "common people" so much have so little faith in their intelligence and under-standing.

The film was finally released—to fine reviews and fine reception. It was a hit, and it wasn't being misunderstood. The Audience Research Institute polled people going into a public showing of the film and polled them again when they came out. The incidence of anti-Semitism had decreased by 14 percent. Of course, like penitents at an evangelist meeting, the good intentions probably leaked away, but maybe just a little did remain. What a triumph for those of us who believed messages could be delivered by someone other than Western Union.

I was on top of the world and so confident of the future that I gladly gave my wife everything when she finally filed for divorce. After all, the way things were going now, I could start from scratch and still be rich in a few short years. Jean and I were more in love than ever. We had bought a hundred acres near Agoura and were drilling water wells and planning our house and horse farm. One Sunday afternoon, after a day spent in pruning some of the great oaks on our land, Jean and I sat on a hill looking out over a lovely landscape. We could see forever, and there wasn't a cloud in the sky.

The next day I was handed a pink subpoena.

THE HOTTEST ACT IN TOWN

The hot-pink subpoena commanded United States Marshal Robert E. Clark to summon Edward Dmytryk to appear before the Un-American Activities Committee of the United States House of Representatives, of which the Hon. J. Parnell Thomas of New Jersey was chairman, on Oct. 23, 1947 at the hour of 10:30 A.M. The subpoena was dated 18th of Sept., 1947 and was signed with the scarcely legible scrawl of the Hon. chairman himself. Little did I suspect that the Hon. chairman and I would both be guests of the federal prison system in about three years.   Adrian Scott and I both received our subpoenas at the studio and were, at first, somewhat elated. The confrontation with the Hollywood rightists, led by C. B. De Mille, John Wayne, Hedda Hopper, Sam Wood, Robert Montgomery, Adolphe Menjou, and a number of less vocal personalities, had been brewing for some time, and we had been looking forward to it.

The Communists had been particularly active in the Writers Guild. Their tactics to gain control of that organization had not only been partly successful, but were extremely annoying. One of their ploys at guild meetings, for instance, was to delay the vote on any crucial issue until long after midnight, by which time most reasonable members had gone home, leaving the more disciplined leftists in the majority. It was enough to put any self-respecting reactionary off his feed.

The Directors Guild was not nearly as susceptible to our machinations. There was only a handful of Communists in the guild, so they confined themselves to pushing liberal issues for which they could get the backing of most guild members. They did succeed in electing a decidedly liberal slate of guild officers, though not one of them was a Communist, nor, in my opinion, was any of them aware that the Communists were responsible for the tactics leading to their election. C. B. De Mille, who had broken with the unions over the compulsory payment of one dollar into a strike fund, was not active in guild matters at this time though he was one of the staunchest right-wingers in Hollywood. He remained very active behind the scenes, however, and was due to come out of the woodwork when the hunting season was on.

There had been a strong movement in the craft unions to establish the CIO as a viable force, led by Sorell of the Painters' Union. Sorell was widely regarded as a Communist, though I'm not aware that this was ever positively established. There was no doubt of his strong left leanings, however, or of the fact that the Communists in Hollywood gave him their full support, particularly in the messy and abortive "painters' strike" in 1945. Roy Brewer, the local head of the IATSE fought Sorell with everything at his command and eliminated that threat in relatively short order. Now he was one of the leaders in the rightists' attempt to get rid of the Hollywood "reds" and "pinkos."

Since the committee had a well-earned reputation for bias, Scott and I knew we would need some kind of legal representation. Scott had recently read *Behind the Silken Curtain* by Bartley Crum, a noted San Francisco attorney, and was impressed by his intelligence and point of view. Besides, he was a Catholic and a Republican. Crum had been one of the leaders of the "young Turks" who had bandwagoned Wendell Willkie to the 1940 Republican presidential nomination. More recently, he had been Truman's representative on an international committee investigating the political and military situation in Palestine. Crum's book presented his own view of the investigation.

Scott and I flew to San Francisco and met Crum at his offices. We found him to be a small, trim, good-looking man of pleasant demeanor. He had the typical liberal Republican's attitude toward HUAC and its continuing attempts to censor by intimidation—he was shocked. He agreed to represent us in Washington, and we flew back to Hollywood in a much more optimistic state of mind. Neither of us realized that we had just sounded the death knell of a very promising career.

In the meantime, some seventeen other Hollywood leftists had also received subpoenas. Those among them who were still party members had immediately organized themselves and hired lawyers. They now set about to consolidate the whole nineteen, since the independence of any one of that group would have put their long-term strategy in danger. Scott and I were asked to attend a meeting at which plans would be discussed for the coming inquisition.

The first meeting, which was to place the stamp of inevitability on the future events of all our lives, took place at Lewis Milestone's home in Beverly Hills. Milestone was not a Communist—he was an easygoing liberal and a soft touch for any leftist with an honorable cause. As a director of great reputation, he had been singled out for a subpoena. Actually, in the group of nineteen, there were a few sheep to go along with the majority of goats, and I believe the committee knew that. But it couldn't hurt to scare hell out of them and teach them a lesson, now could it?

The lawyers present were Charles Katz, Ben Margolis, and Robert Kenney. Kenney had been attorney general of California and was a man with a long history of liberal concerns. He was no longer very active, but he made a most attractive and legitimate front, and front was what was now most needed. Two important decisions were made at that meeting: first, that Adrian and I with our attorney, Crum, would join the larger group in the fight against the committee; and second, that all decisions be made only by unanimous consent, and, once made, must be strictly adhered to. Over the next few years, I learned that the unanimity rule was one of the major weapons in the Communist tactical armory. I have been allergic to it ever since. Where unanimity is required, freedom ceases to exist. But I was scarcely aware of that when Larry Parks moved the rule (at the instigation, he later told me, of one of the Communist lawyers of the group) and I voted willingly for its adoption. Parks later became one of the most tragic victims of the committee and its Hollywood allies.

Now labeled "The Unfriendly Witnesses," we flew to Washington and ensconced ourselves at the Sheraton Park Hotel. Thank God foresight is so limited—we were a cheerful group, looking forward confidently to our confrontation with the committee. We were certain of victory. After all, Howard Hughes had recently faced a congressional committee and had shouted it into silence. We didn't have his billions, but were we any less capable? We thought not.

The committee officially opened its hearings on October 20, 1947.

The first few days were taken up with testimony from the studio executives and Hollywood's friendly witnesses. The bosses were a craven lot, beating their breasts in shame and publicly donning their hair shirts in penitence. It all seemed so unnecessary, since not one of them could remember a single film which had succeeded in sneaking even a tiny pinch of propaganda past their vigilant eyes. I believe it was Louis B. Mayer who did recall that in a Robert Taylor film a scene had been written showing him visiting a Russian family amid expressions of gaiety and good feeling. Mayer had blue-penciled the scene as being unrealistic—no Russian could ever summon up a laugh while living under Communist rule.

Thomas scolded the producers as though they were naughty school-boys—and they took the chastisement in the same frame of reference. They did have a friend on the committee, however. Richard Milhous Nixon, a freshman congressman from Whittier, California, was sitting as a member and asking sympathetic questions that elicited responses which enabled the Hollywood tycoons to get off the hook. He was also building a solid base of support for the future.

Adroitly mixed with the executives were the friendly witnesses who were there to testify that communism *was* a danger in Hollywood and that propaganda *had* infiltrated the screen. Concrete examples, how-ever, were few and unconvincing. Gary Cooper mentioned some script concerning mutinying cavalrymen, I think, which he had read and rejected. Milestone later filled in some of the details. I believe the script was *Jubal Troop*. The studio had sent it to Milestone, and he, in turn, had sent a copy to Cooper. After waiting a couple of weeks, he called Gary for his reaction.

"I'm not through with it yet," said Cooper. "I'm reading it word by word."

Milestone decided that such a reading technique deserved more time, so he waited another three or four weeks, then called again. "Coop" hadn't finished yet.

"How did you like the scene where . . . ?" and here Millie described a scene which appeared at about page 30 in the script.

"Oh," said Gary, "I haven't gotten there yet." And he probably never did. He didn't make the picture, either.

Cooper was no idiot. He was a good and simple man, the ideal embodiment of a great American myth. Politics was a puzzle to him, and the stale smell of a crowded committee room in Washington was no match for the heady air of hunting season in the Montana wilds. He was not an actor in the accepted sense, but when he was impersonating the myth, he was the best there ever was. And he eventually faced slow death as bravely as any person could. He just shouldn't have been sitting there "yupping" and "noping" before a man who wasn't fit to shine his shoes.

Adolphe Menjou was another specimen altogether. Very sophisticated, extremely aware, he was almost psychopathically defending the money and property he had acquired through the years of a successful career. To him there *was* a "commie" behind every tree, and anyone to the left of Hamilton Fish was a "pinko." He was a reincarnation of a witch hunter of the Middle Ages. Once the slightest charge was insinuated, you were doomed. If you denied it, the devil was forcing you to lie; if you admitted it, well, the only cure was death. When asked how an actor could insert propaganda into a film, he answered, "Very simply. By the lift of an eyebrow, a turn of the head."

This brought laughter and ridicule from many people who, at this stage of the hearings, were still strongly on our side. But they were blind to their own potential. I doubt that anyone has ever been turned on to communism by a supercilious stare, but the possibility is always there and the Communists know it better than anybody. That is why such a tight rein is kept on film production in the Soviet Union. At its best, that is what film communication is all about. Eisenstein knew that. A lifted eyebrow, a slight droop of the shoulders, a delicately bent spine, an artful shrug, a well-timed turn of the hand, can be as effective as ten pages of rhetoric. But Menjou was talking about subtleties, and to a good Communist, subtlety is banging a shoe on the desk. I've known a number of Communist actors, and most of them went into a scene like the bull in a beer commercial. And that's the way they started our defense.

At this stage of the proceedings, we had it won hands down. The chairman's ragging and bullying of the executives, the idiotic answers of most of the friendly witnesses, and the long-established tendency of the press to distrust the committee had turned public reaction strongly in our favor. The news media generally treated the cooperating witnesses with contempt. Of course, they generally treated everybody with contempt, but with any skill at all, we could have used this attitude to our advantage. Hollywood figures like David O. Selznick, Samuel Goldwyn, and Dore Schary had come out publicly in our favor. At considerable cost to themselves, a large contingent of film personalities, led by Humphrey Bogart, Betty Bacall, Danny Kaye, and Judy Garland came to Washington to attend the hearings and give us their support. An equally large contingent of Broadway stars was also there. Washington had never seen the like.

There was some trouble in paradise, of course. Bertolt Brecht wanted to testify freely and get out of the country.

"The fascists have chased me around the world," he said. "First they drove me to Siberia, then to Japan, then to Mexico, and finally to the United States. And here they caught me."

Since it was felt that the committee's case against him was weak, he was given permission to testify, which he eventually did. Then he left immediately for East Germany. Another one of the nineteen who was not a party member, but whose wife was, also wanted to testify freely. For twenty-four hours it was touch and go, but his wife threatened to divorce him, and he knuckled under. He was not called.

For days we had been having meetings with our attorneys, preparing evasive answers to possible questions, and writing our separate statements. Any appearance of conspiracy—a felony—had to be avoided, but each of us knew what the others were doing and all our statements were carefully coordinated. Since *Crossfire* was a worldwide smash, my attack, as well as Adrian's, centered on the committee's ethnic bias and its attempts to limit freedom of speech in the area of national self-criticism. But none of our lawyers really expected that we would be heard, and the strategy was say nothing, hide under the possible cover of the First Amendment, and hope for a favorable verdict from the Supreme Court. "Taking the Fifth" was never considered, though it would have kept us out of jail; the implication of guilt was considered too dangerous.

Accompanied by Bartley Crum, who knew his way around Washington, Adrian and I had been visiting various members of Congress who might be able to help us. Our reception was always warm and friendly—after all, we were part of the hottest act in town—but the helping hand was nowhere to be found. Emmanuel Celler, the chairman of the House Judiciary Committee, put it succinctly: "I think you're absolutely in the right, but it's a political matter. I wouldn't touch it with a ten-foot pole." A tired cliche—but apt.

With all the public feeling in our favor, Bart Crum suggested that Adrian and I should testify freely, which we were perfectly willing to do. We felt it might serve to pull the committee's fangs. You'd have thought we were offering to atomize the Kremlin. The unanimity rule was invoked, and that was that. From their point of view, they were absolutely right. If we had answered any substantive questions at all, we would have been legally required to give names if we were asked to. If we refused to name party members, as, at that time, we certainly would have done, we would still be cited for contempt. If we had given the names, the other members of our group would have been in the soup. Eventually, that's where we wound up anyway, but at this point the battle had barely begun and our eyes were fixed on a liberal Supreme Court. With no argument, we put our suggestion aside and on the 27th of October, entered the chamber prepared to face the inquisitors.

20

"THIS IS WAR!"

T he chamber was crowded; the real fun was about to begin. Only one familiar face was missing—that of Congressman Nixon. Like Marlon Brando, he suddenly had to go to the toilet—only his was in Whittier, California. He had nothing to gain—and possibly something to lose—by sitting on the bench for the next few days. But everyone else was there. Dore Schary sat beside me as we watched John Howard Lawson being sworn in. He was the leader and would set the tone of our attack. Unfortunately, Lawson was tone-deaf.

It started with the usual identification by name and address. Then Lawson requested permission to read a statement. After a bit of bickering, Thomas asked to look at it before making his decision. He was, as they say in court, making a record. The statement was handed over to the chairman, who made only a slight pretense of reading it, then ruled that it was irrelevant. Lawson started to argue; Thomas banged his gavel. The exchange got so hot that the chairman nearly forgot to ask what came to be called "the sixty-four dollar question": "Are you now or have you ever been a member of the Communist party?"

Now Lawson started shouting in earnest, trying to enumerate his reasons for refusing to answer the question. Between gavel poundings, the chairman screamed, "Answer yes or no!" Shouting and banging— banging and shouting. It was a miserable scene. I was hit by a feeling I had had once before, when a car skidded into me across a wet street. "This is it," I thought. I scrunched down in my seat and turned to Dore.

"What are my chances at the studio now?" I asked.

"You have an ironclad contract," he replied.

And so it went for the rest of the hearing. I could literally feel the listeners' sympathies oozing away with each shout from one of our group. Thomas had made a ridiculous show of himself with his shouting and free use of the gavel; now we were matching him shout for shout—it was a fight we couldn't win. Few people expect taste and restraint from a congressman, but we were supposed to be artists. Now and then there was a little relief. When asked the obligatory question, Ring Lardner, Jr. had replied, "I could answer that, but I'd hate myself in the morning."

It got a pretty good laugh, but it did little to help our cause. Dalton Trumbo, usually suave and smooth, got involved in another shouting match with Thomas. Our moderate supporters were exchanging embarrassed looks. Adrian and I both spoke quietly. At one point, reacting to one of my remarks, Thomas asked sarcastically, "When did *you* learn about the Constitution?"

"I'll be glad to answer that, Mr. Chairman," I said, and prepared to launch into an interpretation of the Bill of Rights. Stripling, the committee counsel, saw that Thomas had fallen into a trap of his own making, and quickly insisted I answer the previous question. Thomas was always getting himself in trouble, but that didn't change things either. Once or twice, in his anxiety to gavel a witness out of the chair, he forgot to ask the sixty-four-dollar question—a must if the committee was to get a contempt citation. Stripling always straightened him out. When Larry Parks' turn came, he actually *was* in the toilet, so another unfriendly witness was called instead. Larry never did appear before Thomas, but it didn't save him from a life of quiet frustration.

A funny thing happened to me on my way to misery. I was sitting in the witness chair, waiting while the chairman made the usual short pretense of studying a copy of my statement. Crouching in front of me, at the base of the arced bench at which the committee was seated, were about twenty-five news photographers, cameras at the ready. I had wondered briefly why no pictures had yet been taken, but at the moment my thoughts were far away. Unthinking, my hand, with index finger extended, went to my nose in an unconscious gesture of mine. It took only a fraction of a second, but in that short time all twenty-five bulbs popped simultaneously, as if activated by a common switch. Then all the photographers got up and left. As they moved out, I heard one of them say to another, "Are you satisfied now?" That picture, "up" angle, with my finger pushing my nose grotesquely out of joint, appeared in the next issue of *Time* magazine.

Much has been said over the years about corruption and dishonesty in politics, law-enforcement agencies, and big business. In my opinion, none of them is even close to our national press when it comes to lack of honesty and integrity. I disliked Spiro Agnew and Richard Nixon intensely, but I could always sympathize with them when they wailed about the iniquities of our news corps. The press is the guardian of our freedoms, and it occasionally comes through, but who guards the guardians? Self-policing is a dirty word in the newsroom.

In early 1947, while absorbing background material for my forthcoming production of Budd Schulberg's novel, *The Harder They Fall*, I had talked to various fight game figures, accompanied by Budd, who had been over the ground before me. He had spent a lot of words on the arrant dishonesty of the fight game, but he had said little about the sportswriters, without whom the fight game could scarcely exist. Mike Jacobs, the high Pooh-Bah of the racket, himself disclosed what was to me the shocking news that Damon Runyon got a sizable percentage of the purse of every fighter who entered the ring in Madison Square Garden, or he never entered the ring at all. And all reporters who covered the Garden beat got their cuts, the size depending on their papers' value at the box office. Ben Hecht, a former sportswriter, confirmed this to me sometime later.

In my experience with the press, I have rarely been quoted accurately, in context, or in full. Generally the reporters get not what you have to say, but what they are looking for—even if they have to twist, senselessly edit, or even add a few words of their own.

It puzzles me that sophisticated and informed persons will believe anything that's printed. An experience in point: When I agreed to direct *The Young Lions*, the story had been kicking around for years and was now going to be made at 20th as a moderately priced film. The cost, a very nominal $2,000,000, necessitated a cast of nonstars. Wishing to upgrade the picture, I succeeded in getting Monty Clift for "Noah" and Marlon Brando for "Christian."

Tony Randall had been scheduled to play the part of Whiteacre, but although I considered him a very fine actor, he just wasn't the character as I saw it. MCA, which represented both Clift and Brando, also handled Dean Martin, and Martin's agent had mentioned how much Dean wanted to play a decent "straight" role. Because it could mean a great deal for his career, MCA would also deliver him at a price. The more I thought about it, the better I liked the idea. I had had good luck with offbeat casting, and this looked like another good chance.

Dean would have to play a majority of his scenes with Monty. I had made *Raintree County* with Clift, and I was aware of his lack of stability under trying circumstances. I felt it would be wise to consult Clift in this instance in order to avoid possible future complications. So I phoned Monty and mentioned Dean. "Good God, no!" he said. He knew Dean only as Jerry Lewis' partner.

I next mentioned Tony Randall. Monty didn't know his work, but a film of Randall's was appearing in New York at the time. Monty promised to see it that evening and call me the next day. Early the following morning, he did.

"If it's still all right," he said, "I'll go with Dean Martin." And that's how Martin got the job.

If there's anything hard for an agent to take, it's losing a part to another agent. I never heard Tony question this casting switch, but his agent had plenty to say, and he said it often. To save Randall's face, which hardly needed saving, his agent let it be known all over town that Dean had gotten the part only because MCA had blackmailed me—no Martin, no Brando or Clift. The item was printed in the *Hollywood Reporter*'s gossip column, then later reprinted by *Fortune* magazine in a business article on MCA. The story was clearly absurd. If MCA *had* made that kind of threat, it would have lost at least two clients. I brushed it off. Sour grapes are never in short supply in Hollywood.

Some years later, the Justice Department was investigating MCA on antitrust charges. Eventually I was called to testify before the grand jury. The government attorney questioned me about the Dean Martin– Tony Randall affair, quoting the *Fortune* article. I replied that the story was nonsense and related the facts. The attorney looked at me in amazement, then went at me hammer and tongs. It was inconceivable, he said, that the *Hollywood Reporter* and *Fortune* magazine could both be wrong. I pointed out that it was only one story, which *Fortune* had borrowed from the *Reporter*. Nevertheless, said the attorney, I *must* be wrong. *Fortune* was a solid, staid, business journal, not a scandal sheet. "I'm sorry," I said, "but I was there. I alone made the decision."

Before they excused me from the witness chair, after a rough twenty minutes, they promised to subpoena all my records and probably prosecute me for perjury. And if MCA hadn't agreed to a consent decree a short time later, they would have. It was only a jealous agent's bit of gossip, but it had been sanctified by appearing in print, and the truth just couldn't change that.

Oddly enough, some of the cleanest reporting has been done by Hollywood columnists—when they are not engaged in spreading back- biting gossip. Virginia McPherson, writing for the old *L.A. Mirror*, was one of the best. And Louella Parsons could be so drunk at an interview one would swear she had already passed out. But in her next column, everything was there—ungrammatical perhaps, but never out of context.

The hearings ended abruptly, with nine of the unfriendly witnesses still uncalled. Apparently Thomas had become apprehensive about the public reaction to the hearings and had decided to stop short. As far as

I was concerned, it was a standoff. None of the visiting Hollywood stars was inviting any of us to cozy dinners in celebration of the committee's defeat. That fickle finger of fate was beckoning again, and I didn't want to look.

We made it back to Hollywood, basking for a short time in the light of what our leftist friends assured us was a fine and glorious victory, but the decision that would affect our lives was being made at the Waldorf-Astoria Hotel in New York. There, on November 27, 1947, the representatives of the motion-picture industry formally decided to fire any accused worker who would not freely answer all questions asked by the Un-American Activities Committee and who could not clear himself of charges that he was or had been a member of the Communist party. The following day, since Dore refused to be the hatchet man, N. Peter Rathvon called Scott and me into his office and asked us once more to recant and to purge ourselves. With hardly any sense of martyrdom at all, we refused. In that case, he informed us, we were no longer employees of RKO. So much for ironclad contracts. We went back to clean out our respective offices. The next day was Thanksgiving. Even a B writer wouldn't have dared that bit of bathos, but truth, you know . . .

We now busied ourselves with fund-raising activities. A number of the Hollywood Ten, as we would be known from here into eternity, had been insolvent even before the hearings. The rest of us knew we would be out of funds before very long, with a three- or four-year fight ahead. There were a number of good "names," like Thomas Mann and John Huston, still on our side. And there was still a large body of liberal chic to draw on. But the really important battles were being lost.

Herbert Biberman and I were the only members of the Ten who belonged to the Directors Guild. A number of our more liberal colleagues now called on the guild to take a stand against the Waldorf-Astoria Declaration. A meeting was convened, and we had a full house. But when I saw that De Mille was in attendance for the first time since his fight with AFTRA, and had even been given an honorary seat at the guild officers' table, where he didn't belong, I knew it was all over. The liberals didn't have a chance. Early in the evening, one of them moved that all votes be by secret ballot. This vote was by show of hands. As those in favor raised their arms above their heads, Michael Curtiz jumped to his feet, shouting, "Take their names! Take their names! Take their names!" Even the secret ballot was now un-American.

In the midst of the general uproar, De Mille rose to his feet and screamed at the mob: "This is war!"

So it was, and I didn't have a gun.

WHISTLING IN
THE DARK

We weathered Christmas and the New Year in relatively good spirits. Then the reaction set in. At this point, with the contempt trials still some months away, the accent was on staying alive, and the weekly meetings of the Ten concerned themselves mostly with that problem. Any money collected at fund-raising affairs was earmarked for the legal battle. Lawyers can spend money faster than film directors. Even though our attorneys were getting precious little in personal salary, transcripts, pretrial actions, and trial preparation were gobbling it up as fast as we could collect it. If we wanted to eat, we had to fend for ourselves.

I was the only straight director in the group; the others, including Biberman, were all writers. There were many sympathetic colleagues willing to front for them, and some work was sold in this fashion. There were also producers who, out of sympathy or out of greed, were willing to accept scripts "under the table" as long as they were also under a pseudonym. The prices they paid were ridiculously small—but one has to take advantage of a falling market.

Nobody got rich. Retrenchment was the order of the day. Homes and furnishings were sold, households consolidated.

A much larger number of other writers and actors in Hollywood and New York were now suffering from the effects of a general blacklist. A former FBI agent was hired as the industry watchdog. Anyone who had ever signed a questionable petition, been a premature antifascist, or, in some cases, even associated with leftists, lost his job. This condition was general in films, radio, and TV. It lasted for many, many years.

Phones were tapped by the hundreds. Sometime during our first stay in Washington, we had learned that listening devices could be frustrated by sharp sounds. Now, few conversations were held without the constant noise of snapping fingers. It must have been a funny scene, but it was all deadly serious to us then.

Under these conditions, rumors were rife. It was whispered that all suspects were to be rounded up and sent to jail. An exodus to Mexico resulted. (Escaping to Mexico for freedom! Think about that.) For some time Cuernavaca was the second largest film writers' colony in the world. Eventually, of course, fear ebbed away, money ran out, and the writers returned to town. But that was still a long time in the future.

I had given away literally everything except a small bank account and my car in my divorce settlement. The money was soon gone. I was not a writer and had no scripts to sell. I don't know how long I could have avoided the rescue mission if a strange man hadn't come to town. Rod Geiger was a short, somewhat rotund man in his late thirties. His speech was a strange mixture of half a dozen New York dialects, but his mind was razor-sharp, and all his own.

Before the war he had been a secretary for New York's leading importer of foreign films. He was also some kind of artist. These two qualifications led to a cushy job with the army—he oversaw the decorating of the officers' clubs wherever the war took them, and he designed VD posters. When the United States Army entered Rome, he met a relatively unknown Italian director named Rossellini. Using discarded Signal Corps film, Rossellini had managed to make a picture about life under the German occupation. It was called, *Rome, Open City*. Geiger brought the film to New York with him and persuaded his former boss to release it. It was a smash. Now Geiger had the bug.

He got together some money and a few American actors and went back to Rome for another film with Rossellini—this time as the producer. The result of that collaboration was *Paisan*, another hit on its American release. Rossellini never made another first-class feature. Geiger was a little luckier.

The two Italian films had made him some money, which he spent with a lavish hand. He owned a lodge on Lake George in upstate New York and now rented a suite at the Hollywood Roosevelt Hotel, where I met and talked with him for the first time.

Geiger had purchased the rights to Pietro DiDonato's *Christ in Concrete*. A script was being written by John Penn, and Geiger wanted me to make the picture. I warned him that there was no way he could get backing in the States if I directed the film. He shrugged it off with the most delicate of gestures—the mark of a really fine operator. If he's fool enough to try, I thought, what have I got to lose. Sight unseen, I agreed to the project.

For the duration of the preparatory period, Rod and his girlfriend Katya leased a house in Mandeville Canyon. Since I could no longer support my exwife in MacDougal Alley in the style to which she had become accustomed, she had moved back to what was now her apartment house in Beverly Hills. Aside from one unit in which Alvah Bessie had been living rent-free for some months now, the house was bringing in an income, and she and my son could live a modest but reasonably secure life. I had no place to go, so, since there was plenty of room, I moved in with Geiger. I had a roof over my head, food in the refrigerator, work to do, and Jean was by my side. Things could have been worse.

Penn was taking forever with the script, whose turns and twists were now flying off in all directions. Without too much difficulty, I persuaded Geiger to hire a new writer. Ben Barzman had done a good job for me on a difficult project (*Back to Bataan*), he was a close friend, and he, too, was blacklisted (though he was not one of the Ten). Geiger signed him to write the script. He read the book and we agreed that though it had a great final sequence and excellent and honest characters, it was far too rambling for a film. He read what there was of Penn's script—nothing could be salvaged. We sat down and put our heads together.

DiDonato, a Brooklyn bricklayer, had written a short story about his Italian-born father, who had been buried alive in concrete following the collapse of an undershored, underpriced, demolition and rebuilding job in the early days of the Great Depression. It appeared in *Esquire* magazine and was highly praised. Then they published the whole novel under the title of the short story, *Christ in Concrete*. Its depiction of life in the Italian immigrant community was vibrant and interesting, but there was no true plot line as such.

Barzman and I sat down to "one-line" a plot. Ideas flowed like wine at an Italian wedding, and in a few hours we had a story line from which we never deviated. Simplicity was the key. Geremio is a carefree young Italian-American bricklayer. One day, while working near the top of a skyscraper, he narrowly escapes falling to his death. He realizes that if he had died, there would have been no one to mourn him. His Irish-American girlfriend wants no part of marriage responsibilities, so he gets a bride from Italy through the intercession of a mutual friend. But Annunziata has laid down one condition before agreeing to come to America: No matter how small, she must have a house of her own. Geremio lies and writes her that he has such a house in Brooklyn. At the marriage feast, he makes arrangements to buy a house on terms which include the right to stay there for the three days of their honeymoon, but no permanent occupation rights until $500 has been paid. At the end of an idyllic three-day honeymoon, Annunziata discovers the house is not theirs to live in. She is desolated, then forces Geremio to agree to save every penny until the $500 can be paid. In the meantime, they live in a cold-water flat in New York.

The money comes hard, but eventually they almost achieve their goal. Then comes their first baby. And so it goes; every time the goal is in sight again, a new baby arrives. Just as they are within a few dollars of finally owning their home, Wall Street collapses, taking the building trade with it. Slowly their money and their dream slip away. Eventually, in desperation, Geremio takes a job on which all safety regulations have been ignored in the interests of economy. In a harrowing scene, a part of the building collapses, and Geremio is buried in wet concrete. His life is worth $1,000 in compensation, enough to buy Annunziata the house.

Barzman started to flesh out the script, and Geiger started to look for backing. As I had predicted, making the film in the United States was impossible. The migration back to Europe in search of the right to work and think as one pleased, though still a trickle, had already begun. Now we had to join it. Though I was as yet unaware of it, Geiger had squandered all his assets and was now living primarily on credit cards. But, as must be the case with any self-respecting promoter, his facade was magnificent. Jean went with me. The divorce would become final in the next few weeks, and we expected to get married in England. But first I had to get the court's permission to leave the country. It was forthcoming, but with a three-month limit. That was good enough for a start.

Using an air travel card, Geiger, Katya, her young son, Jean, and I boarded a plane for London—but, for some reason, we were going by way of Sweden. It seemed the long way round, but what the hell—where else did I have to go? We spent a few lovely days in Stockholm, where, at a restaurant in a park with a name that translates into something like "The Fortress," I had the second best non-Chinese dinner of my life.

Next we flew to London, checking in at a "drummers'" hotel in Oxford Street. Now, for the first time, I was able to watch a first-class operator at work. As usual, we were short of funds, and we didn't know how long we would have to stay in London to set up a deal. Money was an absolute necessity. A few days after our arrival, Rod and I were walking down Oxford Street. Suddenly he touched my arm.

"Excuse me for a few minutes," he said. "Just wait here for me." I watched as he entered a small Blue Cars office, the equivalent of an Avis or a Hertz in America. I knew that Rod had never been in London before and was acquainted with no one here, and I wondered what business he could possibly have in a car rental agency on Oxford Street. I didn't have to wait too long to find out. After about fifteen minutes, he came out of the office, a small smile on his face. He pulled his hand half out of his pocket in a gesture that was to become quite familiar. In his fist was a wad of British money.

"Five hundred pounds," he said. At the going rate, that was more than $2,000. And the donor had been a complete stranger fifteen minutes before. A miracle, I thought. I didn't know then that I would see Geiger perform enough of them to warrant a high place on the calendar of saints.

We moved to the Selsden Park Hotel, on the outskirts of London. It was a sort of middle-class residence hotel. The rhododendrons were in bloom, and the grounds were beautiful. Inside were all the stereotypes I refused to believe still existed. The mere sight of an American was enough to make most of the Colonel Blimps and their ladies frown. But it was lovely to be awakened early in the morning by the haunting cry of the cuckoo, and we weathered the next few weeks rather well.

In the meantime, Geiger had run into a producer who had access to money, and who agreed to help Rod get the financing for our picture— on one condition. He wanted me to direct another film for him first. I hadn't felt so wanted in months; of course I accepted. But first I had some old business to take care of. Leaving Rod in London, Jean and I headed back to Washington.

In April, 1948, Lawson and Trumbo had been tried for contempt of Congress. The rest of us had stipulated that we would be bound by the decision in their cases. Two trials were held because the charges against each differed somewhat. Now the verdict was in—guilty as charged— and we were starting on the long, slow trail leading to the Supreme Court. But first there were certain technicalities to be observed, and my presence in Washington was desired.

Jean and I had hoped to marry in England, but my ex-wife had refused to pick up the final papers. I got in touch with my business manager, who was still doing an occasional odd job for me though there was no business to manage, and he arranged to have the final papers picked up in my name. Jean and I drove up to Ellicott City, Maryland, and applied for a marriage license. On the way back to the Capitol, we were picked up for speeding and booked at the station for driving five miles over the limit. I was beginning to think Washington didn't like me. Two or three days later, our business completed, we headed for Philadelphia in our rental car, accompanied by another of the Ten, Albert Maltz.

When we reached Ellicott City, the first order of business was to find someone to marry us. We located a Protestant preacher who agreed to perform the ceremony if I could swear that I had been the injured party in the divorce. Since that is largely a matter of opinion, and it was my opinion he was asking, I could swear wholeheartedly. The next item on the agenda was to pick up our license. As we pulled up to the small, gold-leaf cupolaed city hall, we noticed people looking out of the windows. We craned around, but there was no one behind us. They were looking at us. Oh, God, I thought, here we go again! The word has gotten out, and things are going to be rough. I didn't care about myself—I had asked for it—but Jean had never had a subversive thought in her life. Apprehensively, we got out of the car and entered the city hall.

As Jean and I approached the license counter, the most beautiful tenor voice I had heard in years started singing, "Drink to Me Only with Thine Eyes." We looked around. They were standing in the doorways, smiling at us, and a short, pleasant, middle-aged man (we later learned he was the city treasurer) was singing his heart out. We could hardly stand it. There was a little charity in this country after all.

We got our license, borrowed the girl at the desk as a second witness, and drove off to the minister's home. There, with Albert Maltz as my best man, we went through a simple ceremony and exchanged the fifteen-dollar gold bands we had bought in Washington the day before. When we dropped the girl off back at the city hall, our welcoming committee was there again, and as we drove away a lovely tenor rendition of "I Love You Truly" followed us down the road. In the middle of the swamp, a flower bloomed.

That night—the first night of our married life—we stopped in Philadelphia, where Paul Robeson, Maltz, two or three others of the Ten, and I spoke to a gathering of supporters. We said all the nasty things about the committee we were expected to say and uttered all the clichés about freedom of speech that were demanded. I never agreed with W. C. Fields—on the whole, I would rather have been some place else.

A DOG'S LIFE

The case of the Hollywood Ten was now on its way to the Supreme Court, so I was able to get a year's leave on my passport. Jean and I made a quick trip back to Hollywood to sell my car and settle a few small affairs. Jean's mother was pretty broken up. She was convinced that once I got Jean to England, the next step was Russia. Once behind the Iron Curtain, she would never see her darling daughter again. Well, that was one solution to my problems, but not the one we were looking for. I briefly considered reclaiming my Canadian citizenship and moving permanently to England, but that wasn't the answer, either. However difficult, Jean and I decided to see it through.

Back in England, we found that Geiger had leased a large house in Staines and was living in luxury. Lacking his magic wand, we holed up temporarily at the Atheneum Court Hotel in Piccadilly. One day Jean visited the American embassy to inquire about housing and met an employee who was moving back to the States and had a house to sublet. It turned out to be a charming residence in Glebe Place in Chelsea, just around the corner from Carol Reed. Like most London houses, it was one room wide and four rooms high. The stairs were barely wide enough for a cat, and we had to learn the proper way to bank the charcoal fire if we wanted hot water in the morning. But it was within walking distance of the Thames, had a pleasant back garden, and the price was right. Like most of London's buildings after the war, it was a dirty slate-gray. Soon after we moved in, I scrubbed the whole four-story front with sugar soap. It was like removing the surface muck from a fine old portrait. Its original high quality paint now gleamed a soft off-white. We were to spend a happy year there.

The producer whose film I had agreed to make was a man named Nat Bronston. He had the rights to an unpublished novel, *Man About a Dog*, by Alec Coppel. Alec was going to write the screenplay, and Bronston suggested that Alec and Myra Coppel, Jean and I, and Bronston and his girlfriend Marushka, retire to a resort hotel at Lake Annecy, in the foothills of the French Alps, to work on the script. It seemed like nice retiring to me, and we agreed. I figured there had to be some method in his madness, but at the moment everything seemed to be aboveboard.

Alec, of course, was doing most of the work. He and I would meet whenever necessary to discuss an upcoming sequence. Then he would go back to his room to work while Jean and I, sometimes accompanied by Myra, would swim or sail, or just lie around drinking in the sun. In the evenings we got together for dinner, sometimes at the hotel, sometimes at one of the many fine French restaurants that ringed the lake. Once in a great while Bronston and his lady love joined us for dinner.

Marushka was a Russian opera singer. As an artist, she was merely competent, but she had an outstanding gift. She could hit an extremely high note. She was the girl who stood behind the backdrop and hit the X above high C which the diva onstage couldn't reach. For the first time I learned that lip-syncing wasn't a creation of the film industry. Marushka's skin was ultrasensitive to light, so we never saw her in the daytime. She was also sensitive to crowds, so we rarely saw her for dinner. I wondered why she had come with us at all. Three or four weeks later, as Alec was finishing the draft, I found out.

Bronston read the nearly finished script and couldn't find a scene for Marushka and her voice. *Man About a Dog* was a pure suspense story. The leading character is a doctor who has a philandering wife. Her latest love is a young American. Having tired of his wife's infidelities, the doctor logically decides to punish her by doing away with her lover. He imprisons the young man in the sub-basement of a bombed-out building, where he keeps him chained within a limited area. His plan is ingenious. He will keep the American captive for a few months. If the police find him during that time, no action will result since the American, considering the circumstances which led to his imprisonment, would be too embarrassed to bring charges. If the police fail, then the doctor will feel free to do away with him. To this end, every time he visits the sub-basement with supplies for his prisoner, he also brings a couple of hot-water bags full of sulfuric acid, which he empties into a tub in an adjoining room. By the time his self-imposed time limit is up, the tub will be full, and the acid will be used to dissolve the dissected portions of the young man's body. Then the whole concoction will go gurgling down the drain. (By a weird coincidence, while we were filming this story, one of London's periodic sensational murders hit the press. The culprit had been sweet-talking his victims into turning over their assets to him for various kinds of trumped-up investments. Then he would kill them, dissolve their bodies in sulfuric acid, and go on to his next job. He had eliminated fifteen or sixteen persons in this fashion before the undissolved plastic handle of a victim's handbag led to his undoing.) Our young man is saved by his lady's wire-haired terrier, who follows the doctor into the sub-basement one evening, is collared by the prisoner, and becomes his companion. The American teaches the dog to pull the plug out of the nearby bathtub. The disappearance of the stored acid gives our prisoner the additional time needed for his rescue.

Problem: Where can you honestly use a singer with a facility for hitting extra-high notes in this story? Incorporate a cabaret scene, suggested Bronston. After a few very uncomfortable hours, we finally convinced our producer that Marushka would have to wait a little longer for her big break.

The next morning, Bronston and Marushka had flown the coop, leaving our bills unpaid. Alec had a little change, but I had been living completely on expenses and had hardly a franc to my name. After some frantic cabling to England, Alec's agent sent enough money to ransom us out of the hotel and the Coppels, Jean and I returned to England.

When we arrived, Bronston greeted us like long-lost friends, which we nearly were. Obviously, Marushka had not committed suicide, and he had weathered the storm. I often wished that I had been able to eavesdrop when he told her of our decision. I would have heard the high note of all time. We learned, in due course, that Bronston, a plastics engineer during the war, had gotten into films for the sole purpose of advancing his girlfriend's career. But he had taken this project too far with his own backers to be able to cancel now, so the film went into production as scheduled.

Jean and I were doing reasonably well. Since the Bank of England would not allow the export of any money, I could not get a salary. My total pay for the film was my expense account—£50 a week. Jean had been asked to headline a revue at the Embassy Club, a cabaret in Bond Street. It was a nice show. Jean was very well received, and she made some good friends, but the backstage entrance was off Piccadilly. The prostitutes in Piccadilly were having a rough time defending their few yards of pavement, and nightly fights were the rule. The pimps had a trick of sewing a few safety razor blades into the bills of their caps. A few quick slaps across the face and major surgery would be in order. About 3:00 A.M. one morning I pulled my car up to the curb to pick up Jean. She was pale and shaking. Just seconds before, one of the street girls had come up to her, eyed her up and down, then walked into a nearby bar and started talking to a man who was obviously her pimp. As Jean got into the car, they came to the door of the pub and watched. We figured we could do without the extra income, so Jean gave the club her notice.

Man About a Dog, later called *Obsession* in America, was being made at a comparatively low budget and our schedule was (for England) a skimpy 30 days. Robert Newton played the doctor; Sally Gray, his wife; a good, expatriate American actor, Phil Brown, played her paramour; and Naunton Wayne, an excellent English comedian, played the police inspector.

I now learned one of the disadvantages of filming outside Hollywood. There were no picture animal trainers in England. So Bronston bought a dog and had someone train it for our special needs.

Robert Newton was a classic example of a type I have run into over and over again. One of the nicest, most considerate, most sensitive of men when sober, he was a holy terror when drunk, though sometimes amusing. He had a vintage Bentley which he used to drive when it permitted. Laurence Harvey, then a struggling young actor, lived near Newton's flat in Chelsea and often cadged a ride to the studio. Early one morning they got into the car and Newton pressed the starter button. The starter whirred but nothing happened. Again and again Newton pressed the starter button, but the Bentley was stubborn. Finally Newton got out of the car and reentered his house, emerging in a few moments with a huge Australian bull whip. In a frenzy, he lashed the car's hood, its top, its trunk, shouting at it all the while in his best Shakespearean manner. Finally, out of breath and energy, he coiled his whip, got into the car, and pushed the starter button. Dutifully, the engine turned over. With a triumphant roar, Bobby motioned Harvey into the car, put it in gear, and drove off.

Our film was ideal for Newton. He had to post a £20,000 bond guaranteeing his sobriety during production. If we had been a few days over schedule, I doubt he would have made it. As it was, on the last day of shooting, with liberty in sight, he started drinking ale at lunch. By the time I had said "print it" on his last scene, his face was glowing a deep red. By the time our set party was over, he was already Mr. Hyde.

The photographer on the film was a bearded young man named C. Pennington Richards—Penny for short. He was one of those rare Englishmen with whom an American can find no fault at all. Cheerful, witty, hard-working, and ingenious, he was always ready to try something new. Rank had just invested a few million pounds in developing the "instant frame" process, a rather ridiculous scheme for shooting all scenes against prephotographed process backgrounds and on a rigid time schedule. This was supposed to correct one of the main problems of British films—long schedules. Starting with a program of twelve productions, they had already completed three or four, the schedules generally running 32 to 36 days.

Our schedule was a tentative 30 days, which no one considered realistic for a film shot in orthodox fashion. However, I was able to use the short-day technique I had developed on *Crossfire*, and Penny cooperated with the camera. I have always disliked overdetailed lighting. First, it takes too much time away from what is really important—the playing of the scenes. Second, it is usually dull to look at, like a photographically detailed painting compared to an impressionistic one. I have always discussed this point of view with photographers before I start making a picture. Occasionally, with men like Russ Metty, Harry Wilde, and J. Roy Hunt, I got what I wanted. Often I didn't. Penny was more than willing. For example, our main set, the sub-basement, was supposed to be lit with two bright overhead hanging work lights, shaded with those large green enamel shades so common in old workrooms. Penny inserted a photo-flood bulb in each. When we walked on the set in the morning, a pull on the lamp cords lit the set. When an actor walked close to a light, he was hot; when he backed too far away, he nearly disappeared in the background. But God, did it look real!

We finished right on schedule, proving that an all-English crew could shoot a film as quickly as anyone else. And that was the end of instant frame.

Oh yes—about the dog. He had been highly insured, since his loss during production would have been costly. A few weeks after completion of filming, he apparently disappeared from the producer's apartment. The insurance company offered a reward. Someone found him at the other end of Hyde Park and returned him to a somewhat reluctant owner. A couple of weeks later, the ungrateful pup ran off again. Once more a sizable reward resulted in recovery. Sometime later, he ate some poisoned meat. No reward could save his life. Moral—too much insurance is not good protection.

CHRIST IN CONCRETE

L ondon in 1948 was not much different from London of 1946, except that Jean was with me. I suddenly found I loved the town. Life was still hard for the British; food was scarce and monotonous. Many things we had considered necessities at home were luxuries here, and nearly impossible to get. Britain's industrial output was still "for export only." But, unlike other European countries I visited, here there was still the unselfishness, the pulling together, that had been for most of us the finest aspect of the war.

Sometime in November, Jean discovered she was pregnant, and diet assumed a new importance. She received a special ration card entitling her to extra foods, orange juice concentrate, and vitamins, the latter two items at no cost. The card even permitted her to go to the head of any queue. Since I was earning no salary and paying no taxes into the health-care fund, Jean and I insisted on private medical care. Later, I was to wish we hadn't.

Real happiness was a weekend in Paris. Not because of the friendliness of the Parisians—God no!—but because of the quantity and quality of food. When we could find the time and the money, Jean and I loved to go by train. The Golden Arrow of the late forties and the fifties was the finest train in the world. We would come aboard at a decent hour of the morning, recline in easy chairs in a private compartment, and watch the beautiful countryside slip by as we savored our breakfast and coffee. By the time we had finished, we were in Dover. The boat trip across the Channel gave us a chance to stretch our legs and fill our lungs with salt sea air. In Calais we boarded the French continuation of the train—the *Flèche d'Or*—without going through customs or immigration. Again we were seated in armchairs at our own comfortable tables and spent the duration of the run to Paris eating an excellent lunch and drinking fine wine. The customs and immigration officials wandered casually through the cars conducting their formalities under the most comfortable circumstances. Ah! There's a great deal to be said for elitism!

In Paris we had a couple of expatriate Communist friends who knew every little family restaurant in town. The food was wonderful; far better than any we had years later when we could afford the four-star palaces. My one real regret in renouncing the Communist party was losing our Paris friends. I've never been able to find any of those cafés again.

In London our chief source of amusement was ice hockey. We lived not too far from Earl's Court Arena, and the Earl's Court Rangers became "our team." We never missed a match, not even during the great green fogs. London's many power installations still burned coal, as did practically all houses and buildings in London, and the fall and winter atmosphere was full of soot. This particulate matter gave the autumn and spring fogs something to hang on to. These unbelievably heavy fogs could last for days and pretty well inactivate the city. People actually got lost after taking two steps away from their doors.

Jean and I had them licked. On hockey nights, we would get into the car and start moving very slowly—as slowly as the engine would turn without stalling. Jean would stick her head out of the window and give me a running report on our distance from the curb. I would keep my eyes glued straight ahead, watching for parked cars which would loom up so suddenly out of the fog. But those primitive cars had working bumpers (at no extra cost), and the slight bump which often resulted would cause no damage at all. A recurring moment of high adventure was at crossings—leaving one curb behind and hitting the one across the street was touchy business. Thank God the streets were narrow. Since there weren't too many other idiots on the streets under these conditions, we never got into trouble. Two or three times we found games cancelled because of the density of the fog within the arena itself. I like the cleaner air of London now, but I miss the challenge. It's making a softie out of me.

By the time *Obsession* was out of the way, preparatory work on *Christ in Concrete* was moving well ahead. It was a constant struggle. First of all, there was a cast to set. Geiger had made a tentative commitment for Louise Rainer to play Annunziata. It's hard to argue with two Academy awards, but I felt she was very wrong for the part. She was too mature to play a twenty-year-old girl, and her accent was not right. Accents are always a problem in films—no one has yet found a way to please anybody.

I had had an experience some years before which had left its mark. We had just previewed Leo McCarey's *Love Affair* in Santa Barbara. The film was very well received. We picked up some 450 cards after the preview, and most of them were raves—except for one thing. At least 50 percent of them read: "Why do you use Charles Boyer? I can't understand a word he says." I was shocked. He had given a beautiful performance, and I had always considered him one of our best actors. I decided to check it out. Boyer was indeed difficult to sell, I was told—English-speaking audiences had no ear for him. In fact, as a top star, his popularity steadily diminished. After the war, he went back to France.

The problem has been compounded in recent years by the trend to cooperative productions. With the notable exception of the United States, all major countries of the world have some method of subsidizing films. By spending a formula-determined share of a budget for labor and talent within a particular country, a producer can benefit from that country's subsidy scheme. Lately the move has been to ventures involving as many as three or four countries.

This has given rise to some very strange casting. In one film of recent memory, the father was American, his wife was French, one son was an American, the other Swiss, the daughter-in-law was Italian, and they were all playing Germans. Of course, dubbing can solve the problem, but the American audience does not react kindly to this. What's more, if the members of the family are supposed to be speaking in their native tongue, does one have them speak in accented English, or English with a German inflection? I've often had a nonprofessional give me a hard time over this problem—but I've never had one come up with a satisfactory answer of his own.

We knew we would have this problem to face in *Christ in Concrete*. The number of American-speaking actors with work permits in London was small. The number of *good* actors in this category was even smaller. I wound up with two Americans, a Greek, an Austrian, and a South African (who spoke perfect American). The only male in the cast whom everyone thought was a real Italian was Bonar Colleano, a Brooklyn-born Irishman whose circus family had adopted the Italian name. His real name was Sullivan.

Now, Annunziata. Rod had told Miss Rainer that I didn't like her for the part. She asked us over to discuss it. We expected an explosive show of temperament. Instead, we got an underplayed performance. As we entered, we barely had time for a "hello" before she motioned us to silence and started to say her piece, a thirty-minute recital of decapitated expectations, fancied slights, and delicately revealed hurts. We sat there dumbly, uttering not a single word. As she was finishing her scene, the doorbell rang on cue. A bellboy entered, carrying an imposing-looking envelope.

"Excuse me, gentlemen," she said, holding the missive to her heart. "I have just received a letter from my dear husband, and I would like to read it at once—in privacy."

Tears welled up in her eyes. Rod and I got up and headed for the door. We had been told, but good. But we were free to use the actress of our choice, if we could find one. I had seen a young player perform exceptionally well in an obscure Italian film. Her name was Lea Padovani. We found that she was now under contract to Orson Welles, who had started filming *Othello* with Padovani in the role of Desdemona. He had run out of money (as he was to do a number of times before *Othello* reached completion), and the girl was free. We cabled Welles for permission to make a test. He cabled back that he would make the test himself—when he had the time. It finally developed that Padovani was *not* under contract to Welles—he had not been able to meet his contractual salary obligations—and we were free to approach her agent directly. He agreed to send her to London for a test.

She arrived, looking much as we expected her to, but she couldn't speak a word of English. There was a painful interview in my office. After all the effort, and some expense, I wondered how I could gracefully and kindly send her back to Rome. There was no way. Rod and I agreed we would have to make the test, then say that it just hadn't worked out and send her home. We made arrangements for shooting at Denham and put her in the hands of Phil Brown, who was to work as my dialogue coach.

The test started out as I feared it would. Lea was nervous; her speech was awkward. Then, somewhere down the line, it suddenly came together beautifully, and Rod and I knew we had our Annunziata.

Geremio was another problem. We couldn't afford to hire a top American actor (most of them would not have worked with me, in any case). But Sam Wanamaker, who had received good notices playing opposite Ingrid Bergman in *Joan of Arc* on Broadway, was free. He looked a proper immigrant, and he was also being blacklisted. A perfect setup—but he wanted to be paid in dollars. And that was impossible.

Nat Bronston had carried out his agreement and was now helping with the financing of our film. But his sources, who had backed *Obsession*, could barely go halfway. Geiger had gone to Rank for the rest of the money. Rank had asked to see me first. I met him in his office. He expressed his sympathy for my professional predicament and said he cared nothing about my political affiliation. But he did have a question to ask.

"Do you believe in God?"

I sat there for a moment quietly. I am an agnostic. I don't *know* whether a God exists. I couldn't honestly say I believed in Him, but then, I couldn't honestly say I disbelieved in Him, either. So I stretched a point and said yes.

I have been lucky in the people who have crossed my path in critical moments of my life. J. Arthur Rank almost made a believer out of me.

THERE'S MADNESS IN THE METHOD

D ollars. We had to have dollars. With Rank's participation, we could scrape through production (maybe), but Ben Barzman wanted dollars in full payment for his script, and Sam Wanamaker wanted dollars to come to work. Getting them seemed an impossible task to me, but not to Geiger. He was in his element.

I've often thought that if anyone had offered Rod a choice between a million dollars straight or the equivalent value in pounds, he would have taken the latter. Then he could trade the pounds for escudos, make a deal with the Bank of Macao or Zanzibar, meet a couple of mysterious men in a dark alley, and wind up with a half million in dollars. That would have made him happy. Dealing and manipulation made the world go 'round for him, not money. He was very generous with what he had, and if he didn't have it, well—it would please him if you asked him for a hundred. Then he could finagle two and give you half. If he could only have been honest and still retained his manipulative skills, he could have been the greatest producer in Hollywood's history. Like Rathvon with Orson Welles, if I were to run into Geiger today and knew he'd con me out of my last cent, I'd still go into business with him tomorrow.

Barzman wouldn't deliver the script until he got his final payment—
something like $5,000. (I've known many artists in my life, and the
only ones who wouldn't even *talk* a deal when you were in trouble, with
an eminently worthwhile property at stake, were my Marxist comrades,
like Ben and Sam.) So Rod set out to get the money. Hoping to start
intensive work as soon as he succeeded, Jean and I made a last weekend
trip to Paris. Wanamaker went along—his first trip ever to France. In
Paris, we ran into John Garfield and decided to spend the afternoon at
Barbizon, the artists' village not too far from town. It was a memorable
day in the country.

We arrived back on Monday evening and were met by Geiger at the
station. He was in a euphoric mood. He quickly steered us off to a quiet
corner.

"Look!" he said, and he took a large stack of greenbacks out of a small
briefcase. I looked. Then I looked again.

"What's that green stuff on your hands?" I asked.

"What green stuff?"

He put a hand out into the light. It was smeared with ink—green
ink. With an incredulous look, he started leafing through the stack. It
was all the same—so fresh that the ink was smearing off one bill onto
another. Rod deflated like a pricked balloon.

"I'll get it straightened out," he finally said.

And so he did. Fortunately, the black marketeer who had arranged
the deal was an honest man (on a one-to-one basis), and he made good on
the transaction. Barzman was paid, Sam's first payment was made, and
we were ready to make a film.

A dark, wet, dingy street, lined with cold-water flats, stretches away
into the night. Steam spouts from under manhole covers and is raggedly
dispersed by a biting wind. Scraps of newspapers flap helter-skelter
through the scene. A man's feet stumble into the foreground, narrowly
miss an elevated railway pylon, then stagger on down the street. After a
few steps, the man comes to a spastic stop and stares up at the tenement
above him. It looks as if the building is about to come crashing down.
With a wide sweep of his arm, he drives away the fear and scrambles up
the stairs, into the nearest doorway.

We were in New York. But New York was a film set in Denham,
England. The studio had given us their largest stage, and we needed it.
We had to build an entire block of cold-water flats for little money, and
make it look real. I had started work while still in Hollywood with a
young assistant art director named MacDonald. He understood our
needs and his own—he needed a reputation. He went to work to devise
a number of ingenious sets. This was the first. The elevated railway

pillars in the foreground were fully equipped with train shadows and sound effects. Cardboard cutouts simulated one whole side of the street. The distant cross street was live and would accommodate full-sized cars and wagons. Behind that the street continued into the distance by courtesy of a forced-perspective backdrop.

I was proud of the steaming manholes; they were my idea. One of my strongest impressions of New York had been the dirty streets and vaporous manholes. Now, for the first time to my knowledge, they were put on the screen.

The one other set requiring great ingenuity was the four-story building which eventually collapses, killing Geremio. It was a half-demolished structure in the process of reconstruction, and the whole four stories had to be built on the stage. In Hollywood, the set would have gone outside, and there would have been no difficulties. In England, with its completely unpredictable weather, an outside set would have invited disaster, so in it had to go. But all the scenes shot on this set were supposed to be played in broad daylight. Lighting a set that occupied the whole of the largest stage in England was a sizable problem in any case, but I also wanted reality. In the sunlight, reality is a single shadow. Lighting a large set inside a stage normally requires a multitude of light sources—hence results in a multitude of shadows. Normally, the audience is not aware of the anomaly, but I have always felt that there is a subconscious awareness of such inaccuracies that leads to sensory resistance on the part of the viewer.

I discussed the problem with Penny. He sucked air through his teeth and looked worried. While the set was in the process of construction, he spent all the spare time he could find in studying it. On the morning we started to shoot it, he was ready. He had taken the four largest sun arcs he could find in England and put them together in a tight four-leaf-clover cluster in the highest, most distant corner of the stage. The heat emanating from the four closely packed arcs was a serious problem—like that of shooting a baby. The scene would be set up and rehearsed in the dim light of the ceiling lamps. Then, with everyone set to jump off his marks, the camera would be turned and the arcs would be struck. The second I said "cut" on a finished scene, the switches would be pulled, leaving us to stumble around in the relative darkness. But, by God, we had only one shadow! Even now, when I sometimes run my 16-millimeter print, I marvel at Penny's skill. I'd swear we shot those scenes out of doors.

The first setup of our schedule was a shot of Geremio and Kathleen in her bedroom. Penny was working with a new gaffer. The two principals had been lit, and Penny turned to my assistant.

"Ready," he said. The gaffer looked at him in amazement.

"We haven't lit the background," he said.

"Oh yes we have," said Penny. He proceeded to pull the light chains on the two or three lamps that helped furnish the set. He had inserted photo-floods in the light sockets, and the light and shade they threw on the walls were all the background lighting that was needed. How real it looked—perhaps because it was.

All of us believed in the film so much that it was almost a crusade. We had a 60-day schedule (at a ridiculously small cost of $500,000) and though the work was particularly demanding, most of it was a pleasure. There were constant problems, but these were mostly offstage and involved our producers.

Padovani's hotel and living expenses were not being paid. Eventually she had to move in with Geiger's family. One night there was shooting down the street from Rod's home. Gunfire in the streets of an English town is rare, and the local residents all ran out of their houses for a look. Not Geiger. He sent Katya into the street and sat tight himself. He had guessed right. The shooting was a diversion designed to get him out in the open where his creditors could get at him. He spent a couple of days indoors until arrangements could be made to get the culprits off his back. For him it was no big deal.

We were nearly finished shooting, and now it was Wanamaker's turn to create a problem. Acutely aware, along with everyone else in town, of our financial difficulties, he demanded that his final payment, due on completion of photography, be given him before he finished his part in the film. Bronston and Geiger had a day or two to get the dollars. The next day the two producers had a meeting. Nat had a suggestion. There were still a few thousand dollars in the personal drawing account of each producer. He would put his share into the pot if Geiger would do the same. Rod readily agreed. He left Bronston's office and headed off across the lot to his own. He just happened to run into our accountant, and the accountant just happened to mention that, the day before, Bronston had drawn out his personal account to the last penny. Rod laughed it off, got the money somehow, sent it to Wanamaker's agent, and the shooting rolled on.

One day I dropped into Sam's portable dressing room. Sam was showing the various charts which he prepared and used to keep his performance in line. They occupied the greater part of one wall of the room. The one he was explaining when I entered graphed his emotions, scene by scene. The peaks and valleys looked like a chart of the Dow-Jones stock-market averages in a very skittish year.

"I can walk in here," he explained, "take a look at the chart, and know at exactly what level I have to go into the next scene. It also helps me to understand the character." He turned to Lea for her admiration and approval.

"You're full of shit," she said. (She was learning English fast.) "I understood Annunziata when I first read the script."

I'm still a mathematician at heart, so I am completely in favor of the intuitive approach. Actors are playing people, and people are creatures of habit and instinct. Rarely is any action the result of slow, considered thought or planning. In real life, a husband and wife usually scream at each other first; only after the emotions have been drained is there room for sober thought and rational evaluation of the problem. Like all animals, human beings build up reaction patterns, starting at birth, and most actions taken in the course of their lives are set off by these established patterns rather than by conscious evaluation of stimuli. No person thinks about the way he holds his coffee cup at breakfast or the way he hitches up the blankets of his bed.

That is the basic fault of most "method" schools of acting. I'm not just talking about the Actors' Studio, though it is one of the worst offenders. It also pervades the system used by RADA (The Royal Academy of Dramatic Art) and many others. You can practice for hours being a broom in a closet—it won't help you in the least to play the part of a man discovering his wife in bed with his best friend.

I worked with a very important actor whose most noticeable idiosyncrasy was a long pause for thought before any action or reply. As I approached him on the set one morning, I said, "Hello, Mar."

"Hi, Eddie," he responded immediately.

"You see," I said, "you *can* react to someone without mulling over what he's said." He smiled, but I don't think it changed his technique in the least.

The rise of the "I've-got-to-be-me" cult has brought an increase in another manifestation of the artist's inner struggle. More and more often today one meets the young performer who protests, "I wouldn't say anything like this," or "I wouldn't behave that way." Of course not—unless he's doing an autobiographical film. Good acting absolutely requires one to concede that one's own ways are not the only ways or the best ways. Many a young actress who says, "I wouldn't do a thing like that" will be only too happy to play the part of a whore—which doesn't necessarily indicate she admits to being a prostitute.

The shooting was finished, and I was due to return to the United States in a few weeks, but there was still a great deal to be done. I had to put in some overtime. I had already gotten permission to work one evening a week with my cutter. Now I wanted two. The shop stewards rejected my request.

"You simply can't finish the work in the time you have left," they said, "so why try."

Fortunately there is a board of appeal, consisting mostly of management. They gave me their okay. Benjamin Frankel, the composer, had started writing while we were still in production. Now he was in full swing. Within four weeks we had cut, scored, and dubbed our picture and were ready for our first answer print.

While this was going on, Jean was delivered of our first child, a boy, at 4:00 A.M. on July 27, 1949. It was a short but difficult birth. During the next day, the nurses at the private nursing home where Jean was hospitalized complained they had to change the sheets so often—there was so much blood. When the doctor arrived in the afternoon, he found Jean in a coma. She was bleeding to death, and no one had noticed. There was a hurry-up call to me at the studio. When I got to the nursing home, the doctor told me that Jean had a fifty-fifty chance. In the next few hours I learned what had driven the British to socialized medicine. First our doctor called in his old teacher for consultation. They decided to bring Jean out of her coma. Adrenaline, injected directly into the heart, was indicated, but for that they needed a specialist. Eventually he arrived, accompanied by an assistant carrying his bag. The shot brought her out of the coma, but she was still bleeding to death. More blood was required, and, of course, another specialist. He finally arrived, accompanied by *his* assistant. The transfusion seemed to have little effect (Jean is Rh-negative, but they hadn't taken the trouble to find that out), so they opened a large hole in her ankle and poured blood in by the bucketful. How she survived I'll never know, but she did. I brought her home the very first moment I could. A few days later, when we decided to have our son circumcised, our doctor had to call another specialist—a rabbi.

A day or two before we had to leave England, I was ready for my executive showing. Rod and Bronston, Rank, and several members of his staff were there, as well as key members of my crew. When the film was over and the lights came on, nobody moved for a full five minutes. No word was spoken. I had never had such a successful showing, and I never would again. When my guests could finally speak, their compliments were effusive. I left England with a very full heart to fly back to uncertainty and disaster.

Because the English were very touchy about what they considered blasphemy, the name of our film was changed to *Give Us This Day*.

The film played in Europe to critical raves. I won the First Grand Masterpiece Award at the Venice Festival, the Paris-Presse Cup for direction at the Vichy Festival, the First Prize for direction at the Prague Festival, and others, as the carnival barker says, "too numerous to mention." It opened to good reviews in the United States, too, but unfortunately few Americans got to see what the shouting was all about. The American Legion moved in. They warned the exhibitors playing the film that all their future releases would be boycotted if they didn't pull my picture. Not being stupid, they did. The Rank organization didn't know what was happening. All they knew was that nobody was showing the film. They decided a title change might help and changed it to *Salt to the Devil* (from a line in the film). Of course, nothing could help.

But I knew little of any of this at the time. By then I was #3568, and only bits of this information were coming to me through the good graces of the warden of the federal prison at Mill Point, West Virginia.

THE FIGHTING IS OVER

Hollywood had hardly changed. The studios had adjusted easily to a sizable blacklist, and the drop in the quality of their product was scarcely noticeable. Jean, our son Ricky, our Maltese terrier, Beau, and I found a small apartment in the low-rent district near Pico and Robertson and settled down to wait out the Supreme Court appeal. I got an occasional undercover job as a script doctor, which paid for our rent and food bills, with enough left over for a down payment on a Chevy coupe. My ex-wife and her lawyer didn't take that away from Jean until after I'd gone to jail.

While still shooting *Christ in Concrete*, I had talked Geiger and Bronston into giving me $10,000 besides the £50 a week expense allowance. Then, with Rank's support, I had prevailed upon the Bank of England to let me send the money to my ex-wife. That still left me somewhat in arrears, and she went to court to collect. My business manager's lawyer pleaded hardship, but the judge obviously never read the papers and refused to believe him. He appointed my ex-wife the receiver over what little I had left—principally a plane, worth about $2,000, and the Chevy. He also ordered me to pay all back alimony, which made me subject to a prison sentence if I failed to comply. To top it off, her attorney charged me $9,000 for one hour in court! Even the judge was shocked, but, agreeing that lawyers had to live, allowed him $5,000. Of course I couldn't pay, but for the next few months, I managed to stave off disaster.

The Hollywood Ten were still holding their weekly meetings. They were still preoccupied with the same problems; preparations for the coming trials, though these would be largely a matter of form, and planning fund-gathering affairs to finance them. Two of these meetings remain in my memory, since both of them had an important bearing on a decision I knew I would someday have to make.

The first of these concerned Robert Rossen. His film, *All the King's Men*, had been released to great reviews and was breaking box-office records. Now Lawson decided to haul him on the carpet. It was *Cornered* all over again. The film was being acclaimed for its exposure of corrupt politics and politicians, and widely boosted for a number of Oscars (which, in fact, it did win). But for some reason the party disapproved. For at least two hours, he was scolded, upbraided, and generally humiliated. It was a scene out of Kafka. Here was a man who had dramatized one of our group's most quoted slogans, "Power corrupts," and he was getting hell for it. Bob was as startled as I was, and he tried to fight back, but it was useless. Finally, having had enough, he told them all to stick it and walked out of the house, and, I believe, out of the party.

At another meeting, one of our lawyers posed a hypothetical question. "The prosecutors are likely to ask, 'Do you believe in freedom of speech for Communists?' The answer is obviously yes. Then he will ask, 'Do you also believe in freedom of speech for fascists?' What answer do you give?"

"Why, 'Yes,'" someone said. "We believe in freedom of speech for everybody."

"It's not as simple as that," said Lawson. And for two meetings we debated that difficult question. At some point during the second meeting, when a straw poll showed us to be 6-3 in favor of unequivocal free speech (Trumbo rarely attended meetings), Lawson called a halt to our discussion.

"This is your answer," he said flatly. "You believe in freedom of speech for the Communists but not for the fascists."

"Why not?" I asked. I should have known the answer.

"You believe in freedom of speech for Communists because what they say is true. You do not believe in freedom of speech for the facists because what they say is a lie."

Honest to God!

This was when I decided that, sooner or later, I had to part company with the Hollywood Ten.

In April of 1950, the Supreme Court, by a 6-2 majority, decided not to review our case. The fighting was over. There was the usual meaningless second appeal, which merely took up more time. Finally we got the word that we would be sentenced on June 29, 1950.

About a week before I left for Washington and jail, fate had one more surprise for me. At that time I received a call from an attorney friend of mine. He had been at the courthouse to file some papers and had glanced at a subpoena lying on the counter. It bore my name. He looked at it more carefully. I was being summoned to answer contempt of court charges for failing to pay up my back alimony. I hung up the phone in a daze. Over the past two and a half years Jean and I had used up all the old clichés to bolster our sagging spirits, but there was just nothing to fit this situation.

The next morning I was dressed and ready very early. About 7:00 a strange car pulled up in front of our apartment, and a strange man got out and walked toward our door. Sure enough, the man wanted to talk to me; Jean wouldn't do. She told him I was out for my morning walk. He went back to his car and settled down to wait. I said a quiet good-bye to Jean, went out the back way to the downstairs garage, got into my car, and drove away. Nobody followed. I drove out to Brentwood, stopped at Bill Castle's home, and explained my predicament. He invited me to spend the next few days at his place. Jean arranged for a friend to bring her out to pick up the car, and for the next few days she had to lose the process server whenever she left the apartment. Under other circumstances it might have been exciting, now it was just plain miserable.

Dalton Trumbo and John Howard Lawson, whose trials were pilot cases for the rest of us, had started serving one-year jail terms on June 9. On June 29, Maltz, Bessie, Cole, and Lardner were each sentenced to one year in prison. Biberman and I were lucky enough to appear before a somewhat more humane man, Judge Keech, who sentenced us to six months each. Adrian Scott was ill, but was sentenced to a year in prison some weeks later. Sam Ornitz, an old man in frail health, had asked for probation. On June 30 his request was denied, and he, too, got the full one-year term. Each of us was fined $1,000, the maximum under the law.

Handcuffed, we were taken to the federal prison in Washington directly from the courthouse. I had never been in jail before. It was to prove both frightening and fascinating. Everyone should try it at least once.

On arriving at the prison, we were herded into "the tank," where there were already some twenty to thirty miscreants waiting to be processed. As our names were called, we first gave up all our possessions, then took off all our clothes. Jaybird naked, we went from desk to desk, being fingerprinted and filling out forms. Putting a bare bottom onto a cold chair is punishment enough, but the worst part of the admittance routine was the indignity itself. And that, I was to find, is an essential part of prison practice.

Finally we were sent into a huge sunken shower room where we bathed, powdered our hairier parts with an antiseptic powder, then went back to put on our own shirts, shorts, pants, socks, and shoes—all of which had been put through some sort of disinfecting process. I had been warned of this before I came east and had worn only nylon socks, shorts, and shirt, since they would dry quickly when washed. For the duration of our stay in the Washington jail, I washed these items out every evening. By the time I left, they were pretty well in shreds.

Ever since 1950 I have wanted to make a prison picture. No film I've ever seen—not even *The Birdman of Alcatraz*—has come anywhere near telling the real story or portraying the feelings of despair, lost hopes, maniacal irritability, and the constant watch over the passage of time.

We were housed in a wing of the prison that had five tiers of cells on one side of a huge room. The wall on the other side was broken by a five-story-high window of frosted glass, topped by a rose window near the ceiling. The top tier was a bare, fenced-in concrete floor on which no cells had yet been placed. It served as an exercise area on rainy days or when the guards just didn't feel like letting us out into the yard. From the exercise floor one could look across the room, out through a broken pane of glass in the rose window and see a distant portion of the street which fronted the prison.

A guard brought me to tier three, warned all the inmates to stay away from the cell doors, then pushed a button. The doors to all the cells slid back automatically. He led me through the double doors and along a narrow walk to a cell halfway down the row. I stepped inside. The guard returned to the entryway and pressed the closing button. I will never forget the crashing sound of the closing steel doors, like those of a gigantic tomb. As I looked out through the bars I was convinced that I would never see Jean and my son again, nor the outside world, nor any of my friends. This feeling of complete and utter loneliness stayed with me until the first visit of one of our attorneys a couple of days later. It was really something while it lasted.

I finally turned to look around my 6 by 8 foot cell. There were two metal cots, one above the other, a small sink and an open toilet, the size of a boat's head. There was also a stool and on it sat the cell's other occupant. He was a skinny, gimpy, "rumdum," awaiting trial for selling a bottle of booze. I have so often heard nice, middle-class Americans say casually, when discussing the advantages of living in God's country, "In America you're innocent until proven guilty." That is a crock of shit! (If the language bothers you, I'm sorry. I'm in prison now and that is the way we all talk in prison. Every other word is a four-letter word. It is one way of getting rid of a little of that unmeasurable frustration.) My cellmate was a case in point. Unable to raise bail, he had already been in jail more than two months, and now the summer recess was starting. Justice had to have a vacation, and it would be at least another three months before he would be tried. If he were found innocent, there would be no possible way for him to retrieve that lost portion of his life. In those days the time one served before sentencing was called "dead time" and did not apply to one's sentence. In my cellmate's case, he might serve a year working off a six-month sentence. In truth, the old saw ought to read, "In America, as in any other country on this earth, if you're rich, you're innocent until proven guilty. If you are poor, you are guilty as hell the moment the law lays its heavy hand on your shoulder."

Our meals were served in the open space opposite the cells on the ground floor. My cellmate warned me to take only as much food as I was sure I could eat. Not cleaning one's plate was a capital offense. We queued up to be served from a hot table. Each inmate had a tray, a plate, a cup, and a spoon—no knives or forks. The spoons were picked up and accounted for before any prisoner could leave his table. If the count was not exact, everyone sat in place until the missing spoon was found. Any ingenious inmate could turn a spoon into a lethal weapon—and you'd better believe it.

One day at lunch I noticed a new face—a pasty-white-skinned face belonging to a boy who looked about nineteen or twenty years old. He had just come up from twenty-four days in "the hole." As the meal ended, I noticed a commotion at one of the long tables up front. A guard was standing over the pale-faced boy, exhorting him to finish his food. The boy said nothing, just sat there with his hands in his lap looking down at his plate which contained some gristly material. The guard called for assistance, but assistance didn't help. Eventually the boy was taken away from the table and sent back to "the hole." But, by God, he had proved to the guards and all the rest of us that he existed.

Nights were sometimes spooky. A few lights were always left on, giving the section an appearance that would have delighted Roy Hunt.

After the 9:00 P.M. lights-out, complete silence was required. But there were always a few who couldn't sleep. Some man on the fourth tier might start a conversation in an odd singsong tone.

"Hey, Joe, I got the All-American band." A pause.

"I hear you, man," from the first tier. A pause.

"Ol' Satchmo on the trumpet."

"Yeah, man."

"Barney Bigard on the stick."

"I hear you, brother."

"How 'bout Jess Stacy on the piano."

"I hear you, man."

And so it would go, echoing eerily through the cavernous building. Until one night a disapproving screw slithered silently past my cell. In a moment I heard his triumphant cry, "Gotcha! I gotcha!" A short time later the doors crashed open, then shut. The guard and a black inmate moved past my cell on the way to "the hole." I never did get the whole make up of his All-American band. Being a jazz nut—I was sorry.

Once or twice a week we filed out into the yard where, for an hour or two, we could walk around and talk freely with each other. More usually, however, our exercise was taken on the empty top tier within our building. There some of the men would play cards for cigarettes, others would stand around, smoking, while others walked, more or less vigorously, to loosen up their cramped frames. Maltz and I walked. Albert would often complain of his lack of communication with the outside. The Korean War had broken out a few days before we were sent to jail, and he still hadn't heard what the official party position was on the invasion. Until he did, he could have no opinion. I had other problems on my mind.

On one of these daily walks we noticed a tall, pleasant-looking young man clutching at the wire that caged in the tier. He was staring out through the rose window. We made several turns of the tier, and he still hadn't changed his position. Curiosity moved me to speak to him.

"What are you looking for?" I asked.

"My family," he said.

We didn't understand until he told us that on his wife's last visit she had promised to bring their two children to the small portion of the street that could be seen through the rose window. Sure enough, in a few minutes, a car pulled up to the curb. A young woman got out, followed by a child of three or four. The woman reached into the car and lifted out a baby. Carrying the baby in her arms, with the other child tagging along hanging on to her skirt, she walked back and forth on the distant sidewalk while the man inside hung on to the wire and cried. I couldn't take it. I started hitting him on the arm. "Why did you do it?" I cried. "Why did you do it?" Maltz pulled me off. What could the poor guy say?

We of the Hollywood Ten knew that we were due to be transferred to minimum-security prisons since our crime was a misdemeanor, not a felony, but the prison system seemed to be taking its time about it. It was important because we would earn more good-time benefits in a prison camp than in a maximum-security facility. Finally, after eighteen days in the D.C. penitentiary, we were to be transferred. Maltz and I were going to the prison camp at Mill Point, West Virginia. They put us in handcuffs, leg irons, and chained us to each other. We rode in a car with two deputies as driver and guard.

About 100 miles from Washington, we had to take a leak. Our driver pulled the car to the side of the road, then took out his gun while the other one unlocked our leg irons. We limped over to the bushes, with both deputies keeping a close, armed watch. I pictured myself driving by in a car and seeing this tableau. A couple of hardened criminals, I would have thought. I had to laugh.

BUILDING TIME

The West Virginia mountains looked beautiful and free. We had been riding through backcountry for some time and were now approaching a sawmill, complete with logs, flume, and barracks buildings.

"Mill Point Prison Camp," announced one of the guards.

"Where's the wall or fence?" I asked.

"Don't need none," he answered. "You can walk out, but there just ain't no place to go."

The place looked like a C.C.C. camp with sawmill attached. The mill was part of the prison industry—logging native hardwoods and sawing them into lumber. The boast of the camp administration was that Mill Point was the only unit in the whole prison system that showed a profit, and that might very well have been true.

Maltz and I were checked in, fingerprinted, photographed, and taken to quarantine. This was a small building housing eight iron double bunk beds, packed as closely together as possible, a shower room, and a toilet. (In prison, shower and toilet facilities are always open, a feature that discourages lingering and misbehavior.) Here Maltz and I were put through another prophylactic routine. We stripped to the buff, showered, and dried off. Then the guard sprayed a white powder disinfectant over our private parts. But this time there was a difference. The open shower was not eight feet away from the nearest bunk, and here five or six hillbillies stood at stolid attention, watching the guard do our thing. In time they turned out to be simple human beings; now they looked like the mountain folk in the *New Yorker* cartoons, but much more menacing. Their slack-mouthed, dead-eyed stares showed not a spark of friendliness. Maltz and I wondered what we were in for.

The prison population varied between 600 to 750 inmates, two-thirds of whom were black. A large percentage of the population was composed of hillbillies, serving sentences for brewing booze, selling it, or both. At least half of the inmates were completely illiterate, barely able to make their marks. Moderate segregation was practiced; the blacks lived in two dormitories, the whites in a third. Blacks and whites also ate in their own sections of the commissary, but in work details and recreation there was complete integration. Friendships between blacks and whites were occasionally established, with no adverse reaction from either the largely Southern inmates or the administration.

The most noticeable separation was between the hillbillies on the one hand and the more sophisticated urban types on the other. Recreation was usually baseball, played during the long summer evenings and on weekends. Once in a great while there was a movie, but the budget could rarely afford one. The warden told me that the prison received about 70 cents a day per inmate—this for clothing, food, and recreation. Even in 1950, 70 cents did not go far, so in the summer the camp grew its own vegetables, many of which were canned for winter use. The only meat ever served was chicken, on infrequent occasions and, on a high holiday like Thanksgiving, pork—both from stock raised at the camp.

The seasonal gardening and strip-mining led to what I considered an odd practice: In the spring and summer most of the lawbreakers arrested and convicted seemed to be farmers. In the fall and winter, they were coal miners. A small number of my fellow inmates were winos. From them I learned of an odd judicial practice. Some of the states serving the prison, which included Kentucky, Tennessee, Virginia, West Virginia, and parts of Ohio and Pennsylvania, still employed magistrates to try and sentence petty wrongdoers. They were paid by piecework; $15 for each joker sent to jail. When a poor "rumdum" was dead broke and badly in need of a drink, he would be welcomed by one of these magistrates and given a couple of bucks to buy a gallon of cheap wine. The only stricture placed upon the recipient was that he turn himself in to the magistrate after he had slept off his drunk. He was then sentenced to sixty to ninety days in jail. The arithmetic of justice: $15 minus $2 leaves a fat $13 profit.

I would like to dispose of several common prison myths in a hurry. I never met a prisoner who claimed to be in on a "bum rap." Each owned up to his crime, often with a kind of simple pride. Most did complain that their imprisonment wasn't justified since others committing the same crimes were not punished—and that is a legitimate complaint. Our warden, K. E. Thieman, once pointed out to me that almost every inhabitant of this country had broken some law for which he could have been jailed if all the laws were strictly enforced.

Then there is the question of rehabilitation. A number of inmates at Mill Point became friends of mine. Only one swore he would never repeat the crime for which he was serving time. A hard-drug pusher was a typical example. He admitted only one mistake—putting himself in a position to take the rap for a higher-up. In the future, he said, he would do business on his own. How about remorse for selling hard drugs to victims of this dreadful habit? Are you mad? Anyone ameliorating the agony of an addict who needs a fix, at only a small profit, deserves a medal, not society's condemnation—at least that was his position.

The attitudes of the hillbillies were more amusing. There was a father-and-son team with the good mountaineer name of Jeeter, whose term was nearly up. I asked the father about his plans for the future.

"I just want the feds to stay off my back while I cook a couple of hundred gallons. I'll sell half and drink the other half. Then they can have me again."

And he meant it. This was his fifth turn at Mill Point—he was our best chain-saw operator. In time I reached the conclusion that most of the hillbillies had been turned in by their wives. It got the men off their backs and bellies for a few months, and they received a share of the prisoners' work pay—which is more than they got from them when they were on the outside.

And, of course, homosexuality. At Mill Point, the only evidence of homosexuality was between two or three youthful inmates and the prison chaplain, a young divinity student from Duke and a raving poof. It meant an occasional trip to town for the inmates in the chaplain's company, and no one in the camp begrudged them that privilege nor envied them for it. My own experience was much more typical of the general prison population. I put any thought of sex out of my mind and never discussed it with any inmate. Nor did any of the inmates show any inclination for such discussions.

Maltz and I had to stay in quarantine for two weeks, doing odd jobs about the prison in the meantime. We mowed the rather extensive lawns in the administration living-quarters area, plucked chickens, peeled boiled beets, and performed a number of other menial tasks. The office personnel consisted largely of trustees, so all pertinent information about us was soon the property of the whole camp. At first the guards with whom we came in daily contact regarded us with a mixture of awe and suspicion. They knew that I had earned more in two weeks than they did in a year. They also suspected that we were intellectuals, and that concerned them. Most of them had had experience with conscientious objectors during the war, and these, apparently, had been a very troublesome lot. When they discovered that we worked willingly at whatever job they handed us and engaged in no disruptive activities, their attitudes, with a few exceptions, changed. Some of them, including the warden, became good friends.

When we had arrived at Mill Point, we had been surprised to find that Clifford Odets had preceded us. He was one of several members of the New York–based Antifascist Refugee Committee who had received three-month sentences for contempt of Congress and had gone to jail ahead of us. Odets and another member of the committee, a professor of Germanic languages at NYU, had been sent to Mill Point. The professor had undergone a partial withdrawal, whether political or psychological I never knew. He worked willingly enough, but avoided us and the other inmates as much as possible. Odets, on the other hand, was all outgoing friendliness—there were times when I wished he were more like his professorial associate.

Our stay in quarantine completed, Maltz and I were assigned permanent duties. We had been allowed to express our work preferences, with only one area excluded—that of teaching. Here were four of us—two novelists, a director, and an actual professor—and we were not allowed to teach those few illiterates who came to class. Maltz was assigned to orderly duties in the four-bed hospital that adjoined quarantine, which was a stroke of luck for the inmates. The medical officer at the camp was an ex-army medic, an alcoholic who didn't even know the remedy for athlete's foot. He was content to sign Maltz's requisitions and let him take care of the patients. The mentally ill just had to suffer out their terms.

I was made garage clerk. My duties consisted of opening up the facility at 6:00 A.M. every morning (except Sunday), handing out the keys to the forty or fifty trucks and vehicles that were used in the camp's lumbering activities, ordering parts for trucks and tractors as needed, servicing and fueling the fleet as well as the passenger vehicles used by the prison staff, then refueling and parking all the trucks as they were brought in after the day's work was finished. I also kept the garage records. The servicing and repair work was handled by a staff of three prisoners under the direction of the garage guard, a Mr. Farmer. As for the rest, I was on my own. Because I worked much longer hours than the other inmates, I was entitled to a few privileges. I was excused from standing count, which was taken about five times a day, I ate breakfast and dinner pretty much at my own convenience, and, along with Maltz and a few of the kitchen staff members, I was allowed snack privileges in the commissary before bedtime, which offered a chance for relaxed conversation with the few inmates and guards who dropped in for a cup of coffee. It was a welcome break in the day's routine. I also talked the warden into giving me a free hour in the usually slack period of the early afternoon, during which I could do my weight-lifting exercises. I even organized an evening weight-lifting class, attended by three other inmates. One of my black students developed into a first-class lifter.

Another member of my weight-lifting class was a thirtyish man who was completing a sentence for murder. The prison camp served as a halfway house for long-termers before their return to the streets, which can be a terrifying experience. This man, whom I had met through Clifford Odets, had been a merchant seaman during the war. In a North African port, a fellow crewman had attacked him with a knife. He had succeeded in taking the knife away from his assailant but had killed him in self-defense. The military court which tried him conceded the self-defense (there were witnesses), but ruled he had defended himself too vigorously. He was given a ten-year sentence, with no possibility of parole. With good-behavior time, he was finally being released in the fall of 1950. He was luckier than most; Odets had gotten him a job with a publishing house.

Legally, a prisoner can leave the prison immediately after midnight on the day of his release. In practice, in order to minimize disruption of the day's routine, he is released after the camp is awake in the morning. In this instance, the warden had agreed our friend could leave at midnight. Further, he allowed Odets, Maltz, and me to stay with him until he left the prison. It was a very wise decision. Long before midnight, the poor man, in spite of our prattling attempts to get his mind off the future, was a sweating, shivering mess. By midnight he was nearly ready to commit another murder to avoid going out into the streets.

"Out in the streets"—that's the convicts' phrase, and how apt it is. In the opinion of most of the old hands, about two years is all a person can take before going stir-crazy or becoming prison-simple. The difference between the two terms was explained to me, and I had examples of both before me in plenty. The stir-crazy inmate becomes psychotically irritable and rebellious; the prison-simple inmate retreats into a state of quiet semi-idiocy. It is this second type who is most frequently a recidivist. In prison he feels protected; in the streets he is terrified. One elderly kitchen worker had the most benign temperament of any man at Mill Point. He was released while I was still in residence. A friendly guard named Balzer, with whom I talked frequently, assured me that the freed man would be back in a week. He overestimated by three days. This kindly man, terrified of the outside world, had found an occasion to attack someone with a knife (he did not wound him). He got his wish: a speedy return to the kitchen detail at Mill Point.

Even I experienced this feeling of security, to some extent. I had long suffered from the directors' occupational disease—an irritable stomach. It had never reached the ulcerous stage, but I always kept a roll of Tums in my pocket. I dreaded being in jail without them. Yet, throughout my stay in prison, I experienced not one moment of heartburn. I almost felt guilty. I had always said my incarceration would be harder on Jean than on me, and now I was proving it. It is logical enough. At Mill Point I didn't have a single decision to make, hence nothing to worry about. Freedom is more conducive to gas on the stomach than captivity.

The warden was particularly careful to protect his charges against possible outside irritation. One day he called me into his office. He chatted casually for a bit, then handed me a newspaper clipping. He watched me closely as I read it. It was Walter Winchell's column and that considerate man was reporting that Jean Porter Dmytryk was filing suit for divorce. Like most good citizens, the warden knew less about the excesses of the press than I did. He was really concerned that if I heard this news from some other source, I might try something rash, like escaping from prison. I assured him I had the utmost faith in Jean and he believed me. After a few more minutes of conversation, in which I did my best to get him to share my own jaundiced view of the press, he sent me back to the garage. He wasn't nearly as careful sometime later when he told me I had won the First Masterpiece Award at Venice for *Give Us This Day*.

THE BIG DECISION

I t's a beautiful morning on Cranberry Mountain." Whether it was raining torrents, bitter cold, or dark as Hades, each day we were awakened by that cheery phrase. To our resident sadist, every morning was beautiful.

But life at Mill Point wasn't all routine. I learned how to make a good electric weld and how to operate a bulldozer. I also learned how to build a still, complete with thumper keg, and how to turn a file into a first-class knife. Knives were plentiful in jail. Guards could shake down the entire prison, confiscate dozens of weapons—within two weeks there would be just as many more. The most popular place for carrying a shiv was inside the double layer of cloth covering the fly. Guards never touched that area when searching for fear of being accused of homosexual advances, a cause for dismissal—at least so the prisoners believed. I never had occasion to test the theory.

As for stills, at one time there were five in operation on the premises. One, located under the floor of the kitchen, made alcohol out of various fruit juices which were surreptitiously sidelined whenever we had canned fruit for dessert.

There was an occasional fight between inmates, usually broken up by their own leaders to avoid punishment. I narrowly escaped my own battle one Saturday night. In that masochistic part of the country, Grand Ol' Opry ran for a full four hours. Warden Thieman allowed the speakers in the dormitories to stay on until the end of the program—around 11:00 P.M., I think. Unfortunately I slept on a top bunk, and one of the speakers was about a foot over my head. "If you've got the money, honey, I've got the time" was sending me right up the wall, so I turned off the speaker. Within fifteen seconds, a young hillbilly from the other side of the room had climbed my bunk and turned it on again. By the time he was halfway back to his bunk, I had snapped it off once more. He turned, glared at me, started toward me, then stopped. I glared back at him. Eventually, he decided not to try me, and I was just as glad. Besides, all the other speakers in the building were blasting, as they continued to do for the duration of my stay. I've never been able to stand country music since.

One of the greatest sins committed by our American system of injustice is the ridiculous disparity in prison terms. One of my fellow inmates had been a postal clerk in Cleveland. He had conceived a beautiful caper. He learned the names of all the major philatelists in the area and routinely opened their mail. He learned when and from or to whom a valuable stamp would be sent. He would intercept these stamps and appropriate them. When finally apprehended, he had several hundred thousand dollars worth of rare stamps in his possession. This is mail robbery, a federal offense, a felony, a Jesse James crime, right? He got 90 days. A young, skinny, pimply hillbilly, just married, was sentenced to two years for selling five gallons of moonshine—his first offense. The odds are that his life is ruined forever.

Maltz and I first noticed him when a guard complained that the young inmate was giving him a hard time—he refused to work as directed. Maltz talked to the boy and learned of his recent marriage and of his fear that the two years in prison would ruin that particular relationship completely. He was obviously on the edge of an all-out crackup. Over the next few days, he began spending an ever-increasing amount of time in bed. The next Sunday morning, as I was waking up at the regular reveille, I heard a voice repeating sharply, "Look, look, look!"

By the time I had climbed down from my bunk, there were already eight or ten inmates staring at the young hillbilly's bed. He had pulled the blankets up over his head, and they were bouncing up and down in a regular rhythm. To the delight of the onlookers, the boy was masturbating. And he never stopped. A guard tried to pull the blankets down so he could talk to him, but the boy hung on for dear life. I called off the guard and went to the dispensary for Albert. He came, he saw, and he suggested that we take him to the hospital. We eventually got the warden's permission to transfer him, brought down a stretcher, loaded him on it, and carried him to a hospital bed. What a classic case of withdrawal into self-abuse.

We talked to the warden about shipping the boy to a prison where he could get psychiatric help. Warden Thieman laughed to keep from crying. There was only one federal prison with that kind of service in the whole country, he told us, and that was reserved almost exclusively for homosexuals, who didn't need or want it.

One day we had a fire drill and I learned that the garage clerk was the fire chief of the camp. I also learned what was inside the tightly locked

little building next to the garage—a fire truck. But first I had to find the
key, which took some time, and open the rusty lock. Inside was
something right out of the Smithsonian—or Toonerville—a red fire
truck, vintage about 1925. (If it still exists it's worth $100,000.) The
tires were nearly flat and the battery was dead, but with the garage next
door, that wasn't much of a problem. We finally got it going, piled on,
and chugged around looking for the fire and feeling like a troop of
Mack Sennett's cops. Eventually we found the small bonfire that Balzer
had set. It was nearly burned out. We jumped off the truck, grabbed the
extinguishers, and started spraying. Nothing. They were dry as bone.
We stamped out the fire with our feet. For the next few days, we
scrubbed and scraped and cleaned and filled, and finally had a functioning fire engine. Then I put it back in its garage and locked the door. I
didn't tell my successor in the job about his fire-chief duties when I left.
After all, he, too, deserved a little fun.

The all-consuming interest of the inmates was the passage of time. It
was never off their minds. They called it "building time," and the usual
daily greeting was not "Hi," or "Hello," but "How're you buildin' it?"
Every con knew to the minute how many years, months, weeks, days,
and hours he still had to serve. What's more, he knew as much about his
friends' time. It was quite common for a lumber-truck driver to pull up
for gas and say, as he jumped out of the cab, "Hey, Dmytryk, two
months and nine days, right?"

"Right," I'd answer. "And yours is one year, three months, and
seventeen days. How are you buildin' it?"

"Great," he'd say. "No sweat."

Without ever discussing it among ourselves, we all developed similar
techniques for making time pass more quickly. For instance: We got
our laundry twice a week. When I picked mine up, I would say to
myself, "Hot damn! Only thirty more laundry days—thirty more
laundry days." Sunday was a special day—"Fifteen more Sundays—just
fifteen more." The best was the full moon—it marked such a relatively
long period of time, yet you could literally see it grow—"Just three
more full moons—three more." It worked—it helped to make time
pass more quickly. It worked *too* well; I haven't been able to turn it off. I
look at each full moon and think, "How many more full moons—how
many more?"

Jean was coming to visit me. Next to the day of my release, that was
obviously the best day of my entire prison term. The federal prison
system has minimum-security prisons much nearer Hollywood than
Mill Point, West Virginia, but none of the Ten had been sequestered in
any of these. I wouldn't say that this was a conscious action on the part

of the Superintendent of Prisons, but then I wouldn't say it wasn't, either. Anyway, it made it very difficult for any of us to have visitors. Jean and I decided that one visit was all we could afford, and that should be at the end of August. Margaret Maltz was coming with her. They flew to Charleston, West Virginia, and drove to Mill Point in a rental car, where they spent the night in a motel. Bright and early the next morning, they were at the prison camp.

Up to a couple of years before our Mill Point sojourn, the prison administration had allowed the inmates to take their visitors out into the surrounding woods; a wonderful custom, particularly when a wife alone came to call. But they soon found that many of the mountaineers were lending their wives out to their friends—for a small fee, of course. It was a very hospitable and commendable practice, but not to the prison authorities. So it was stopped.

Because of the single visit, Warden Thieman had given us the whole day off, and even allowed us to use a spare office as a visiting room. Among the many things Jean and I talked about that day was something that had been on my mind since long before I entered jail. I wanted out—not just out of jail, but out of my real imprisonment, my associations. I had known for at least a year that my comrades' protestations that they were fighting for "freedom of thought and speech" was just more window dressing. The meetings on *Cornered* and *All the King's Men*, the debate about the right of fascists to free speech, as well as a number of lesser, but related incidents, had convinced me that what we were martyring ourselves for was the right of the Communist party to exist and function freely. Possibly a laudable cause, but I believed every martyr had a right to choose his own reason for martyrdom. Protecting the Communist party, which I had grown to detest, was not going to be mine. Though I had considered no specifics, I had reached a tentative decision to take some sort of action even before I went to Washington for sentencing. I knew that if I broke with the Ten before going to jail, everyone would think I was doing so to avoid prison, so I decided to postpone any move until I had served my sentence.

But the waiting was too much. Jean had already been in touch with Bartley Crum, who was standing by for my decision. I decided to set the wheels in motion. Jean was ecstatic. She agreed to call Bart as soon as she returned to Hollywood. The whole procedure had to be carried out with great secrecy. Ever since I had refused to take part in the last of the fund-raising campaigns, the hard-core members of the group had been uncertain of my continuing cooperation. Jean, who, aside from this sad business, had never had anything in common with the other wives, was also considered a weak link. From time to time, one of these dour-faced women would call on her to keep her firmed up. She was actually a little frightened of them and didn't want them working on her. So, until the announcement came out in the press, no one was to know. Naturally, I didn't confide in Maltz.

When Jean gets into action, fur flies in all directions. Here are portions of my letter to her, dated September 10, 1950:

From: Edward Dmytryk   Sept - 10 - 1950
           #3568   8338 DeLongpre Ave.
To: Mrs. Jean Dmytryk   Hollywood, 46, Calif.

Darling—It's done! I don't know whether it will turn out good or bad—but we'll just have to sit back and see what happens. The reason I'm writing this air-mail is that things have happened so fast the last few days, I haven't had time to warn you of some possibilities . . . you will be on the receiving end of a lot of stuff. Most of it will be good, I think, but some of it might be pretty unpleasant. Probably the wives will be pretty brutal. . . .

Bart came in style. Brought the lawyer Diamond (the one who almost succeeded in negotiating the settlement with the studios) with him, and a secretary. He dictated the statement, which was just what I would have wanted to say—no more, no less—then several other papers having to do with substituting Crum for the other attorneys in my civil cases, and kept the office in a general uproar with calls to the White House, Attorney-General McGrath, places for plane reservations to Washington, etc. I'm sure the local telephone central has never had such a day. I told them I'd have to get back to work to pay their expenses, but they have high hopes for a decent settlement with the studios on my civil cases . . .

Darling, the next few weeks may be a bit rough—hang on—we'll make it—then it'll probably be smooth sailing again. I love you more than anything, and hope you're happy about everything. Love to Ricky. Edward Dmytryk #3568

(The formal sign-off was a prison regulation.)

My statement, witnessed by the warden, Thieman, on Sept. 9, 1950, said simply that I was not now a Communist nor a Communist sympathizer, and that I had not been a Communist at the time I appeared at the Congressional hearings. I did not refer to my previous membership. Bitter medicine, I was to learn, is best taken in one gulp. I was trying to sip mine.

At the time the statement was released, Odets had already been freed.

Maltz was shocked and disappointed. He thought I had made a great mistake. I thought I had done the first sensible thing in three years. Since we had never been close, there was little change in our relationship. In Hollywood there was a mild stir. With one or two exceptions, our friends were not Communists—they were very happy with the statement and called Jean to tell her so. Our few Communist-oriented friends never spoke to Jean or me again—at least not until after the events of Hungary and Czechoslovakia.

At Mill Point things went on just as they had before. When a fellow inmate at the garage got very angry with me one day, he shouted, "You—you congressman, you!" (Americans are the best informed people in the world.) The weather got colder, the waiting got harder, but each day did finally end and soon it was nearly time to leave. Some days before my release date, I turned over my garage duties to another inmate and settled myself to wait out the longest week of my life.

Balzer had told me that, at least in a minimum-security prison, the last few days of a man's sentence was the period during which he was most likely to attempt an escape. Now I found out why. As I mentioned earlier, on coming to jail, I had put all thoughts of sex out of my mind. Now they came flooding back. There is no aphrodisiac like the thought of a beautiful, desirable, and ultimately attainable woman. Each day got worse. Jean was driving back to pick me up this time, and day by day I pictured her getting closer and closer to West Virginia. The morning of November 14 finally arrived. I don't remember sleeping at all. At 6:00 A.M. Jean pulled up in the car and brought in a suitcase full of fresh clothes. I changed and signed out. I don't remember saying good-bye to anybody. Thank God, it was still pitch-dark. We must have gotten a whole mile away from the camp before I pulled the car over to the side of the road and turned off the lights.

OUT OF THE PARTY
AND IN THE RED

For a few days more, everything bore a strange air of unreality—I felt removed from the world—but I was brought back to earth soon enough. My agents, Charles Feldman and Jack Gordean, had been working quietly since September to ease me back into the industry, and were having some success. Harry Cohn, always a rebel in his own way, was willing to take a chance. Feldman and Cohn were talking a deal that called for $60,000 a picture to start with. To me that sounded like a million. Then Herbert Biberman knocked on my door.

Both Biberman and I, with six-month sentences, had applied for parole, and both appeals had been denied. (I received official notification of denial two weeks after I got home.) Now the other eight were making similar applications, and Herbert wanted me to write the Board urging that paroles be granted. We all knew that was totally unlikely, but it seemed little enough to do. I agreed, on one condition—that they would not publicize my name locally as one of the group recommending parole. I explained the delicate state of the contract negotiations with Columbia, and Herbert agreed not to release my name. Two days later, it was plastered over the front pages of both trade papers, and Feldman phoned to tell me that, as a result, Cohn had called off our deal.

That was the last straw. I was boiling mad. I had been walking a tightrope between abandoning an extremely distasteful affiliation and protecting my few friends in the Party. And my "friends" were giving me no help whatever. Of course, I had another choice; I had received offers of work from J. Arthur Rank and other European producers, but Jean and I had decided that the U.S. was our country and this is where we wanted to live, work, and raise our family. Now, thanks to Biberman's "humanitarianism" all hope of work had disappeared. The amount of money I owed for back taxes, alimony, and assorted debts ran well into six figures. My ex-wife and her attorney were still trying to bleed the turnip, and the IRS was adamant. Over the next few months, I had several meetings with its Hollywood representative. At one point, I broached the possibility of a settlement, noting that a certain sports figure had recently made a deal to pay a small percentage on the dollar.

"His situation is different from yours," I was told. "We feel he no longer has any earning potential, so we'll take what we can get. You, on the other hand, are only forty-two, and a long way from finished."

Very encouraging. If only I could have taken that expression of faith to Louis B. Mayer and traded it in for a job. At the same meeting he told me, almost with glee, that Lionel Barrymore had had to come to them for permission to buy a new car battery. He was so far in arrears that the IRS could never hope to recoup its just due. They gave him a small weekly allowance and took the remainder of the rather reasonable salary paid him by MGM. Whenever an emergency arose, as with the dead car battery, he had to plead with them for the extra money needed.

Bart Crum and I had been looking into every possible means of breaking the blacklist. There was only one: I had to purge myself. Hollywood's right wing had to have its pound of flesh. They were riding high just now, and there was no way they were going to let anyone off the hook. It was an eye-for-an-eye attitude, but who could blame them? On the whole, they had taken a pretty bad public-relations beating from a bunch of pretty bright men. The most notable of the blacklist personalities had been remarkably clever at avoiding being pinned down. They always refused to answer the sixty-four-dollar question on the grounds that it would compromise their principles, while at the same time implying most ingeniously that they had never been members of any group more subversive than the Boy Scouts of America. And they convinced a lot of people. In the early days of the struggle, when it was a little easier to laugh, we often chuckled in appreciation of some of the cleverness displayed, particularly by someone like the very witty Ring Lardner, Jr. Now the whole joke seemed rather stale, but it still stuck in the right wing's craw. They needed confirmation, and they insisted on getting it.

Bart Crum made the necessary contact with the Motion Picture Industry Council, a committee that was charged with the rehabilitation of blacklisted workers. I had known most of its members for years. All were interested in putting the whole business behind them, but it had to be done *their* way. There were several requirements; some merely suggested as desirable, some absolute. The suggestions involved primarily public relations activities which they felt important in paving the way for favorable acceptance by the public at large. The absolute was a second appearance bedfore the House Un-American Activities Committee, with full and open answers to all questions asked.

Meeting the voluntary requirements was easy. I was put in touch with Richard English, a well-known Hollywood writer who often did articles for national magazines. He wanted to write my story for the *Saturday Evening Post*. We spent a couple of weeks together, during which he questioned and cross-questioned me like a prosecutor. He edited the material down into a lengthy and fairly comprehensive article explaining my involvement with the Communist party. It appeared in the May 19, 1951 issue of the *Post*. It mentioned no names, yet led to some interesting reactions. But before it was released I was involved in a much more publicized process.

I now had a decision to make—the second independent decision since 1947. My first decision, on September 9, 1950, from jail, had separated me from the Hollywood Ten, but not from their control over my life. I weighed the facts. I had long been convinced that the fight of the Ten was political, that the battle for freedom of thought, in which I believed completely, had been twisted into a conspiracy of silence. I believed that I was being forced to sacrifice my family and my career in defense of the Communist party, from which I had long been separated and which I had grown to dislike and distrust. I knew that if it ever got down to a choice between the party and our traditional democratic structure I would fight the party to the bitter end.

On the other hand, I would have to name names, and I knew the problems this would cause. Though the principle remained the same, my decision was made easier by the fact that my experience as an actual party member had been rather meager, and I couldn't name anybody who hadn't already been identified as a party member. Weighing everything, pro and con, I knew I had to testify.

I was put in touch with committee investigators. Naturally, they were pleased that I was going to cooperate. They were tired of getting hit on the head with the bladder of "freedom of thought" by people who would have abolished it overnight if their positions had been reversed. They (as did the FBI in future interviews) laid down one stricture: They did not want to hear a name mentioned unless his (or her) membership in the party was certain and verifiable. None of the names I gave was a surprise to them, though they were interested in some of the party procedures. I found out at this time that Larry Parks was also going to testify before the committee, and we discussed the timing of our appearances. I suggested that I be called first, but for some reason which escapes me, Larry wanted that position. His tortured testimony was so copiously reported that it haunted him throughout the rest of his life. (After our testimony, the committee changed its procedures to allow other "name" witnesses to testify in closed session.)

My appearance before the Committee on April 25, 1951, was a complete surprise to everyone. As I approached the door to the hearing room, I ran into one of our former Communist lawyers, who was there to represent a new batch of questionees. He looked at me in astonishment.

"What are you doing here?" he asked.

"I'm making an appearance," I said.

He turned white. I entered the hearing room. Representative Thomas, our nemesis, was no longer on the committee—he was no longer in Congress. He was in jail. He had been convicted of malfeasance in office and had served a sentence in the same prison and at the same time as Lester Cole and Ring Lardner, Jr. The new chairman was Representative Walters, a much quieter man than Thomas, who was doing his best to demonstrate that the committee could function with a certain amount of dignity. All of the shouting was now being done by recalcitrant witnesses.

In my testimony I gave the names of a number of persons I had seen at closed party meetings whom I could positively identify as Communists, and described some of the party methods and practices as they related to the motion-picture establishment. There was no new or startling information in any of my testimony. Its chief value was that it was a confirmation of the committee's statements by an actual former member of the party. Everything I said had been verified by the committee's investigators in advance. For the first time in three and a half years, I felt free of guilt.

The press gave my appearance full and surprisingly accurate coverage. The reaction was as I had anticipated. My non-Communist friends were relieved and pleased; if any of them felt in the least betrayed by my past dissembling, they never showed it. My former comrades and their many leftist supporters were shocked. The vituperation of these people when injured, as any ex-Communist can testify, can scarcely be believed. They had always specialized in the "big lie" technique, and their main tactic was to call anyone who charged them with wrongdoing a liar. They now started just such a barrage against me, which was intensified when the *Post* printed English's article some three weeks after my committee appearance. Their cry of "Liar!" became so shrill that the *Post* worried about a possible suit. English asked them to conduct their own investigation into the facts. They did, and their fears were laid to rest.

My disclosures had obviously hurt the party's continuing campaign, or it wouldn't have felt the need to fight back quite so hard. In answer to the *Post* article, the party bought the center spread of the trade papers to publish an "answer" by Albert Maltz. Maltz had been my best man and my prison mate, so he was chosen to be the hatchet man. He put together a series of half-truths and distortions in an effort to discredit the *Post* article.

I now proceeded to put the whole nightmare behind me and tried to find work. The Communists had stated as fact that I had been signed to a $5,000 a week, long-term contract by MGM as an inducement to get me to testify. To the contrary, the major studios were still following that economic axiom, "nothing is as easily frightened as a million dollars," and my agents were getting nowhere. But the King brothers, an independent outfit, were willing to take advantage of my situation, and I was willing to take advantage of theirs. The King brothers also bought and produced Robert Rich's *The Brave One*, for which Dalton (Robert Rich) Trumbo later collected an Oscar. For $5,000 (total) I agreed to make a small-budget film called *Mutiny*. It featured Mark Stevens and Angela Lansbury and a good supporting cast. Made in something like 18 days, it was a potboiler which helped the King brothers sell one of their cheap pictures. It served as a finger in the wind for me. Nobody protested my employment; the American Legion remained quiescent; no theaters were picketed. I had demonstrated that I was no longer "unclean."

But there was no miracle, and we settled down to more waiting. Jean was pregnant again and I was spending three hours a day with my weights. At 5'7", I weighed 172 fat-free pounds. I was in the pink, but also in the red. I just couldn't get rid of that damned color.

Then Stanley Kramer, a noted "chance taker" and progressive film-maker, approached me with a four-picture deal. Manna from heaven. Maybe, after four years of famine, the harvest would be full again. I was sure going to find out.

The author at age 25, while assistant to cutter (editor) LeRoy Stone at
Paramount (1934).

Courtesy of RKO General Pictures

The first "A" film: *Tender Comrade* (1943) "Ginger Rogers—oh, boy!"

Courtesy of RKO General Pictures

Directing Dick Powell and Claire Trevor in *Murder, My Sweet* (1943). "I wanted Marlowe played as I believed Chandler visualized him— really an Eagle Scout with the patina of toughness only skin deep." Tenor Dick Powell never had to sing again.

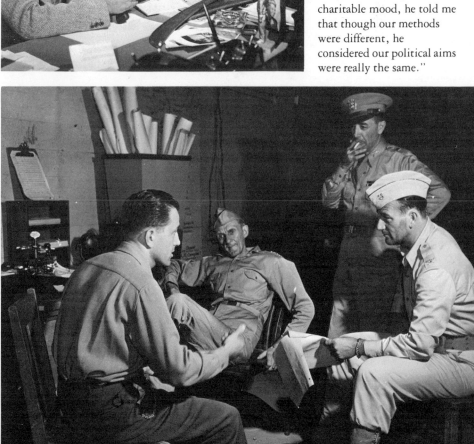

The author and a young Anthony Quinn match swords while filming *Back to Bataan* in 1945.

Dymtryk's only experience with John Wayne was *Back to Bataan*. "Once, in a charitable mood, he told me that though our methods were different, he considered our political aims were really the same."

"Mr. RKO" (1945).

Till the End of Time (1946). Dmytryk discusses a scene with Dorothy McGuire and producer Dore Schary. During this picture, the author met his future wife Jean Porter, who was cast as the girl next door. The director already knew how to skate, but Jean and leading man Guy Madison had to learn.

Directing Robert Young and Robert Mitchum in *Crossfire* (1947), a milestone in Dmytryk's career.

Dmytryk worked with producer Adrian Scott on *Murder, My Sweet,*
Cornered, and *Crossfire.* Both received subpoenas from the House
UnAmerican Activities Committee at the RKO studio in 1947 and
became members of the Hollywood Ten. Both went to prison in 1950
for contempt of Congress.

On location in Israel for *The Juggler* (1953) with Kirk Douglas and
Paul Stewart. "On the set, Kirk is a man activated by a tightly coiled
spring."

The Mountain (1955). On location in the Alps, Spencer Tracy had to be
lowered by rope to the side of the mountain. Dmytryk tried it first,
while Tracy and crew watched. Tracy (who was afraid of flying)
eventually played the scene. Inset: The director with stars Tracy and
Robert Wagner. When Wagner balked at an especially exerting scene
at such an altitude, Trace told him: "Young man, you ought to get
down on your knees every night and thank God you work in the most
overpaid business in the world."

Clark Gable, the King, starred in *Soldier of Fortune* in 1954. Actor and director discuss
a scene at the studio (above), and sample *sake* with friends while on location in Tokyo (below).

Raintree County (1956). (Above): a conference with Elizabeth Taylor and an impulsive Montgomery Clift. (Below): The director surrounded by his cast on location in a hot and humid Natchez.

The director of *The Young Lions* (1957) mugs with one of its stars,
Marlon Brando.

Robert Mitchum played an American journalist in *Anzio*, filmed in
Rome in 1967 and produced by Dino De Laurentiis. "Mitchum is an
unusual man, tough and taciturn on the outside, soft and sentimental
on the inside, and very insecure."

Shooting in New York for *Mirage* with Diane Baker and Gregory Peck.

Richard Burton and the author during the filming of *Bluebeard* (1972).

The Dmytryks attend Liz Taylor's gala fortieth birthday party in Budapest during the filming of *Bluebeard*.

A NEW DEAL

S tanley Kramer was a highly successful producer of short-budget
films, but short-budget films with a difference. He had made a
number of pictures in much the same way that Scott and I had
made *Crossfire*. His scripts were tight and well written, his casts,
while not expensive, were much better than competent, and the productions were well planned and efficiently shot. They had earned him a
reputation as a man of taste and a producer of moderately controversial
films. When I joined his company, *High Noon* had just been finished. It
was a somewhat more ambitious project than any of his previous ones,
and the last film under his old United Artists deal. A new partner, Sam
Katz, had been instrumental in negotiating a contract with Columbia
which was probably the best since Orson Welles' original deal at RKO.
Under its terms, the Kramer Company had the unsupervised use of
some twenty-odd million dollars to make some twenty-odd films. Aside
from an upper limit on budgets and on running time, Kramer was free
to operate how and with whom he pleased. When I started my first film
for him, he already had two or three others under way.

Edward and Edna Anhalt had joined the outfit as writer—producers.
Their first effort was an original script called *The Sniper*. It was now
given to me as my first directorial chore for the company. It was a piece
of cake—a moody suspense story about a psychopathic sniper. It was
one of the first modern films to make an attempt to understand the
so-called criminal, and, though not exactly a financial success in the
United States, it was highly regarded by the great majority of critics,
criminal psychologists, and students of *"film noir,"* particularly in
Europe.

For star rating, the cast was undistinguished; for quality of performance, it was tops. Arthur Franz played the role of the confused killer
beautifully. Other parts were played by Richard Kiley, Marie Windsor,
and Adolphe Menjou. The casting of Menjou brought a blast from the
Daily Worker of November 15, 1951. It said in part:

Movie director Edward Dmytryk, ex-member of the Hollywood Ten who turned informer for the FBI, is now palsy-walsy with his erstwhile foe—the rabid witch-hunter and haberdasher's gentleman—Adolphe Menjou.

Now Dmytryk and Menjou are together again—this time as friends. Menjou has a leading role in *The Sniper*, which Dmytryk, gone over to warmongering and restored to favor of the Big Money, is now directing for Stanley Kramer productions.

Typical. We—Kramer, the Anhalts, and I—agreed on Menjou because we considered it to be excellent offbeat casting. As a run-of-the-mill police detective, Menjou shaved off his moustache, wore cheap suits and shoes, and was as far removed from the haberdasher's gentleman as we could reasonably get. Regardless of his extremist views, he had always been a fine actor, and he did an excellent job in our film. We were still at opposite poles politically, though neither of us, as far as I knew, was doing any warmongering. Menjou also received some criticism from his fellow-reactionaries—one of whom asked why he had agreed to work with me.

"Because I'm a whore!" he snapped.

There always has to be a place in my heart for honesty.

The film was a bonanza for those who seek symbols and hidden meanings in every work of art. At an early point in the film, Menjou seeks information on homicidal psychopaths from a psychiatrist, played by Richard Kiley. Since the story was laid in San Francisco and the police headquarters of that city was in its famous Chinatown, I decided to stage their luncheon meeting in a Chinese restaurant. Menjou, as an old Chinatown habitué, eats with chopsticks. Kiley, unfamiliar with the utensils, tries briefly, then gives up in disgust at his clumsiness and picks up his fork. I introduced this common vignette simply to add a little action to a "talky" scene. The symbolists jumped on it with glee. I couldn't begin to understand the esoteric meanings read into this simple scene.

We did have a number of "symbolic" scenes in the film. One, which was rarely commented on, was a chase scene near the end of the picture, unique because there was no one chasing the sniper. He had been discovered in the act of shooting and had fled the scene of the crime, running for dear life to reach his apartment. My intent was to indicate that he was trying to escape his own conscience. But symbol buffs preferred the chopsticks.

On this film I used a sketch artist, something I do on infrequent occasions. Sketch artists are exactly what the name implies—they do more or less rough pencil, or pen-and-ink sketches of scenes to be shot in a film, something in the nature of a comic strip. Using sketch artists is not a common practice. One or two directors, like Alfred Hitchcock, do their own sketching. A few others use the artist to sketch scenes and setups as they—the directors—have conceived them. I consider that a waste of time and money. Any experienced director thinks in terms of setups, reads in terms of setups, dreams in setups; he hardly needs an artist to draw his own mental images for him. I ask the artist to sketch out his own interpretation of the scene, or perhaps to develop an idea of mine which is incomplete. That way I have an opportunity to broaden my creative base. If the artist can come up with just one original, usable conception on a film, he has earned his salary.

For example, our film included a rooftop chase of a "copycat" sniper. Everyone has seen dozens of rooftop chases, and I wanted something different. After a brief mental bout, I came up with the idea of rooftop clotheslines hung with laundry, which I had never seen used in chase scenes. Having too many other problems facing me at the moment, I tossed the laundry idea to the sketch artist. In a couple of days, he brought me a very unusual and photogenic conception of a chase through a sea of flapping sheets. It made an interesting and unusual sequence out of what might otherwise have been something quite routine.

My next film for Stanley was *Eight Iron Men*, a film version of the play that brought Burt Lancaster to Hollywood's attention, *The Sound of Hunting*. This one, too, was produced by the Anhalts. Like all of Kramer's films, we had a good script, a fine group of actors, but no names—and that was at a time when names were very important. Occasionally I voiced my desire to have someone—anyone—that an audience might recognize. Stanley would pat me on the back and say, "You can bring it off—I know you can do it." Highly flattering, but until we made *The Caine Mutiny*, most of his taut, tasteful, inexpensive films fizzled like wet firecrackers. Kramer did learn his lesson, however. When he started directing his own films, he went to great expense to get the biggest best-sellers, scripted by the most highly regarded writers, and cast with the biggest star names available. That's what comes of not having someone else around to pat you on the shoulder and say, "You can do it."

The cast of *Eight Iron Men* consisted of Richard Kiley, Arthur Franz, Bonar Colleano, Nick Dennis, Jim Griffith, and Lee Marvin. Lee was fresh from the Marine Corps—almost. He had played a small part in a Hathaway film. We liked his work and gave him a somewhat fatter role in ours. He proved to be an unusual actor and an unusual man with a highly developed observational ability. He re-dressed our entire squad until it really looked like a group of working GIs. He could imitate the sound of every type and caliber of shell, and he showed me the way men really died on the battlefield and how their bodies looked in death.

Our story was simple. A squad of men has to destroy a German machine-gun post that blocks the American advance in their sector. Naturally, the machine gun was authentically German, and just as naturally it always jammed when we needed it most. The gun experts who had rented it to us could do little with it. After two or three frustrating days, Lee, who had served only in the Pacific, said, "Let me take a look at it."

What could I lose? He spread out a sheet, took the gun completely apart in a few minutes, then reassembled it. It never jammed again. Some men have a way with dogs, some with kids. Lee had a way with war.

Eight Iron Men was well liked by the critics. Unfortunately, they get in free.

Film number three for Kramer—*The Juggler*. The screenplay was written by Michael Blankfort from his own novel of the same name. It starred Kirk Douglas, and was about as sweet and sour a picture as I have ever made.

First, the sweet. It started in the worst way possible. About half the film was to be made in Israel, so the art director, cameraman, unit manager, and I flew to Tel Aviv in June of 1952 to scout locations. The El Al Constellation which carried us over had no air conditioning, and as we started our descent into the airport, it was stifling hot. I looked forward eagerly to getting out into the open air and was standing in the front of the plane when it came to a stop and the door was opened. What a shock! I thought we were entering the biblical fiery furnace! We soon found out that we had arrived in the middle of a *chamsin* (the Semitic word for "forty")—the Near East desert wind that traditionally blows for forty days out of the year—not consecutively, thank God!

Mad dogs, Englishmen, and film crews go out in the noonday sun. We checked in at our hotel, climbed into our hired cars, and started out to see the country. The natives thought we were nuts, but over the next two weeks, we explored every foot of every road and highway north of the Negev Desert. Even I felt the thrill of standing on land and in towns I had studied as a child, reading the Bible. We had a few things to learn though, like how violent an Orthodox Jew could be if he caught you driving or smoking on the Sabbath. Our art director lost his pipe and nearly half his teeth when an old, white-bearded, gentle-looking man slapped it out of his mouth as we walked unheedingly in Jaffa.

In 1948 Jean and I were spending an evening with Bart Crum when he got a call from Harry Truman. Bart was an old friend of the Zionists, and the president wanted him to be the first to know that the United States was recognizing the brand-new nation of Israel. Now, just four years later, I was seeing that nation pulling itself up by its bootstraps. The hotels were completely inadequate, the food made me long for the awful "wiener schnitzel" at Mill Point, and the weather was brutal, but the spirit of the people was the greatest I had ever witnessed and it made our stay unforgettable. Our job was nearly done when I got word that my ex-wife had died. Leaving the others in Israel, I flew back to California to meet a son I hadn't seen or talked to for five years.

Kirk Douglas wanted to take advantage of the 18-month, tax-free break allowed Americans living abroad at that time, so we had reversed our usual scheduling procedures: We were shooting the interiors first, in Hollywood, then traveling to Israel for the locations, after which Douglas would remain in Europe for his 18-month hiatus. That meant our studio shooting had to be done strictly to schedule, since our departure date had to be set well in advance.

Thomas Wolfe had said that the act of creation was a battle that must be fought within oneself. Unfortunately, Douglas had never learned that. Kirk always does best in the role of a man activated by a tightly coiled spring. On the set, Kirk *is* a man activated by a tightly coiled spring. As was the custom at Kramer's, we had spent a number of days reading the script and in rough rehearsals, with Kirk's active participation. We had reworked the dialogue and sharpened the scenes. Kirk seemed quite content.

Then we started shooting. It was as though we had never read or rehearsed—the same old doubts and insecurities surfaced all over again. Kirk circled a scene in an ever-decreasing spiral, like a dog finding a spot on which to lie down. Eventually he made it, but it was only back to where we had always been, and a great deal of time had been lost in the process. Also, like a man putting on a heavy diving suit, the minute we were ready to shoot, he had to go, and he was a very slow goer. All this wasted time made us fall behind schedule. I had to use every trick I had learned in B films to try to get us up to par.

Three or four days before departure time, I was shooting scenes in what was supposed to be a small auditorium at a kibbutz. In order to save lighting time, I was finishing all scenes in one direction without regard to direct continuity. This meant that a couple of Kirk's close-ups had to be put off until late in the afternoon. About 3:00 he came storming onto the set, having apparently worked himself up into a self-righteously frenetic mood. He wanted to know why he, the star, was being forced to stand by. I kept my cool and put him off with sweet-talk. He slunk back into his cave. In about an hour, I was ready for him. We had lit his close-up using his stand-in, then called him to the set. He came in somewhat sullenly, took his place for a rehearsal, then started to beef again. By this time I had a self-righteous peeve on myself. So I let him have it. I pointed out that I was trying to save time, which he had largely been responsible for losing, so we could get him to Europe in time for some effective tax-dodging. He was outraged and stormed off the set. I asked the assistant to sign everyone off for the day, gave Kramer my version of the battle, and went home. Rather late that evening, a delivery van pulled into our driveway. I was presented with a large bouquet of flowers, a box of cigars, and a note of apology. The next morning I had a short talk with Kirk and we went on with the film as though nothing had happened. But it had, and it was never quite the same again.

Working in Israel was an experience. We had only one thing in full supply—free advice. A minor instance: I had hired a young Israeli actor as a third assistant—literally, a messenger boy. He had had no film experience, but wanted to learn. On the second day of shooting, he strongly objected to one of my camera setups. I tried to ignore him, but you can't ignore an Israeli. So I fired him. The next morning he was back on the set in tears, full of remorse and apologies. If I would only give him another chance, he would never misbehave again. I relented and he came back to work. Within a few hours, he was pressing his views again. The third time I fired him, I realized I just had to learn to do without his advice. And somehow I did.

One day, I exchanged a few words with Israel's chief of police, who was visiting our location. He had inquired about our reception in the country, and I had replied we were more than satisfied. Then, for lack of anything more clever to say, I asked if they had been satisfied with our behavior. (A film crew in a foreign land is like a company of soldiers and can sometimes raise just as much hell.)

"No," he said. "I've been getting complaints."

I was startled. We had a hand-picked crew, and I had heard of no trouble.

"Good Lord!" I said. "What kind of complaints?"

"It's about the way you work," he answered. "My men all agree they haven't worked so hard in their lives."

I've said it before and I'll say it again. No one works as hard as a film crew on location, unless it's a southern chain-gang. But it was good to have my belief confirmed by a citizen of the hardest-working young country in the world.

Work finally finished, we went our separate ways. Jean met me in Rome for a few carefree days in that city, then we flew to Paris for some dubbing with Kirk. Finally, back to Hollywood for the cutting of the film. Like the other pictures I had made for Kramer, *The Juggler* was well received by the press and went on to a modest success with the public. But by then I was getting ready for another important step in my career. Kramer had asked me to make *The Caine Mutiny*.

THE CAINE MUTINY

Kramer's deal with Columbia was nearing its end. Besides his series of what were essentially intelligently made "quickies," he had taken a gamble on a "far-out" film, a fantasy, *The 5000 Fingers of Dr. T*. It was a dismal failure. As a matter of fact, his whole program had been a decided financial disappointment for both Kramer and Cohn, and now he was making his final picture for Columbia. It was a great story and we had a great cast, but the shadow of Harry Cohn hovered over the undertaking from first to last.

The Caine Mutiny is probably one of the four or five best sea novels ever written—it is almost certainly the finest to come out of World War II. It was the first best-seller that Kramer bought, and, for him, it established a pattern. In the beginning, its production seemed somewhat in doubt. There were constant rumors of Navy Department objections which, if true, would have been disastrous, since the film could not have been made without the navy's cooperation. The rumors didn't seem to bother Stanley as he went ahead with his preparations.

He hired the novel's author, Herman Wouk, to write the screenplay, but that turned out to be a disaster. It is often true that when an author has finished writing a book, that particular vein has been worked completely, and knocking out a script becomes a sterile occupation. Wouk, I believe, was a victim of boredom. He wanted to write something new, and he did. It was very good and very funny, but it wasn't *The Caine Mutiny*. Kramer reluctantly parted company with Wouk and hired Stanley Roberts. It was an ideal choice. Roberts was an excellent literary editor and he had a rare ability to transfer the selected portions of the book into a screenplay virtually verbatim and still consider the material essentially his own.

The average novel runs to several hundred pages (*Caine Mutiny* is nearly 500 pages long) and each of its pages is at least twice the length of a page of script. Yet a 140-page script will run a good 2 hours on the screen, which means that a novel like *The Caine Mutiny*, if transferred to film in full, would run 15 hours or more. Obviously, novels have to be edited severely, and the fact that so many of them have been satisfactorily translated into films speaks well for the good Hollywood film writers—or badly for the verbosity of the novelists. In the case of *The Caine Mutiny*, Roberts was able to produce a 190-page script that was the distilled essence of the novel, and with the dialogue of the selected scenes nearly intact.

During his three years at Columbia, Kramer had treated Cohn in rather cavalier fashion, never seeking his advice or asking for his recommendations, but pointedly avoiding him at all times. It would have taken a very big man to overlook such youthful arrogance, and Cohn wasn't quite that big. Now he had the upper hand. Though I did not know of it until sometime later, he insisted that *The Caine Mutiny* be made strictly in accordance with the terms of the deal, that is, the cost could not exceed $2,000,000 nor the running time two hours. (The alternative was full control of the film by Cohn.) That was a pity. *The Caine Mutiny* should have been at least three hours long; there was more than enough exceptional material to keep an audience's interest for that length of time, and the additional shooting could not have cost more than another million.

A couple of years later, I asked Columbia's head of distribution why they had insisted on the two-hour limit.

"We were able to get one extra showing a day," he said.

"But if it had been a better film at three hours, couldn't it have played to a larger audience in the long run?" I asked.

"Quite possibly," he replied, "but it would have taken a good deal longer to get our money back." So much for the economics of excellence.

Cohn's shadow appeared first upon the completion of the script. It was beautifully done, but it was 50 pages too long, and that without "the girl." Columbia wanted "the girl." Putting her in was not particularly difficult (though she didn't really belong), but it meant making even more deletions. Roberts couldn't suffer the violation of his masterpiece, so he quit. I wasn't happy about it either. An uptight Kramer called in Michael Blankfort. Closeting themselves for a week or two, they went to work with the scissors. The script that emerged was still Roberts' script, but with great chunks excised. Sad, but necessary—a case of cut off the legs or let the patient die.

Even in Hollywood, the show must go on. There was no time to cry over fine scenes being thrown into the ashcan. Casting had already been started and fell into place easily. That's one advantage of working with a best-seller—every actor in town wants to be in it—and that's one of the reasons best-selling novels are so eagerly sought after by filmmakers, even when they are not good screen material. The casting process becomes more a matter of exclusion than selection. Eventually, the following players were lined up: Humphrey Bogart for the infamous Captain Queeg, Van Johnson for Maryk, the executive officer, Fred MacMurray as the novelist, Keefer, and Jose Ferrer as the lawyer, Greenwald. Kramer decided to go with a newcomer, Bob Francis, as the young ensign, Willie Keith. A dozen girls were tested before another unknown, Donna Lee Hickey, was cast in the role of Keith's girl friend, May Wynn. A nicely balanced cast.

CINCPAC headquarters was in Hawaii, so that was the next stop. Observing protocol, we started with Admiral Radford and worked our way down the chain of command. No director would ever have cast Radford as a commander-in-chief—he was too on-the-nose. A tall, extremely handsome man, his manner and charm were upper-class navy to a T. We had, as yet, no sure knowledge of the official attitude toward our production and felt we were walking on coals. The meeting with Radford was encouraging; he had enjoyed the novel and had no objection to its being filmed. But there were other admirals, each one in charge of some phase of naval operation, whose cooperation was essential. We had been warned about one such officer who ranked not too far below Radford. He was considered a tough nut, a 100 percent no-nonsense navy man, and he was in complete command of the Pearl Harbor port and repair facilities.

The morning we were to meet him, he was attending some formal naval ritual (a transfer of command, I believe), and he was still attired in his full-dress whites when he arrived, a few minutes late, at his office. His appearance was as forbidding as his reputation: a short man with cropped, white hair over a stern face. He had been formed in the "Bull" Halsey mold.

After the formal introductions, Kramer started a tentative conversation, looking for some sign of a direction in which to go, when the admiral cut short our suspense. He pointed to the stripes on his sleeve.

"There is no star on my sleeve," he said bitterly, "because I had a Captain Queeg for a commanding officer early in my career." The absence of a star indicates the officer can never aspire to sea duty or command.

"I think," he continued, "that *The Caine Mutiny* should be required reading for every man and officer in the United States Navy."

What sounded like a roller sweeping in at Waikiki was just the combined sigh of relief that filled the office. It was all downhill from then on. Only one obstacle remained: my security clearance. Our technical adviser, Lieutenant Commander Shaw, hd requested it but had run into an unexpected snag. He made a special trip to Washington and found out that though there were copious entries in my dossier preceding my prison sojourn, all further surveillance had stopped. Shaw was able to clean up the situation in a few days, and I had freedom of access to the naval installations.

My first move was to look at hundreds of thousands of feet of actual wartime footage. The Signal Corps had done a remarkable job of covering every phase of the war in the Pacific. I had been reading official histories, but actually seeing so much of the action, both in and behind the battle lines, was invaluable in giving me the look and feel of a navy ship at sea.

We began shooting in San Francisco. The U.S.S. *Caine*, as described in the novel, was an old four-stacker. The navy was unable to furnish us one of these since they had all been dispersed to foreign allies during the war. Only one or two were still in service, and these were in Latin American ports. Instead, we used two "small" destroyers—sister ships. One was now in San Francisco and would leave for duty in the Far East as soon as we were through with her. The other was being pulled back from Korean duty a couple of months early and would be at our disposal in Hawaiian waters, after which she was due for refitting, refurbishing, and R. and R. in San Diego. It was an arrangement that pleased everybody.

The crew members of the San Francisco "Caine" insisted that we had miscast the role of Captain Queeg—it really belonged to their skipper. Sure enough, one day in his cabin, he pointed to a row of buttons near his bed.

"I love to push those one after the other and see everybody come running," he said.

A clear case of the Queeg syndrome. Another time, his self-esteem damaged by the fact that he had never conned his ship into or out of its berth, he tried to handle the job himself. He handled it well through casting off the hawsers that snugged the vessel to the dock, then steamed out into the channel, tearing out all the auxiliary electric cables and telephone lines that had been plugged into the ship.

A captain I met in Pearl Harbor had an interesting comment to make.

"I used to know a lot of Captain Queegs," he said, "but now that I've made that grade, I'll be damned if I know any."

We shot some boy-girl scenes in Yosemite, then took off for Honolulu. In 1953 Hawaii was still an idyllic group of islands, with clean white beaches washed by a clean, warm sea. The heady fragrance of flowers was all-pervading the moment the arriving plane's doors were opened and stayed with you long after you had left. The Hawaiians, whatever their racial origin, were a rare people, whose warmth and hospitality could hardly be believed. Tourism has changed all that. Once a bather on Waikiki Beach could see the rainbows in the mountain valleys, or a valley resident could look down at the surfers in the sea. Not anymore. The solid wall of high-rise hotels and condominiums has made a most effective screen. Hospitality is down to the level of any other city in the United States and the pervading odor is that of gasoline and exhaust fumes.

Working in Hawaii was tough, but it had its compensations. We would board ship in the crystal-clear early morning and head out to sea. After a full day's shooting, we would steam back to Pearl Harbor, counting the rainbows which spanned the cloud-filled valleys as we skirted the coast of Oahu. Evenings were always soft and warm and filled with music, and we could slip into the ocean for a midnight swim without shocking a single nerve-end.

The work at sea was something else. The schedule was tight and so were the working spaces. However, the navy personnel was completely cooperative and helped us greatly along the way. Still, with a motion picture crew, things will go wrong *even* in the navy. Little things. Like the Marine Corps captain during the "yellow stain" incident who got so seasick riding in the landing craft that work had to be stopped while he was taken on board our ship so he could "die" in comfort. Or the mine-sweeping drill, done at my request, during which the chief in charge almost lost his thumb. The cables were old, the fittings were rusted into immobility, and the paravane turned turtle and floated because it had a leak. (It seems the gear hadn't been used since World War II. The ship got a new paravane, a new towing cable, and a few oil cans while she was in port that night.)

Story action called for a general-quarters drill. On our first day at sea,

I asked the skipper to stage one for me. The necessary commands went out over the ship's loudspeakers, and I watched from the bridge as the members of the crew strolled casually to their respective stations, few, if any, bothering to don the required protective gear. In about twenty minutes, the ship was battle-ready—or as battle-ready as she was going to get. With Commander Shaw's help, I took the skipper aside and pointed out that I couldn't take that much time for a drill, that I needed to show a top naval crew under wartime conditions. He saw my point. I put off shooting the sequence until our final day at sea. In the meantime, during nonshooting periods, the captain would signal general quarters. By the time the sequence was photographed, the men were at their battle stations, in full gear, within a minute or two. The old navy pride was still there—it just needed stirring up a bit.

We were shooting the target-towing sequence. This incident, as related in the novel, is an example of dramatic license. No battle wagon, not even a destroyer, can steer a circle tight enough to cut its own towline. But the sequence was too good to permit an irrelevant little thing like impossibility to scuttle it. So we cut the target free and steamed a circle back toward it. The first time around we missed it by a good 200 yards. The captain promised to do better on the next try. And he did. As we completed our circle, we found ourselves heading straight for the target—a large steel floating platform with a steel framework (the target) mounted on top. The cameras were rolling, and I was scared to death. So, I noticed, were the officers and men on the bridge. The captain gave the order for starboard engines full ahead and port engines full astern, then realized that was just the opposite of what he really wanted. There was an extremely long five seconds, during which the ship started a slight heel to port, before the captain corrected himself. The ship agonizingly leveled out, then slowly heeled to starboard. In slow motion, the bow moved off the center of the target. As we steamed by, one corner just barely touched the ship, leaving a long streak of yellow paint down the entire length of the hull. Later the executive officer told me that with a few inches less clearance, the platform would have sliced the ship's thin skin like a can opener slitting a tin of sardines. But luck was with us and it looked awfully good on the screen.

Then there was the other side of the target incident. I needed some shots of the ship's rifles firing and the skipper agreed to activate his 5-inchers—the crew needed the practice anyway. Indeed they did. I placed my cameras in the bow of the ship and waited for the ready sign. When it was flashed from the bridge, I turned the cameras and waited. And waited. After about five minutes, I figured out what it was costing me in film (I was using three-strip Technicolor), so I signaled the bridge and cut my cameras. A quick exchange informed me that something or someone had fouled up in the gun room. It was soon corrected, and in a few minutes I got the ready sign again. I turned the cameras and signaled that we were shooting. The guns fired once, then stopped. Again we waited, but there was no further firing before the cameras had to reload. The third time was the charm—everything worked. With an attempt at lightness, I turned to an embarrassed Commander Shaw.

"How did we ever win the war?" I asked.

"They made more mistakes than we did," he said quite seriously. And that, as I have found out in a long life of working in a lot of places, is the way it really is. Like a game of tennis—more points are scored on your opponent's mistakes than on your own skillful placements.

An aircraft carrier (I believe it was the *Kearsarge*) was arriving at Pearl Harbor, then leaving almost immediately for the Far East. Since they could give us only one day, everything was carefully planned. The navy experts had decided to position the carrier some distance off Waikiki, but its Captain had decided to exercise his prerogative. When our seagoing tug arrived at location early in the morning, we found the carrier was anchored much closer to the beach than originally planned. Our first shot was to show Johnson, MacMurray, and Francis approaching and boarding the carrier. The actors were in their gig and I was about to turn the cameras when all hell broke loose on our tug and I realized we were moving backward at a good clip. We signaled the gig to return to the tug, and I dashed up to the bridge. The skipper had just received word that the carrier was slipping its anchorage and drifting onto the beach. All hands were busy getting the ship out of trouble.

By the time the carrier had maneuvered itself out to the spot originally designated and we were free to shoot, it was nearly noon. By early afternoon, I was in a Marine helicopter ready to shoot a general assembly of the ship's full crew. I had asked to see the action from the air; it was a replay of the first general quarters on the destroyer. Crewmen, in their varicolored uniforms, sauntered casually across the huge flight deck taking what seemed forever to reach their assigned positions. I asked the officer in charge for two changes. I wanted everyone to run, and I wanted all men to start at the opposite end of the ship from their final positions. Then I went aloft again and we started shooting. What a sight! On signal, over two thousand sailors suddenly appeared from under the periphery of the flight deck and dashed madly through, past, and over each other to reach their positions in record time. From our height the men in red, green, and yellow uniforms resembled bright-colored atoms flying wildly in all directions until they suddenly coa-

lesced in formation. I had to radio down and ask the commanding officer
to repeat the action a bit more slowly for our second shot—at a trot
rather than at a gallop. When I landed on the carrier, I found that the
original rush had resulted in one broken leg and a large assortment of
less damaging injuries.

We got down to the business of shooting our dialogue scenes outside
the bridge. Two thousand noisy sailors were watching, the light was
getting yellow, and MacMurray was getting nervous and lousing up his
lines. He stopped short and turned to me with a request. Since the
background of the scene was a mere few square feet of bulkhead, which
could be duplicated at the studio for a few hundred dollars, wouldn't it
be possible, he askd, to skip the scene and do it back on the lot? It was a
reasonable request. I turned to relay it to Kramer, who was sitting some
distance behind me, but he had heard Fred. He suddenly jumped up
and shouted, "No!" There could be no waiting—it was now or never!
Somewhat abashed, we went on with the scene and got it in the
can—not good, but serviceable—with just enough time left to get off
the ship before it sailed for Japan.

The outburst was so uncharacteristic of Kramer, normally rational,
pleasant, and easy to talk with, that I determined to find out what had
caused it. I cornered the production manager and finally learned of the
budget and time restrictions under which the picture was being made.
A few words early on could have made the whole job easier, but pride is
often at cross-purposes with reason.

Working with the cast was a delight. Johnson and MacMurray had
always been known as hard-working, cooperative professionals. Bogart
and Ferrer, on the other hand, had no such reputations. Bogart, in
particular, had been known as a drunk and an unpleasant character in
general. Obviously, Lauren Bacall had been able to turn him around.
No one could possibly have worked harder, stayed more sober, or been
more cooperative than Bogey. And his performance was superb. His
transition from self-control, to petty truculence, to paranoia, then back
to full awareness in the court-martial scene, is one of the finest I have
ever witnessed—and transition is what acting is all about.

Ferrer, too, belied the scuttlebutt and behaved like the gentleman he
really is, while turning in a smooth, suave performance. It's not easy to
walk into a film already near completion and mesh gears immediately
with the rest of the company, but he managed it with great style. Lee
Marvin was in this one, too, playing a gob slob, learning his trade and
waiting in the wings. We all knew he was good, but few of us knew just
how good. We'd have to wait a few years to find out.

We finished in 54 days, exactly on schedule. I completed my director's cut and left the studio. Ordinarily I stay with a film to the bitter end, but I didn't want to get mixed up in the wrangling I was sure would follow. Besides, I had a promising film to make at 20th Century–Fox.

As I had anticipated, *The Caine Mutiny* got a number of Oscar nominations but few awards. But it made enough money to more than take the whole Kramer-Columbia operation out of the red. Reputed box-office figures are always suspect, but the last one I was aware of was some $30,000,000 or $35,000,000. At an original investment of $2,00,000, that's not a return to be ashamed of.

A TURN WITH
THE GREATEST

S ol Siegel had fired me from Paramount in 1940. Now, thirteen years later, he wanted me to make a film for him at 20th. The script was excellent, the star was Spencer Tracy, in his first film since leaving MGM, and the price was right. The added soupçon of personal vindication made the whole package irresistible. There was one slight hitch, and its name was Darryl Zanuck. I had heard frightening things about him: he was arrogant, domineering, he interfered, and he considered himself a good writer and a great cutter. Not the kind of executive with whom a slightly head-strong director wants to break lances. But, sooner or later, I had to breast the big waves, so why not now?

As usual, rumor and truth did not coincide. I found Zanuck to be a collection of contradictions, but never a difficult man to deal with (which means I got my way more often than not). A man of great physical energy, he was sophisticated yet extremely naive, independent yet subject to the importuning of sycophants, possessing limited taste yet recognizing and appreciating taste in others—he worked hard, played hard, and made some damned fine pictures.

Sol Siegel was a tall, well set-up, good looking man, quiet in speech and manner—the director's perfect producer. He organized well, surrounded the director with the most competent help available, then left him alone. (During production I tried a number of times to get him to visit us at work, both on location in Arizona and on the set in the studio. He always promised to try, but somehow never found the time.) Still, at the slightest sign of trouble, Sol was ready to stand back-to-back. No director can ask more than that.

The film was *Broken Lance* (not to be confused with *Broken Arrow*) from a screenplay being completed by Richard Murphy. It was a very loose rework of an earlier Fox film, *The House of Strangers*, the story of a New York banking dynasty, which starred Edward G. Robinson and which was a financial washout. Murphy had transformed it into an excellent "adult" Western. ("Adult" signifies more of substance and less of six-shooters.) Dick was just finishing a second draft when I entered the picture. A few days later, he, Siegel, and I went to Zanuck's office for a story conference.

I had never had a story conference with a studio head before, and I was apprehensive. Now, I thought, all those intimidating things I've been hearing about Zanuck will prove true. Sometimes it pays to fear the worst—the eventuality has to be a pleasant surprise. Darryl had a number of suggestions, but he was never dogmatic. He had a keen nose for character or situation weakness, but his own attempts at correcting these faults left a good deal to be desired. The treatment was often more damaging than the disease. However, to my surprise, I found he was never adamant. For instance: Tracy's death scene was weakly conceived. Zanuck launched into his version of an alternative—lightning, thunder, galloping horses, the whole corny (not to mention expensive and difficult-to-shoot) bit. Feeling it was now or never, I interrupted his performance and suggested that though his analysis of the scene's weakness was correct, it might be better for Murphy and me to take some time to work out a new version to show him. He looked at me for a moment, then said, "Why not?" And that was the end of the conference. We did create an effective scene that bore no resemblance to Darryl's extemporaneous conception, which he accepted with enthusiasm.

Once more I had a little less than $2,000,000 and 55 days in which to make a film, but it was not nearly as difficult as *The Caine Mutiny*. There would be 15 days of location in southern Arizona and 40 days at the studio and on local locations. Besides Tracy, the cast included Katy

Jurado as his Indian wife; Richard Widmark, Robert Wagner, Earl Holliman, and Hugh O'Brian as his four sons, Jean Peters as Wagner's sweetheart, E. G. Marshall as her father, and Eduard Franz as the Indian foreman. With the exception of E.G., all of them were new to me, but families are quickly formed in Hollywood and just as quickly torn apart.

For the first time, I was working with Cinemascope. I had tried to get Kramer to use it for *The Caine Mutiny*, since I thought it would serve the horizontal lines of ships and sea horizons particularly well; but the technique was very new, and Stanley is quite conservative. Ordinarily, I prefer the "Golden Mean" frame, but in semidesert Arizona I felt the old experimental thrill. The soft, distant mountains formed a low, broad horizon; men on horseback filled more screen horizontally than vertically; even the squat, spreading architecture of the American West suited the new dimensions perfectly. I was thirty again.

To me, the Western cowboy myth involves the Western horse, with tossing head, flying mane, and flaring nostrils—the whole equine bit. I remembered such horses in the early thirties Westerns I had cut for Hathaway. I was dismayed to find this type of horse no longer existed— at least not in the stables that customarily supplied Hollywood with its stock. There were only plugs. I asked Bill Williams, TV's Kit Carson, what had happened.

"A spirited horse is a handicap today," he told me. "Most Westerns are now made for TV, and TV is quick. If my horse moves me out of the frame while I'm reading a line, they're simply going to cut to someone else. So I make sure I have an animal that never quivers." That's when I first decided that a potentially great medium was being horribly used.

We finally got our horses, all from private owners. They were big, they were beautiful, they were alive, and they added immeasurably to the feel of the film.

The first day on any film is discovery day. I had had a number of meetings with Spencer Tracy, but personalities are often different under the gun. It seemed that every new star I worked with had a reputation as a bastard on the set. Tracy was no exception. Under such conditions, there's only one thing to do: Behave as though you're working with Mr. Nice Guy himself. It can't hurt, and often it turns the trick.

Tracy was the guest of ex-ambassador to England, William Douglas, at his ranch home some 15 or 20 miles from our first location. Early in the morning, one of the crew pointed out that the toilet facilities consisted of crude canvas shelters over buckets of lye. Most studios had been using more sophisticated equipment for years—multiple dressing rooms cum toilet facilities built into huge, long trailers. Even Columbia used them, and Columbia was then the cheapest studio in town. I approached the production manager and hit a stone wall, so I decided to use force. The greatest force at my disposal was Tracy. I explained the situation to him briefly.

"You wouldn't want to get your ass burned with lye, would you?" I asked.

He squinted at me in mock seriousness and brought his right thumb around to the left corner of his mouth in a gesture I was going to know so well.

"No, I wouldn't," he said. "And I suddenly feel the urge." He looked for the production manager.

"Get me a car!" he yelled.

"What for?" The production manager was surprised.

"I have to go to the toilet," said Tracy. And go he did, all the way back to the Douglas ranch. Long before he returned to the set, our production manager was on the blower, and the required rig, with two men on board for straight-through driving, was rolling toward Nogales. It was on location when we arrived very early the next morning.

I knew that Tracy had played polo, so I had planned to shoot many of the riding shots with him in the saddle. What I didn't know was that he hadn't ridden in a number of years and that he was already getting prematurely old. When Tracy mildly objected that his pal Clark wouldn't ride, I treated it as a mild joke. Coop, he mentioned, had to be lifted into the saddle and then wouldn't ride at more than a slow walk. I knew that, but I also knew that Gary Cooper had a very troublesome back. Spence did everything but say flatly that he didn't want to ride, and I refused to take any hints. So, when the time came, he rode, and he rode extremely well—all of which added to the authenticity of the scenes. Naturally, we had doubles for long shots and for dangerous scenes.

Though it is often true that a stunt is beyond the physical capabilities of some actors, there are others who could match a stuntman stunt for stunt. The main reason for the existence of stuntmen is economic. Stunts are dangerous and even the best of stuntmen get hurt— frequently. If a stuntman breaks an arm, he is replaced and the show goes on. If a leading actor breaks his arm and the film has to shut down for a period of time, it means the loss of hundreds of thousands of dollars.

One of our scenes involved an all-out rip by Tracy, Widmark, Wagner, and Franz down the side of a very steep and rough mountain. The SPCA always had a man on any set or location in which animals were used who went to great lengths to ensure their safety. (Animals were always far better protected than were actors.) In this case, four separate paths were carefully laid out on the side of the mountain, and all were picked clean of any rocks or pebbles that might inconvenience the horses. The riders were all doubles, of course, one of whom, a Papago Indian, was the most skillful horseman I have ever seen. In a rehearsal, the horses were taken down their respective paths at a walk to familiarize them with their routes. Then we turned the cameras. On signal, the horses flew down the mountainside, over bushes, small trees, huge boulders, whatever was in their way, never once touching hoof to a designated path. It was a great ride, and not a horse was scratched. Even the SPCA man finally recovered.

The more arid parts of location consisted of large multicolored boulders and outcroppings. But there was a large bluff—perhaps 150 to 200 feet high and 300 yards long—that was a monochromatic rust-red. Three-fourths in jest, I turned to our standby painter.

"Wouldn't it be nice if that bluff matched the rocks down here?" I asked.

"Yeah," he answered laconically.

I didn't see the location again until some nine or ten days later, when I was ready to shoot it. I was dumbfounded—the whole damned bluff was a subtle mosaic of pastel shades, blending nicely with the more intimate spots we were shooting. (I should mention that the paint used was water-soluble and the bluff was eventually washed clean by the rain which visits even this arid region periodically.) I never learned how he was able to complete so massive a job in so short a time with just one helper but he was a perfect example of what I believe about the workers in a Hollywood motion-picture crew: They are the last practitioners of an old American axiom, "Nothing is impossible."

Though Spence was staying with the Douglases, he usually ate dinner with us at our motel in Nogales. Two or three times he had asked Jean Peters to have dinner with him. She had given him equivocal answers, but always wound up having dinner in her rooms to be near the phone. Like most people who have earned a worldwide reputation, Spence had his share of vanity—an engagingly shy vanity, not in the least objectionable. Finally his pride was punctured. On inquiry, he found that Jean stayed in "just in case" Howard Hughes should call. Hughes was notorious for standing up his ladies—sometimes for months—and Tracy had had a previous contretemps with Hughes, so he blew his top.

"What the hell is it about this guy?" he asked her. "What makes him so damned special? Is it his money?"

"Money!" Jean laughed. "He owes *me* a bundle!" She named a sizable figure. "Whenever we go out, he just doesn't have the change in his pocket, and I have to foot the bill."

Spence was deflated, and he never again asked Jean to dine. As for her, she succeeded in outwaiting Hughes, but whether it brought her as much happiness as a dinner with Tracy, who can say?

Richard Widmark played Tracy's oldest son with the greatest skill. Our relationship was by no means ideal; it was Widmark's last picture under his 20th contract, and he felt that the studio was selling him down the river in forcing him to play a secondary role. So he found himself at odds with any one of the Fox establishment. But he was professional enough to do his job with a minimum amount of griping, and to do it well. Subsequently, I made several films with him, and we got along famously, both professionally and personally.

E. G. Marshall had played the small but important role of the prosecuting counsel in *The Caine Mutiny*. In *Broken Lance*, his part was somewhat meatier. When he and Tracy were on the screen together, it sparkled. He did not have all of Tracy's charismatic qualities, but he had all his talent and abilities. The pleasure of seeing two such actors working together is akin to that of hearing a spectacularly sung operatic duet, and makes the interminable hours and ulcer-making tribulations of filming almost worth while.

Katy Jurado—well, she was Katy Jurado, a woman of sharp intelligence, great bawdy humor, and sensitivity of performance that is rare indeed. She won a supporting actress Oscar for her performance in this one, and she deserved it.

Zanuck exhibited another side to his character while we were on location. He saw rushes at the studio at least a day before they got back to Nogales, and he kept us fully informed. I hadn't received a memo from a head of Production since *Golden Gloves* at Paramount. Zanuck sent them in droves—to the cameraman, to the players, and to me. The first were highly complimentary and got the whole crew off to a great start, but he could be critical if he felt criticism was deserved. However, this production was like the weather, which held perfectly, giving us sun when we needed sun and clouds when we needed clouds. We finished location in the time estimated.

Once back at the studio, I was able to use my short shooting-day technique. It worked like a charm, particularly for Tracy. Spence was an insomniac and was up in the small hours of the morning. He was always ready for us long before we were ready for him, but he tired easily and the short day suited him to perfection. For a man reputed to be a roaring tiger, he turned out to be a pussycat. Like almost all great actors, he did his homework in private, but made a pretense of playing everything off the cuff. Yet I've never been able to print so many first takes on any other film. Spence had developed a trick of naturalistic hemming and hawing, which he used most effectively to cover brief lapses of memory, but sometimes he would go a bit too far. I called for another take on one such occasion. He feigned hurt surprise.

"What was the matter with it?" he asked.

"You flubbed just a touch too much on that one," I said.

"Young fella," he drew himself up. "I've spent a lifetime perfecting that flub."

"Well, you flubbed your flub. Let's go one more time."

He laughed and we shot it again, this time with no flubbing, perfected or otherwise.

At first, I had been a bit diffident in working with Tracy, but as the film progressed, I found he was very receptive to changes in inference or emphasis. Once only, he resisted a suggestion of mine and in doing so exhibited what was one of his greatest talents.

In studying a scene we were to do in a couple of days, I found one long speech that was rather stiffly written. I had reworked it until I felt it was more playable.

"Look, Eddie," Tracy said, "I've already learned the words. Why don't you let me try them the way they are. If you don't like it, I'll look at your rewrite."

I agreed, and later we shot the scene. He hadn't changed a word in the original speech, but he broke it up and played with it in such a way that it seemed the most natural scene in the world. That is a skill that few present-day actors have mastered. Faced with a difficult line, they will complain until it is simplified to their taste. But Spence had that ability which in jazz singing is called "phrasing," of which Louis Armstrong was the greatest master. Louis could make a ricky-tick lyric sound like poetry, and Tracy could make a leaden line shine like gold. The odd thing was that he felt it was nothing special—that it was just something that every actor owed his art.

The studio shooting went so smoothly that we finished the film 15 days under schedule, and $250,000 under budget. Joe MacDonald, our photographer, had done a beautiful job on the film, and to this day it remains one of a handful of pictures which have utilized the wide screen effectively.

Up to now, everything had gone far more smoothly and pleasantly than I had anticipated. But the editorial sessions with Zanuck were coming up, and here I was convinced that trouble would start. The only occasions on which I have been actually sick to my stomach—to the point of throwing up—have been at cutting sessions with obtuse executives. But, as any cutter will testify, no producer or studio executive exists who doesn't feel he is a superb editor. And Zanuck leads the list.

The big day—or rather night—came. Darryl was a night worker, and he scheduled his runnings for late in the evening, usually around 10 or 11 P.M. Score one for Zanuck. I am a day person and function only sluggishly after 6:00. And Darryl had his claque—a theatrical institution I've always hated. Zanuck—wisely, I thought—never previewed straight dramatic films. He believed that he could judge drama as well as a couple of thousand nonprofessionals, and I applauded him for that. But here in the projection room he had his own little band of nonpros—Nick, who ran the studio restaurant, his masseur, and his barber. Each was an expert in his own field, but why Zanuck respected their theatrical opinions I never learned. Score two for Zanuck. Against these yes-men I had a valuable no-man, my producer, Sol Siegel, and that turned out to be enough. If I got into an argument with Darryl about some cut and Sol thought I was right, he would say, "Now, just a minute, Darryl," and Zanuck would usually cave in under the added weight. This reluctance to yes the boss cost Siegel an important promotion a few years later, but he left the studio and did better at MGM.

So, in the end, the film went out pretty much as we wanted it, and was well received by the public and by the press. It won a few awards, among them the Silver Spurs award for the best Western of 1954, as well as Silver Spurs awards for acting and direction. Besides Katy's Oscar, it also won an Oscar for best screenplay, which led to a change in the Academy rules for that category. The original screenplay for *House of Strangers*, which Richard Murphy had used as a springboard for *Broken Lance*, had been written by Philip Yordan, and though not a single line had been used in our quite different version, the award went to Phil and not to Dick. Though Yordan protested, nothing could be done about it—he had to take the Oscar. But this was about the only serious mistake made on a film which had started under what I thought were threatening circumstances and had turned instead into a truly pleasant experience.

HOLLYWOOD,
INTERNATIONAL

L ife at home was moving forward as smoothly as life at the studios. Relieved of alimony, paying off the IRS was not too burdensome. I traded in my navy Jeep for a Jaguar roadster, and Jean started looking for a house. When Jean looks for something, she always finds it—and fast. This was in old Bel Air, and that scared the hell out of me. I was doing all right, but solvency was still some years in the future. It was a beautiful Norman house on three acres of land, most of it reverting to native underbrush. In contrast to my political views, my taste in architecture tends toward the traditional, and I fell for the place immediately.

I have few incentives to make money, but I've found that working my way out of debt is the most effective. So, in 1952 we signed a two-year lease with an option to buy and by the end of the year we were happily able to exercise that option. It was a good investment, in more ways than one.

It took three winters of cutting, clearing, and burning to clean out the rank undergrowth, but I'm a farmer at heart, and the work eased me through many postproduction doldrums. When I've finished a film, it takes me at least six weeks to recover, during which time I find it impossible to read a book or carry on an intelligent conversation. Production drains me, as I believe it does most persons in the so-called creative arts, and chopping brush is an ideal activity for a body controlled by a depleted mind.

Besides my English-born son, Richard, my first son, Michael, was now living with us, and a daughter, Victoria, had been born in November 1951. We had a full and happy home. We had hardly gotten well settled in before David Rose and Columbia asked me to make a film in England—an opportunity I could scarcely refuse. Jean and I had not seen London or our many English friends for five years, and we needed little urging. The story, a Lenore Coffee script of Graham Greene's *The End of the Affair*, and a cast including Van Johnson and Deborah Kerr, were added inducements.

At that time, Van was one of the most admired and least understood stars in the world. As an actor, he was a pleasure to work with. He loved films, and when he wasn't working in one he was usually watching one. When there was trouble at home—and often when there wasn't—he'd head for a theater as soon as the doors opened and stay until they turned him out at closing time. This activity undoubtedly served to take his mind off the constant battle being waged within him. He was painfully shy, yet realized that occasionally he had to mix with people, so he allowed his wife or his agent to drag him to parties where he would spend a miserable evening hiding out in some secluded room. Yet in the hustle-bustle of a movie set, he felt completely at home.

Van worshiped Spencer Tracy, and for good reason. Early in his career at MGM he was cast, along with Tracy, in *A Guy Named Joe*. A nearly fatal car crash injured him severely. The studio named a replacement, but Tracy refused to carry on until Van either died (a distinct possibility) or recovered sufficiently to return to work. Van refused to die, but his recovery was slow, necessitating a production postponement of several months. The waiting proved worthwhile for both Van and the studio: *A Guy Named Joe* boosted Van to stardom and added another asset to MGM's account.

Deborah Kerr was a revelation. A superb artist, sensitive and passionate on the screen, she seemed to have no trace of temperament or ego. Like Johnson, she was usually on the set a half hour early, drinking tea with the crew and straining at the leash. Rarely have I seen two people of comparable skill and talent work together so effortlessly and with so little self-indulgence.

Two other names were added to the cast: John Mills and Peter Cushing. John was an old friend, of course, but Cushing was a new name to me. He proved to be completely professional, utterly charming, and extremely friendly. As with so many other British actors, all the superlatives are justified. Anglo-Saxon culture (not necessarily race) turns out fine actors by the hundreds—more, I believe, than any other society. The attitudes of London and Hollywood toward each other are remarkably similar. Hollywood actors have said to me, "Working in London must be a wonderful experience—there are so many excellent actors there." Quite true. On the other hand, British actors have said to me, "Working in Hollywood must be a smashing experience—you have so many great actors there." Also true. It would be hard to say which town has the most or the best actors, but one thing is certain: Today, the British artists are more disciplined, more versatile, and much less self-indulgent than their American counterparts. But then, that may be just another instance of art holding the mirror up to life.

Jean, the two younger children, and I settled down in a flat in Kensington, not too far from Hyde Park. It seemed as if we had hardly been away. We spent a pleasant few months, but then Jean and the kids got homesick for Southern California and flew home, leaving me in the lavish but impersonal care of the Claridge Hotel. There was nothing for me to do but finish cutting the film as quickly as possible and chase after her—which I did.

This film, released in 1955, was the story of an adulterous love affair—the kind of plot which today would not lift a single eyebrow. In Europe some critics called it the most adult love story ever made. But in the United States the critical reaction was generally one of puritanical shock. Even Sheilah Graham, of all people, thought the relationship disgusting. It seemed that things had hardly changed since 1938 and *Zaza*. There are times today when I wistfully wish I could still say the same.

Back in Hollywood, I was barely able to reset my watch to local time before 20th called me in on a new project, the first of a five-picture deal, made after the success of *Broken Lance*. It seemed that Clark Gable felt lost at MGM without his screen buddy, Tracy, and now he, too, was out free-lancing where the green grew high. First Van Johnson, then Spencer Tracy, and now Clark Gable—I was getting all the Metro émigrés.

In the middle fifties, the disintegration of the major studios was in its early stages. We knew something was wrong, but none of us was aware that Hollywood, as we knew it, was showing the first signs of senility. A story went around about Spyros Skouras hitching a ride to the airport with Barney Balaban just to ask, "Barney, what's it all about? What's happening?" But Barney had no answers. None of us did.

One of the first signs of old age was the not-so-slow erosion of the studio contract lists, but we didn't see it that way. When the great MGM stars started to leave the fold, we simply blamed Dore Schary and his ego. Perhaps the studios' efforts to conceal the degree of their malaise contributed to our misunderstanding. Only recently has it become clear that the breakup of the major studios, as producers of theatrical films, was economically inevitable. Dore, I apologize.

The new story was Ernest Gann's *Soldier of Fortune*. Buddy Adler, the producer, was somewhat apologetic. He realized that it wasn't the greatest script in the world, he said, but Gable had read it and liked it, 20th wanted very much to get a Gable film on its next year's release schedule, and I was the only contract director on his approved directors' list. Buddy assured me that the studio would expect no miracles, but would appreciate my agreeing to do the film.

It would be nice to report that directors, given the choice, recognize artistic integrity as their only guide. It would be nice, but it wouldn't be honest. I read the script and recognized that it was indeed a potboiler, though possibly one of the better ones. It wasn't up to the quality of films I'd been doing lately, but—there was Clark Gable, the King, Susan Hayward, a fine actress, and Hong Kong.

I had been a Sinophile practically all my life. I had studied Chinese as a written language since my days as a cutter, when I had composed sentences in Chinese characters on the large ground-glass viewing panels in my cutting room and a young Japanese janitor had complemented them during the night with his own comments, also in ideograph form, but I had never gotten closer to China than Wo Fat's restaurant in Honolulu. I convinced myself that the furtherance of my personal education was worth a slight diminution in my status as an artist.

Susan Hayward's marital problems would keep her from going to Hong Kong, so we decided to shoot her exterior scenes only in long shots, using a double, but Gable, Michael Rennie, and Gene Barry were going with us, as well as a sizable number of key crew members. On this trip Clark and I spent a number of days in Tokyo.

Hong Kong exhilarates me. But Tokyo depresses me. It may be the general grayness of the city, or the dreadfully congested traffic, with its accompanying heavy smog, which makes L.A. seem like the clean-air capital of the world, but I always feel ill at ease until I'm on my way out. Still, there was a certain amount of public relations work to be done, so we stayed. First, there was a huge press conference, complete with television cameras. Gable spotted them in the back of the room and refused to go on with the meeting until they were removed.

"You are my competitors," he told the TV crewmen, "and I will not work hand-in-glove with my competition."

The TV crews politely withdrew. History is repeating itself, I thought. I had been around long enough to remember when many actors from the theater held much the same view of the upstart flicks.

One night we were invited to visit one of Tokyo's all-girl musical theaters like the one depicted in *Sayonara*. We had been seated for only a few minutes when the manager came around to say that the star of the show, a famous Japanese kabuki dancer, would very much appreciate meeting Gable and would we be so very kind as to come to her dressing room. Gable was willing. We followed the manager through a back-stage maze that looked like an ideal setting for a suspense movie, climbing dark stairways, traversing narrow hallways where chorus girls peeked diffidently out of doorways, and finally reaching a dressing room on the fourth level. The manager went in to fetch the star, who turned out to be a tiny person of near middle age, dressed in a long white kabuki dance robe. Her eyes were lined with mascara, and the rest of her face was completely covered with a heavy coating of rice powder. As the introduction was made, Gable reached out his hand and she took it, looking up into his eyes (she was about 4'8", he was 6'3"). She said not a word, just held his hand and looked at him while huge tears rolled slowly down her cheeks, tracing crooked paths in the rice powder. It's the only time I have ever seen Rhett Butler nonplussed. Like a frozen frame, they stood there for what seemed like a full minute, the silently crying Oriental and the tall, inscrutable white man. Then she broke away and glided into her dressing room. I had seen the power of the King.

Some years later, while making *The Carpetbaggers* at Paramount, George Peppard and I were crossing the lot when he noticed an old *The Misfits* poster, bearing Gable's picture.

"What did he have that we haven't?" he asked. "What made him and others like him such superstars?" I didn't have a satisfactory answer then, but at least one of the reasons has become clearer with time. Organization—the same thing that made Hollywood and the names of the major studios known throughout the world. Tracy once asked Hepburn why she continued to work for MGM, a studio that was far too patronizing for her tastes.

"It's worth it when you go through Chicago," she said.

For the enlightenment of the great majority who were born too late, Chicago was the changeover on the Hollywood-to-New York train run, and the process took several hours. Studio representatives picked up commuting stars and executives, took them to hotels where they could clean up in comfort and enjoy a leisurely lunch, then escorted them back to the 20th Century Limited for their trip's continuation. All the majors furnished such service, but none on a level as luxurious as that of MGM. The same was true of the local studio representatives abroad who seemed to have unlimited resources for entertaining visiting VIP's whether they were coming to work or just passing through. The majors' global downfall was signaled in the sixties, when the local reps had to look for a gourmet dinner and a possible evening on the town on the VIPs' expense accounts.

Each studio had tremendous exploitation and public relations departments, and these were made to work for every star thought worthy of the effort and the expense. The stars, in turn, were usually more than happy to cooperate, not only with interviews but with personal appearances. Today, once a player thinks he has it made, he usually can't be bothered. And that is why, perhaps, names like John Wayne, Jimmy Stewart, Fred Astaire, and Marlon Brando still mean much more abroad than names like Dustin Hoffman, Al Pacino, or Elliot Gould. Or, for that matter, George Peppard.

Working with the Chinese was a revelation. At every level, whether coolie or intellectual, the people worked hard and uncomplainingly. We shot for a number of days at the typhoon harbor in Kowloon. This is the home of the Hakka, a Chinese people with its own distinct dialect and customs. By tradition they are born, live, and die on the water—only after death do they finally rest on land. We hired a Hakka family as "gofers." Most of the work was done by two girls, aged about eight and ten. They sculled their sampan at top speed through the most crowded waters, often with a few-months-old baby brother, tied to a loose line, on board. They never failed to complete an assignment in record time.

A most revealing example of Chinese organization and skill was demonstrated during the shooting of our climactic action sequence. In this scene Gable, fleeing in his junk from a Red Chinese gunboat, is met in the open sea by a huge fleet of junks and sampans sailed by his Hong Kong friends and associates. He makes good his escape by simply getting lost in the midst of the armada. We were able to collect nearly a thousand boats, from junks nearly 100 feet long to sampans as short as 15 feet. Since only a handful of these boats had radios and most depended on wind power, I was apprehensive that maneuvering this unwieldy fleet to get the large number of shots necessary would take many days. But I finished long before the light got yellow on the first day of shooting.

Our camera, sound equipment, and a small generator were on board a large seagoing raft, towed by a small tug. To begin with, we were hauled to a position which would allow the armada to sail past us on a favorable tack. The fleet was divided into basic units, each with an officer in charge, and these were further subdivided into still smaller units, the final minimum groups comprising about ten craft. We communicated with the flagship, a large junk, by walkie-talkie (a very typical pidgin English word, by the way). It, in turn, relayed orders to the rest of the fleet by means of simple flag signals. There was a good wind, so we started our day's work.

The first shot of the fleet of nearly a thousand vessels, with their myriad-colored sails, silently but swiftly gliding toward and then past us was electrifying. Now came the test. Since the fleet was at the mercy of the wind, we couldn't simply ask it to turn collectively around and sail back for another take. We had to quickly figure the wind, the best direction for the next tack, and have our raft towed to the proper position for the next shot. The second I cut the cameras, our tug was under way for the next position. On arrival, my assistant was in touch with the disappearing fleet. Like a flock of pigeons, all the boats came about as one and sailed back toward us for the next shot. This went on with never the slightest hitch, nor a moment's rest, until we had gotten every shot I had planned, plus a few more thrown in for good measure. I have worked in almost every country of the so-called technically superior Western world, but I have never seen planning, organization, or execution anywhere near that shown by this group of fishermen, lightermen, and smugglers.

Like the other established stars I had worked with, Gable was a director's dream. Never a moment late, always well prepared, he insisted on only one condition: Except under the most unusual circumstances or regularly scheduled night work, he stopped work at 5:30. Since that was late for me, we had no problem on that score.

Clark prided himself on his acting ability. He felt that overexploitation of his charismatic image had deprived him of his just due as a skillful actor. I'm inclined to agree with him. The hero's role was not always to his taste.

"I was doing my umpteenth film with Spence," he told me once, "when I suddenly realized that for at least the third time I was holding him in my arms while he played a glorious death scene. I dropped him to the ground, went to the director, and asked that, for once, I be allowed to die in Tracy's arms. Nothing ever came of it," he added wryly.

When we bought our home, Jean and I had been told that Gable and Lombard had lived in it for a number of years before building their own house in Encino. Gable confirmed the information and said that he himself had commissioned the solidly built tennis court which I was now tearing out with the greatest difficulty. He related one incident which took place there: He and Carole had had one of their not-infrequent battles royal. She had finally maneuvered him into a small aviary located in what we liked to call "the woods," locked the door from the outside, then turned on the sprinklers. By the time she turned them off again and released him from his confinement, he was not only all wet but thoroughly cooled off.

I mentioned earlier that I've received the most severe criticism for my most "worthwhile" efforts. *Soldier of Fortune*, an admitted potboiler, offended no one, got good reviews (though no raves), received no awards, and made *Variety*'s list of All-time Box-office Champions. I've never spoken to anyone who has seen the film who didn't say he thoroughly enjoyed it. Hidden in all this, somewhere, there is a message. But I refuse to see it.

BOGEY

Hawaii is a mantrap which first anesthetizes, then smothers you with its soft, redolent air and its milk-and-honey existence. Jean and I chose to succumb to its siren lure. We bought a 37-acre farm on the outskirts of Kealakekua, in Kona, on the big island of Hawaii. Now that our trips were tax-deductible, we flew to the Islands as often as we could. In the past, like many film workers, I would feel out of touch and forgotten if I left Hollywood on a three-day holiday. Now I was cured. Relaxing in an easy chair on the volcanic shore of a truly blue Pacific, watching an occasional whale or giant manta sporting in the sparkling water, I didn't care whether school kept or not.

Since my Congress-imposed hiatus, my attitude toward my work had also been changing. Through the Depression thirties, past the war years, and to a considerable extent even today, the "well-informed" have been influenced by behaviorism and, though many refuse to admit it, by a Marxist approach to human development. Simply put: Change society and you change man, or its corollary; whatever is wrong with man is the fault of society. In spite of Lorenz and what came to be known as the sociobiological movement, we insist on having a scapegoat for our very human weaknesses—for those who have outgrown the devil, it is "society."

I had moved with the tide, concerning myself with the "pill"—a tiny core of sociological concern thickly coated with sugar to make it more palatable to the public. The coating consisted of an engrossing plot line—usually mystery or suspense—and a heavy dependence on catchy camera and lighting techniques. It is amazing how often this combination, well executed, succeeds, even with those who should know better, the critics. Sometimes, particularly with the critics.

I don't know whether it was my experience with communism (which still believes that a contrived society can create a contrived man), with jail (which believes in the change of neither), or just the films I had lucked into since leaving Cranberry Mountain, but my point of view was executing a slow 180. Though I still felt some satisfaction in contriving an unusual setup or photographic effect, it was of no importance to me unless it helped accentuate a point about some human characteristic or conflict of relationship. It seemed to me that the crusaders of the last few generations, who had been blaming society for all our ills while excusing misbehaving individuals as its victims, were looking through the wrong end of the telescope. I also began to understand why so little attention was paid to this approach by filmmakers: It is damned difficult.

Give me some lights, some high-speed film, a good cameraman, and an actor who looks like Boris Karloff, and I'll deliver a hair-raising suspense sequence with absolutely no sweat; supply three cars and three stunt drivers and I'll shoot a breathtaking chase, whether it's on city streets or an Iowa corn farm. So will any journeyman director. In spite of the logistical problems involved, it is creatively easier to shoot a gigantic battle scene than to write a sequence that can adequately investigate the measure of human greed and twisted human logic which leads to the sacrifice of millions of human lives. I realized that the phrase "man's inhumanity to man" was a copout. It was man's "humanity" to man that was at the root of our problems. And the question for the filmmaker was not "How do you say it?" but "How can you make them listen?"

Shortly after my return from England, Zanuck asked me to get a script to Humphrey Bogart. I was a little surprised that Zanuck was diffident about approaching Bogey himself, but that should give you some idea of the awe with which Hollywood's top stars were regarded, even by the men who had created them. The script was Alfred Hayes' version of William Barrett's novel, *The Left Hand of God*. As is my custom, before passing a property on, I read it first, liked it, called Bogart, and got his permission to drop it by. This may all seem rather formal to those not conversant with Hollywood customs, but there is a strict procedural chain in these matters. Agents are very jealous of their prerogatives—justifiably so. But, though strong industry rules require that they pass along any offer to their clients, no matter how unrealistic, the suspicion remains that this is not always the case, and, particularly in more recent years, independent promoters, eager to get bankable names and more reasonable deals, often try to bypass the strongly protective curtain set up by the players' representatives. Sometimes this results in the setting up of a project beneficial to all; more often, it is merely annoying or embarrassing to the artist involved.

In this case, Bogart liked the story and arrangements were quickly made for its production. A first-rate cast was assembled. Lee. J. Cobb played the Chinese warlord, E. G. Marshall and Agnes Moorehead, a husband-and-wife missionary team, and Gene Tierney, the feminine lead. Gene had bouts of mental illness from time to time and had not worked in films for some years. She had recently come out of a sanitarium and had indicated her readiness to resume her career. Zanuck, who could never be faulted for his kindness, lost no time in asking Bogart and me for approval to cast her in our film. No problem. My Jean, equipped with rubber eyelids, played Bogart's Chinese girlfriend in the film's opening episodes.

There were few topflight ethnic actors in Hollywood in 1955. There just wasn't enough demand. Our national sense of shame had grown sufficiently strong to eliminate ethnic caricatures from the screen by the late forties, and now it was almost impossible to cast a black. Except in historical films, a black could not be a servant, a Jew could not speak with an accent, a Mexican or an Indian could not play a heavy. All very laudable, but, in the absence of more positive ethnic roles, a sizable vacuum was created. Even well-known players like Hattie McDaniel and Louise Beavers found little demand for their talents, and Harry Green, the excellent Jewish comic and actor, moved to England.

Our several hundred players, bits and extras, provided a field day for Bessie Loo and her Oriental clients. An old friend, Cam Tong (he later played Hey Boy in the TV series, "Have Gun, Will Travel"), was required in one scene to bring in an urgent message on horseback. He had never ridden before, but he refused to fall off the cantering beast until he had brought it to a full stop in front of the camera. Then he rolled out of the saddle like a sack of potatoes, getting both a good laugh from the crew and an extra close-up.

Franz Planer, my cameraman, who had photographed *The Caine Mutiny* and would work with me again on *The Mountain*, was a wonderful human being. I believe he was a Czech, though to my knowledge he never admitted to any specific nationality. He had done outstanding work in a number of European films and was brought to Hollywood in the late thirties by Harry Cohn to photograph *Holiday*. He had entered the States on a limited visa, and at the completion of his assignment, the studio sent him across the border to Tijuana to await official certification of his immigrant status. Then they forgot him. For several years he and his wife survived on refunds for Coca-Cola bottles they collected in the bullring. Not long before Cohn finally remembered him and helped arrange his return, Franz was lucky enough to buy a quarter-share in a winning lottery ticket, and the Planers lived out the last few weeks of their exile in relative comfort.

Most cameramen can give you what you want; a very few can give you what you wish you had wanted. Franz, like Roy Hunt, was one of those very few. True artist that he was, he made the transition from black and white to color with no strain. He was one of the first to bring out pastel shades or the soft, warm colors of the great Dutch and Flemish painters. Of course, that was on the negative, and we usually saw it only in the rushes. The finished product was as hard and postcardy as Herbert and Natalie Kalmus, who originated Technicolor, could make it. They were selling color so, by God, they were going to give you color, and color to them was all in the primaries. James Wong Howe was fired off a film because he made a scene that was supposedly lit by a single candle flame *look* as though it were lit by a single candle flame. Hollywood, as a whole, took some hard knocks for Technicolor's sins. But all that is in the past. Today Technicolor will strip as much color as you desire as effectively as any other lab, and better than most.

The shooting on *The Left Hand of God* went smoothly. The scenes with E. G. Marshall and Aggie Moorehead were a total delight. I've often wished that the thrill of watching superb actors practicing their art could somehow be "laid under" the finished scene, like a music track, to add to the audience's enjoyment. For me it is a rare bonus.

Bogart, as usual, worked hard and well. The demands of this role were by no means as severe as were those of Captain Queeg, but the physical pressures were much greater. He had a great deal of horseback riding to do while nursing an exceedingly painful slipped disc, but I heard no complaint. His chain smoking was really getting him down. Before the start of a scene, he would slip into a paroxysm of coughing that would elicit concern from almost every member of the crew. At one time or another, nearly every one on the set begged him to cut down on his smoking, but Bogey would just shrug his shoulders and light another cigarette.

Bogart had had a well-earned reputation as one of Hollywood's foremost topers, but I believe all this was scaled down after his marriage to Lauren Bacall. I saw no evidence of intemperance on the set of either of the films I did with him, nor do I ever remember seeing him embarrassingly drunk on any of the occasions we visited the Bogarts at their home.

When 4:00 rolled around on the set, he usually asked if I still had important scenes to shoot with him that day. If the answer was no, he would unlock the door of the small refrigerator in his set dressing room, take out a bottle of Scotch, and pour himself a drink. And that was it until the day's work was finished.

At one of his birthday parties, one of the few Hollywood occasions I liked to attend, he got into an argument with one of his guests and invited him "out back." On their way to the field of honor, Bogey turned to his antagonist. "Can you fight?" he asked.

"Yes," was the answer. "Pretty well."

Bogey stopped in his tracks. "Let's forget the whole thing," he said, and led the way back into the living room. Now that doesn't sound very drunk, does it?

"READ THE LYRICS, KID"

During the filming of *Broken Lance*, Spencer Tracy had given me a copy of *The Mountain*, a prize-winning novel by the Russian-French author, Henri Troyat. It was a short and simple story: An airliner crashes in the French Alps near the top of a nearly inaccessible peak. Only one of the local guides has ever made the ascent at this time of the year, and he is now retired. When he is asked to lead a party in search of survivors, he adamantly refuses to go. A rescue party makes the attempt without him, loses its guide, and returns in defeat.

Motivated by avarice, the younger brother of the retired guide finally goads him into making the climb in secret. After a hair-raising ascent, the two reach the downed airliner. While the younger brother greedily collects cameras and wallets, the guide finds a survivor, an unconscious young Indian woman. The next morning he makes a sled out of a plane door and prepares to take the girl down the mountain, but the brother wants no witnesses and would rather see her die. The shocked guide sets off down the steep, snow-packed slopes, leaving his unskilled brother on his own. Weighed down by his booty, the brother attempts to negotiate a false snow bridge over a crevasse and falls to his death. The guide brings the Indian girl down to the safety of the village.

Tracy's representatives had set up a deal with Paramount to make the film, and Randy MacDougall had written an excellent script. When I had completed my work on *The Left Hand of God*, Paramount, at Tracy's request, asked me to produce and direct it. I had fallen in love with the Alps and with mountain climbing when I had scouted locations for *The White Tower* in 1946, and I accepted with pleasure.

I set up offices at Paramount around the end of May, with A. C. Lyles as my production assistant. As usual, the script needed some reworking, but I felt this could be more effectively done after we had selected the locations, so we set up our entourage—the writer, Randy MacDougall, the cameraman, Franz Planer, the art director, John Goodman, the production manager, Harry Kaplan, me, and two freeloaders, my wife Jean and Mrs. MacDougall. Taking a writer on a "reccy" was not usual Hollywood practice, but I have always felt that an acquaintance with a story's physical background can result in important script modifications, and I've usually been right.

Early in June we flew to Paris, then drove in two cars to Chamonix, in the French Alps. This charming village is the center for most of the mountain-climbing activity in the Mont Blanc massif, the most imposing and concentrated group of peaks, needles, ridges, and glaciers available anywhere in the world—at least under those conditions required by a film unit. Housing for the cast and crew should be comfortable and convenient to the locations, travel time from the hotel to location should never exceed two hours, or shooting time is reduced to an uneconomical minimum. Beyond that, it is axiomatic that the greater variety of locations available within a limited area, the more efficient the operation. Our film required a small village, meadows, a glacier, and a variety of climbing backgrounds (ridges, chimneys, overhangs, rock faces, ice walls, etc.) and all this was available in Chamonix in profusion. I was already convinced that this would be the center of operations, but, not to shortchange ourselves, we had to look around. We set off for Switzerland and the Italian Dolomites.

Spring was late that year, and we reached St. Moritz in the middle of a snowstorm. It was not as suitable for our purposes as Chamonix, and after a day or two, we drove on. I would never have believed anyone could tire of beautiful scenery, but I got so bored with lovely lakes, beautiful valleys, and alpine passes that I would have given a good deal for an hour in Death Valley. We reached Merano, in the Dolomites, late that afternoon and checked in at the Bristol Hotel, at that time one of the most beautiful and modern hotels in the world. The Dolomites have a very special grandeur, quite unlike that of any other mountain chain I have ever seen, and the valleys are the quintessence of rustic beauty. But a couple of days of scouting convinced us that our first choice was still the best, so we returned to Chamonix.

Feeling more at home now, we spent a few days in Chamonix zeroing in on locations, then headed for Paris and the long flight home. The whole trip—and this before jet planes—took about two and a half weeks.

Back at the studio, MacDougall started his final polish while I started casting. Aside from the role of the guide, which, of course, would be played by Tracy, there was only one fully rounded character in the film—the younger brother. Spence had had a good relationship with Robert Wagner during the shooting of *Broken Lance;* he also had a very realistic attitude regarding his own box-office appeal. He felt that Wagner might attract the younger and larger audience and suggested we try to borrow him from 20th. I agreed with his analysis (as it turned out, we were both somewhat in error) and 20th was willing, so R.J. was set. We got excellent support from Claire Trevor, E. G. Marshall (no, I don't know what the initials stand for), Dick Arlen, and Harry Townes. In 1955 an all-expense-paid trip to Europe was still a considerable inducement, and it was easier to get people for small parts than it is today, when a sojourn in southern Spain or Yugoslavia can mean scorpions, bad beds, and boredom.

On the basis of what we had seen in the Alps, work was started on the interior sets and wardrobe. The camera department designed and built two remarkably small hand cameras, utilizing Leica lenses, for use with Paramount's VistaVision process. Unlike Cinemascope or Panavision, this system registered a scene on two frames of standard 35 mm. film, side by side, thus giving the "big screen" effect without squeezing the image into one frame, as was done in the anamorphic process. However, this meant running the film through the camera at a speed of 180 feet per minute instead of the standard 90, which, in turn, necessitated 2,000-foot film magazines and exceptionally heavy and unwieldy cameras and blimps, each weighing around 200 pounds. Hardly the sort of equipment to drag up vertical rock walls at rarefied altitudes. Though they needed frequent reloading, the small hand cameras were a godsend for the silent scenes.

As I've remarked, a Hollywood crew on a foreign location resembles a small army and can have the same effect on the local residents, so we try to pick our crews with care. We do our best to avoid drunks, troublemakers, and loudmouths. This is not too difficult, since most of the workers I know are at least as circumspect as the average politician. But there is an occasional exception, and we do our best to eliminate him on the basis of past records.

Shortly before leaving for France, I called our location crew together for a briefing on the Alpine facts of life. I warned them that our work would take us to altitudes as high as 14,000 feet. There would be hard hikes and climbs and long working days. Anyone with a weak heart or an aversion to too much physical exertion had a chance to back out. None did. But now I found I had a problem with Spence. He and I were going over a couple of weeks early. I still had to cast the Indian girl in Paris, and Tracy, who had been leading a sedentary life for a number of years now and was soft and overweight, hoped to spend some time getting himself into shape and acclimatizing himself to the location. Except that at the last minute he didn't want to leave—he didn't even want to be in the picture.

I had gone through a bit of this on *Broken Lance* and was not completely unprepared. This great artist, considered by many to be the finest actor in Hollywood, if not in the world, always had an attack of the insecurities before the start of a film. His behavior with me was typical.

"I can't do it," he said. "It's just not the part for me. How about Gable? I think he's free, and he'd be perfect. Or Robert Young?"

It went on this way for an hour or more at several different sessions— Tracy backing off, hedging, and I gently but firmly reassuring. I had to cancel our first reservations and almost canceled the second. Then I realized that what he wanted and needed was a firm hand. When he stalled again, I simply said the car and driver would be calling to take him to the airport at a certain time, and I would expect to see him there. That was it. He showed up. Only later did I learn, to my sorrow, that he was not only insecure about starting a film, he also feared and hated flying.

Our first stop was London, where Tracy wanted to spend a few hours with Katharine Hepburn, who was on her way to make a theatrical appearance in Australia. On our first evening, Tracy, Hepburn, Ambassador Douglas (whom I had met in Arizona), and I had dinner at an excellent Italian restaurant in Soho. We dined well and stayed late, then walked back to the Claridge, where Spence and I were staying. On arriving at the hotel, Douglas excused himself, and Spence went up to his room while I took Miss Hepburn around to the tradesman's entrance at the rear of the building. We took the freight elevator up to Tracy's floor (the operator knew her well) and joined Spence in his suite. There Katy made coffee for him and we chatted until it was time for her to say good night. Again I escorted her to the freight elevator, through the rear entrance, and a block or so down the street to the Connaught, where she was staying.

It seems that on some previous visit the management of the Claridge would not allow Miss Hepburn to walk through the lobby in slacks. She immediately moved out of the hotel and ever after refused to enter the lobby, even when, as on this particular evening, she was wearing a dress. A wonderfully principled lady is Katy Hepburn.

In Paris, Tracy and I spent an easy few days interviewing Indian actresses and eating in fine restaurants. There were plenty of the latter but very few of the former. I think we saw only four or five young women, and of these only one was suitable. Her name was Anna Kashfi, she came from London, and she looked lovely in a sari. The passport she carried bore an Irish name, but that made little difference to us. She looked Indian and she got the part. As an added inducement, my assistant, A. C. Lyles, promised to introduce her to Marlon Brando when we got back to Hollywood.

Early in August we arrived in Chamonix, a week or two before the start of shooting. I spent most of my days pinpointing my locations, but there was time enough left over for an occasional stroll with Spence as he conditioned himself for the film. At the end of one of these walks in the foothills of Mont Blanc, we made our way up a small rise. Spence was full of good spirits and a sense of accomplishment. As we started back down the road, we spied a local woman making her way up the hill toward us. She was about five feet tall and at least ninety-two years old, and on her back she carried an old-fashioned five-gallon milk container which, judging by its movements, appeared to be full. Her pace was much faster than ours had been, and her breath was completely under control. When he spotted her, Tracy stopped dead in his tracks, watched her until she had gone well up the hill, then turned without a word and headed for the hotel, his good spirits flown somewhere up the mountain with the spry old lady. It took very little to puncture Tracy's ego balloon.

On another occasion we took the mountain railroad up to the Mer de Glace glacier. We were just sitting down to lunch in the station restaurant when we were approached by a small group of men who wanted to meet Tracy. The main member of the group was a young Italian mountain climber who had just come down from a five-day and four-night solo climb of the vertical face of the *Aiguille-Vert*. When Tracy started to shake his hand, he presented his right forearm, then showed us his hands in explanation. His fingers looked like ten overripe bananas, and the raw tip of each finger was gouged out as if by a melon-baller. It turned out that this had happened on the first day of the climb, but he had continued on to the top, tying himself upright on narrow ledges (no more than six inches wide) with ropes run through pitons pounded into the rock, to doze fitfully through the freezing nights. It took him at least thirty minutes, he said, to thaw out sufficiently to start climbing again each morning. But he had been the first, and that made all the agony worthwhile. Tracy was very impressed with the man's will and courage. I believe it did much to inspire his subsequent performance.

Tracy had asked if he could hire a friend of Hepburn's, an English script girl, as his secretary for the duration of our stay in Europe. I had no objection, and she was put on the company payroll. It was one of my more fortunate decisions. Our script "boy," who had been present when I briefed the crew in Hollywood, now disclosed that he was not up to the necessary hiking and climbing since he had lost the toes of one foot during the war. I hit the ceiling, since the man had known from the beginning that he couldn't do the job and had conned himself into a free trip to Europe. Tracy's secretary agreed to take over, and she performed admirably, quietly making her way on our most difficult climbs and outperforming most of the men in the bargain. Of course, some of the men figured that since she suffered from tuberculosis and had quite recently left an Alpine sanitarium, she had an unfair advantage.

When shooting started toward the end of August, our working crew consisted of about fifteen people from Hollywood (not counting players), an excellent French crew, five or six local mountain guides (two of whom doubled for Tracy and Wagner), and about forty-five porters, who, of course, had the toughest jobs. The two heaviest burdens were the camera and its blimp (the soundproof camera cover), since each weighed around 200 pounds when stripped. Two porters were assigned to each of these pieces of equipment—not to carry it simultaneously, but to spell each other at regular intervals. Watching a man carry a 200-pound camera worth many thousands of dollars up and down a knife-edged snow ridge at 14,000 feet was enough to give one *mal de montagne*, even if a normal supply of oxygen had been available. But we never had a serious accident nor lost a single piece of equipment—not even on the day when a sudden and violent Alpine thunderstorm sent us clambering for our lives over a half mile of huge broken boulders. One bolt of lightning struck ground a few feet from one of our porters, sending him flying 50 feet through the air, but he survived both the strike and the fall, and was back at his job the next day.

In order to truly acclimate both ourselves and the nonclimbing crew, I started with the nearest and lowest locations. I also encouraged actors who might not be working on a particular day to come to location anyway, so each day furnished at least a minimum amount of workout time. As usual, the only complaints came from a few of the extras, who worked very little and only on the valley locations.

The first morning Bob Wagner worked in a small village, he was astounded to see the local cows, bells clanging loudly enough to force us to temporarily cease shooting, come in from pasture and walk deliberately into what he considered the living areas of most of the village houses. When he learned that the animals lived on the ground floor and thus furnished heat for the human quarters above, he was filled with admiration. From then on all cows were "heaters" to R.J. If the energy squeeze gets much worse—and it will—we may all be borrowing a trick or two from the Alpine villagers.

Day by day we worked our way out of the valleys and hills and up into the mountains. Fortunately for us, the Chamonix–Mont Blanc area has two aerial tramways—one on either side of the valley. These made it possible for us to get much closer to our work areas before having to strike out on foot, though even then one location was a good two-hour hike from the nearest station. The Mont Blanc tramway carried us to an altitude of roughly 12,000 feet, and this was about 5,000 feet higher than Tracy could go. He did try to pay us a visit one day when we were working at that altitude, but as luck would have it, the cable car he was riding got hung up at about 10,000 feet, and it was some forty-five minutes before they could get it unhung. He never tried again, and I didn't blame him. Those damned things are scary enough when all is going well, but to be caught in one of those claustrophobic cubicles, swinging in the void a couple of thousand feet above sharp rocks and hard snow, is an experience to avoid, particularly by someone with a fear of flying.

Franz Planer had a heart problem and couldn't work at our higher altitudes, either. Fortunately, Til Gabani, our camera operator and a fine athlete, was able to take over on the heights, and our photography did not suffer. After one day's work in the Val Blanche, Wagner, who had run a few dozen yards at that extreme altitude (while I shot several takes) complained to Tracy that I was working him too hard. "Young man," said Spence, "you ought to get down on your knees every night and thank God you work in the most overpaid business in the world." Where, oh where, have these sane attitudes gone? (Wagner's complaint only emphasizes the difficulty of our locations. He was on all other occasions the most amiable and cooperative of men.)

I had my own mishap in Chamonix. The evening before our last and most difficult day on the mountain (a two-hour traverse halfway across

Mont Blanc itself), I was sitting on my high French bed after coming in from a cold and tiring day on the mountain. I reached down to unlace my climbing boots and popped my sacroiliac. Some fifteen minutes later, I finally reached my phone and summoned help. Our head guide suggested a miracle man from the next village who healed such things by touch. In time, he arrived—a small man, about five feet tall, who reeked of stale wine. He spent five or ten minutes touching various parts of my anatomy, then announced my cure would be completed within the next thirty minutes. Fortunately, he didn't wait to verify his prediction. Alas, I have never seen a miracle, or experienced one. I took twenty minutes to roll out of bed the next morning, an interminable time dressing, then led my crew across the mountain, mincing like a man with a broom handle stuck up his rear end. But I made it. It was six months before I could take a free, full stride again, and from time to time, the ruptured disc has plagued me ever since.

It was on one of our less arduous locations that an incident occurred which has since been related in several different contexts. Our company was resting between setups on a path above the glacier. Somehow or other, a young, English-speaking hiker got through our lines and approached Tracy, who usually avoided people. The young man was interested in the theater. Before Tracy could escape, he was asked that dreadful question, "Mr. Tracy, what is the secret of great acting?"

Spence fixed him with a fishy eye. "Read the lyrics, kid," he said. "Read the lyrics."

But how many could read the lyrics like Spencer Tracy?

In a scene near the end of the film, Tracy tells his story of the climb and the rescue, slanting it in an attempt to make his dead brother the hero and himself the heel. It is a long scene, running 5 to 6 minutes, interrupted only by one short question from E. G. Marshall near the beginning. I shot Tracy's close-up first, as was frequently my custom, to ensure that this shot, in which most of the scene would be played, had all the freshness and spontaneity possible. As usual, Spence nailed it on the first take. At the finish, most of the crew was crying. I said, "Cut," and looked over at E.G.

Tears were streaming down his face. "I wish all the method actors could watch this man work—just once!" he said. He said it all.

On our last evening in Chamonix, the guides' association threw a big party. It was quite a wingding, and, naturally, many toasts had to be drunk with the excellent local wines. Just as naturally, Tracy had to drink them. And so started my first and only experience with a periodic alcoholic.

When we left Chamonix for Geneva early the next morning to catch a plane for Paris, Spence was decorating the countryside with empty beer bottles. In Geneva he switched to wine. Once in Paris, we discovered that our flight to Los Angeles was delayed for six hours. That was a long time to wait at the old LeBourget airport, so Tracy tried a more effective time-killer, whiskey. Our Constellation finally took off, and most of us took refuge in our berths. Not Tracy. For him it was the beginning of a night out that was to last a week. He drank all that flight's available alcohol and cursed the stewardess for running short.

Los Angeles Airport had been alerted, and when we deplaned, a limousine was waiting. Tracy was sneaked into the car and whisked away from the airport, leaving his welcoming family in tears. For the next six days, I received daily progress reports: This quiet, very private man was on the town, and in spades. I shot what few scenes I could without him, then closed down. On day seven, he was in the hospital with a bleeding ulcer. I planned to restart production a week from that day, and in a week he showed up, ready to work. For a few days he had a bottle of milk constantly at hand. Then it was back to Cokes again and what Warren G. Harding called "normalcy."

Two weeks out of two pictures and a total of more than 100 days is not too bad. It could have been worse, and was with other actors I've worked with. As Tracy himself once said, "If I have been drunk as often as many people say I was, how the hell did I ever get all those pictures made?"

I have often been asked if Tracy actually did any of the climbing in *The Mountain*. I reply that he did, though he never got higher off the ground than the height of an apple box. I do not say this facetiously or with disdain. Tracy was an actor, not a mountain climber —yet no one, in my opinion, ever made mountain climbing look more real, more harrowing, or more perilous than he did. In one scene, while supposedly standing on an inch-wide ledge (I used inserts made with his climbing double to establish this) he reaches for a crack, finds it filled with ice, carefully takes out his ice ax and chips it away, replaces his ax in his belt, and finally, after a breathless pause, makes the short leap necessary to reach the next handhold. Throughout the scene, shot in close-up, he was standing on the bottom of an upturned apple box, perhaps 8 inches off the ground, but you would have sworn it was a matter of life and death on Everest. That's acting. In the final film I let the scene run without a cut, except for a couple of foot inserts—it must have lasted a full 4 minutes. Only an actor of Tracy's caliber could have sustained a scene of this kind for so long.

And only a cutter who was also the director and producer would have dared play it that way. That's one of the advantages of producing as well as directing your own film. People sometimes comment that wearing two hats must require twice as much work. On the contrary, I think most—if not all—director-producers will agree it makes the whole job much easier. It eliminates the need for compromise, and that's a great advantage, both mentally and artistically. Compromise is the single most difficult problem facing any creator.

In the usual situation, either the producer or the director always dominates. In most cases, especially those involving a "name" director, it is the producer who takes the back seat once the director appears on the scene. In a few cases, particularly with men of the stature of a Selznick or a Goldwyn, the hand of the producer is dominant, and sometimes it is a confrontation of titans and all hell breaks loose. But in all these cases, some degree of compromise is necessary. A director-producer has only to worry about disciplining himself, and though that can be a sizable chore, it rarely makes you sick to your stomach. Compromise frequently does.

Excluding the two lost weeks, the film was finished more or less on schedule, was beautifully scored by Daniel Amphitheatrof, and eventually released to a world that didn't really care to know why men climb mountains. It did quite well abroad, where Tracy was still something of a box-office draw, but only so-so in America. Still, Anna Kashfi got to meet Marlon Brando, the man with no toes got to see Paris and the Alps, and even Paramount didn't seem too unhappy. They gave me a nonexclusive play-or-pay four-picture deal.

MONTY

For untold years artists have been demanding "freedom of failure." It is an important right, and in those arts that require only the expenditure of an artist's time, it has been exercised at frequent intervals, sometimes at the risk of slow starvation. Picasso invoked it constantly in his earlier years, it is a familiar story with composers, and even playwrights experiment with new themes and strange forms. But for the filmmaker, the right to fail hardly exists. It takes a great deal of money to make even a relatively small picture, and to the bankers or businessmen who foot the bill, including the studios' boards of directors, failure is the dirtiest word in any language.

It is true that a film can be made for a few hundred thousand dollars; if one wants to risk nonunion labor and inexperienced actors, it is even possible to make one for under $100,000. But the short-budget film almost always suffers from a short schedule, and time is usually the most important ingredient in the recipe. Actually, films made cheaply are, with rare exceptions, just the opposite of experimental efforts. They are hackneyed stories produced by promoters out to make a quick buck, or they are TV productions, which amounts to the same thing.

Crossfire had been regarded by those of us who made it as an experimental film. However, we had insured its very nominal cost by spending most of the budget on a cast which almost certainly guaranteed its return. My next film, *Raintree County*, was in some respects a similar undertaking. This best-selling novel by Ross Lockridge, Jr., had won the 1948 MGM Semi-Annual Award of $150,000, and was a Book-of-the-Month Club selection. A long, rambling, involved story of small-town life in Indiana during the middle of the nineteenth century, it was anything but film material, and many writers had blunted their ballpoints on it.

Dore Schary, now production head of MGM, decided to make a final effort. *Raintree County* was taken down from the shelf, dusted off, and assigned to a fine writer, Millard Kaufman, as a do-or-die project. He did pretty well, mostly by ignoring a good deal of the novel and striking off in new directions. The script was judged good enough to risk production, and David Lewis, an old associate from *The End of the Affair*, was assigned to produce it. With Schary's acquiescence, he asked me to direct it. It turned out to be the lengthiest and most costly film I ever made—and also one of the most successful.

The script ran to over 200 pages, and amazingly, no one asked that it be cut down to 135. It didn't concern itself with great battles or the burning of cities, but with the unfulfilled hopes and unrealized dreams of a small number of rather unremarkable people. That's why I con- sidered it experimental, though I would never have used that word within the hearing of any of the studio management. There was an almost universal belief at that time (1956) that few human bottoms could survive a plush movie-house seat for more than 2 hours. True, *Gone With the Wind* had run for 4 hours, but it was considered the exception that proved the rule, and Selznick, of course, was just crazy enough to get away with it. But in general, as demonstrated by *Caine Mutiny*, "Thou shalt not subject a derriere to more than two hours of torture" was one of Hollywood's prime commandments. However, for some strange reason, no one at the studio seemed concerned about the problem, at least not until I had finished the film, and by then, fortunately, it was too late. (Dore knew, of course, but he was on our side, and it was probably his "magic," still working at that time, that dazzled the studio hierarchy long enough to get the picture made.)

The film cost somewhat more than $6,000,000, a whopping sum in 1956, though minuscule today, when a practically unseen *Doctor Do- little* can cost $25,000,000. *Gone With the Wind* had cost "only" $5,000,000 some sixteen years earlier, but inflation was not a great factor then, and though Selznick's $5,000,000 probably bought more than MGM's $6,000,000, it was almost certainly far more carefully spent. The cost was, however, more or less insured by the cast: Eliza- beth Taylor, Montgomery Clift, Eva Marie Saint, Rod Taylor, Lee Marvin, Agnes Moorehead, Walter Abel, Nigel Patrick, DeForest Kelley, Tom Drake, and Jarma Lewis. With the exceptions of Aggie and Lee Marvin, I had met none of these players before, and, as always, when long, intimate relationships are to begin, I looked ahead to the coming months with some misgivings. I didn't know the half of it.

Montgomery Clift was a formidable name at the time. His back- ground, the solemn, almost dour quality of many of his previous roles, and my mistaken notion that he was an Actors' Studio alumnus, made me rather apprehensive. Obviously, I had to confront the "enemy" as soon as possible so I arranged a dinner meeting even before my deal with

MGM was concluded. Jean and I met him at Dominick's. He was pleasant, easy to talk to, with a quick, light sense of humor, and a surprisingly wide range of interests and knowledge, absolutely no sense of self-importance, and a hatred of "method acting"—obviously a man to be liked and respected. He drank very little that evening, and by the time we parted we had known each other for years. It was an auspicious beginning.

I had never worked at MGM before—I found it quite unlike any other studio in my experience. Like most tottering empires, it exhibited an opulent exterior which concealed some very anachronistic, profligate, and inferior practices. Behind the scenes, the "departments" ran the studio—or at least thought they did. The production department set up shooting procedures and schedules without much feedback from the director or producer, and the art department still designed huge sets that could be shot from only one position, conveniently staked out by the set designer. There is a story that in Cedric Gibbons' heyday, an all-glass department-store set was constructed—a beautiful thing to see. When the cameraman (James Wong Howe, I believe) came onto the stage for his first look, he was flabbergasted, but not for long. Turning to his grip, he asked for his hammer, then proceeded to shatter all the glass within reach. He knew, of course, that glass reflects, and that it would be impossible to light the set—something the art department, from its lofty position, had neglected to consider.

Late in the film, I had occasion to shoot some process. The equipment was a travesty, obviously designed during the silent era. It was immovable and so noisy that no dialogue could be directly recorded. When I gently informed the technician in charge that more modern equipment was available, even in 1930, he seemed surprised. I'm sure he had never bothered to find out. If it was used at MGM, it had to be the finest. I demanded changes, which were grudgingly made. Needless to say, I never worked at MGM again.

On the obvious, money was spent recklessly. Elizabeth's wardrobe demanded a large number of elaborate antebellum (and postbellum) hoopskirts. In spite of the fact that nobody can finger cloth on the screen and appearance is far more desirable than texture, only the finest materials were purchased, even for concealed petticoats. This cost the picture a lot of money but at the usual mark-up of about ten to one, it made a lot of money for the studio. The director's profit-and-loss record scarcely benefits from this practice.

Following another outdated custom, tests were made of every dress and suit worn by the leading members of the cast. In the days of uncertain color techniques, this practice was a necessity; but by 1956 what you saw is what you got—unless you had the most incompetent of cameramen—and one could hardly call Bob Surtees anything but the best. He could even shoot white and make it *look* white—no mean achievement before the days of Eastman color. I didn't mind the testing too much since it gave me an opportunity to get acquainted with my cast and a good many of the crew, and made for much easier going when I finally started shooting.

Before we started the film, Schary called in the cast for a reading of the script. It was rumored that he did this so that he, a closet actor, could have the pleasure of reading all those roles to be played by actors not yet on salary. I don't like to credit this rumor, but it is true that he considered himself to be the only person in the whole wide world capable of playing the offstage voice of God in the film, *The Next Voice You Hear*. Be that as it may, Dore didn't count on Monty, who arrived late and in "high" spirits. Clift was one of those actors who couldn't read *Dick and Jane* with any conviction. His attempts were so ludicrous (possibly by intention) that Dore was forced to call off the reading by the time we reached page 5—we were all sick with laughter.

The first 6 weeks were easy sailing. We filmed a number of scenes in the studio and on the back lot before leaving for locations in the South. Monty was obviously on top of the world—he was playing a twenty-year-old in these early sequences, and looked it. Eva Marie Saint had always been a trouper and a topflight actress; working with her was a gratifying experience. Lee Marvin finally came into his own. I like to think that it was his performance in this film that gave him the opportunities he so richly deserved. Elizabeth Taylor—well, so many things have been written and said about her anything I add will only gild the lily—still, Liz was a hard worker, late for social engagements but rarely late on the set. She was—and still is—a remarkably caring person: Everyone's problems are her own. Within her range, she is one of the best actresses around, as a couple of Academy Awards and more nominations testify. On the set she is quite untemperamental—almost phlegmatic at times—but she does have fire and can achieve a fine anger at some stupidity, though I've never seen this anger directed at a coworker on the set. She also has great inner strength, and she needed a lot of that on *Raintree County*.

We finished our first 6 weeks of shooting at the studio and were scheduled to leave for New Orleans the following Monday morning. On Saturday night Elizabeth and her husband, Michael Wilding, had a few guests for dinner: Rock Hudson and a lady who was doing a story on him for a leading magazine, Jean, and me. Monty had also been invited, but showed up late, clearly the worse for wear, unshaven, suffering from a hangover, but stone-cold sober. He refused Liz's offer of a drink, and when Jean and I left the house near midnight, he still hadn't had one. That was probably his mistake.

Jean and I lived about fifteen minutes from the Wildings, and we had been home only a short time when the phone rang. It was Elizabeth, informing me of the accident. Monty had left her house a short time after we did (he was driving himself, then) and had hit a telephone pole only a short distance down the steep, winding road from her home. The car was a total wreck, as was the telephone pole. A large transformer had broken loose and fallen not two feet from Monty's head. As for the cause of the accident, I see no reason to question Monty's succinct explanation: "I had one blink too many."

He had fallen asleep and had failed to negotiate a sharp curve.

I saw Monty in the hospital and was surprised that so little showed. His nose had been broken, and he had the usual accompanying black and blue eyes. His jaw had been broken in three places, but had been wired together so skillfully that nothing showed, and he had a slight cut on his upper lip. A broken nose is no problem for a modern specialist and leaves no lasting sign of injury. The cut lip healed quickly, leaving the slightest of scars, perhaps a quarter of an inch long. The broken jaw, though causing him intense pain until the wires were removed, healed properly. Still it's amazing how many people professed to see a physical change in Monty. I have photographs of Clift taken before and after the accident, and no such change is discernible.

It's true that Monty showed signs of physical disintegration over the next few months, but I believe the disintegration was due to his excessive drinking and drug indulgence. Falling off the wagon can be more damaging than hitting a telephone pole. I've seen greater physical changes in Richard Burton after a few weeks on the booze.

Monty was damaged psychologically, too. He fell apart after we resumed production and became less and less responsible as the picture progressed, but this could have been due to any one of a dozen reasons. Checking his behavior out with some of his friends, I learned that he had been prone to such periods of instability at various times long before the accident. There has been a lot of nonsense printed about Monty's accident. Clift was a very complicated man, and the behavior he exhibited over the next few months stemmed from causes far deeper than the simple trauma of an accident, particularly one that occurred while he was asleep.

On another Monday, six weeks after the one originally scheduled, our chartered plane prepared to take off for New Orleans, but one of our cast was missing. Elizabeth was late. We waited for half an hour. Then I asked the pilot to shove off. We had just reached our takeoff position when the tower radioed that Miss Taylor had arrived at the gate. We taxied back, picked her up, then went on our way. I ignored her. She wept a bit. Then the whole thing was forgotten. She wasn't late again until the last day of retakes, but that's another story.

We picked up a few enemies at our stopover in New Orleans, when Liz and Monty refused to talk to the press. The PR man was upset but I could hardly blame them. In the hundreds of interviews I've heard or taken part in, rarely has an intelligent question been asked. I'm sure the representatives of the press must be as bored with the whole business as are the people they interview. Yet each new star, each new personality in any field, has to put up with the same routine ad nauseum.

Our first center of operation was Natchez, Mississippi. The people were friendly—aggressively so. Our chief problem was finding lodging for a couple of black players we had with us. In our travels through the South, they usually wound up staying with a local black minister, one of the few places where Christian charity was practiced.

We were making the first 70 mm. film with the first Panavision camera. It was a huge affair, much larger than the one used for VistaVision. Special steel rods were provided to enable eight grips to move it from one setup to another. Almost as heavy were the dresses worn by Elizabeth—I believe each weighed about 75 pounds. It was August—hot and very humid, and the result was inevitable. Near the end of a particularly uncomfortable day, Liz collapsed with an acute attack of hyperventilation complicated by tachycardia. Either attack alone would have been incapacitating; the two together were frightening. Hyperventilation is a deceptive syndrome. The victim feels that he is getting no oxygen in his lungs while actually suffering, as the name indicates, from too much of that element. The more the victim gasps for air, the more oxygen fills his already overoxygenated lungs, and the greater the pain and fear. Death feels imminent, though there is actually no possibility of such a result. It's not pleasant to watch.

Our company doctor had no license to prescribe drugs in Mississippi, and our local medical contact was unavailable. A strong tranquilizer was urgently needed and our doctor was at a loss. Clift came to the rescue. From somewhere he produced a nearly full bottle of demerol and a syringe. The doctor's eyebrows lifted, but he accepted the drug without comment and administered it to Liz. The hyperventilation slowly subsided, but the tachycardia continued, and Liz was taken to the hotel and put to bed, where a solution of sodium amytal was administered on a continuing basis. It was about a week before Elizabeth was able to return to work.

During this enforced hiatus, Millard Kaufman, our writer, Clift, and I generally had dinner with Elizabeth in her suite. One evening Monty was missing. A phone call to his room went unanswered, so Millard and I went down to find him. The door to his room was slightly ajar and we walked in. Monty was asleep in his bed, his head not two feet from the phone, dead to the world. We attempted to awaken him, but with no success. He still clutched a cigarette in his hand; it had burned deep into the flesh of both his index and his middle fingers and finally gone out. I pried the butt out with a pencil. Then Millard and I quietly left the room, returned to Elizabeth's suite, and ordered dinner. Monty arrived before our order, dressed and groomed, Band-Aids covering his burns. Our not-quite-routine inquiries about his health brought the answer, "I'm feeling great." We had already learned from experience not to press him any further.

Our doctor had ordered some chloral hydrate capsules (Mickey Finns to anyone who spends his time in cheap bars) for Liz, to be used in case of dire emergency. Fortunately, she had no need of them. But one evening the doctor noticed that a number of the capsules were missing; there had been forty, now only twenty were left. The capsules had to be recovered, and the culprit was not hard to find. While the doctor called Monty to Elizabeth's suite for a conversation, Millard and I made a strictly illegal search of his room. What we found was a little frightening but educational. Stashed away in desk drawers, medicine cabinet, and coat closet were at least a hundred containers—bottles, packets, small boxes—of pills, powders, and capsules. There were two bottles of demerol and a beautiful leather case fitted with needles and syringes. There were also a few bottles of liquor, which to me seemed unusual only because, like many people, I had labored under the delusion that persons who took drugs did not drink. I finally found the missing capsules in a bottle that had been emptied of a white powder which now coated the capsules, making them difficult to recognize.

For a number of reasons, we felt it unwise to confront Monty, so our doctor got the local druggist to open his store, and we finally located some B–1 capsules whose outward appearance was quite similar to chloral hydrate. We placed these in the bottle and returned to join Liz and Monty, feeling like CIA agents after a dangerous mission. Monty had an amazing ability to recognize and name almost any drug, and he must have noticed the exchange when he next opened the bottle. Nevertheless, none of us ever heard a word regarding the incident, not even Liz.

Our work in Natchez completed, the company moved on to Danville, Kentucky. Our first official affair was dinner with Governor and Mrs. "Happy" Chandler. Monty's behavior was faultless. The same could not be said for our first (and only) dinner in a public restaurant. The place was full; the sidewalk outside was crowded with local residents trying to catch a glimpse of Taylor and Clift through the plate-glass windows. Monty was in a soaring mood. He ordered his usual steak, blue-rare. When it was served, he went into an all-too-frequent routine: He coated the steak with a thick layer of butter, took the cap off the pepper shaker and covered the butter with pepper, then picked the steak up with his bare hands and started tearing it to pieces. The sight of him, gnawing away at the meat while melting butter dripped through his fingers did little to endear him to the local gentry. Or to our PR man. Nor was his image enhanced when a few nights later, blown out of his mind, he ran naked through the upper-class residential area of the town. After that we put a policeman on his porch every night for the duration. The officer was quite won over by Monty's charm (as who wasn't?) and told me he had some delightful conversations with Clift while gently encouraging him to go back into the house and to bed.

Monty's eating habits were the despair of all his friends. My wife Jean thought she could outwit him. She invited him to dinner at our home and decided to serve meat fondue, thus enabling him to cook his own meat to his own satisfaction and in his own way. Like most people of central European background, I like my meat very well done. However, Jean had hardly put the sirloin strips into the boiling butter when Monty plunged a hand into the pot, brought forth a number of barely seared strips of meat, and deposited them on my plate. And he seemed utterly unable to understand both my concern for what must have been a severely cooked hand and my protests about the uncooked state of the meat.

Monty's intemperance had been taking its toll of our schedule. I tried patience, understanding, reason, firmness—the result was always the same, a kind of puppy-dog eagerness to please, but no positive improvement. Finally, I had had it—or so I thought. After a morning during which he had started to fall apart a bit earlier than usual, I went into his dressing trailer during the lunch hour, accompanied by my assistant (I needed a witness), and told Monty that he was no longer capable of performing that day and I would have to send him back to town. His eyes filled with tears and he asked to stay through lunch. I agreed, but in a short while he called for his car and left the location. After lunch, there was little I could shoot without him, but I puttered around for appearance' sake. Soon there was a call for Millard to attend Monty. A half hour later, it was Elizabeth's turn. In another half hour the doctor was called for, and he left the set. We were running out of cars. Further pretense was useless, so we packed it in for the day.

Back in town, I found that Monty had been taken to the hospital for X rays. He had apparently broken a big toe during a scene that morning, but, as usual with his injuries, had mentioned it to no one. When he came back from location, he had pounded the broken toe into the floor in a fit of self-abuse and had smashed it to shreds. It was set as well as possible, bandaged, and the next morning he was back at work, acting as though nothing had happened. Not even limping.

During our stay in Danville, Elizabeth occupied a house across the street from Monty. Millard and I shared one on the edge of town. One morning we dropped by to pick up Liz. We had hardly arrived when Monty's housekeeper ran in, crying that Monty was hurt, but had disappeared. We hurried across the street. The shower door had been slid back against the glass enclosure and both panels had apparently been kicked through. Sharp shards were scattered in the tub and over the outside floor. Huge splotches of blood led from the shower through the living room and kitchen and out the back door—but Monty was nowhere in sight. We organized searching parties and finally found him—in our makeup room at a nearby motel. I tried my best to look calm and untroubled.

"How are you, Monty?" I asked.

"Great," said Monty. "What's up?"

"Oh, nothing," I said. "Just thought I'd say good morning."

"Thanks," said Monty. And that was the end of that.

Except that later that day Monty suggested that he throw himself under the wheels of a caisson that was traveling as fast as six horses could pull it through a scene I was shooting. He assured me he could roll out of the way in time. He was serious, and I was tempted, but I turned him down and asked one of my assistants not to let him out of his sight.

Just as I was getting to the point where falling under the wheels of a cannon seemed an attractive idea, we finished our location work and flew back to Hollywood. There it was more of the same. Each day I postponed lunch as long as possible, since each afternoon was a replay of *The Lost Weekend*. The studio executives had been getting reports from location, reports which lost something in the sending, but now they could see for themselves. They were incensed. Eddie Mannix himself, MGM's number two, was coming to the set to read Clift the riot act.

Mannix drove out to the back lot in a long black studio limousine, arriving just as we were getting ready to start a scene of Monty frantically wading through our studio-made swamp in search of his lost son. He watched as I started the cameras and signaled for Monty to come on. Clift smashed his way through the undergrowth, waded through knee-high stagnant water, then finally, as I yelled, "Cut!" he fell face forward into an algae-covered pond and stayed there. And stayed. For a half-minute I ignored him. Then I worried. I motioned to my assistant, who waded in and yanked Monty's head out of the water. He came up laughing! Then, spotting Mannix, he sloshed out of the pond and threw his arms around him in a bear hug.

"Hi, Eddie!" he yelled. "How the hell are you, and what are you doing here?"

"Hello, Monty," smiled a somewhat damp Mannix, "I just wanted to tell you how great the rushes are. We're going to have a great picture—a great picture!"

And as soon as he could disentangle himself from Monty's wet embrace, Mannix got back in his car and fled to the safety of the administration building. There's nothing like a little firm discipline to make a film run smoothly.

All good things come to an end, and eventually we finished shooting. The first cut, about 4 hours long, was to be shown to Dore in the private projection room at his home. Included in the viewing group were Dore's wife, his children, and his oldest daughter's new husband. (I object to outsiders, even when they are family, looking at a first cut as much as McCarey objected to producers' girlfriends at a sneak preview. My stomach was churning.) Monty had an agreement that he could see the first cut. He was late and we were all seated, waiting for him, when he burst through the viewing-room doors. Waving a cheerful greeting to all, he threw himself into Dore's lap.

"Hello, Fuckface," he beamed. That was the happiest 4 hours I've spent in a projection room.

Before the final cut was finished, I had an opportunity to see a bit of the MGM executives in action. Schary had fallen into disfavor and was fired. One of his best friends, under contract to the studio, a man who had dined with the Scharys two or three times a week, called Millard Kaufman to ask, "Would it be safer for me not to see Dore again?"

David Lewis was fired. I finished the film on my own. Our sneak, for reasons which will become obvious, was held at a theater in Santa Barbara, a notoriously difficult town to preview in. All the studio executives were there, and MGM had a lot of studio executives. (Clark Gable once commented that one executive got $2,000 a week just to sit in his office on the north side of the administration building and watch for encroaching icebergs. That was a slight exaggeration—he got only $1,500.) Also present was Sol Siegel, my producer from *Broken Lance*. He was due to take over soon as production head at the studio.

The running, some 3 hours and 45 minutes long, was a smash. I have rarely attended a more satisfying sneak. Feeling elated, I waited in the lobby. The executives came out with long faces. "They *liked* it," said one sourly. I'd already had an inkling; it was nothing new in Hollywood. They *wanted* it to fail. It was a Dore Schary enterprise, and the hierarchy didn't want him to look good after his firing. My cutter later reported that on the ride home one of the executives had asked Siegel's opinion. "I'd ship it," said Sol, direct as ever. Very good advice, but that wasn't the way the studio worked.

A few weeks later, I was called back to the studio to shoot some retakes. Zimbalist and Franklin, two company producers, had taken over the reins. They had wanted to use a contract director, but Monty and Liz (bless their souls) had refused to work without me. Millard handed me about thirty pages of new script. I read them. About five were okay.

"What for?" I asked.

"Beats me," he said. "I don't like them either, but I do what I'm told. Why don't you ask them?"

In due course, Millard and I were called to Zimbalist's office. Franklin was also there. They asked us to be seated, then informed me that we were going to read the changes.

"What for?" I was getting repetitive.

"That's the way we always do it," said one of the producers.

"Not me," I said. "I've never done it that way. I don't even agree with most of the changes. I've read the pages, and if you want to discuss them, I'll be happy to oblige; but I'm no actor, and I'm not going to read the stuff out loud."

I don't usually behave this way, but it had been a long grind, and I'd had it up to here. The meeting was cut short, and I eventually retook about 5 pages.

On the last day of retakes, Elizabeth was late. Unlike Monty, she could take a scolding, and when she finally arrived, I was ready to let her have it. She beat me to the punch, flashing a huge twenty-carat headlight in my direction.

"I'm engaged," she said. "To Mike Todd."

She had flown to New York and back the day before, getting in very late. What could I do except remind her that she was still married to Michael Wilding. But, again unlike Monty, Liz could take care of any problem with a mere shrug of her lovely shoulders.

The story of *Raintree County* has been largely the story of Montgomery Clift and his somewhat dicey behavior. It will probably surprise everyone to learn that I enjoyed working with him more than any other actor in my experience. Unlike the other drunks I've worked with, Monty never got mean when under the influence—he simply fell apart. And he never hurt anyone except himself. He was intelligent, thoughtful, humorous, and caring—oh, how caring. He was a man with no skin—all his nerve ends were exposed.

In his work, Montgomery Clift was a genius, the most quickly creative actor I've ever met. He was so secure in his profession that he was never stubborn or combative. Other actors have given me suggestions, then argued interminably if I demurred. Monty would throw out an idea, and if I hesitated, he would say, "Forget it."

When I'd say, "No, Monty, let's examine it. There might be something there," he'd say, "Nope. If there's the slightest doubt, forget it. We'll come up with something better." And we usually did.

Still, much as I liked Monty personally, I swore I'd never go through that scene again. Besides, I thought he'd soon be dead. Six months later, he was still alive and I had changed my mind. I'd found a part that only he could play.

THE YOUNG LIONS

I needed a long period of recuperation after *Raintree County*, and we spent a number of weeks in Kona. My distaste for the business slowly dripped away, and after about four months, I could think of films again without a tic or a tremor—which was lucky, because 20th was sending smoke signals in my direction. Al Lichtman, a long-time Fox distribution executive, now retired, had obtained the rights to Irwin Shaw's *The Young Lions*, considered by many the best novel to come out of World War II. 20th had agreed to finance its production—more, I gathered, out of gratitude for Al's many years of faithful service than out of any enthusiasm for the property. They planned a $2,000,000 budget, a 64-day schedule, and a cast of contract players. I felt that none of these was adequate for such an important project.

Though Shaw, in my opinion, was one of the best short-story writers ever, a fine novelist, and a reasonably good playwright, his screenplays had never been successful. His mediocre attempts at adapting *The Young Lions* had been at least partly responsible for keeping the novel off the screen for nine years. The ability to be equally good at all forms of writing is reserved for the very few, and I've forgotten his name.

Edward Anhalt, who with his wife Edna, had written and produced two of my films for Stanley Kramer, was doing a solo job on this one. (He and Edna had divorced, personally and professionally.) When I came into the picture, he had just completed a first draft of about 200 pages, not a bad rendering of a novel that was just short of 700 pages. It was a difficult story to lick—very episodic—following the separate lives of three men, one of which didn't even touch either of the other two until the last scene of the picture. But what was there was enough to arouse excitement.

The three main characters in the story represented three distinct aspects of the effect of war on its participants: one, a decent man destroyed by its senselessness and brutality; two, a man able to come to terms with his own cowardice and fear of involvement; and three, a very ordinary young man who learned, grew, and was even ennobled through meeting its challenges. It was the last character, the young Jew, Noah, who was the heart of the story, and if I could get the right actor, I knew we'd be a long way ahead. There was only one right actor at the time, so I sent a script to Monty Clift. A few days later came the shortest telegram I've ever received: "Yes." In 1957 that was a commitment, honored by actor, agent, and studio.

At about the same time, Marlon Brando's agent, Herb Brenner, dropped into my office. Marlon had heard, he said, that we had a good script (it helped, of course, that *The Young Lions* had been a best-selling novel) and, since Marlon still owed 20th a commitment (at a ridiculously low price) in settlement of their suit against him for his long trip to the toilet, there just might be a possibility of getting together. That possibility was very exciting, but I was a little reluctant to give Brando a script since the German, Christian, was the only unrealized character in our story. Anhalt and I had been beating our brains about the problem, but had not yet come up with a clear solution. However, Brenner assured me he'd relay my reservations and my hopes to Brando—at least it was worth a try.

Marlon read the script, saw its possibilities, and asked for a meeting, which promptly took place one evening at his home. He and I talked for about two hours; at the end of that time, Brando agreed to do the film. He also helped us resolve the character of Christian. Like Monty, Brando was—and is—a very creative actor, though his methods are slightly different; Monty's ideas flashed like sparks from a pinwheel, while Marlon wrestles with his interminably.

In the novel, Christian is a reasonable man, non-Nazi, but sympathetic to many of Hitler's aims. His participation in the war brings about a moral degeneration until in the end he is a complete Nazi, as black-hearted a villain as was ever conceived. Anhalt and I felt that little was to be gained by keeping this characterization. Twelve years after the war, the dyed-in-the-wool Nazi heavy was a cliché, and everybody accepted the proposition that a brutal war furnished brutal opportunities for a brutal man. Besides, we had all learned by now that many thoroughly Aryan Germans had also been hanged to lampposts for refusing to cooperate in Hitler's war.

Brando concurred with our analysis, showing a willingness to go even further than we had anticipated in changing the character. Eventually, Christian was established as a man who is in sympathy with many Nazi ideas and ideals but finds that these degenerate into barbaric brutality as the war progresses. He resists the trend with growing intensity and finally, with Germany itself in its last throes, he walks unarmed into an American bullet. Here we had a developing character, although a tragic one, who could demonstrate the weaknesses of totalitarianism far better than the more-or-less one-dimensional figure of the novel.

In order to make the transition work, we promoted Christian from sergeant to lieutenant. As a noncom Christian simply would not have been in a position to make certain dramatically necessary decisions. Many people thought the change was made to enable Brando to wear more handsome uniforms, which, of course, was nonsense. Noah was a kind of "nebbish" character. In order to be more effective, Clift dieted down to 135 pounds (at 6 feet), cut his hair unfashionably short, and made his ears stick out. A few critics peevishly complained that Monty was not handsome in the film—probably the same ones who delight in calling Hollywood "Tinseltown." Others took his appearance as proof that he had indeed been disfigured by the accident. Sometimes you can't win for trying.

I've already mentioned the circumstances surrounding the hiring of Dean Martin for the role of Whiteacre. Hope Lange played Noah's fiancée and wife. Barbara Rush played Whiteacre's girlfriend. Liliane Montevecchi and Dora Doll played two chance friends of Christian and his photographer buddy, played by Parley Baer. The very important role of Christian's captain, Hardenberg, still remained to be cast when I took off for Paris to start preparation for the considerable filming we had to do in Europe.

But first came the obligatory production meeting. I mention it only because it illustrates so neatly the bureaucratic thinking of some studio department heads. The original budget was $2,000,000, based on a 64-day schedule. I was only slightly surprised to learn that in spite of the upgrading in our cast, the studio not only adhered to the original budget but wanted to cut the schedule down to 60 days. (I suppose because it's such a nice, round figure.) I pointed out that casting either Monty or Marlon automatically required doubling the schedule—having both in the film placed it beyond reckoning. In my opinion, the cost would go over $3,000,000, and the schedule would run about 120 days. The studio production manager was obstinate. I finally agreed to the 60-day figure for the record, but still insisted I'd double it in actuality. That bothered him not at all; he returned to his office in a happy frame of mind. He was on the record, and safe—I would be responsible for the overages which he knew would eventuate as well as I did.

We set up offices in Paris and started to round up a crew. European crews are not as consistent as those in Hollywood. That is true of every country I have worked in, without exception, though the English tend to be the best. When planning *The Mountain*, Paramount had wisely "reserved" our excellent crew a good many months in advance of production. The Fox people, on the other hand, rather arrogantly assumed they could pick up a premium crew at the last minute. They were quite wrong and we paid for it, over and over again.

I still had to find a Captain Hardenberg and his wife. A few days in Munich proved fruitless, though one of the German films I saw there turned out to be a help later. Back in Paris, I turned to the local agents. One left me a brochure of a young actor named Carl Schell. He was a touch too on-the-nose for a Nazi officer, and I set him aside. I awaited the arrival of some tests made in Hollywood after my departure. None proved satisfactory. In desperation, I called Schell's agent and asked if Schell were available. I was told he was not only free but he could be in Paris by midnight to meet me. I agreed to the rendezvous, then promptly forgot it.

Returning from a late dinner, after midnight, I found Schell and his agent waiting in front of the Raphael Hotel. I had just started to apologize when I realized that the young actor standing there bore little resemblance to Carl Schell. Quite naturally. It was his brother Maximilian. I had neglected to use a given name when I had inquired about

Schell's availability, and the agent had thought Max while I was thinking Carl. As luck would have it, one of the German films I had seen in Munich had starred Max, though I had been looking at the leading lady. His performance had been excellent, and he was much more the physical type I was seeking. But there was a slight catch. When he said hello, he'd used up his whole bag of English. Out of desperation, I decided to take a chance. I had brought Walter Roberts, a former playwright and English professor, with me as a dialogue coach, and Max agreed to work with him for a couple of weeks before I made a final decision. About three weeks later, when we shot his first scene at Sacre Coeur on Montmartre, his English was so good that none of it had to be dubbed. His excellent performance in our film earned him the role of the defense counsel in *Judgment at Nuremburg*, and that earned him an Academy Award. Not bad for a man who couldn't speak English a year before.

Story: Stanley Kramer was filming *Judgment at Nuremburg*, and Maximilian Schell, playing the German defense attorney, had just finished his opening address to the justices. Spencer Tracy walked over to Widmark, placed his hand on Dick's shoulder.

"Richard," he said, "we're in trouble."

Tracy was usually right.

The Young Lions was one of the most trying jobs of my entire career. Bad luck plagued us from the beginning. A few days before we started shooting, Marlon had an interesting accident. He, Dean Martin, and some friends were in the George Cinq bar. Marlon, a nondrinker at the time, had ordered tea. As a large pot of scalding water was placed on the table, someone managed to tip it over, emptying the entire contents over Marlon's—excuse the expression—loins. He hastily unzipped his fly and sprayed the affected parts with seltzer, which caused quite a stir among his eager fans but had little effect on his third-degree burns. He spent a number of unforgettable days in the hospital (unforgettable to the sisters who nursed him), then reported for work with no complaint.

We started shooting near Chantilly, about 30 miles north of Paris, and the weather, which had been beautiful up to this point, turned sour. (In all, during our European stay, we lost 35 days due to bad weather.) As the delays piled up, so did the cables from Hollywood. It was suggested that I shoot in the rain. That's an old bone of contention. On occasion it's possible to work in a drizzle, or even a light rain, but in our case, the rains were minor deluges and cascaded off our actors' helmets like miniature Niagaras. And if we decided to start a sequence in the rain, the next day could bring a skyful of sunshine. It was a dilemma, and the studio had specifically barred the use of cover sets, so we had to sit and play gin rummy.

On our first day of shooting, Parley Baer broke a leg jumping down into a concrete ditch. His steel-braced cast was covered with ersatz leather to match his other boot, and we went right on working. (I have, with very few execptions, been blessed with the best-natured, most decent actors in the world.) After a few weeks and a dozen more communications, the studio suggested that I shoot the Berlin scenes on the back lot. At that time Berlin still had the huge bombed-out, rubble-filled areas so necessary for our film, and I objected to the studio's proposal. Stalling for time, I suggested that if they could send me sketches proving they could construct a ruined Berlin on the back lot, I would acquiesce. Half-heartedly, they sent me some pitiful sketches and another demand for an early return. I riposted with an offer to quit the film, which I sincerely hoped they would accept. Instead I received a 28-page wire of rationalization and apology (I still have it). I had lost again.

Paranoia was setting in much earlier than usual. I have always found Paris the least hospitable city in the world. In the many months I've spent there, I have been invited to a private home just twice, both times by Franco-Russian producers. The French Communist party took my defection from the ranks with more bad grace than most. Their press, to this day, reviews me rather than my films, and certainly not kindly. Our crew was about half red and did its best to sabotage the film. If it hadn't been for two young women (both Franco-Russian, by coincidence) who started as interpreters but soon were our jills-of-all-trades, I probably would never have finished the picture. Both girls were threatened with ostracism as, later, was Dora Doll for reporting that she loved Hollywood—a mortal sin in some Parisian circles. With the weather, the studio, and a good part of my French crew all bugging me, I was ready to flip. The only things going well were Monty and Marlon.

Clift and Brando had never met before. Quite naturally, each was interested in the other, and soon after we arrived in Paris arranged to have dinner together. During the course of the evening, Brando, who had been observing Clift closely, suggested that Monty might profit from a few sessions with a shrink. A possible (though doubtful) beautiful friendship was nipped in the bud.

Monty was on his best behavior. I can remember only one instance of work stoppage due to his drinking. Considering that a full bottle of wine for each member of the cast and crew was practically a state requirement at our location lunches, that was quite extraordinary. There were a few near-misses, but Monty had developed a great affection for our production manager, Ben Chapman, and somehow or other Ben succeeded in keeping Clift functional.

Because of its opportunities for positive statements on anti-Semitism, Monty was very enthusiastic about his role. When shooting his sequences, we usually rode out to location together, using the travel time to work on his scenes—not the scenes for that day but those a week or two in the future. Several nights he awakened me at 3:00 or 4:00 in the morning, asking me to come to his room to discuss some particular line or piece of business. One such morning I found him traveling a very high road, but though he was climbing walls, he was doing it in relation to the film and that was significant. On the whole it was a good way to work; by the time we got around to the actual shooting, all the creative work was done and it was just a matter of recording the scene on film. Like Spencer Tracy, Monty was a one-take man. If, for some reason or other, the scene ran past three or four takes, his acting, like his reading, became awkward and mechanical. It was necessary to take a long breather then, during which he could recover his spontaneity, or turn to another scene in the meantime. To insist on crashing on regardless (as a few directors did) led only to serious trouble and inferior scenes.

Marlon Brando was a whole different kettle of fish. In the first place, Brando is one of those actors, rare today, particularly in Hollywood, who uses makeup freely to help establish or enhance a character. Judging by that and by his past work, I had always thought that he was an extremely dedicated actor: I found him instead to be one of the industry's great goof-offs. Brando is an extremely cynical man, and a great practical joker, with an unquenchable penchant for boyish horsing around. When Brando was preparing for *The Men*, Stanley Kramer's film study of paraplegics, he regularly accompanied a number of them to a bar near their hospital. In order to get the feel of their daily lives and patterns, he, too, maneuvered around in a wheelchair. One evening a kindly old busybody lectured the men on "faith"—her message was that if they *really* believed, they could get up and walk.

Hardened to this sort of altruistic advice, the men listened politely, but Brando soon had all he could take. "I believe," he breathed. Then, more loudly, "I believe!" And pressing his hands on the arms of his wheelchair, he slowly pushed himself up to his feet, then started to totter toward the kindly old lady.

Her own faith was not quite up to the miracle. She let out a small scream, then turned and fled the bar, while the men nearly fell out of their wheelchairs in stitches.

Like a comic or a pop singer, Brando surrounds himself with a small (I could almost say "weird") coterie of sycophant-friends. Their duty seems to be to keep his mind on anything but the work at hand.

Once Brando had agreed to do the film, I had made my usual

inquiries about his work habits on the set. Admiration for his ability was unanimous—for his work habits, less so. The consensus seemed to be, in the words of one man, "He will go through thirty or forty takes, listlessly—nothing happens—then suddenly, on the next try, everything comes together, and everybody on the set knows he's seen a perfect take." In one instance, he had done seventy takes of a silent shot, a reaction to something seen through a window, before a satisfactory take was recorded. I've seen directors go this far, either while on an ego trip or because they didn't quite know what they wanted, but never an actor—except in those rare instances when one ran into a mental block. (Those few with a constitutional inability to remember lines were usually furnished with "idiot boards," a common practice in TV filming.)

Brando and Glenn Ford reputedly had a run-in on *Teahouse of the August Moon*. Ford was typically Hollywood, always well prepared and ready. In the scenes he played with Brando, he gave his all and ran dry long before Marlon began rounding into shape.

All this discouraging information made me glad that Monty and Marlon worked together in only one scene, and in that Christian was already dead. That, at least, I felt Brando could handle in the one or two takes necessary for Monty to do his job.

I approached our first day's shooting with misgivings and a pocketful of Tums, but some dim hopes. I was disappointed. Marlon was in the proper wardrobe, but had little idea of what the day's work was about. He was given the information (for at least the fourth time) and glanced cursorily at the scene over the script girl's shoulder. It was a simple scene with only a couple of lines of dialogue. After 18 rehearsals (the number, for some silly reason, is etched in my memory when far more important things have been forgotten) I was whistling in the dark. Deciding that more rehearsals were a waste of time and emotion, I called for takes. It was rehearsals all over again, but after a ridiculous number of false starts and incompetent renditions, Marlon finally said, "Oh, *that's* what the scene is about!" as if making a discovery.

"It always was," I said, which he took more lightly than I had meant it. The next take was a print.

It went on like this for a few days. Then Marlon began to develop a real interest in the project and the part. The goofing diminished, the attention increased, and the performance improved. Before we finished our European shooting, I was getting prints in three or four takes, and this continued after our return to California, particularly when Schell's obviously great talent put him on his mettle. "Eddie," he said one day, "I haven't had such a solid working relationship since I worked with

Gadge (Elia Kazan)." I thanked him for the compliment. Then I suddenly realized that Marlon's early horsing around may have been merely his way of testing my own strength and dedication to the picture. He is notorious for trying his directors to the breaking point.

One of our locations took us to Strasbourg, in Alsace. Near there, at Schirmeck, the Germans had built a concentration camp (the only one in France, I was told, though the Nazis would have considered Alsace a part of Germany). Much of the camp was still standing and received a steady flow of tourists from all parts of the country. I had visited Dachau, near Munich, and I had seen the original newsreel film of liberated concentration camps released by our Signal Corps during the war. In Paris I had received permission to review a great deal more of this film at the War Museum. I was unprepared. I do not easily show emotion, and kept myself well under control while looking at about three hours of unbelievable atrocities, but I had no sooner gotten into my car with Joe MacDonald, my cameraman, and two or three other members of my company when, to my complete embarrassment, I broke into uncontrollable crying which lasted about an hour. Now I had to make the whole thing come to life again, a sheer impossibility. It could be done only by indirection.

With Ben Chapman's help, we had circumvented 20th's "no cover sets" edict. For example, during our shooting at the French Army's tank proving grounds near Paris, we had blacked in a cottage set to enable us to shoot the interior scenes. Ben had scouted the city for tarps or drapes large enough for our purpose, finally finding some at a mortuary. Now he authorized the reerection of a couple of the inmates' barracks under the guise of repairs to standing construction, thus enabling us to salvage a couple of days more on our schedule and to use many of the ex-inmates of the camp as extras. How could we beat that at home?

The entrance to the camp enclosure was made of huge, 20-foot-high, tarred telephone poles, double in depth and copiously strung with barbed wire. The fence around the camp was also doubled, the two fences 6 or 8 feet apart. Reputedly, this "run" had been guarded by police dogs. But the booklets on sale at the camp office contained sketches made by some of the inmates themselves and these showed a simple, single-wired gate (no telephone poles) and a single barbed-wire fence circling the camp. I asked the local priest (a former inmate) about the seeming contradiction.

"Oh, the booklet is correct, of course," he said. "But the gate and fences didn't look barbaric enough for our tourists, so we rebuilt them. Now we have no complaints."

He also told me the story of the inmate who managed to escape the camp one night, only to be recaptured. The camp commandant was intrigued.

"Show me how you got out," he said, "and I'll let you go this time."

The inmate gladly agreed. He had secreted a long pole in the camp and had easily vaulted over the 8-foot fence. Now, for the edification of the commandant, he repeated his escape. He made his jump and continued running down the hillside. At the officer's command, a guard shot him in the back.

Our technical expert had been a tank corps commander. Coming from a long line of titled German soldiers, he was strictly a military man. He was also the husband of our script girl, who browbeat him shamelessly. On our first day at the camp, he requested and received permission to accompany us on our tour of the place. It's hard to tell what his true feelings were, but he came out crying.

Our Berlin shooting lasted about a week, during which Marlon, in an interview, stated, "The picture will try to show that Nazism is a matter of mind, not geography; that there are Nazis—and people of goodwill—in every country." His speech moved a Berlin journalist to observe, "Brando speaks more like a statesman than a movie actor." Why not? Didn't we give our country Ronald Reagan and George Murphy?

An example of the sort of skulduggery a film company occasionally runs into: We arrived at a bombed-out area to shoot a scene at a strangely isolated apartment house. We were photographing only the exterior and had made the usual financial deal with the owner of the building. But we had reckoned without the tenant and his son, who seated themselves on chairs in the driveway and refused to move unless paid a large sum of money. On principle, I refused. The police pleaded, but could take no action, since the sit-down strikers were on private property. Some of the bystanders reminded the two of America's generosity during the recent Big Lift. Nothing. They sat and we sat—for about four hours. Finally, shamed by the continual goading of the watching crowd, they went inside, and we got our shot. Now and then something like this happens in almost any place in the world. It happened to me once on the Columbia Studio "ranch" in Burbank, California, when a truck farmer on a lot across the street started plowing his land at 1:00 in the morning, and quit only on the payment of $50.

We finally finished our European locations and took off from Paris, leaving an airport filled with the sobs of "location wives." On our flight back, Max Schell watched the prairies of the Dakotas, Wyoming, and Utah sliding under our Constellation. "Christ!" he said. "What a lot of empty country you have in America!"

Once back in Hollywood, we left almost immediately for the Borrego Desert, northeast of San Diego, to film the desert battle scenes. But first I had to cast the captain's sexy wife. I decided to take another chance. Based only on an interview test taken in Italy, I picked Mai Britt, a former photographer's assistant from Sweden. She had a good deal to learn about acting. But sexy? My, yes. Fox had another leading lady overnight.

There followed two weeks in Borrego Springs, working in 118-degree temperature (in the shade). I lost my cameraman, Joe MacDonald, to the heat, and two members of the crew to scorpions, but our operator, Duke Callaghan, took over nicely and we forged ahead. Anna Kashfi came down to visit Brando, the first time I'd seen her since *The Mountain*, and Christian Brando was conceived. I never learned whether he was named after his father's character in the film, or Marlon's friend Christian Marquand, but I always assumed the former. And one night when Jean came down with Rickie for a visit and we wanted to go out to dinner, Marlon baby-sat for us, which won him a personal Oscar from my wife. A man of many parts is Brando.

From the desert filming come two examples of Brando at work. It is just before sunrise and Christian, Hardenberg, and twenty German soldiers lie on the crest of a hill overlooking a British encampment, where some two hundred British Tommies are rousing themselves from a night's sleep and collecting their morning cups of tea. Marlon had an intuition—some kind of comment seemed appropriate. He, Max, and I retired to my trailer-office and went to work—that is, we lounged around and tried to be creative. Eventually (after about two hours) we came up with this bit:

As Hardenberg and Christian watch the British soldiers drinking their tea, the captain speaks:

HARDENBERG
Do you like tea, lieutenant?

CHRISTIAN
(watching the British)
Hm?

HARDENBERG
(turning to Christian)
Do you like tea?

CHRISTIAN
(turning to Hardenberg)
Oh . . . No, sir.

Hardenberg turns his attention back to the British. Then, with great contempt:

HARDENBERG
Tea!

Very simple—but also very effective. In a few words and a couple of expressions, the captain makes clear his contempt for the English and helps us to understand why he would dare to engage in battle a force ten times the size of his command. (The battle sequence was considered so effective by the British they requested a copy for the Imperial War Museum.) I can't remember who came up with the actual germ of the scene, but without Brando's insistence on finding it, the sequence would have been shot without it, so he must get the credit. In passing, you will notice that it is not his scene, but Schell's.

In another sequence, following the British breakthrough at El Alamein, Christian and the captain are on a motorcycle, fleeing for their lives. Frightened, dead-tired, and angry, Christian flails out at the war and its unpleasant conditions, but briefly, as befits the situation. The scene is cut short when they hit a land mine. Some days before we were to shoot the sequence, Marlon suggested that he might be able to use the opportunity to deliver a more involved condemnation of the world's ills. This was hardly a scene for a crusading speech, but I had no time to argue, so I suggested he write out his version as a basis for discussion.

He did, and brought it to my motel room a couple of nights later. It was 8 pages long and mentioned the Scottsboro Boys, our treatment of the Indians, a bit about Zen Buddhism, and a few other items close to Marlon's heart. Over the course of a half-hour's discussion, I pointed out that these subjects were all worthwhile—so much so that each deserved at least one complete film in its own right. He finally laughed, tore the pages in half, and threw them into the fireplace. A very good man to work with, Brando—at least when he is involved in a film worthy of his talents.

Each production is a lifetime in miniature, and each comes to an end. As I had predicted, we finished in 125 days, at a cost of a little over $3,000,000, truly a tiny budget compared to its eventual take.

The *Variety* prerelease review said, "A few more like this and the picture business' 'comeback' will be here. It's a kingsized credit to all concerned, from Edward Anhalt's skillful adaptation to Edward Dmytryk's realistic direction and not the least the highly competent portrayals of virtually everyone in the cast."

Weekly *Variety* of March 19, 1958 called it a "B. O. Blockbuster!"

But before the film was released I had one more surprise. Following procedure, we held a running for the New York brass. As the film ended, the executives broke into unrestrained applause. Everyone was crying, and the compliments flew thick and fast.

"It is so beautiful, so perfect," said Spyros Skouras. Then, as an afterthought, "How long is it?"

"Three hours and twenty minutes," I told him.

"You'll have to cut out half an hour," he said.

In the textbooks, they call that a conditioned reflex.

THE FASTEST GUN
IN THE WEST

After the seemingly interminable strain of *The Young Lions*, I was looking forward to an easy year in 1958. I had anticipated a call from Paramount, but production at that studio was moving at a snail's pace. Buddy Adler, at 20th, asked me to read the novel, *Warlock*, by Oakley Hall, one of the first, and, to my mind, still the best of the writers who were treating the Old West as something more than mere grist for the pulp mills. *Warlock* had nothing to do with male witches—it was merely the fictional name of a town in Western territory which, believe it or not, is torn not by a battle between cattlemen and sheepherders, but by a dispute between miners and mine owners. The owners hire a band of "regulators"—actually a lawless gang of cowboys and ranchhands—to keep the miners under control. (This not-uncommon practice is little known except to scholars of the Old West.) The regulators terrorize not only the striking miners but the townspeople as well, so they, in turn, pool their resources to hire a gunfighter, a Wyatt Earp type, to regulate the regulators—and there the fun begins.

Two aspects of the project were intriguing: First, I was to produce as well as direct the film. Though I had actually been the unofficial producer of a number of my films and had produced *The Mountain*, the first draft of that script was just about completed by the time I got involved. In this instance, I would be in a position to select my own writer and proceed from scratch. Second, the depth of the novel furnished us with a number of opportunities to examine life in the Old West in a serious and "adult" manner, while retaining the obligatory action and gunfighting of the standard Western. I accepted the assignment with pleasure, since I knew I would have a long rest while the first draft was being written.

The old saws hold true in the arts as much as in other fields—you get what you pay for. A top writer might easily saddle a production with a story cost (including the price of the original property) that would be prohibitive. Even in 1958 a $500,000 total story cost was by no means unheard of. There is a way out for the producer who is looking for great ability at a nominal price, but it is risky and definitely a one-shot deal: Find a new talent, a writer whose early work shows a superior gift, but whose lack of credits renders him relatively cheap. (I find it interesting that the Italians have no word for "cheap," meaning inexpensive. Instead they use the expression "a buon prezzo," literally "at a good price." Now isn't that a positive attitude?)

Some writers can only write comedy, others only drama. Some write clever dialogue, while others weave skillful plots. Some can write great individual scenes but have little sense of organization or continuity; others organize well but write dull scenes. Some talk a great story which somehow loses its magic when committed to paper, while others stammer like bashful children but write like Boccaccio. Perhaps the chief reason for teaming writers, a much-criticized Hollywood practice, is simply to overcome these natural weaknesses through the collaboration of two (sometimes more) writers who complement each other. And very, very few can properly visualize a scene; they are accustomed to expressing everything through dialogue—even, for example, to the point of saying "all right" when a nod of the head would serve better. Which is why so many directors, and *all* good directors, collaborate on the scripts they eventually direct, even though, more often than not, they take no credit. After all, visualization and communication through properly timed action are supposed to be a good director's chief skills.

In this particular instance, I wanted someone with original ideas—a risk taker—someone who could write a totally unexpected line or an apparently bizarre scene which, on brief consideration, would prove to be honest and in tune with reality. There is a very fine line between stifling a scene by overanalysis of its consistency and relevance (after all, it is the very fact that a character does something untypical or unexpected that makes for drama) and resorting to purposeless flights of fancy. Continuity I don't worry about—linear organization has been my bent since childhod. I finally decided to "take a gamble" on Robert Alan Aurthur, a New York TV writer who, as far as I know, had never been in Hollywood, and who had written only one screenplay for a New York-based movie.

Each producer works with writers after his own fashion. Some prefer to have each sequence presented for their perusal, analysis, and subsequent discussion. (I have known producers who insisted that every 4 or 5 pages be handed in, even if the sequence were incomplete.) I feel this inhibits a writer considerably and diminishes any possible inclination for chance taking. Other producers hand over a book or previous script and leave the writer completely on his own, and sometimes find themselves the owners of a screenplay bearing no similarity to the original story. I prefer to discuss the story and the characters in fairly broad terms, arrive at some tentative decision on the story's main thrust, and then let the writer retire to do his work, keeping only the lightest rein on his progress. (A certain amount of watchfulness is recommended. I once hired a writer who tripped off to the Caribbean to sit in the sun, then dashed off a totally unusable script in the last few days of his subsidized "holiday." And I couldn't return the goods and get a refund.)

Our novel had enough material for two good films—a Western and a story of labor conflict. For our purposes, the Western aspect was dominant and we decided to concentrate on the civilizing of a frontier area through the gradual and painful imposition of law. Not an original theme, but what made it more interesting in *Warlock* was that the process continued through several steps: First came the willful dominance of a lawless mob; then the rule of the mob legitimatized (comparable to baronial rule in feudal times or that of a Chinese war lord prior to World War II); third, the rule of the gunslinging marshal (comparable to that of a dictator); and finally, the accession of a popularly elected sheriff. It was the development of a society in microcosm. At the same time, these transitions, following closely one after the other, gave rise to dramatic personal conflicts as values suddenly changed and attitudes became anachronistic.

After we arrived at an understanding on the story's general structure, Aurthur went home to work (home meant New York) while I set about recovering from the mental and spiritual wounds inflicted by *The Young Lions*. That meant Hawaii, which, for me, was as soft and soothing as ever. For Jean, too much lassitude can be trying, but, as always, she was understanding.

Eventually, Aurthur appeared with a first draft, and I had to return to my real world—the world of make-believe. I always advise writers against severe self-editing in the beginning for fear that something potentially good may be eliminated without getting a chance. Bob had taken me literally, and his first draft was very long—and very dull. I was a little frightened, but experience has taught me never to over-react to first appearances. The necessary pruning, judiciously done by both of us, exposed the shape of an unusual and exciting Western. Besides the broad sweep of the plot, already mentioned, there were an unusual number of those offbeat incidents and character touches that are the salt in most filmmakers' stew. Our heroes did not gallop into town on untiring chargers, but plodded in on worn-out, dust-covered mustangs, accompanied by a wagonload of their worldy goods. Our gunfighter, before accepting the marshal's job, insisted on taking over the gambling concession because, as he said, "My salary as marshal will hardly pay for the ammunition I use up while practicing." This one comment alone broke ground in several areas. First, it showed a gunfighter of notoriety using his reputation to enhance his earning capacity—a very true but rarely mentioned fact of Western history. Second, for the first time, to my knowledge, it mentioned (and we later showed) that, like any other trained professional, a gunslinger had to practice his craft to stay on top of his form. Again, in a later scene, the marshal gives the new sheriff a few pointers on the "quick draw," just as Hank Aaron might give a rookie some hints on hitting the long ball—there are tricks in every trade.

There was an interesting relationship between the marshal and his right-hand man. Many critics and viewers thought it might be homosexual (a no-no at that time). Actually, it wasn't—it was a good deal more complex than that and of more than passing interest to the audience. The big duel on the street was not between the hero and the villain, but between the hero and his best friend—and not for reasons of hate but of misdirected love. And in the climactic face-off between the gunslinger and the sheriff, the marshal easily outdraws his opponent, not once but twice, then throws his guns down into the dirt and rides out of town and into a world with a declining need for his particular gifts.

The traditional Western permitted only two kinds of women: the brazenly dressed, or undressed, dance-hall girl (though she might have a heart of gold), and the "good" woman, God-fearing and clothed from throat to ankle. In actual fact, pioneer women throughout history have been rough, tough, and ready, as capable of firing a gun, plowing a field, butchering an animal, or accepting sexual gratification as were their men. The natural functions of dogs and cattle, and of mom and pop in a one-room sod shanty, were not mysteries to them, and with the nearest inside toilet or bidet hundreds or even thousands of miles away, few pioneer women ever swooned at any functional or sexual display. We tried to keep our women as honest as we could.

I was able to put together an excellent cast. Henry Fonda played the gunslinging marshal. To me he was the epitome of the lean, wind-bitten, Western man, second only to Gary Cooper in the long history of Hollywood. His somewhat shady sidekick was played by Anthony Quinn. The third leading part, that of a bad guy turned honest, was played by Richard Widmark. Quinn, always an excellent actor, was getting better and better and did a beautiful job. Widmark, free now of any feeling of being had, gave his usual top-notch performance.

Dick is an extremely conscientious workman, a study in concentration and creative irritability, and has a very short fuse. This combination erupts now and then with interesting results. Dorothy Malone, though not our leading lady, was our most important female character. In the film she tries to use Widmark to revenge herself on Quinn for some past wrong. At this time, Dorothy was head-over-heels in love with Jacques Bergerac, and, I'm afraid, was not up to doing her homework. Late one afternoon I started to rehearse a rather long and complicated moving shot which was to be our first setup on the following day. Dick, as always, was fully prepared. Dorothy wasn't, but guided by me, she managed to stumble her way through the scene, reading her lines. The end of the scene required that she slap Widmark. Now, slaps are one thing one doesn't put one's heart into in rehearsals, but after I had tugged her around the set a couple of times, and Dick had scarcely disguised his displeasure at her lack of commitment, she wasn't exactly feeling like Goody-Two-Shoes. At the end of the third rehearsal, she delivered a mighty wallop to Dick's left ear. He grabbed her hand, and, showing exemplary self-control, reminded her that this was a rehearsal, that his left ear was his bad ear (it really was), and, if she *did* want to hit him in rehearsal, he would appreciate her using her other hand on his other ear. In the meantime, I had decided that we had reached the point of diminishing returns and asked my assistant to excuse the actors for the day.

The next morning, all was ready at 9:00. Somehow, Dorothy had found time to study her lines. I called for a final rehearsal for camera, lights, and sound. All went well until the slap, which Dorothy (carried away by the scene, no doubt) delivered with full force to Dick's left ear. She hit the jackpot. Widmark's arm shot up in instantaneous reaction, landing a terrific clout on the side of Dorothy's head. Tears popped out of her eyes—not from crying but from the concussion—and she flew backward clear across the set. Then, quite literally adding insult to injury, Widmark proceeded to lay her out.

"You no-talent bum!" he started . . . I felt that he needed a safety valve and that she had asked for it, so I let him carry on in that vein for a few moments, then asked them both to retire to their dressing rooms.

Dick later admitted that he was being a bit unfair. Dorothy Malone is by no means a no-talent bum. When the chips are down, she surprises with performances of depth and understanding, with all the right nuances in all the right places.

In half an hour tempers had cooled, but so had the atmosphere on the set. I decided to start shooting directly—in case of further action, I wanted it all on film. As the scene finished, Dick was to make an exit through the front door. He stopped suddenly, halfway across the room, and broke into a belly laugh. So did Dorothy, who was watching him leave. Over the door our cameraman, Joe MacDonald, had placed two crossed boxing gloves, surmounted by a sign which read, "Hail the Champ!" Joe had ruined the first take, but he had certainly saved the day.

As an actor, Hank Fonda has gotten about all the kudos a modest man can handle, so I'm going to give him a knock. Hank was one of the few leading actors who worked in the theater as much as he worked in films, perhaps more. Though Hollywood acknowledged him as a superactor, it had never quite given him the accolade of superstardom, and it was for this reason, perhaps, that he was inclined to prefer the legitimate stage. I had been warned that Fonda tended to hold back a little when working in a film, and indeed I found this to be the case.

Hank seemed surprised when I suggested he wasn't delivering 100 percent, but on due consideration admitted it might be so. He responded immediately, but was not completely convinced until he played a scene with Frank Gorshin, in the role of Widmark's hotheaded brother. In this scene, the regulators were faced, for the first time, by Fonda and Quinn. Fonda tries to get the cowboys to withdraw peacefully, but Gorshin goes for his gun. Fonda speaks quietly, pleadingly, "Billy . . ," as though begging him not to commit suicide, then pulls his own gun and shoots him. All this was timed to the split second and was very effective. And simple—but it convinced Fonda that we were trying for something outside the usual run. It's truly remarkable how little it sometimes takes to make things come together.

One of the most effective suspense-in-action scenes that can be staged is the call-out, with its fast-draw climax. We had several in our film. I was ready to try every trick known to get really quick gun action—

undercranking the camera, double-cutting the film, using experts as doubles—but none of these proved necessary. When I rehearsed the first such scene, I found that Fonda could draw almost faster than the camera could register, though he professed himself to be unaware of it. I wound up looking for ways to slow up the action so the audience could savor it properly, and not miss it with the blink of an eyelid.

For my supporting cast, I rounded up Tom Drake, Wally Ford, Richard Arlen, Don "Red" Barry, Regis Toomey, Vaughn Taylor, and Whit Bissell. I received a sharp note from Lou Schreiber, Buddy Adler's assistant, suggesting that my casting of so many "old-timers" was giving our film the look of a reissue. This attitude had always been a bone of contention between me and the studios. It seemed to me that the older performers had earned their spurs, had demonstrated their abilities, and deserved the right to make a decent living, so I always tried to use a number of veterans in my films, especially those who needed the work. And since new blood is a necessity in any continuing enterprise, I tried to balance out my cast with as much fresh talent as I could get away with. Today, TV is a heartless machine in its treatment of our veterans. Just as it chews up and spits out plots by the thousands, so it uses up our human talent. One of the grimmest appellations that can be applied to an actor is the word "overexposed." The Italians are more honest than we are about these things. There I heard the word *"sputanato"* used frequently in the same context. Very plainly, it means "spit out."

My more youthful half of the supporting cast included Dolores Michaels, DeForest Kelley, Paul Comi, and Frank Gorshin, who, besides being a good actor, kept us well entertained with his inimitable imitations.

The film was a ball—good story, fine actors, no strain, no paranoia—I scarcely needed a holiday when I had finished. But I was going to get one anyway. While I was still in production, D. A. Doran of Paramount had called, offering me an exciting new property. And, whether I liked it or not, I had to take a trip around the world.

FITS AND STARTS

Han Suyin is a collection of contradictions. To begin with, her real name is Elizabeth Macomber. She is a Eurasian, half white and half Chinese. She has a fine reputation as a doctor, but she is better known in the West as an exceedingly skillful writer of romantic novels. A staunch feminist who fought for women's rights in that most difficult arena, the Orient, long before women's lib was a catch-phrase in America, she nevertheless creates heroines who are traditionally feminine and extremely "giving." She is tall, lanky, and plain; yet men scramble for her attention. She preaches freedom—and is denied a visa to the United States. Some people have everything.

Han Suyin had written *A Many-Splendored Thing*, which 20th and Henry King proceeded to turn into a record-breaking film starring William Holden and Jennifer Jones, appending "Love Is" to the title. I can remember no love story, well and intelligently made, failing to clean up at the box office. The men who control the purse strings today, however, must know something that I don't—they rarely film a love story.

Paramount had bought Miss Suyin's latest book, *The Mountain Is Young*, for $250,000, a fairly staggering sum in 1958, and now they wanted me to produce and direct it. There were so many imponderables involved in its production that it was necessary to go to the source, and the source was the mysterious kingdom of Nepal.

I arranged to postpone final editing on *Warlock* until after my return, and on January 16, 1959, we set off for Katmandu. Six of us were making the trip. Besides myself, there were Bob Aurthur, whom I had asked to write the script, Luigi Luraschi, our liaison man, John Larson, the art director, Don Robb, a production manager, and, of course, Jean. Prop planes were still the order of the day, so we arranged a rather leisurely itinerary. There would be two days in Hawaii, one in Tokyo, a day and a half in Hong Kong, three days in Singapore, and one in Calcutta—then Nepal for a couple of weeks. Jean had never traveled west of Hawaii, so each new city was a treat for her, and Paramount's representatives did their very considerable best to make each stopover, however short, a pleasant one.

Our longest en-route call was Singapore, where we were to meet Han Suyin. The Raffles Hotel was all we had imagined it would be, but our fabulous Royal Suite, with its built-in waterfall, was almost beyond imagination. I usually drink tap water wherever I go, without bad results, but Singapore gave me my comeuppance. I spent the first day in bed, but with Jean bathing my brow and Han Suyin taking my pulse, it was almost worth it.

Miss Suyin was operating two clinics in the Singapore area, but she managed to give us her evenings. My colleagues fell all over themselves escorting the gal to dinner, but she managed to play them off against each other quite neatly. One evening of good conversation was spent at the home of Lok Wan Tho, but during most of our time together, Bob and I tried to learn what she was trying to say in her novel. (We knew what *we* thought she was saying, but authors' and readers' views are by no means necessarily identical.) She could tell us very little, which wasn't surprising. Most artists create from a gut feeling, and digging into the motives, ideas, and attitudes behind the expressed manifestation would require deep, lengthy, and probably painful probing. In fact, I have a natural suspicion of an artist who can tell me exactly what his work is meant to convey. In deep water, the lower layers are usually murky.

Our reception in Calcutta was warm, but the city presents such a depressing picture of poverty and human degradation that it hardly encourages lingering. We were relieved to take off for Nepal the next day.

The aerial view of the valley of Katmandu is breathtaking. To the north the Himalayas rise in all their majesty, but the valley itself, a rich, alluvial plain, is an Oz-like patchwork of small towns and cultivated fields in all shades of brown, tan, gold, and green. From the moment we landed until the moment we left, our stay was a delight—the sights were almost bewilderingly exotic, and the people, from the wealthiest Rana to the poorest peasant, were extremely warm and friendly.

Nepal had been a closed kingdom for a hundred years. Then, in 1952, a bloodless palace revolution opened the country to visitors from abroad, but the only way in was by DC–3, and no rush of tourists had yet developed. The country was almost completely untouched and unspoiled. The only hotel in Katmandu was a renovated Rana palace, operated by an aging Russian ex-ballet dancer and his attractive young Scandinavian wife. (We already have here the ingredients of a first-class thriller.) Its rooms were large and colorful and its power source was dependable—it could be counted upon to cease functioning several times a day.

The city itself was full of exotic beauty. It seemed that three out of every four buildings were temples—religion was everywhere, and in all forms. There were Buddhist stupas, Hindu and Tantric temples, a number of them pagodas, a style of architecture the Chinese reputedly imported from Nepal. One had to walk carefully—any rock on the road might have some spiritual significance. Shrines, some as large as a house, others as small as a breadbox, were scattered everywhere throughout the country.

In the village of Patan, we passed a family sacrificing a water buffalo. Its head had just been severed from its body and placed on a fire. The odor got to Jean, and we made a dash for the car. We got all the way back to the hotel, a half hour away, before she lost control. On the other hand, at a temple marking the spot where the god Vishnu had wielded his huge sword to cut a gorge in the mountains, thus draining the valley of its hundreds of square miles of water, I watched a family of four celebrating some occasion. When the officiating priest handed the father a chicken and a knife with which to slit its throat, the man rebelled at the small act of violence, and I felt a little better about the human race.

On another day, our party, accompanied by some of our new Nepalese friends, was flown in the king's private plane to the town of Pokhara. I had always considered height a relative phenomenon, and had thought that the Himalayas, in their own setting, would scarcely look more imposing than the Alps or the Canadian Rockies in theirs. How wrong I was. As I sat in the copilot's seat and looked out at the massive grandeur of the mighty range, I was left absolutely speechless. There are no East-West roads in mountainous Nepal, and the first wheel the natives of Pokhara had ever seen had been on the first plane to land there not many years before.

We came down in a meadow on the outskirts of town. Behind it rose a beautiful mountain, a twin of the Matterhorn, but loftier by a full two miles. And directly in front of the town was a huge and solitary sign—"Drink Coca-Cola." The town's chief, a Buddhist priest, had brought civilization to his Gurung subjects—he owned the local franchise.

Bagwan Sahai, the Indian ambassador, invited us for an evening of Indian food and music. Ravi Shankar, the famous sitar virtuoso, and his three fellow musicians played for four unforgettable hours. But the young Rana prince who was with us requested only that we send him more Rock records.

After ten days of beautiful countryside, exotic temples, and warm hospitality, I felt I had seen all I needed to see—at least for this trip. Nepal could certainly furnish a most unusual and exciting background for a superior film. Leaving the others behind to take care of some unfinished business, Jean and I headed for Bombay, by way of Calcutta. We should have waited.

We had left a few days earlier than scheduled and, arriving at Patna, found all flights already overbooked. It meant an overnight train ride to Calcutta. We bought our first-class tickets and spent the greater part of the afternoon at the railroad station. Most of the people on the platform had huge mounds of bedding with them, and Jean and I felt sorry they were burdened with so much extra baggage. We soon found out why. The train pulled into the station and we entered our compartment—a large, empty room, with bare iron shelves serving as berths, but no bedding or amenities of any sort. Also, there were two other names posted as occupants of what we thought was a private compartment. We awaited the arrival of our fellow passengers with some anxiety, but by departure time, neither had arrived. Just as the train pulled out, a young Indian stepped through the doorway. He was an employee of the railroad, and he asked permission to ride with us a couple of stops down the road. He was a pleasant fellow and spoke English quite well. Just as he left the train at his stop, he advised us to lock our doors for the night and keep them locked. That did little to relieve our already apprehensive mood.

It was a very long night. Our train stopped at every little hamlet along the route. We had purchased packaged "lunches" for our dinner—only the hardboiled eggs were edible. Once I ventured into the toilet—the overwhelming odors bounced me out in a hurry. It was bitter cold, and only Jean's full-length mink coat kept us from freezing. We were both fearing the worst when, during a stop at one of our way stations at about 1:00 A.M., there was loud shouting and a furious banging on our door. We cowered on our bare shelf, holding each other tightly, like Hansel and Gretel before the old witch. After what seemed an eternity, the train pulled out, leaving our "attackers" behind. (The next day, in Bombay, the English-language paper headlined a thuggee attack on a train in which several passengers had been killed.)

We finally arrived in Calcutta at 6:00 A.M. It almost looked good. As our taxi pulled out of the station it nearly ran down a tall, slender, bearded, dhoti-clad man. Our driver spewed out a stream of vituperation. The jaywalker turned and looked at us—on his face was the most gentle smile I have ever seen on a human being. Jean and I reacted simultaneously—this was the India we had been hoping to find.

Calcutta and Bombay are literally East and West. Bombay is cleaner (the sacred cattle are kept out of the central city) and less depressing (so are the starving people). The odor of human urine and excrement is not so all-pervading. Some years later, I came to know a Pakistani sudent-observer on my set well enough to casually broach the subject of objectionable odors in the Orient. "I know what you mean," he said. "When I first came to this country, I found the smell of gas and oil fumes nearly intolerable."

In Bombay, we visited Meboob Khan's studio to check his facilities, meet a number of his stars, and look at a few of his films. I was impressed by all three, but not by the Indians' working procedures. Stars played simultaneously in a number of films, and a producer had to grab a scene or two whenever he could. A star's agent would say—"Sajit is available on the thirtieth and thirty-first of January, the eighteenth of February, and the eleventh, twelveth and thirteenth of April." And so it would go over a long period of time. In between the available dates, the production marked time. I witnessed one frustrating scene. Meboob took us down to one of his stages to watch a company at work, but the set was deserted. On inquiry, Khan learned that the star had failed to show up for his scheduled day's work. A rather volatile man, Khan ordered the set to be struck immediately and it was. Sometime after lunch, the tardy star arrived, found the set demolished, and stormed into Khan's office. There was little meditation at the studio that day.

After a couple of days in London, Jean and I returned to the warmth and security of our home in California. Paramount was itching to get under way. Doran suggested that the studio would appreciate anything I could do to ensure my availability by the time the script was finished. I was more than willing—I, too, was excited at the prospect of a story which, I felt, could be one of the most unusual films in many a year. My enthusiasm clouded my judgment. I had one more film to make at Fox, and in my eagerness to have it out of the way, I agreed to do the first property I was offered: *The Blue Angel.*

There was nothing wrong with the script, nor with the actors already committed. It was just that it had been done before, and had become a minor classic. There is one ironclad rule for directors in Hollywood: Never remake a classic (major or minor). You just can't win.

I've mentioned that I have always been puzzled by the tendency to lump many old films together in the "classic" category. I believe far greater discrimination should be practiced. Some of the old classics I've seen, like *Greed* or *The Cabinet of Doctor Caligari* are, to my mind, scarcely unforgettable art. They may be admired for their attempts at handling difficult or profound subject matter, or for certain technical innovations, but the acting, for instance, was excruciatingly bad, even for its day. Films like Murnau's *Sunrise* or Lang's *M*, on the other hand, hold up surprisingly well in all categories, and truly deserve the accolade of "classic."

I looked at von Sternberg's *The Blue Angel* a couple of times (not *many* times, as Josef von Sternberg suggested in his autobiography), and didn't find too much to frighten me, except for one thing—Marlene Dietrich. She was a little overweight, her voice was a good octave higher (and reedier) than I had remembered, but she was extraordinarily charismatic and oh, so honest. Much as I had admired Emil Jannings in silent films, here he was a ham. The other actors were not particularly competent, but Marlene—no one could spoil her. She—and she alone—made the picture.

Our script stayed close to the original because that was hard to beat. Kurt Jurgens, as the professor, gave a beautifully shaded performance. John Banner and Theodore Bikel furnished solid support. But the girl . . .

We went round and round when casting. The studio, Jack Cummings, the producer—all of us realized we had a problem. Dietrichs don't turn up every day—not even every decade. Eventually, we had to admit there was probably nobody around who was any better than Mai Britt. She had been a moderate overnight sensation in *The Young Lions*, and had played a nondescript part in a Dick Powell melodrama. As far as acting experience went, that was it. But she was attractive and leggy, necessary requirements for the part, and she did her best. She worked very, very hard, and we eventually wound up with a film none of us had to be ashamed of. We even received a number of reviews (and a number of letters) comparing it more than favorably with the original. But, on the whole, it got lost in the shuffle, and that was probably just as well. The rule still holds—never remake a classic, even a minor one.

But at least my deal with 20th was completed. There was some talk of a new contract, but I wasn't particularly interested. There was a great project awaiting me at Paramount, one that would obliterate any disappointment I felt over *The Blue Angel*. Or so I thought.

The script for *The Mountain Is Young* was finished, and a very good script it was, but Paramount was taking no action. I had been in touch with Doran during the production of *The Blue Angel*. We had discussed the progress of the script, and possible casting. But now that we were ready to move, there was nothing but silence—officially, that is. Rumors were plentiful—some executive of Southern extraction had finally read the book and found that the male lead was a "black" Indian, the production department wouldn't risk such a long and distant location, the budget was too high, the situation in India was shaky—they went on and on. But none of the brass would ever give me a straight answer—not even a yes or a no. I don't remember that the project was ever officially closed—like an old soldier, it just faded away. For years and years I have tried to puzzle out the reason.

Just recently I was reviewing my records and came across copies of two telegrams, both dated May 18, 1959. The first is to Y. Frank Freeman, at Paramount, and reads: "Very sorry to hear of your resignation but happy if easing of labors will help to add more years to a long and very useful life—Eddie Dmytryk." The second is to Jack Karp, also at Paramount: "Congratulations on your new well-deserved post. I hope for long, prosperous and pleasant association—Eddie Dmytryk." I realized that these two wires said it all. Once more I had been squeezed by a change in administration. Freeman had been a freewheeling executive. Karp believed, it seemed, that if you didn't make a creative decision, you couldn't make a mistake.

But I was at the studio and being paid for films I hadn't made yet, so Doran presented me with a property and an actor. The property was Michael Barrett's novel, *Appointment in Zahrain*, and the actor was Clark Gable. The story was a better-than-average melodrama, and the prospect of working with Gable again was pleasing. I agreed to take on the project.

After one hit and a near miss, Aurthur was already financially out of reach, so I looked for a "new" writer. I decided on Richard Matheson, author of *The Beardless Warriors* and a number of excellent out-of-this-world horror tales. He was intrigued with the idea of tailoring a script for Gable and started work with a good deal of enthusiasm. A few weeks later, when Gable was at the studio shooting his last "process" scenes for *The Misfits*, we had a short discussion about the nearly finished script. He, too, was looking forward to the film. But two weeks later he was dead.

All of Hollywood felt the shock, as did many people of the world. It hit Matheson particularly hard. He lost heart completely and found it impossible to finish the script. Every line had been written with the King in mind and now it had died with him. At the studio's insistence, I hired another writer, but my heart wasn't in it either. Finally I was allowed to beg off. The film was made some months later with another star—it was a dismal failure.

Before the *Zahrain* project had started, my agent, Charles Feldman, who had turned to producing as a sideline, asked me to direct his production of Nelson Algren's *Walk on the Wild Side*. But Paramount's preemption of my services, censor problems, and a few other things had prevented our getting together. Now the way was open for me to accept the offer. It wasn't easy sledding—nothing ever was with Feldman— but, one by one, most of the obstacles were overcome, at least on the surface.

Charlie, at one time, had been an avid art collector. There was a story that he bought one young artist's painting, found it too cheerful for his taste, and had the artist add clouds, rain, and a deep, dark mood in general. True or not, the story was descriptively accurate, and I should have taken the hint. Besides, I had done some script-doctoring for him during my blacklist period, and I really knew better. But Feldman was not one of the town's best agents for nothing—he could have sweet-talked Hitler into making Ben Gurion his Minister of Culture.

Feldman could not get a studio deal until he had the censor's okay, and up to now it had been withheld. So my first job was to get the script (written by a whole gaggle of writers) past Shurlock, the industry censor. I rewrote and cut a number of scenes and eventually got the needed approval, and Charlie got his studio deal, with Columbia. Almost immediately, he started replacing the censored material, and I started objecting to being immorally and unethically used—a tug-of-war that continued throughout the film.

At this point I tried to get out of both my picture and my agency contracts, but Feldman was adamant. (A new seven-year agency agreement had been one of his conditions of my making the film, though Charlie verbally agreed to cancel the deal if our association turned out to be an unhappy one.) As a concession, however, he promised to go to Europe the day shooting started and leave the production in my hands. Stupidly, I took him at his word. Now started the hemstitching that Feldman was so fond of—I never knew how many closet writers he had already used on the script, but the first acknowledged one was Clifford Odets. I had known Odets at RKO when he was preparing and shooting a heavily dramatic picture with Cary Grant—perhaps the only Grant film to fail at the box office. Clifford was now living in Beverly Hills, posing—and being accepted—as a serious authority on modern painting—a gratifying status which pays very poorly. He needed the money.

"I can make any scene interesting," he told me with dubious pride, "even though it may have nothing to do with the story."

The three or four scenes he wrote for the film fit this description to a T. They were not used.

Next came a very pleasant interlude with Ben Hecht. Feldman hired him to polish the script, and for two weeks I "lived in" at his home in Nyack, New York, while he conscientiously and meticulously reworked the dialogue from page one to the final fadeout. Ben was perhaps the most "organized" writer I have ever worked with.

Besides enjoying the company of Ben himself, the highlights of my visit were a dinner at which his nearby neighbor, Helen Hayes, was a guest, and being a vicarious "insider" at the second Johansson-Patterson fight. Johansson had knocked out Patterson to win the championship in their first battle, and was an odds-on favorite to whip his glass-jawed opponent in the rematch. A day or two before the fight, the nation's sports reporters converged on New York City. Many were friends of Hecht and called to pay their respects. In spite of what I had learned years ago from Budd Schulberg and Mike Jacobs, I was surprised to hear that the writers, without exception, predicted Patterson would be the winner by a knockout in the fourth. And the fight followed the script—Patterson knocked out Johansson in the fourth by hitting him on top of the head, and there's just no way you can get enough power into that kind of a punch to hurt a twelve-year-old.

Back at the front, though Feldman criticized Hecht's work as not sexy enough, we got on with the job of casting. As might be expected, most of the leads were Feldman clients. This helped establish a new guild rule in Hollywood—one could be either a producer or an agent, not both. This was the second exclusionary rule brought about primarily because of Feldman's activities. The first was the Writers Guild rule prohibiting an agent from buying a client's work, then reselling it at a profit. We had Laurence Harvey, Anne Baxter, Barbara Stanwyck, Joanne Moore, Jane Fonda, and Feldman's paramour, Capucine—on the whole, a cast of quality. (As you can see, this was a woman's picture.)

We started production on location in New Orleans. We made good friends, savored its food, listened to its music, and enjoyed working in the old quarter, the above-ground cemeteries, and other colorful areas. Everything was going well, with one exception: Feldman had not left for Europe as he had promised.

We came home to a foreboding change—the period of the film was 1931, and all the costumes had been artfully designed to suggest that period without being too bizarre. Feldman decided that Capucine must wear only Cardin, and of the latest design. Our other ladies all dressed 1931 and looked fine. Capucine dressed 1961 and looked out of place and time. I contrived my setups to minimize the contrast as much as possible.

Now Jane Fonda entered the picture, and with her came a young Greek exquisite, reputedly an ex-ballet dancer. I had heard of Fonda's propensity to work with outside advisers, but I had gotten assurances from both Charlie and Jane that her "secretary" would in no way interfere with her work in the film. I could do nothing but sit back and wait for something I knew had to come.

As the film progressed, the polarization continued—on several levels. Feldman kept sending me rewrites and added scenes (written by Lord-knows-who) which I would show to the actors involved and then, with their agreement, throw them out. Mostly they were scenes which today would be called soft porn, and in 1961 stood not a chance in hell of getting by the industry censor. Charlie was just a few years ahead of his time.

Stanwyck and Baxter, the old pros, were steady as rocks, trying hard to do their best while ignoring the silly backstage shenanigans. Harvey, less stoic, but just as conscientious, was working hard at staying on an even keel. But Capucine, Jane, and her secretary, were in the enemy camp. I didn't blame Capucine. She was living with Charlie and had to go home every night to face his questions. There they were often joined by Jane and company, who added fuel to their fire. The inevitable blowup came one morning on the set.

It was a very important scene—Capucine's death scene, the climax of the film—and we had rehearsed it thoroughly the afternoon before. Everyone had gone home feeling good and secure about everything. But now, as I was setting up a final runthrough, Capucine informed me she had worked on the scene the night before and had a few ideas of her own to offer. Taking Larry by the hand, she played her own version of the scene. It looked like something "choreographed" for an amateur ballet. When she had finished, Harvey was seething. The other players looked embarrassed. I started to point out some of the more obvious weaknesses of her concept, but the poor girl, obviously under strong inner pressure, began a spirited if illogical defense. At this Larry erupted. It was Widmark all over again, without the slap.

Eventually, I cleared the set of everybody, including the crew. Then I sat down with my assistant and the production manager and laid down a few regulations. Jane's secretary was to be barred from the lot, and our New York art director, who was a member of the cabal, was barred from the set—both for the duration of the picture. Work would start again after lunch as if nothing had happened—and, strangely enough, it did.

Somehow or other, I finished shooting, completed my cut, and turned the film over to Feldman and Columbia. Saul Bass conceived and executed a main title which was a masterpiece. After all the tribulations of the production, the picture was well received by the critics and the public, and made a little money for everyone involved—except me. I gave up $70,000 in deferment to get out of my contract with Famous Artists Agency.

BEFORE *THE FLYING NUN*

T here was this Italian who died and found himself at St. Peter's gate. But the holy doorman wouldn't let him enter.

"I don't understand," protested the Italian. "I was a good Catholic. I went to church on all high holidays, and I am buried in hallowed ground."

"There are a few other requirements," answered St. Peter, "but because you occasionally went to church and are buried in hallowed ground, I'll bend the rules a little and give you a choice. You can go to regular hell or to Italian hell."

"What's regular hell like?" asked the Italian.

"Well," said St. Peter, "for twelve hours a day, you eat, drink, love, and live it up. Then they nail you to a cross, light a fire under your feet, and for twelve hours you burn."

The Italian shuddered. "And what is Italian hell like?" he asked.

"Well," said the good saint, "in Italian hell, for twelve hours a day, you eat, drink, love, and live it up. Then they nail you to a cross, light a fire under your feet, and for the next twelve hours you burn."

"But there's no difference!" complained the Italian.

"Ah!" said St. Peter. "In Italian hell, sometimes they forget to bring the nails, sometimes the matches won't light . . . ."

That's an Italian story, and only the Italians could take such a perverse pride in this picture of the Italian state of affairs.

I was in Rome to make *The Reluctant Saint*. It was the one collateral reward for the misery of *A Walk on the Wild Side*. While at Columbia, I had read *The Saint of the Satellites*, a tale by John Fante and Joe Petracca, a somewhat fictionalized, semi-biography of St. Joseph of Cupertino, who lived in the first half of the seventeenth century. St. Joseph was a simple man, a bumbling near-idiot. His mind was an empty vessel, and, since nature abhors a vacuum, it was filled with the grace of God. As a result, more miracles have been credited to this simple man than to any other on the long list of saints. Among other miraculous acts, there were over one hundred recorded instances of levitation, one in the presence of Pope Urban VII and his retainers.

Fante and Petracca had written a delightfully funny yet touching treatment of a few key years in the saint's life. I gave it to Mike Frankovich. He read it, and after a few minutes of conversation, committed Columbia to finance the picture. Once in a while it could be done as easily as that.

Laurence Harvey had wanted to play St. Joseph, but was now unavailable. Jerry Lewis would have been right, but nobody would have believed him. Since the perils of living dangerously have seldom concerned me, I decided to try offbeat casting again. I flew to Munich and offered the part to a man who had played nothing but Nazis— Maximilian Schell. He was entranced. He had just won an Oscar for his role in *Judgment at Nuremburg*, and I thought I had a winner.

In England I enlisted the services of my old friend and coworker, John Sloan, as production manager and coproducer. Together we went to Rome, holed up at the Excelsior Hotel on the Via Veneto, and started asking questions. The answers didn't cheer us. It was impossible to round up a totally competent crew, we were told. Time meant nothing; cheating and stealing were rampant; contracts were worthless.

"The three most apt Italian mottoes," said one informant, "are, 'Non funzione' (It doesn't work), 'Non e' mea culpa' (It's not my fault), and 'Non so niente' (I know nothing)." Like most scuttlebutt, it was just talk—the truth was much worse.

Jean, our two children, two dogs, and a cat were coming to Rome, and I had to find an apartment. Our Italian secretary found an attractive flat at a not unreasonable price. When I went to see it, the price was doubled.

"You're an American," explained the owner. "For Americans the price is always twice that for an Italian."

"Even if it stays empty?" I asked.

"Even if it stays empty," she said. It stayed empty.

I had them block off four rooms at the Caesar Augustus Hotel, complete with balcony where we could watch the cars crash into each other on the Via Francia on a quiet Sunday afternoon, and they served us very well.

What can't be faulted in Italy are the locations. Twenty miles from the Via Veneto are villages which, outside of electric lines, have not changed one whit in the last three hundred years. The housewives still get their news and their water at the town fountain, and the garbage is still dumped out of the window or into the nearest ravine. And the pickers still bring their grapes to the wine presses by donkey. Going back to St. Joseph's time would be no trick at all. Our problem was with the present. My art director kept stalling on a couple of important locations, saying the owners did not wish to cooperate. Since they had been quite affable when we had first talked, we were surprised. John Sloan decided to investigate. The owners were quite willing, he found, but they refused to pay the exorbitant kickback the art director demanded. John straightened it out in a hurry.

At a restaurant outside of Rome I had a happy accident: I ran into Ricardo Montalban. He was just finishing some Italian swashbuckler and would be available to play an important role in our film. Fortune couldn't have been kinder.

My cast included Max Schell, Ricardo Montalban, Lea Padovani, Akim Tamiroff, Carlo Crocollo, and a combination of expatriate Americans and eager Italians. As far as the actors were concerned, there wasn't a bad egg in the lot. The same could not be said for the crew. I had brought Penny Richards, my cameraman, from England. As always, he was a lifesaver. The Italian electricians were very good, as were the grips, but there it stopped. The rest of the crew were living proof of Murphy's Law: "If anything can go wrong, it will." Not one day passed without its unpleasant surprise. Mara Blasetti was my bilingual assistant production manager. Each morning, as I came to the location or the set, she stood waiting, wringing her hands. And her first line was invariably, "Oh, Mr. Dmytryk. It's nobody's fault, but . . ."

"But what, Mara?"

"Well, it's nobody's fault, but we can't start shooting, *maestro*. (Anyone with the least standing or authority must have a title in Italy. If you disclaim the right to use any, they will supply one—or half a dozen.) The wardrobe isn't here."

"Why isn't the wardrobe here, Mara?"

"It's nobody's fault, but the wardrobe trailer ran off the road."

"For Christ's sake, Mara, stop saying it's nobody's fault! Who was pulling the trailer?"

"It was being pulled by a jeep, sir."

"And was anyone driving the jeep?"

"Oh, yes, sir, but it wasn't—"

"I know, Mara. It's nobody's fault."

The special effects department is a very weak link in a European crew, particularly down in the boot. One scene called for our simple-minded young Joseph to cut down a huge pine, which falls on and demolishes a farmer's hut. First, the hut: I found it was being built of solid cement blocks, well mortared. It would stand up under a major California earthquake.

"Don't worry." The crew chief was confident. "It will go down like a house of cards."

"*Spero,*" I said, crossing my fingers.

Next, the tree: It was about 12 feet tall, with a girth of about 4 inches. Obviously, it wouldn't smash a doghouse.

"But we can't find a bigger tree," wailed the chief.

Now, just four or five days before there had been a violent windstorm, and the road from Rome to Sutri was literally lined with huge, fallen Aleppo pines. The chief's eyes lit up.

"Of course!" he said. "We'll get one—*subito!*"

And they did. On the morning of the shooting, I asked if they were sure the tree would destroy the hut. The crew chief took me inside and pointed to a huge hydraulic ram, set up to smash the walls from the inside. They had moved in a cannon to do the work of a flyswatter. But a people who would design a machine the size of a small locomotive to brew a cup of coffee—well, I was willing to be convinced. I had no choice.

The tree was felled. It crashed into the roof of the hut and stopped dead. Not a tile crumbled. From inside the hut came a loud pounding sound, but the walls of the house stood firm. I yelled, "Cut!" and waited for the hydraulic ram to cease pounding. The harried chief came out of the hut, looked at me, then delicately shrugged his shoulders.

"*Non funzione,*" he said.

I moved on to the next location.

For some reason, which is a complete mystery to me, only Hollywood has good property men. They are usually better than good, and compared with those of any other country, they are miraculous.

I am normally a very quiet director—I won't even let my assistant raise his voice. Early on in Rome, I was being briefed by an American director who had made some films in Italy.

"You have to shout at them," he told me.

"Not I," I said. "I never shout at anyone." (Not on the set, that is.)

"You will," he said smugly.

And I did.

There was a special rock we used on location to prop up the broken head of a terra-cotta Madonna. There were a number of scenes with this prop, some on location, some at the studio. As we shot it for the last time on location, I summoned the prop man.

"That rock is very important—*molto importante.*"

"Si, dottore."

"Please take very good care of it—we will use it back at the studio." I had Mara translate it into better Italian—I wanted no mistakes.

"Certo," he said, a little put out.

A couple of weeks later, we were shooting the head of the Madonna in the studio. It was propped up on a couple of small rocks. I summoned the prop man.

"Where is the rock for the Madonna?"

"There," he said, pointing to the two rocks.

"Those aren't correct," I said. "Where is the original one?"

"That's it," he persisted. "The same one."

I called over the script girl, who had taken stills of the Madonna on location. The prop man caved in—he was almost crying.

"Now where is the original rock?" I asked.

"Non so," he whimpered. "I don't know."

"Cretino!" I screamed. *"Stronzo!"* Two hours later, when I had personally found a workable substitute and made my shot, he came up to me smiling.

"You see?" he said. "Everything worked out fine. There was no need to get excited."

I started screaming again.

I kept reminding myself of Archimedes, of Galileo, of Giordano Bruno and Leonardo, of Marconi and Fermi. If balance is a requisite of nature, it is no wonder Italy has bred so many geniuses. The answer, of course, is not too difficult to find. For over 2,000 years, Italy has lived a kaleidoscopic political life—and it has bred a nation of cheerful anarchists. In many respects it is the freest nation in the world. There are many laws, many strictures, legal, religious, and social, but nobody really gives a damn, though the bloody acts of the Red Brigades may soon bring a change in this attitude. That anarchy translates itself into something else in their work. Every Italian workman believes he is a master of improvisation—and that may be so. But most improvisation can in no way compete with careful planning. In some of my discussions I pointed out that I, too, liked to improvise, but always on a very solid base. But it's hard to change the habits of centuries.

In the meantime, Jean, who was then pregnant, was having problems. Her obstetrician was the most highly recommended specialist in Rome—and a very pleasant fellow indeed. But though she tried not to show it, Jean was none too sure of Roman efficiency. Some of her anxiety manifested itself in false labor pains. I made a practice run to the Salvator Mundi Hospital at least once a week—I wanted to be sure there were no detours when the time came. Sure enough, one night, though it was about three weeks early, Jean experienced what seemed to be real labor. We tried to reach the doctor, but he was nowhere to be found, not in his city office, not at home, nor in his office at the hospital. I put Jean and her small suitcase in the car and we arrived at Salvator Mundi in record time.

The next day, in the late afternoon, she called me. "Pick me up on your way home. It was a false alarm."

"What does the doctor say?" I asked.

"I don't know," she answered. "They haven't found him yet."

When I picked her up, I got the rest of the story. Against the strong objections of the nurses, she had packed and walked out of her room. The corridor was crowded. A young woman was taking her baby home, and there had been the customary party. As the young couple and their friends moved away down the hallway, Jean's doctor stood waving good-bye. Jean brushed past him.

"Good-bye," she said.

The doctor reacted with a classic double-take. When he recovered, he ran after her. "You shouldn't worry if you can't find me," he said. "We have a very good midwife at this hospital."

Jean returned to the hotel, called TWA, and booked tickets for herself, the two kids, the dogs, and the cat. She had to fib a little about the length of her pregnancy, but the next day she was on her way to California. I worried a little, but fortunately Dinah Shore was on the flight, and she helped take care of Jean, the kids, and the animals all the way home. Three weeks later, my daughter Rebecca was born.

Despite what I've described, Italians and some Hollywood directors have made some exceptional films in Italy. The answer is—time. The average Italian director moves into a set, sits down, and thinks. His crew waits. Eventually, he decides what he wants to do and what he needs to do it. Now it is the director's turn to wait while the crew works to fulfill his requirements—which might take a day or a week. When all is ready, he starts shooting. If something has been overlooked, he screams a lot, suspends work, and waits until the oversight has been corrected. Then he begins all over again.

The average American director does not work in this fashion. He plans ahead and expects everything—at least everything the script calls for—to be ready and waiting when he moves onto a set. If special props or equipment are required, he usually tells his A.D. a good deal ahead of time—if he pulls a surprise, he must pay the consequences. But most Hollywood crews have a rare sense of anticipation and even, when needed, improvisation.

When John Wayne worked his first picture for John Ford as a prop man, so the story goes, he asked around.

"Always have a coffin handy," he was told. "Ford always needs a coffin."

Nothing remotely resembling a coffin was called for in the script, but Wayne decided to take no chances. He loaded a coffin on the prop truck and for weeks carted it around from location to location. He began to think he had been had. But one day near the end of the film, far out in the desert somewhere, Ford called him over.

"I want a coffin," said Ford.

"Yes, sir!" said the Duke, and in a few minutes hauled it in on his back. It was the start of a long relationship and a fairly successful career.

We had been farsighted and had set our schedule at 60 days. That's what it took to make a simple film I could have made in Hollywood in 30. But, I wouldn't have had the colorful medieval towns, the typical southern Italian countryside, the interesting churches, or the Roman ruins. They were worth far more than all the pain, the strained vocal cords, and the additional 30 days.

While Bel Air burned, I finished the cutting and the dubbing in Rome. My dubbing mixer was a Milanese—precise, intelligent, and very efficient. I couldn't have asked for better. Nino Rota composed the score. When I dropped in at his flat to hear some themes, I found him whacking away at his music. He assured me it was not for the film but for an opera he was writing. He seemed a little harassed.

"If only I knew English well enough to work in your language," he complained, "I would be much further ahead." I was surprised.

"But Italian is *the* language of opera," I said.

"Not at all," said Nino. "English has such a large vocabulary, so many words that mean approximately the same thing. If I want to write one note, I could use a one-syllable Anglo-Saxon word. If I wanted to stretch it over five, I could find a five-syllable word of Greek or Latin origin—and so on, in between. In Italian, there is usually only one word for one meaning, and it's usually polysyllabic. That makes it very hard—the music has to fit the words, never the other way around."

He wrote the score in a universal language, and it was beautiful.

Something about the Italian temperament makes one forget the hurts, the foul-ups, the settling-for-less. I left Italy in a relaxed and pleasant state of mind. My first stop was New York. I showed the film to the Columbia executives. They were delighted—with the picture, but not with its prospects.

"I don't know how we're going to sell it," said Columbia VIP Jaffe. I was sure they would find a way.

In Hollywood we had a number of private showings, and the reactions were gratifying. With very few exceptions, everyone loved the film. I was so pleased that I failed to pick up an ominous undertone. Ruth Waterbury, a veteran fan-mag editor and critic, approached me after one showing. She was an old friend. "I didn't want to come tonight, Eddie," she said. "I expected to be completely bored. But I enjoyed it thoroughly. You have a great film here."

There was one other small fly in the ointment. A few—very few—people thought I had to be kidding. They couldn't believe that an ex-Communist and self-professed agnostic would make an honest film about a levitating saint, and nothing I said could change their minds. So I gave up trying. The priests and monks and nuns and rabbis and ministers who saw *The Reluctant Saint* laughed with it and loved it, and some of my friends thought it was the best film I'd ever made. That was enough for me.

And it had to be because, like Ruth Waterbury, most of the people expected to be bored and stayed away in droves. As Jaffe had said, Columbia didn't know how to sell it—but neither did I. It was just one of those pictures people love *if* they happen to catch it, but something discourages them from wanting to see it in the first place. It was perhaps the only film I've ever made that honestly never came out of the red. It won the National Catholic Theater Conference's Drama Award for 1964, but, on the whole, I can only say in the words of the Italians, *"Non funzione."*

HOLLYWOOD
ON HOLLYWOOD:
THE CARPETBAGGERS

No one finds it strange that an experienced carpenter or a veteran butcher lacks a finger or two. A working cowhand will exhibit permanent marks of his skirmishes with barbed wire, and a football player lives with shaky knees. It is taken for granted that a manual laborer will carry the scars of his craft, but few people consider that attrition is inevitable among men and women who work with their minds.

By 1962 I had been in the studios for 39 years, about twice the length of time required for honorable retirement from the average civil or military service job. Physically, I was in my prime, but, mentally, I was hamstrung. I decided to take it easy. Hollywood was in the doldrums, and I wallowed in the calms—but from choice, not from necessity.

We had found absentee landlordism too great a luxury and had sold the Kona coffee farm. Our acreage in Agoura also went on the block, since we decided we would never build there, and the offers from land developers were too good to resist. But after a year or so the irritating effects of the pull of the land and a sizable bank account prompted me to look for a way to scratch both itches. To this day I don't know whether my dear, unselfish wife was anxious to please me, or whether she, too, carried a bucolic streak (I suspect it was mostly the former), but she wholeheartedly joined in my search for another farm.

In the meantime, a year of minimum mental strain had done wonders for my brain lesions, and when Paramount surprised me with a call, I was in a receptive mood. My old home studio had a new production chief—Marty Rackin, whom I had known only casually as a first-class raconteur and a second-class screenwriter. I had stopped reading the "trades" some time before and I was surprised to learn he held the post—I was even more surprised to learn how he had "earned" it. This is his story as he told it to me.

Marty had produced a few Alan Ladd action films when that actor's career was in its sunset phase (a euphemism for sharp decline). Lately he had been involved in some third-rate (his own evaluation) TV fare in Italy. He had tried—unsuccessfully—to sell it in Hollywood, and on his way back to Rome had decided to drop in on one of Paramount's New York executives in a last-ditch attempt to peddle his product. An hour's sales pitch, which included about 50 minutes of funny stories, brought an invitation to return the next day for a meeting with Barney Balaban. Though he considered the prospects slim, he postponed his flight and returned to Paramount the next day primed to ballyhoo his Italian goods. Marty had hardly gotten his first laugh of the day when Balaban suggested, "How would you like to work for us?"

Rackin was startled, but though he was willing to sweep stages if that would keep him in the country, he knew his agent would be annoyed if he made a decision without consultation, so he stalled for time.

"As what?" he asked.

"As head of production in Hollywood," said Balaban.

It takes a great executive to make such snap decisions—or a very desperate one. And those were desperate times. But in all fairness, Marty Rackin proved to be as good a production executive as any the studio had had since the voluntary retirement or demise of the Hollywood tycoons, and probably better than any who came after him.

After the usual prologue of rapid chatter and surefire jokes, Marty got down to business. Had I read Harold Robbins' book, *The Carpetbaggers?* I read tons of nonfiction, from archaeology to zoology, with accents on history and mathematics, but my fictional intake is usually limited to the comics, the sports pages, and science fiction. I knew about the book, of course, since Hollywood had been buzzing for months about Robbins' tour de force—even though the guessing game concerning the novel's real-life prototypes was hardly a challenge. But pornography leaves me cold, and I had found the temptation easy to resist. Now I rued the oversight.

"No problem," said Marty. Paramount wanted me to make the film, but there were still a few things to sort out with the owner of the property, Joe Levine, so I would have time to read the book and get back with my reaction.

I read the novel that afternoon and evening and found it very intriguing. Robbins had capitalized far more than most writers on that old cliché: Truth is stranger . . .

The novel's leading character, Jonas Cord, had hardly had a change of costume. Howard Hughes had always fascinated me—he was a man of such great talents, great eccentricities, and great fears. I had heard a few anecdotes from people who had firsthand contact with the billionaire. The first two came from Lewis Milestone, who made some of Hughes' early and excellent products, including films like *Two Arabian Knights* and *The Front Page.*

One evening Milestone walked into his usual projection room to look at his rushes. The operator informed him that he'd have to use another room; this one was out of order. On his way past the booth, Millie stuck his head in to see what was wrong. There, on the floor, was a spread-out sheet, and on the sheet sat Howard Hughes, surrounded by the hundreds of parts of a completely stripped-down projection machine.

"What the hell are you doing?" asked the surprised director.

"Just wanted to see how it worked," replied Hughes. But it must have been child's play to a man who later helped design the Constellation and the Spruce Goose.

On another occasion, Milestone had just finished his final cut of one of Hughes' films—*The Front Page*, I believe. He had turned it over to the lab for negative cutting and was enjoying a few days' rest at his lodge on the shores of Lake Arrowhead. One morning his cutter called to report that Hughes, scissors in hand, was in the cutting room, snipping his way through the film. Milestone's contract stipulated that no one could tinker with his films—not even Hughes himself. Filled with righteous rage, Millie jumped into his car and broke all records driving the 70 miles to the studio. Dashing into the editors' building, he paused at the door of his cutting room to watch Hughes at work.

Millie waited until he was sure that Hughes was actually cutting the film, then burst into the room under a full head of steam. Hughes tried to cool him down, with no success. Finally, grabbing his arm, he pulled him out of the building and down to the parking lot, while Milestone continued to give him a large piece of his mind. Hughes was not yet secure enough to wear tennis shoes and drive a Chevrolet—he owned a beautiful boat-shaped Duesenberg, probably the most powerful car of its day. Shoving Milestone into the passenger seat, he got behind the wheel and burned rubber out of the parking lot, over Cahuenga Pass, and out into the San Fernando Valley, then almost entirely farm country, with long, narrow unfrequented roads. The farther they went, the faster he drove, until Millie was slumped down in his seat, begging Hughes to stop. Eventually, he did, and turned to Milestone.

"Are you cooled off now?" he asked.

Millie could barely essay a nod.

"All right," said Hughes. "Look, I wasn't cutting your film. I happen to have enough money to indulge my whims. And I wanted to see what the film would look like if I removed ten percent of every scene, so I ordered an extra print, just for myself. Your cut and the negative are untouched."

Then he turned the car around and drove a much smaller Milestone back to town.

My old friend and cameraman, Franz Planer, told another story. He handled the photography on *Vendetta*, a film Hughes and Preston Sturges were partners on, though Hughes was putting up all the cash. The main location was in a deep canyon in the Santa Monica Mountains, where the sun cleared the hills about 10:30 A.M. and disappeared about 2:30 P.M., affording a very diminished shooting day. According to Planer, Sturges and his girlfriend would arrive about 11:30, saddle up a pair of horses, and ride off for a cozy lunch in the hills. By the time they returned, the sun had disappeared and decent photography was impossible. The 200 or so extras were enjoying the routine as much as Sturges—it was a long, well-paying run.

Planer's nervous stomach and high ethical standards could take only so much, and he decided to quit the film. That night he was summoned to Hughes' bedside at the hospital, where that eccentric was recovering from his airplane crash.

"Why are you quitting, Franz?" he asked. Franz didn't want to get Sturges in trouble.

"It's my stomach," he said. "I've got to take a rest."

Hughes took a large notebook from his bedstand, and started to read. Sturges' day-by-day activities were recorded in minute detail, including even passages of dialogue. One of the extras was a Hughes informant.

"I want you to stay with the picture," said Hughes. "I'm buying Sturges out."

And he did, for a reported $1,000,000 in cash.

It was on the same film, after a new director, Stu Heisler (with a new leading lady) had taken over, that another typical Hughes decision was recorded. Ever since *Hell's Angels*, Hughes had loved fleecy white clouds, but fleecy white clouds are rare in Southern California. Hughes could afford to wait. Heisler, on the other hand, had grown impatient, and finally decided he had to shoot. Planer advised against it, but Stu insisted, so they shot. Howard saw the rushes the next day and sent Stu a short message: "Am dumping everything. Wait for clouds."

Then there is the only story which doesn't come to me firsthand. It almost certainly is apocryphal, but it's in the right spirit. A very famous and busty blonde beauty had convinced herself that she and Hughes had a wedding date. (She was by no means the first or the last to make that mistake.) On the important day, Hughes was nowhere around. Finally, after hours of trying, she got him on the phone, only to be told that he had no intention of getting married.

"You can't do that to me!" wailed the star. "I've already had all my luggage monogrammed H.H."

"Then marry Huntington Hartford," said Hughes and hung up.

I was taken with the Hollywood episodes, since Hollywood rarely makes an "inside" film that bears the slightest resemblance to the truth. I told Marty Rackin I was available. There was a slight hitch—my contract called for me to produce, but Joe Levine insisted on the credit. I could have refused and still collected my full salary whether I made the film or not, but credit above or below the line means very little to me. I assumed that since Levine's office was in New York, there would be little interference from that direction, and what really mattered was who did the work, not who took the credit. I agreed to waive the producer clause.

John Michael Hayes had written the script, and an excellent script it was. It isolated the story of Jonas Cord and retained all of its drama and tragedy, though it was overlaid with more humor than was to be found in the novel. The industry censor was still active, so Robbins' porno sequences were played down to a passable minimum. They would certainly get a P.G. rating today.

Happily, Paramount agreed that the book and its title were the attractions, and star power would be a needless expense. We set about finding the right actresses. The studio was interested in a newcomer, Elizabeth Ashley, and Marty thought she could play Cord's wife, Monica. I looked at a couple of her TV performances and was impressed. Levine agreed and we penciled her in.

And now there were two. At the start of their Jonas Cord periods, the book portrays Rina and Jennie as in their late teens or very early twenties, yet certainly "all woman." That was typical of many of Hollywood's early actresses. As a callow youth at Paramount, I had been struck by Jean Harlow's beauty and demeanor when she was still an extra—and sixteen. As far as maturity was concerned, she could have played Mata Hari or Camille. Loretta Young was another sixteen-year-old who played mature roles.

So I started a search for overdeveloped teen-agers in whom the instincts of womanhood had come to early flower. But times had changed. Every female was a "girl" now. I met twenty-year-olds who looked like schoolgirls, and forty-year-olds trying to look twenty, but not one eighteen-year-old who could have kept Cord's interest past the stage of introduction.

We tested about ten girls—among them Katharine Ross, whom we had brought down from a little-theater group in the Bay area. We found her to be a good actress, but not the type we were seeking. Universal saw our test, liked it, and signed her to a term contract. Rackin and I were stalling for a "miracle" when Levine solved our dilemma. Exercising his producer's prerogative for the first and last time during production, he informed Paramount that he wanted Carroll Baker to play Rina, and Martha Hyer to play Jennie. Neither of these choices thrilled us, but we had no one to offer in opposition, so we gracefully acquiesced.

The rest of the cast was our choice—though Levine had veto power, he found no reason to exercise it. George Peppard had played a couple of good roles, but was still well short of star status. We thought his hard, poker-faced personality would serve our character well and, since he had not yet established a popular image of his own, he could well wind up being Jonas Cord. It worked out that way.

Alan Ladd was not the man I had known in 1940. Then he had been a nondrinker and an athlete of Olympic caliber, still in top physical condition. Now he was a heavy closet drinker, and physically not even a caricature of his old self.

Size has rarely been a requisite for stardom. Men like James Cagney and Edward G. Robinson were short, and couldn't have cared less. Nor did their sizes make them less believable in "tough guy" roles. Ladd, at one time the top draw in the business, just couldn't handle it. Many stories concerning his reactions to tall leading ladies made the rounds of Hollywood. Rackin told me of his own technique for casting Ladd's costars. In his office, a picture was hung on the wall near the door, its distance from the floor corresponding to the maximum height permissible. Sooner or later in the interview, the actress was maneuvered to a position near the picture. One quick glance could tell whether the candidate passed or not.

I had serious doubts about Ladd's ability to handle the part of Nevada Smith, but Rackin felt a strong obligation to Alan for past favors, and insisted we take a chance. My fears proved well founded, but somehow we nursed him through the film, and what eventually appeared on the screen was one of the best performances of his life. It was also his last—he died not too long after the film was finished.

Marty Balsam, as the producer who outwits Jonas Cord, was at his best. As was Lou Ayres as Cord's long-suffering attorney. I had not seen Ayres since I had cut *Hold 'Em, Navy* for Paramount in 1937. *The Carpetbaggers* started a friendship which continues to this day. And Tom Tully, who had garnered an Oscar nomination for his role as Queeg's predecessor in *The Caine Mutiny*, played the short role of Monica's father to the hilt.

As Monica, Elizabeth Ashley proved a find. I predicted great stardom for this exceptional actress, a prediction that hasn't yet been fulfilled.

Personal problems have hampered her career, but a recent success on Broadway may be the start of a second climb to the top.

Levine's two nominees held their own. Carroll Baker, always a fine actress, worked extremely hard. In retrospect, I find our struggles with the censors amusing. Our first sight of Carroll in the film is when Cord arrives to announce his father's unexpected death. She is at her makeup table, in the nude, as Jonas unceremoniously bursts into her bedroom. Even partial nudes were shot only in skin flicks in 1963, and most of us were embarrassed that Carroll should appear nude on the set, even though we were photographing only her back. The set was lit, Carroll, in a robe, seated herself at the dressing table, and a screen was placed around her. When all was in readiness, those members of the crew not absolutely necessary were excused from the stage. I started the camera, the wardrobe mistress took Carroll's robe, the screen was removed, the scene was shot, and we all breathed a little more easily. And all that eventually showed on film was a bare back which was quickly covered by a robe. (A few years later, I was driving into Rome from the airport, and passed a poster of Carroll's latest Italian film. It was titled *Orgasm*. I wondered what the hell I'd been such a gentleman about.)

The film was finished more or less on schedule and at a cost of about $3,000,000, and it eventually grossed more than ten times that much. Joe Levine came out for the wind-up party, saw a few reels of cut film, expressed his satisfaction, and flew back to New York. The next time I saw him was in Chicago, the day of our first preview.

A lingering fear of our subject matter led us to undertake a double preview in the Midwest—one in Chicago and one in South Bend, home of Notre Dame, America's best-known Catholic university. The brass reasoned that if our film could get by in the Bible Belt, it would do well everywhere.

We were all tense before the Chicago showing, and it was a relief to get it under way. About halfway through the film, I decided to go out into the lobby. The audience reaction was extremely good; there had been only two or three walkouts, unusual for such a controversial film, and I felt we were in. Levine followed me out into the foyer. He looked worried.

"They're laughing a lot," he said.

"And all in the right places," I said. "I planned it that way."

He looked a little unsure, but the preview cards convinced him, and the next night, South Bend confirmed it. We had a hit.

TIME OUT

The sale of our Agoura acreage left us with a considerable amount of money in the bank, so, with Jean's enthusiastic collaboration (Jean is *always* enthusiastic), I started looking for workable land. We had always enjoyed the wine country north of San Francisco, and now we spent a number of weekends exploring the area, without much success. Finally, a Santa Rosa real-estate dealer took us to see a small dairy ranch just off the Petaluma-Bodega Bay Highway, about 7 miles in from the sea. We knew it was for us the minute we saw it.

It was a completely run-down, class C dairy, on about 500 acres of land, of which about 200 acres were in barely passable grazing condition. There was a two-acre lake, a couple of old barns, and a hundred-year-old house. A two-story, L-shaped structure, it had seventeen rooms and no baths, but there were four fireplaces, including one in the huge, high-ceilinged kitchen. There was also a beautiful curved stairway off the entrance hall.

We bought it, cleaned out the garbage and decay, and Walter Tyler, my art director on *The Carpetbaggers*, helped Jean to redesign the place. While all this was in its preliminary stages, my son Michael purchased twenty virgin heifers and a bull, all Black Angus, and we put them out to pasture. In nine months' time we anticipated twenty healthy young calves. We loaded one of the barns with alfalfa to augment the rather skimpy pasture then available and bought a small trailer to serve as living quarters for the man I hired to look after the ranch and the cattle. With my dream project safely in hand, I now concentrated on my last film for Paramount.

The studio had already paid off for a film I hadn't made, and one more was called for in my contract, which would soon run out. But production activity in 1964 was extremely lethargic. The only project on the books was another Robbins novel, *Where Love Has Gone*. It is not one of his better works. John Michael Hayes, who had written the screenplay for *The Carpetbaggers*, was doing the same for *WLHG*, and Susan Hayward was tentatively scheduled to play the lead. The script was not up to Hayes' standard, but in a moment of overconfidence, and feeling I couldn't decently take money for another unrealized picture, I agreed to take on the assignment. I felt that, given a good cast, I could rewrite the material and wind up with a decent enough movie. I had done it a number of times and had usually succeeded.

The first mistake was Susan. She had serious misgivings about playing a promiscuous woman. Yet, for some now-unremembered reason, Marty Rackin felt she was the only actress for the part, and he made a number of character concessions to win her agreement. The concessions improved the moral tone of the script, but diminished its dramatic possibilities.

For the role of Susan's mother, we cast Bette Davis. Not long before, Miss Davis had created a stir in town with trade ads in which she asked for work. Having suffered a rather lengthy lean period, she struck out at a heartless industry. She was quite justified—Hollywood has always had a short memory and a minus pool of gratitude. But in this case, the studio executives felt a little ashamed, and the role in our film was one of a series she was now offered in an impressive resurgence of her career.

Vincent Sherman once made a film at Warner's which starred Bette Davis and Miriam Hopkins. He was asked how it felt to direct two such stars.

"I don't direct them," he said, "I referee." It's always funnier when someone else is involved.

Most female stars come on pretty strong—it comes with the territory—but Bette was undoubtedly the champ. She was (and still is) an extraordinary actress and an unusually hard worker. A diplomat she is not. It began when I had been shooting for some days, rewriting as I went along. Early one morning, I came on the set with a handful of new pages and found Miss Davis in her dressing room, ready for work. (She was always ready before her call.) I sat down with her and went over the proposed changes, with which she heartily concurred. Then, since Susan was still being made up, I went back to my office. Bette walked out on the set, where the crew was preparing our first setup, with her usual cheery greeting.

"Hold everything, boys," she said. "We've just made a few changes in the scene."

The "boys" were used to Bette, and didn't miss a beat, but the scuttlebutt factory went to work and in a few minutes Susan heard that Bette Davis was rewriting her scenes. Unlike her opponent, Susan was an insecure actress, and suspicions immediately flooded her mind. Her agent was soon at the studio, and the three of us were in Rackin's office. We discovered that Susan's contract specified that she was bound only to the script she had originally read, and, good or bad—and even Hayes admitted it lacked quality—that's all she was going to do. And that's all she did.

Mike Connors, as Susan's husband, and Joey Heatherton, playing her daughter, contributed excellent performances, but the pedestrian script gave them little help. We all tried hard, but none of us had wings on his heels when we finished the film. For me, the capper came some weeks later. The New York executives, who hadn't broken into unrestrained cheering after the finish of *The Carpetbaggers*, which was to make them a fortune, called me after viewing *Where Love Has Gone*, to say they considered it one of the best films Paramount had turned out in a number of years.

The Double D Ranch was an ideal hideaway for licking my wounds. We put our Bel Air home up for lease, crammed our belongings into two huge vans, and moved, lock, stock and barrel, up to Sonoma County. While Jean slaved away inside the house, I turned over about a hundred acres of pasture land, reseeded them with the right mixture of legumes and grasses, and topped off the whole area with a generous helping of fertilizer. As soon as I had finished with the plowing, I started work on paneling the library. Next, the oat hay had to be mowed, windrowed, and baled, and then we discovered that seven of our "virgin" Angus heifers had had clandestine relations with a Hereford bull before we had bought them. The Hereford has a much larger head than the Angus, and the birth of a large-headed calf to a cow not constructed for such delivery can be a trying ordeal, both for the cow and for the rancher. Our hand, Felix, my son Mike, and I spent many a weary and frustrating hour pulling calves out into the world. We lost only three.

It was the end of summer. Fencing, clearing, and corral building were getting to be a bit of a drag, and our kids were about to start school. So my agent's out-of-the-blue call was welcome. U-I wanted me for a film. Jean nearly cried with relief. Our L.A. home was still vacant, so we called in the moving vans and trekked south once more.

Universal had changed a great deal in twenty-one years. It had suffered through two more ownerships and a great many alterations in policy. Even the physical structure of the lot was different. But, once inside my office and at work on a script, I found everything very much the same. Even the reproductions decorating my office walls were exactly like those in any other studio in Hollywood, or, for that matter, in the world. The minute a filmmaker walks through the gates of any studio in the world, he is at home. The smell of film, acetone, and makeup remains constant—as do the "studio chaps," as the British would call them. Just as I was able to recognize an unknown cameraman on sight in the confines of Mill Point prison, so I could spot a sound mixer, a prop man, or a wardrobe mistress as easily in a Bombay studio as I could at Paramount.

I have found this phenomenon invaluable in establishing the characters in my films. The inner personality of a human being, whether he is kind or cruel, thoughtful or greedy, intelligent or stupid, may be largely a function of heredity, but the outer aspects—manner of speech, appearance, physical carriage, etc.—seem to be much more the functions of craft or profession. Some actors know this instinctively, some learn it through experience, and some are never aware of it at all. It is like a uniform which, once donned, tells the audience a great deal about the character's background, and therefore about the character himself. A man may seem a sanctimonious hypocrite until he puts on a priest's robes. MacArthur in mufti was a small, rather colorless man, but in uniform he was a giant, a figure of great authority. Once an actor has learned how to wear the environmental "uniform" of the character he is portraying, he has taken a giant step toward "living" the part, rather than just acting it.

A correlative of this hypothesis is that of "attitude." The close-up acting of films and TV differs from stage acting primarily because of its accent on attitude. Most of the old-time actors were elocutionists, "reading" the author's lines with varying degrees of skill. Today, the lines aren't nearly so important. It is a truism that a person can say one thing and mean another. In fact, a great deal of our daily conversation is concerned with the concealment of our feelings. Scripts which, at their best, mirror life as we know it, do the same thing. Much of the dialogue of any script is dialogue of concealment. Lines that give information too baldly are called "exposition" or "expository," and are considered inept writing; a director coming across such a line (it happens too often) does his best to change it into something which reveals what we need to know, but in a much more subtle manner.

In the end, it is up to the actor to disclose, through his attitude, what his mouthings have frequently concealed. Our greatest actors do it best. Tracy could speak a very serious line, but a subtle demeanor would make it quite clear that the whole thing was a put-on. Jack Lemmon could do a straight recitation of "Little Red Riding Hood," but if seduction were on his mind, his audience would have no doubt about it. Perhaps, in its simplest form, the whole point can be capsulized in that famous line from *The Virginian:* "Smile when you say that, stranger."

The whole of *Mirage* was an exercise in concealment—and discovery. A first-class story of suspense, scripted by Peter Stone, from an original novel by my old prison buddy, Howard Fast, it followed the adventures of a scientist, suffering from shock amnesia, as he tries to assemble the jigsaw puzzle that is the blacked-out period of his life. Everything possible is done to deceive him; every obstacle, including the murder of potential witnesses, is placed in his path. But, doggedly, he fights through to knowledge and clarification. The fact that the complications were the result of a conflict between those working for the greater good of society and extremely cynical and selfish private interests, gave the story a certain moral orientation which lifted it a notch above the usual suspense thriller. This basic plot has become trite, as have the plots of most private-eye and hard-hitting suspense films, because of the voracious demands of TV. But in 1964, a good deal of what we had to say was relatively fresh, as were many of the characters through whom we said it.

When I came into the picture, Gregory Peck was set to play the amnesiac. In fact, his company was making the film in cooperation with Universal, and he had a proprietary interest in the project. I had never worked with Peck, and I looked forward to our collaboration with mixed feelings. He was well cast for the role. He is a dogged individual, or at least he gives that impression on first meeting. That type can be hell to work with, but if the doggedness is bent toward proper goals, it can also become a part of a rewarding relationship.

Our first script conference was a bit upsetting to Peter Stone. Our script contained a good deal of humor, but not much of it emanated from the leading character. Peck wanted some funny lines, as Cary Grant had had in *Charade*, which Stone had also written. After Greg had left the office, Peter voiced his concern. Stone has a great sense of humor, both as a person and as a writer, but what is sauce for Granny Goose is not necessarily sauce for Gregory Gander. Peck has wit, but it is very dry. What's more, the character of a man seeking his lost persona has hardly the makings of a stand-up comic.

The months at the ranch had been good for me—I found myself not the least bit concerned. I suggested to Peter that he do his best to write in as many "laughs" as he could for Peck—in the long run, I assured him, none of them would be in the picture. I had gotten the impression that Peck was a very honest actor, and when the chips were down, anything with a phony ring would be dropped in the first rehearsal. And that's how it worked out. The film had a good share of laughs, but most of them came from other—and funnier—members of the cast.

In rehearsals, actors often make mistakes or take off in unusual directions. I usually ignore, initially, the errors or the experiments that dialogue coaches, assistants, and, most usually, script girls, bring to my attention. Most actors are aware of their miscues, and will make their own adjustments. Correcting prematurely can cause embarrassment and, in extreme cases, mental blocks, a serious acting problem. Of course, if a mistake persists, I will discuss it with the actor and work it out. As for experimenting, I encourage it. How else can you get that "something extra" into a performance? If the experiment is not suitable to the scene (often the case) the actor himself will usually drop it quickly. If not, it's time for me to speak up. By the time we're ready to shoot, these problems are usually worked out in the best interests of the scene, and with the least chance of unpleasant and nonproductive controversy.

The cast of *Mirage* looks better in retrospect than it did at the time. Oh, we thought it was a very good acting cast, but not particularly strong at the box office. We had Gregory Peck—period. And even his star was on the wane, as far as audience attraction was concerned. After Peck, we had some first-class character actors in Walter Abel, Leif Erickson, and Kevin McCarthy. The leading lady was Diane Baker. Three relatively unknown actors rounded out the cast—Walter Matthau, George Kennedy, and Jack Weston. Today, this trio alone would make an all-star cast. In 1964, it was Gregory Peck and a cast of "distinguished players."

One day I was congratulating Matthau on a particularly well-played scene. I was, perhaps, a little patronizing.

"You should have a great career in films," I assured him. "You can be one of our top character actors."

"Character actor, hell!" said Matthau. "I'm going to be one of the top leading men."

Well, he knew what he wanted, and he sure as hell got it—though I would have given 50-to-1 odds against it.

Matthau's rapid rise was helped in no small way by the beautiful part he had in *Mirage*. I don't remember whether it came straight out of Fast's novel or out of Stone's fertile mind, but it was a honey, and, like all good things, has been imitated into mediocrity. He played a former refrigerator repairman who had always wanted to be a private eye. His techniques came from a correspondence school, his style from Raymond Chandler. His AAA Detective Agency was first in the Yellow Pages, and Peck was his first client. He was different from the usual movie shamus in other ways—he drank Cokes instead of bad whiskey, and was often unsure of himself. But he had the private eye's vocabulary down pat, and, in his honest way, helped Peck a long way toward the ultimate solution. When he was killed, the audience nearly cried, and so did I. He was the freshest character to come along in a decade, and I would have loved to see him share Peck's triumph at the end.

There was another innovation in the film—one for which I will happily take the responsibility. The picture contained a number of flashbacks—and *flash*backs they truly were—very brief scenes, consisting usually of a few spoken words or a single action, as something in the present triggered a snatch of memory recall. During our story conferences, we debated at length the method of identifying these shots. In the script, Stone had suggested oil dissolves, those undulating, in-and-out-of-focus effects commonly used to introduce dream sequences, but I felt the time factor in any dissolve would invalidate the instantaneous triggering that was so vital to our film. In the end, in keeping with my policy of never underestimating the public, I decided to try straight cuts—if they didn't work at the preview, other solutions could be sought. They worked—and have worked in many theatrical and TV films ever since. But at that time, it was a brand-new technique, never before used in a film, certainly not in Hollywood.

We spent 2 or 3 weeks on location in New York City, and I have never had more pleasant shooting. Our excellent production manager had done all the necessary wheel-greasing, the crew was A-1, as were the extras, and the residents, wherever we shot, were most cooperative and hospitable. I almost lost my feelings of hostility to the Big Town, only to have them come flooding back again on my next nonworking visit. It's a hard city to love, even when you want to.

As I had suspected after our first meeting, Greg Peck proved to be a conscientious, honest, and hard-working actor, and the owner of a very fine talent. The whole production (including the writing of the musical score by Quincy Jones) was a close-knit, smooth-working operation—the kind that makes the profession of film directing seem the most rewarding work in the world, recharging your batteries instead of draining you dry.

Mirage was prematurely released, to very good critical reception (*Life* magazine called it a "minor masterpiece"), and it won a couple of minor awards. I flew back to the ranch to take pleasure in my growing Angus herd.

42

BAYOU COUNTRY

 1965 was a good year. The ranch was thriving—a constant source of hard work and spiritual replenishment. I spent many days, sometimes weeks, building corrals, gates, fences, a new water tank, planting, mowing, and baling hay, rounding up and spraying cattle, and keeping records on the development of the young cows and their offspring.

Late in the spring, my agent, Jack Gordean, put together a package. Since leaving MGM Sol Siegel had lived through a few years of professional and personal suffering, and Jack was trying to get him back into the swing of things. He had secured Columbia's backing for a story titled *Alvarez Kelly*, a hybrid of Western and Civil War parentage. William Holden, another Gordean client, was set to play the title role. The script was pretty sick and needed a lot of help, but so did Sol. I had known Holden casually since his early days at Paramount, and I figured that if he could take a chance, so could I. Besides, it's not too difficult to sacrifice six months of one's time for a few hundred thousand dollars. The hypocrisy of such a situation can be quite amusing, if somewhat "black." Tyrone Power died suddenly in the midst of production. The trade press heralded the fact that Yul Brynner, because of his love and respect for his dear, departed friend, had volunteered to replace Power in the film. A few days later, the same press quietly noted that Brynner would receive $600,000 for his act of charity—probably the most money he'd earned for a single film up to that time. It's quite likely that Brynner had nothing to do with either announcement, but the story made interesting reading for those who tend to take a cynical view of life.

Our story was based on an actual Civil War incident. During Grant's siege of Richmond, a herd of some 2,500 beef cattle was rustled from behind the Union lines by a daring and hungry troop of Confederate cavalry. The script broke down into three separate parts: the initial cattle drive from Mexico through its delivery to the Union forces; the planning of the raid in Richmond, during which the original owner, driver, and seller of the herd, an Irish-Mexican named Alvarez Kelly, is coerced into helping the Rebs; and finally, the successful rustling operation itself.

Bill Holden was Alvarez Kelly. Richard Widmark (our third outing together) played the Rebel cavalry commander, and Patrick O'Neal his antagonist, the Union mounted officer. The cattle presented an interesting problem. The American beef herds of the middle nineteenth century consisted of what we now call "wild" cattle: scrawny, long-horned, and belligerent. However, outside of a small private show herd of Texas longhorns, no such animals exist in the United States today. But Mexico is another story—and that is where we went for our steers, about 750 of them, which had to be examined, passed, and transported to Louisiana, where we were shooting the major portion of the film.

The constant stickler, and there are always a few around, will ask, "Why didn't you go to Virginia, where the original action took place?" Well, we went to Virginia, but a lot of changes have taken place in a hundred years. We also spent a number of days exploring Oregon, which would have been more convenient to the studio. But Oregon is one of the most heavily electrified states in the Union, and high-voltage-line pylons were omnipresent. So we wound up where many other location companies have wound up, in the underdeveloped South, where we could find miles of empty and beautiful countryside. (The South is catching up fast and will continue its advances as long as the pay differential is in its favor. God knows what the movies will do for "green" locations in the next 10 or 15 years!)

For this film we had to find a wild stretch of river, completely free of any sign of civilization, where we could build—and eventually blow up—our own bridge, and where we could maneuver a large herd of cattle through enough wooded, swampy, and open territory to film a lengthy cattle drive and stampede. For days we toured the area in cars; nothing the local guides could show us was usable. I finally ordered a five-place helicopter. With my cameraman, production manager, and art director, I flew the length of two of the local streams, coming down whenever we felt the terrain justified a closer look. Within four hours we had found the ideal location, whose well-kept dirt roads made it possible for us to get our cattle and equipment in with a minimum of grading. In these situations, there is nothing to take the place of a look from up on top. Expensive by the hour it is, but, in the long run, it is so much better and cheaper.

For our more civilized location, we found a lovely, modest "plantation," about 45 minutes' drive from Baton Rouge, our home base. It consisted of a couple of thousand acres of sparse pasture and woodland and was the center of much of our work. The owner was a semiretired New Orleans surgeon of some repute, a Southerner of the old school, courteous, pleasant, and hospitable. He kept a small herd of a rare breed of "White Park" cattle, a type I had never seen before. He also had white turkeys, white peafowl, white pigeons, and white horses. One sultry afternoon before the start of production, we were enjoying iced tea and a chat on his rear veranda. He was enlightening us on the attributes of his Park cattle. During a lull in the conversation, my head wrangler casually mentioned my Black Angus herd and started to comment on some of the Angus advantages, when our host interrupted.

"I won't have anythin' black on my place," he said.

But, once shooting started, he did allow a young black boy to peddle cold drinks to the crew—for a share of the profits, of course.

As I mentioned earlier, the script was somewhat short of perfection, and Dan Taradash, one of Hollywood's very best writers, agreed to do a brief doctoring job. He wrote a few excellent new scenes and shored up a number of the old ones, but there was no time for a thorough renovation. With actors like Widmark, O'Neal and Holden, I was sure we could do a cosmetic job on the picture. And for the first few days of production, nothing happened to prove me wrong.

We had a good crew and a good cast of hard-riding actors. But Bill Holden, like many of his colleagues, had a "drinking problem." (It was no problem for him—he liked to drink.) When the film took shape in Hollywood, Bill was on the wagon, and it showed; he looked like a juvenile. I was a little concerned one evening when he told me he had taken "the cure" in France, and the French were not as stuffy as the Americans—they did allow the drinking of wine after the cure. And for a man accustomed to Paris, Rome, and Hong Kong, Baton Rouge can be a boring community—and boredom is the enemy of good sense. One morning, as I was about to call the actors for the first shot, Widmark approached me, took my elbow, and pulled me aside.

"We're in trouble," he said.

"How?"

"Come on back to the trailer," he said, nudging me along the way.

"Holden is out," he explained. "I don't think you'll get anything out of him today. He's gone!"

I have learned to live with problems, and I rarely react excitedly to "catastrophic" news. Instead, I flatten out, become fatalistic. "What the hell. If we can't work, we can't work. We'll all go back to the motel."

"Let's give it a try," said Dick.

What surprised me most about the situation was Widmark's attitude. Knowing his temper and his feelings about nonprofessional behavior, I expected him to blow sky-high. Instead, he behaved like a solicitous mother. He drenched Holden with black coffee, walked him around a bit, and in about 45 minutes Bill was sitting his horse and ready to get on with the scene—a bit surly, but serviceable. (If accurately quoted in a recent interview, Holden has been on the wagon for the last two years. His remarkable performance in *Network* would seem to bear this out.)

The crisis weathered, things went on in routine fashion. Holden *is* a professional, and he did his best with a role I was never quite sure he believed in. There were a few minor skirmishes with the crew, the mayflies, and the weather. One oddity about people working away from home—and this holds true for persons of all nationalities—is that they will happily eat slop in their own environment, but, taken to a distant location, they will demand food of "Pyramide" quality—and they will threaten a strike if they don't get it.

The chiggers, mosquitos and mayflies were hard for Californians to deal with, but anything that will make a man work harder in order to get home sooner can't be all bad.

As for the weather, most of it was hot and muggy. And windy. One of the great hurricanes of the century was due to hit Baton Rouge during our stay there. At about 3:00 P.M. on the afternoon of its visitation, we stopped shooting and battened down the hatches in anticipation of the blow. The storm was to reach its peak about 11:00 in the evening, and I, who had experienced the best earthquakes that Southern California had to offer, looked forward to living through a genuine hurricane. She was roaring pretty good by 10:00—and then I fell asleep. I awoke in the morning to a calm, clear world. Seen through my window, little seemed to have changed. I dressed and went outside. Huge trees, uprooted, lay on their sides, shards of shattered picture windows shimmered on the lawns, and roofs were half-bare, if they were there at all. My one chance to see a live hurricane, and I had goofed it. It was time to go home.

It was our last day on location, and Jack Sabin, who owned a local restaurant most of us had adopted, brought out a vanful of beer and champagne. There must have been at least 250 people on location, and all could drink a toast or two. "Fat Jack," as Widmark called him with respect and affection, turned our last day in Louisiana into much more than the hour of escape it usually is.

Alvarez Kelly was another *Soldier of Fortune*, a potboiler, but we had a great stampede. It always amazes me how well such pictures do abroad, where nuances of language mean little, and action is everything.

I finished the cutting, saw the film through scoring, dubbing, color correction, and a preview, turned it over to the lab, put away my Miltowns, and headed for a few days at the ranch, where my occupational nightmares would steadily diminish, then disappear. That's when I would know the job was really over and done with.

NEVER SAY NO
TO AN ADMIRAL

I t was 1967. Over a year had passed since *Alvarez Kelly*, a period which marked the beginning of a new phase in Hollywood. Psychedelic films were in, and they brought with them young psychedelic directors most of whom would flare up and fizzle out more quickly than the trend that gave them life. But in the meantime, the "old-timers" were dropping like flies.

"Eddie," my agent told me, "it's much easier for me to sell some clown who's never directed a film, than it is to sell George Cukor."

I was only 58, but I'd been in films for 44 years. I was definitely an old-timer. Oh, I'd been offered scripts, viable ones—two by Warners. But I wasn't hungry yet.

"Why do you want to waste your money on such crap?" I asked, a little more diplomatically than that.

In most cases, the films I turned down were made by some other director—and they bombed. That was little satisfaction to my business manager.

"You're short of cash," he said, "and running into debt. You'd better get a job."

I took the next job that came along.

De Laurentiis was in Beverly Hills. He came in at least once a year for some freewheeling recruiting. I went to his bungalow at the Beverly

Hills Hotel. He was charming, as always, and persuasive—but then, I was a setup. He had the rights to *Anzio*, the story of the Anglo-American landing on the Italian coast at the town of the same name. It was one of the greatest foul-ups in American military history.

Dino De Laurentiis was Italy's most important film producer. I had met him some years earlier, when he had brought me to Rome to discuss the making of a film on Simon Bolivar. I had been impressed. At his instructions, his art department had made dozens of color "sketches"—minor works of art, really—of costumes, characters, even key scenes, and some of them were impressive. Bolivar's winter crossing of the Andes, reminiscent of David in its execution, made Napoleon's crossing of the Alps seem like a brief outing of the Polar Bear Club. The script was a great deal less distinguished than the planning and sketches. It had been unreasonably distorted by hand-tailoring the part of Manuela, Bolivar's mistress, into a role fit for Silvana Mangano, Dino's wife. Manuela, too, was a powerful and charismatic person, in every way a fitting companion for Bolivar, but somehow, in Dino's version, the two characters succeeded only in canceling out each other.

De Laurentiis conceded that the script needed a great deal of work. In any case, he said, he would not be ready to start production for a year or two yet. In the meantime—and here he brought out four or five other scripts he thought might interest me.

I smelled a rat, but an all-expenses-paid trip to Rome does place one under certain obligations, so I settled down in my all-expenses-paid suite at the Hassler Hotel and read the scripts in one day.

My nose had been right. When I returned them to Dino, I told him I thought I knew how to lick the Bolivar story, but he wasn't listening. He wanted my reaction to the other scripts, particularly one about a group of Yugoslavian women guerrillas. I gave it to him. He thanked me, I thanked him, and flew back to Hollywood. The Yugoslavian guerrilla story was later made by another American director. It wasn't very good. I wondered if Dino had used the same bait on Marty Ritt.

Our second meeting had been in 1961. Columbia had given him the script of *The Reluctant Saint* to gauge his interest in a possible coproduction. He turned it down. He liked the story, he said, but it wouldn't make a lira. He was so right.

Dino didn't have a script yet, but he did have a writer, and he had this idea about a giant German cannon which would be wheeled in and out of its protective cave on railroad flatcars—his art department was even now drawing up the plans and making some sketches. Of course, there had been no such cannon on the Anzio front, but Dino had seen *The Guns of Navarone*, a very successful film, and he was not above copping an idea.

De Laurentiis is a very unusual and interesting man. Nothing fazes him—except honesty—but that's true of many Neopolitans. His is a very active mind—not very original, but very manipulative. He is turned on by the mechanics of films and finances. Putting it all together, setting it all up, is what he finds exciting. Once everything has been organized and, particularly, the deal negotiated, he loses interest, and the director can make his film with relatively little interference from him. And that's the way most directors like it.

There *is* a problem while the story is being written. Dino is epigonous—though, to his credit, let it be said that he borrows only from the most successful—and if he were left to his own devices, his ideal film would consist of a long series of scenes stolen from the biggest earners in motion-picture history. Fortunately, he is amenable to counsel. Before anyone jumps to conclusions, I will say now that I would just as soon make a picture for Dino De Laurentiis as any other producer I know.

Ignoring the cannon, I knew that *Anzio* held enough drama and excitement for a dozen films, and there were still a few things I wanted to say about the waste of war, so I agreed to do it. We shook hands on the deal, and Dino promised to send the writer, with his script, to Hollywood within the next few weeks. And, within the next few weeks, he arrived.

He was a voluble Irishman—a big drinker, but full of Gaelic "charm." He had burrowed his way into the heart and bed of one of our leading female journalists, which is why our script meetings were being held in Hollywood and not in Rome. He was here for a couple of weeks of bundling, at Dino's expense, and the script would have to wait. Finally, the day before he was to return to Italy, I cornered him for an hour's conversation. In spite of a nasty hangover, he was in his most winning mood. I am unreasonably immune to "Irish charm," suspicious even when it's on the level. And in this case, my suspicions were well founded. He didn't have a word on paper, except for a little doggerel he'd written (he fancied himself a poet) and he didn't know where that would fit. (It didn't.) But he assured me that he had a number of ideas bouncing around in his brain and would write a script in very short order. We discussed a sketchy story line, and I heard nothing more for another few weeks.

We had a June starting date, so I finally took off for Rome on my own. I reported to Dino, then ran down the writer. He did have a good deal of script written, and it would have been a great vehicle for one of Laurel and Hardy's lesser efforts. (At one point he had Bob Mitchum escaping from his Nazi jailer by confusing him with a series of perfectly executed bird calls.) I was in trouble, but Dino was not at home with the English language, and he was taken with the man. It had all started when John Huston had confided that the writer was potentially one of the most brilliant playwrights in the world. What Dino didn't know was that Huston is one of the greatest practical jokers in the world. And it cost him a great deal to learn the truth.

On the grounds that I needed an American to filter out the "Irishness" in the dialogue, I succeeded in bringing over Frank De Felitta, a writer who had served in the U.S. forces in Italy. Working "behind" our writer, most of whose work ended up in the wastepaper basket, we were able to put together an acceptable script. .

In *Anzio*, Robert Mitchum played an American journalist. He was supported by an excellent male cast. Playing GIs were Peter Falk, Earl Holliman, Mark Damon, Joey Walsh, Tom Hunter, and Reni Santoni. Arthur Kennedy, Bob Ryan, and Arthur Franz made shorter appearances as American generals. And playing another GI was a young neophyte actor, Giancarlo Giannini. He spoke very little, except in Italian—but my, how he could act.

My cameraman was Giuseppe "Peppino" Rottuno, whom I rank alongside Franz Planer as one of the few color artists I've worked with. Shortly before the picture started, we were in Dino's office, studying a model of the ruins of Anzio. Like an Italian De Mille, Dino was describing the hugeness of the set he was "giving" me. Later, as we left the office, Peppino waggled a finger at me.

"Beware of Dino," he admonished. "In the office, it's always big"—and he stretched his arms out wide—"but when you get on the set, it's always small, like this"—and he opened his thumb and forefinger about three inches apart. Maybe so, but I had little cause for complaint. We covered a lot of ground, shot in many richly photogenic places, and I had little executive trouble until Columbia took over the film for release.

The crew and the people we worked with in general? Well— "sometimes they forgot to bring the nails, sometimes the matches didn't light." Nothing in Rome had changed. Each day still brought its silly, needless problems. One almost stopped us in our tracks. We were shooting the embarkation of the landing forces at the naval base in Taranto, inside the heel of the Italian boot. One day the car of the admiral in charge of the base was held up a minute or two while we finished a shot. Unfortunately, the admiral was in it. Seething at the indignity, he stormed into his office and ordered all shooting to cease. It did. He wouldn't receive our production manager, so we phoned Dino, who went to the top. The top sympathized and asked the admiral to rescind his order. Instead, he threatened to resign. I don't know what it cost Dino to assuage the injured ego, but after the loss of a couple of days, we were back at work.

During that time I had lunch with the commander of the flagship of the fleet. Seated at the table were ten or twelve of the ship's officers—all very friendly and warm. When the question of the work stoppage came up, they were embarrassed. Shrugging, the commander explained, "We, too, have our Captain Queegs."

Then there was the day when I thought I had it licked. Absolutely nothing could go wrong. The scene was simple and had been well rehearsed the evening before. The only participants were Mitchum and one Italian actor. At 9:00 A.M. the camera was ready and Bob was standing by. We also had a visitor—the Yugoslavian Minister of Culture had dropped by with his wife and a couple of friends to see how the Americans made movies in Italy. We were eager to show off, but the Italian actor wasn't on the set yet. I learned that he was in makeup and dispatched a messenger. Twenty minutes later, I saw the messenger and my assistant waving their hands at each other. After a great deal of hemming and hawing, it turned out the actor wasn't in makeup—he wasn't even in the studio. In short, he arrived about noon, a good two hours after the Yugoslavian contingent had left the set. He told me the story.

He lived in Rome, about 45 minutes from the studio. A company car was supposed to pick him up at 8:00. The driver was there on time, but he couldn't bother to get out of the car and knock on the door. When no actor appeared at the curb, he turned around and drove back to the studio. In the meantime, the actor called in to report himself stranded. Instead of being asked to hop in a cab and hurry on down, he was told to wait for a studio car. The dispatcher, in turn, waited until the original driver had returned, then sent him back for the actor. Traffic being what it is in Rome, we were lucky to get the actor by lunch. And a scene that should have been in the bag by noon ran on to quitting time.

Then I was shooting a short scene in a landing craft. The soldiers were crammed inside, guns slung over their shoulders. I was about to turn the camera when I noticed that one of the guns resembled a pretzel. A closer inspection showed all our guns were made of rubber. I resorted to screaming again—a technique I had to relearn when I started shooting *Anzio*—and was told that Dino had had an argument with our gun supplier and had refused to meet his terms. I sat down in my chair and said I'd start shooting when we had the proper weapons. Sometime after lunch, we were back at work.

Still, there were days when we marched a thousand men onto ships, complete with tanks, troop carriers, troops, and onlookers, with the troops parading down the Via di San Gregorio, through the Arch of Constantine and around the Colosseum, and later on that same day, marching around the Forum. All in all, it wasn't a bad show.

All my cast was excellent, but two, in particular, were remarkable. I've already given my opinion of Mitchum's artistry, but his ability to scan a scene is almost scary. In the evening, he might be stoned out of his skull; still, at 8:00 A.M., he will glance very briefly at five pages of dialogue, walk into the scene and never miss a beat.

And Peter Falk. Dino had sweet-talked him into the film by long-distance phone. When he arrived in Rome, Frank and I had not yet worked out his character or his scenes. He read the script and made reservations on the next plane home. Somehow, we dissuaded him. With his cooperation, we eventually developed an excellent and amusing character. One of the best scenes in the film—Falk's saying goodbye to three whores in an ambulance—was completely his creation. Sometimes I worry about the effect "Columbo" will have on his talent.

Jean and my two daughters had spent the summer with me in Rome. With the start of the new school year, they returned to California. I finished cutting the film, Dino expressed his satisfaction, and I took off for Hollywood. A few months later, I was back in Europe on other business and heard that the Columbia executives in London had mangled the film. In white heat I headed for Rome and De Laurentiis. He showed me the latest print. Sure enough, every line in the film which suggested that war was not exactly a glorious pastime had been deleted. Dino was apologetic, but said he had to depend on Columbia's views concerning the unfavorable effect the deleted lines might have on an American audience.

I dashed off a multi-paged letter to London. I was extremely angry and I was not very polite. A few days later, I was in England, and I bearded the lions in their den. I was told that they feared such honest comments because the Americans were involved in the war with Vietnam, but I continued to press my position. Eventually, I won a few concessions. It wasn't quite the film I thought I'd made, still—the *Film Daily*, in its review of June 19, 1968, said: "As an evocation of war—its horrors and heroism—*Anzio* excites both the eye and the emotions. This powerful re-creation of an incident in history should meet with considerable audience response."

I believe it did.

AND NEVER MESS
WITH A MYTH

*S**halako* is a prime example of a man hoist by his own petard. The man was I.

Euan Lloyd was a British PR man just turned producer. Like many Welshmen, he had a quick mind and a glib tongue. While I was still preparing *Anzio*, he approached me with a script based on Louis L'Amour's Western novel *Shalako*. The book was interesting, the script awful. I tried to let Lloyd down lightly. It was a mistake. If I had come down hard, he might have abandoned the project. Lloyd's future as a producer depended on getting a film off the ground, and this was his only property. He talked hard and fast. I thought I had an idea which would get me off the hook—a hook which, I realized, was of my own making.

An actor friend of mine, Jim Griffith (I was surrounded by Welshmen) had long been bugging me for a writer's job. He and a collaborator had written a workmanlike script which I had read and liked. I suggested to Lloyd that he hire the team to rewrite *Shalako*. If the result was good enough to attract an important cast, I would agree to direct the film. Lloyd accepted the proposition and Griffith accepted the job. I had a preliminary story conference with the two writers, then promptly forgot about the whole thing. But by the time I had finished *Anzio*, the boys had finished their version of *Shalako*.

It wasn't exactly *Shane*, or even *Warlock*, but it wasn't bad. Lloyd, like De Laurentiis, is an operator rather than a student of drama. He was delighted with the script and flew off to Europe. I was sure he would find it impossible to line up a decent cast, but I underestimated his talent for persuasion.

A couple of weeks later, Lloyd called me from London.

"Would you consider Sean Connery for Shalako?" he asked.

"Sure," I said. "Or William S. Hart. Give me a blast when you get him." I started to hang up.

"I've got him," said Lloyd, "subject to a few minor considerations. When can you come over?"

"Send me a ticket," I said.

The petard had exploded before I could make my escape.

1967 and 1968 were very confusing years. After fifteen happy years in Bel Air, we sold our house and optioned a beach property at Trancas. Jean found it a rather distant and gritty place to live (I was in Rome), and bought a home in Beverly Hills. Early in 1968, Jean learned our Bel Air house was back on the market. She called me in Spain to get my agreement to buy it back. Naturally, I gave it. It cost only a few thousand dollars to make it look as it did when we had sold it.

The ranch, which I still loved, was becoming a burden. My herd was growing nicely (I had over a hundred head now), but reliable help was difficult to get. And it was beginning to look as if all my work would be in Europe. In the middle of 1968, I sold the ranch and the cattle and said good-bye to another dream.

Meanwhile, I had another project brewing. During the summer of 1967, I had met an Italian writer, Ennio de Concini, one of the authors of *Divorce Italian Style*. We established an instant rapport and have remained great friends to this day. At our first meeting, we discovered that we shared a common interest in Christopher Columbus, and that our ideas concerning his life and career coincided. With me it had all started many years ago.

I had received a Columbus script from a Spanish producer. It was the usual hero-worshiping pap, but it inspired a period of research. I read everything I could dig up on the explorer, but all of it was in much the same vein. Even Samuel Eliot Morison presented a picture of a five-year-old boy, sitting on the beach at Genoa, staring out at the sea and dreaming of new worlds. What nonsense, I thought.

But I had read enough to be convinced that Columbus was a very down-to-earth Italian, and that most of the legends surrounding his career were false. Every intelligent person of his time—and all sailors—knew the world was round and had known so for over a thousand years. All the great Spanish and Portugese navigators knew the Orient could be reached by sailing west, but they also knew that no ship of the day could carry enough water and supplies to reach China. Columbus dared to make the trip because he was in error—he thought the world much smaller than it really is, and that China was only 3,500 miles away. If he hadn't run into the West Indies quite unexpectedly, he would have had to turn back with only a third of his journey completed and no water in his barrels.

Queen Isabella's scientists had vetoed his scheme because of its obvious errors. Then why did Isabella finally decide to spend the equivalent of about $15,000 to send him on his way? He was a very competent con man.

1492 was also the year that the Jews were being kicked out of a very Christian Spain. This explains one Columbian myth and explodes another. Columbus' ships were so tiny because there was more money (and safety) in transporting the fleeing Jews to Holland, Italy, the Near East, North Africa, wherever—and that's how most of the seaworthy Spanish ships were being utilized that year. As for the story of Isabella and her pawned jewelry, the confiscated property of even one moderately wealthy Jew would have more than paid for the whole enterprise.

There was enough honest information of this kind to fashion an exciting and unusual biography. Ennio's ideas on Columbus paralleled mine, and we agreed to collaborate on the project. Later that summer, Marcello Mastroianni found the concept attractive. Over a good Italian dinner, the three of us drew up and signed an agreement and toasted our partnership with champagne, a very treacherous drink.

When I returned to Hollywood after *Anzio*, I received a great deal of publicity on the Columbus project. There were two interesting results. First, an author-composer was inspired to write a musical based on a character surprisingly similar to the one I had been describing, and second, Justice Michael Musmanno went ape.

Musmanno, an associate justice of the Pennsylvania Supreme Court, spent a good deal of his life fighting off all threats to Columbus' position as the first and only discoverer of the Americas. The fact that evidence of previous discoveries, not only from various quarters of Europe, but also from North Africa and the Orient, continued to pile up overwhelmingly, only spurred the good judge to increasing counteractivity. He died firmly believing he had established, "beyond a shadow of a doubt," that Columbus *was* first.

He was also dedicated to the preservation of the Columbus image. Without the slightest knowledge of what our story really had to say (no script had yet been written), he set about to sabotage our efforts, bombarding our embassy in Rome, officials of the Italian government, and the Vatican with letters denigrating our project. He also urged the Italian-American Society to help stymie our efforts and wrote me an hysterical letter. I answered him quite politely, as I do all judges, assuring him that most of what had been printed was purely publicity, that we had great respect for Columbus as a man, and begging him to withhold judgment until he read our script, which I would send him as soon as it was written. But his answering letter continued to scold me on the basis of "Hollywood reports" and to threaten me with unnamed punishment if I persisted in my folly. In an arrogant gesture, he sent me a copy of his book, *Columbus Was First*, which he promised to autograph if I "behaved." Good God!

In one important way, *Shalako* was a different Western, which was its main attraction. It was an ideal vehicle for European casting and European production. The story's participants were Europeans on a Western "safari," in the 1870s. I have always considered most Westerns laid before the turn of the century as quite inaccurate. There were no "Westerners" then, only Easterners making their way to the coast or South-
erners escaping the trials and the indignities of Reconstruction. Many of the cattle ranches that sprang up well after the Civil War were owned and operated by Europeans. It took a few generations to breed the true Western types. I hoped *Shalako* would gain some stature from the presentation of this little-known area of Western history.

I met Connery at the Grand Hotel in Rome. We spent the first two hours watching the World Cup match. Scotland was playing West Germany, I believe, for the cup. Fortunately for Lloyd, Scotland won. It took only a few minutes to relieve a euphorious Connery of any reservations he may have had. I still wondered why he wanted to play a part which did not really seem to suit him as a person or as an actor. When I learned that he was getting $1,000,000, plus 100 percent of the profits from Spain, where he wanted to establish a winter home, I understood.

Lloyd had a few other surprises for me. First, he signed Brigitte Bardot as our leading lady. Then, in short order, he put together a supporting cast consisting of Stephen Boyd, Alexander Knox, Honor Blackman, Jack Hawkins, Peter Van Eyck, Valerie French, and Woody Strode. Lloyd was obviously calling in a lot of IOUs.

In keeping with the "new way" of packaging motion pictures, I was involved in many of Lloyd's activities, most of which are blurred memories. I do remember a few days in Venice at the Film Festival, where Sean and I helped to "sell" the Italian distributors. (They were surprised that I didn't have a long white beard and that I spoke American with no trace of accent.) And Jean, the kids, and I spent New Year's Eve in Rome with de Concini. Then my family flew to California and I left for Spain.

Near the town of Almeria, in southern Spain, there are a few square miles of semiarid desert, a patch of land which could easily be tucked into a corner of a medium-sized Arizona cattle ranch. Here are made most of Italy's "spaghetti Westerns," and here we had spotted our locations, built our sets, and were now going to work. Spanish culture and language was heavily influenced by the Arabs of North Africa, and in Almeria one feels it more strongly than anywhere else in Spain. The country is Moorish, the music is Moorish, and so are the social attitudes. (The women of Almeria disapproved most openly when Jean and my older daughter, in on an Easter visit, wore slacks in the streets of the town.) Most of our crew came from Madrid, and, backed by key personnel from London, were quite efficient and friendly.

Jack Hawkins was making his first appearance in a couple of years. He had undergone a laryngectomy, and with amazing courage and strength of will had achieved excellent pharyngeal speech. Even though its sound was not normal, its appearance was. Later, in London, we replaced his speech with that of a remarkable "voice double," making the performance normal in every way.

Bardot was a pleasant surprise. Except that she couldn't report for work before 10:00 A.M., and her contract so specified, she was a most conscientious worker. Once she complained testily when she thought I kept her waiting too long, and, while she was about it, informed me that her French directors shot more close-ups of her than I did. I excused her for the day (I was shooting a fight, and her close-up reactions could wait), and she made no further complaints.

More than any star I've known, Brigitte has an amazing still-picture instinct. I was convinced that sitting for stills was really her first love, and that she acted in films only because it immeasurably increased her opportunity for such posing. She had no feel for acting and seemed to take no particular interest in it. But I always knew that a still photographer was nearing the set (and the teaming of Connery and Bardot had them flocking to Almeria by the hundreds) when I saw Brigitte move to a suitable prop or background and settle herself into a fetching pose. Her instinct for the proper location and position was absolutely faultless; in that area, at least, she was a consummate artist.

The rest of the actors were typically British in their techniques and abilities. Alexander Knox, who once played Woodrow Wilson for Zanuck, is one of the most subtle and most gifted actors alive. Connery was involved and enthusiastic. Honor and Valerie are both gifted artists, as was Peter Van Eyck. Stephen Boyd was in a class by himself. Extremely presentable, he played heroes and heavies with equal skill.

Filming away from home and family, particularly at Europe's derriere, is almost like being in prison. But inevitably, we wrapped it up and moved to England for postproduction. Here, at least, I was close to friends and in a city I loved.

De Concini was also in London, and together we finished *Columbus*. What a beautiful script it was, funny and serious, comic and tragic, full of rich characters and situations. Dmitri de Grunwald, whose company had furnished completion money for *Shalako*, had agreed to find the necessary financing for *Columbus*. Now came our first great disappointment. Musmanno's pressure had been too much for Mastroianni. Without even reading the script, he withdrew from our agreement. Now we didn't have a package. In the independent field, a complete package is a must, and of the three ingredients—story, star, and director—the star is usually the most important.

To add to our difficulties, the industry was in its deepest trough of all time. The usual money sources had dried up. On any film costing more than a million or two, even the majors were looking for outside help. They were competing for the same Swiss, German, Belgian, and Dutch gold that the independents were trying to mine, and they had a trump card—distribution. Sometime after *Shalako* was released to mixed reception, I flew to Rome and started preparation on *Columbus*, while de Grunwald flew to Hollywood and Paramount for his last try at finding the financing. They liked the script but couldn't stand the cost. The project was a punctured balloon. Like Columbus, a few days out of Spain, I was becalmed, drifting in the doldrums.

LIZ, DICK, AND A DASH
OF PAPRIKA

I t was 1971. I had been idle for nearly three years. Nothing worthwhile was coming my way, and I was getting scared. I was too young to die. And if I didn't die of boredom, we would all die of starvation. Our Bel Air menage, much as we loved it, was chewing up our meager savings at a prodigious rate. So Jean and I finally decided to make a move we had occasionally contemplated. We were going to settle down in England.

We sold our house—again. This time, moving was a traumatic experience, the worst I had undergone since leaving prison. Our house was like the mythical pitcher which could never be emptied. Finally, at 6:30 on a sunny June morning, I parked my neighbor's jeep in his driveway for the last time, and joined my wife and Rebecca at a nearby motel, from which we were due to leave for the airport at 9:00. The last few days had been an absolute nightmare.

England, as always, was peaceful and green. By a stroke of luck, our old friends, the James Clavells, were spending the summer in Canada, and their lovely Westminster flat needed a house-sitter. We moved in. For the next three months we enjoyed a real holiday. I wasn't doing anything different, but I was doing it in a different place. We took almost daily outings in St. James's Park, where Rebecca delighted in feeding the pigeons and the waterfowl. Every two weeks we rode the train to Norwich, where our two cats and our dog were serving out their quarantine. And, occasionally, we drove out into the countryside, looking at houses, one of which might possibly become a home.

But this was a different England from the one we had known. Eggs and butter cost more than they did in California, and the prices of houses were climbing at an ever-accelerating rate. Much against my will, I was slowly beginning to admit that, just possibly, Jean and Rebecca were right: home is best.

While I was still shooting *Shalako*, I had taken an option on Bart Spicer's novel, *Act of Anger*, and I had asked Stephen Boyd to play the lead in what I hoped would be my next production. The project was eventually set up, on a "step" basis, at Warners-Seven Arts. Peter Allen Fields had written an excellent script. I turned it in to the executives, who came back to me with raves: "The best script I've read in years," "This is like one of your great ones," etc. The next morning I read that Seven Arts had sold its holdings to another company, and a few mornings after that, I learned that the new management was canceling all films that weren't already on the floor. For at least the fifth time, I had been caught in a management changeover. Since, in my deal, I had sold them the option, which still had nearly a year to run, I couldn't even try to set the project up at another studio. *Act of Anger* died stillborn.

But Steve and I were planning to set up a company of our own, and we kept in touch. He had just finished a film for Alexander Salkind in Spain. Now he called me to say that Alex had a number of tentative projects ahead and was in need of a director. Could he recommend me? I didn't particularly need the money, but I sure needed the work. I told him to go ahead. Alex called me from Paris, and in a few days his son Ilya flew in to London with an armful of scripts. One, not yet finished, I found interesting. It was the story of Gilles de Rais, Joan of Arc's notorious captain, who had been accused of sadistically murdering literally hundreds of children. Of course, this occurred at the height of Europe's witchcraft hysteria; and the good captain, the richest noble in France, had a number of possessions that tempted both the bishop and the French king. The possibility that he was the victim of trumped-up charges had always attracted me to a thorough investigation of his story. Alex Salkind and I reached an agreement.

By the end of the summer, much to the delight of Jean and Rebecca, who are Southern Californians in every conceivable way, we had decided to resettle somewhere near L.A. They flew back in time for the fall school term, taking with them the dog and two cats who, sadly, were never to set a free foot on English soil. I went to Switzerland to continue discussions with Salkind. Alex was in Montreux, drinking the curative waters, though God knows what he was trying to cure. He picked me up at the airport in Geneva, and apologized that he'd have to take a short side-trip to his bank. When he came out, his briefcase was bulging with dollars. Ah, I thought, another operator.

I had persuaded Salkind to hire De Concini to rewrite the Gilles de Rais script, and Ennio and his collaborator, Maria Pia Fusco, joined us in Montreux. We were in for a surprise. The Salkinds had consulted some of their exhibitor friends and had discovered that a film based on the life of the notorious child-slayer would be difficult to sell. They still wanted me to make a film for them but could it please be something else?

We kicked around a few ideas. Gilles de Rais has on occasion been called the original Bluebeard, a name commonly used for generations to identify mass-murderers. It was a logical step to consider Bluebeard as the subject of a film. The story had been made before, but not for a number of years. We decided to take a crack at it.

That night, Ennio, Maria Pia, and I sat out on the sidewalk in front of our Geneva hotel, sipping our after-dinner drinks and discussing the reasons a man might find for wanting to kill his wife. There were dozens. (We could have found an equal number of reasons why a woman might want to kill her husband, but Bluebeard was traditionally a male.) Our problem was to find seven which would have the greatest identification in the minds of our potential audience.

Some were obvious—the domineering woman who is in perpetual competition with her husband, the guilt-plagued wife with a compulsion to confess her past indiscretions, the nymphomaniac with overwhelming sexual demands, the lesbian who shouldn't have married our "hero" in the first place. . . . We sifted the number down to ten or twelve, then set about the somewhat more difficult task of finding ingenious ways of killing them. By the time we retired to our rooms, about 2:00 in the morning, the framework of our story had been set. The next morning Ennio and Maria flew back to Rome, and I returned to Paris.

There has never been any studio operation in France worthy of the classification. Films have almost always been made by independent producers setting up projects on their own. As a result, the producers are invariably promoters or money-getters, and rarely "creative" impresarios on the order of Selznick or Goldwyn in Hollywood, Korda in England, or Ponti in Italy. This leaves the director much more free to be the boss of the film once it has been set up—in fact, it is taken for granted that he will be. It also means that he is obligated to follow the film through to its final completion, since there is no studio organization to take charge of the postproduction, as is the common practice in Hollywood.

The European financing process worked something like this: On the strength of his contract with me, Salkind was able to borrow money to finance the writing of the script. Once he had a satisfactory script, he could get a bit more money to finance his efforts in obtaining a star. When the star had been signed, Salkind, armed with a script, a star, and a director, could set about the financing of the film itself. The amount of the initial budget depended, of course, on the name value of the star. And each "name" added to the cast increased the film's potential value and enabled Salkind to increase the budget and the schedule. The money came from two sources: the banks, and distributors' advances against the film's eventual distribution grosses. For Salkind, in this instance, it worked out very well. The cast we assembled was strong enough internationally to enable him to show a profit before the production went on the floor, and allowed him to establish a line of credit which insured future production on an ever-increasing scale.

In the late fall, the first draft of the script was ready. The Salkinds were startled to discover we had written not a horror story, but a black comedy. Alex was disturbed, but his son Ilya saw the advantages immediately. Alex checked with some of his distributors, who resolved his doubts, and we got the green light. Casting was difficult at first, since Salkind was still holding a rather flat purse. Then my agent, Kurt Frings, asked for a copy of the script and I obliged him. A few days later, he called me.

"How about Richard Burton for Bluebeard?" he asked.

"Good God!" I said. "Is it possible?" We had been aiming at much more reachable targets.

"I think there's a good chance," he said. "Let me give it a try."

The Salkinds were ecstatic. Burton opened up a whole new vista. They waited impatiently.

A week later, Burton, Frings, and I were having lunch at Fouquet's on the Champs-Élysées.

I had met Burton briefly three years before in London. He looked better in Paris. He was on the wagon, physically trim, and looking younger than he had in years. And he liked our script. By the end of our very pleasant lunch, all that remained was for Frings to arrange the terms of Burton's deal with Salkind. That was no problem, for Burton was craftier than most. He requested a sizable amount for expenses (minuscule, however, when compared to current star salaries) and a hefty percentage of the distributor's gross. For him there were no box-office failures.

With Burton set, all systems were go. The next two months were a whirlwind of activity. I spent most of my time in Rome on a polish of the script, but there were trips to Hungary, Yugoslavia, and Bulgaria, looking for locations, and Munich and Paris for casting. Since our film was being cooperatively financed, we had to get players from the United States, France, Germany, and Italy. This presented a few problems. The major parts were obviously those of Bluebeard's eight wives, and each part was what, in film circles, is called a vignette—outstanding while it lasts, but it doesn't last very long. It meant dozens of interviews in half a dozen cities, and dozens of films to view. Munich was the most painful.

I was being shown film clips of different actresses at the Munich studio, and all of them were obviously excerpted from stag reels. I turned to the man who had organized the showing.

"This isn't exactly what I was looking for," I said. "Can you show me some of your family pictures?"

"These *are* our family pictures," he answered.

And, indeed, they were. During this period, no ordinary American film could make a dime in Germany. The Germans, French, and Italians came late to freedom of expression in matters of sex, but they certainly did their best to make up for lost time. This blatant hard-porn trend is probably responsible, at least in part, for the decline in quality of French and Italian films. Germany, on the other hand, has been a cinematic wasteland since World War II. Today there are signs of a reawakening of talent which may help the German filmmakers regain the prominent position they enjoyed before the rise of Hitler.

With Burton on the team, Salkind found money easier to get. Raquel Welch was offered $150,000 for five days' work. She accepted. Virna Lisi, a legitimate star in Italy, also received a fair amount for a few days' work. Joey Heatherton was imported from Hollywood to play Bluebeard's eighth, and surviving, wife. From France came Nathalie Delon. Karin Schubert and Sybil Danning were Germany's contribution. Marilu Tolo and Agostina Belli, from Italy, completed the roster of wives—as beautiful a bevy of broads as ever graced a film.

In the meantime, we had been touring the Balkans for locations. Among other things, we were looking for castles, and there were none. It seems the Turks, who overran that part of the world in the late Middle Ages, and who fought primarily on horseback, considered them an unsportsmanlike obstruction to their progress. They razed every castle in their path. As one moved further south toward Turkey itself, even a self-respecting palace was hard to find. For this and certain financial reasons, it was decided to make the film in Hungary. Budapest became the center of our activities.

I was excited at the prospect of living for several months behind the Iron Curtain. The Communist description of life beyond the pale is so at variance with that of the red-baiter, there is only one way to learn the truth—one must see for oneself. My first impression was disappointing. Budapest is no longer the city of light, as prewar legend had it. Heavily damaged during the war, it is still trying to pull itself together. But there was one immediately noticeable anomaly I found difficult to accept.

Within a few blocks of the studio stands a statue dedicated to "the salt of the earth," the cornerstone of Communism, the proletarian, the working man. He stands solid and proud, square-shouldered, steely-eyed. On his head he wears the worker's symbol, a cap—a cap which he tips to no man. In theory, that is.

When I first walked on the studio lot and made a tour of the stages, I was amazed to see the workers tipping their caps to me and to the bureaucrat who accompanied me. Those without headgear literally pulled their forelocks, that old gesture of subservience. I later commented on this practice, which I considered so out of place in a Socialist state. My guide gave me an answer that I was to hear a number of times during my stay: "We talk water, but we drink wine," he said.

As time went on, I found the Hungarians were still Hungarians; a bit subdued, perhaps, but still in love with the good and gay life—at least, as good and as gay as they could get it. The restaurants were excellent, and food was in good supply. And the service, quite the contrary to that reported by travelers in Russia, was excellent. Obviously, the Hungarians still took pride in their food and the way they presented it.

We were also quite free to drive anywhere in the country—to visit and to talk with whomever we wished. At no time was there the slightest sign of surveillance, and I am not an amateur in this field. The streets and weekend roads were stacked with cars, and new models were being added to the crush at an ever-increasing rate. The country showed every sign of soon enjoying those extra rewards of Western civilization: smog and traffic jams. The average worker's salary was $90 a month, with a system of small bonuses for unusually good or productive work, but food and rents were ridiculously low, and not one person was unemployed. There is some excellent talent in the local film industry, and I asked one of our interpreters what the top salary of their biggest star might be. About $2,500, she told me, for perhaps six months of his time—just a few hundred less than Raquel was getting for an hour's labor.

Miss Welch was full of surprises. I had heard very bad reports of her behavior in many of her previous films—fights with her costars, with her directors—but in Budapest, she was a doll. She worked hard and enthusiastically, and showed a comedic sense I would never have guessed at.

We started shooting in Budapest soon after the New Year. Our camera crew was Italian, led by Gabor Pogany, a Hungarian who had emigrated from his native country when he was a young man. I had selected him before we had decided to shoot in Hungary because he was one of the best cameramen in Rome. Now his knowledge of the language and the country made things a good deal easier for us. Our sound men were German, and the rest of the crew was Hungarian, and quite efficient. The local equipment was archaic, and we imported most of ours from Italy and France.

Burton was on the wagon, and, it followed, on his best behavior. On closer acquaintance, I found him, like many actors, to be somewhat shy and introspective, but straightforward, extremely literate and articulate, and a thorough professional on the set. His effect on women was clinically interesting. A fifteen-minute conversation was enough to leave most females starry-eyed and sanguine.

"He loves me—I just know he does," one said to me.

"But you've barely spoken to him," I said. "And what about Elizabeth?"

"Oh, to hell with Elizabeth. He loves *me*. I could feel it."

At least a half dozen women expressed themselves to me in remarkably similar words. And they not only chose to ignore Elizabeth, but their own husbands or companions. Like many insects in mating season, I figured Richard must exude an odor that only women could smell.

Sometime in February, I believe, David Frost arrived in Budapest to tape a couple of talk shows with Liz and Dick. We gave him the use of one of our sets, complete with lights, for the shooting, which took place one evening at the end of our day's work. Elizabeth's session came first. Liz has always hated interviews, not only because the end results are often distorted and disappointing, but also because she suffers acute stage fright in any kind of personal appearance. She fortified herself with a shot or two of her favorite tranquilizer, Jack Daniels, and asked me to stay close by for moral support. She was actually shivering. As the cameras started, Burton tried to reassure her.

"Just relax," he said. "You're only talking to a friend."

The "friend" started the conversation rolling, and they were into a session which lasted about two hours.

Liz was sitting on a divan, and under the divan, close to her right hand, was a tall glass of sour-mash whiskey. As the interview progressed, Liz reached for the glass at every break and took a man-sized swallow. One of her sycophants would reload the tumbler whenever it showed any danger of exposing a dry bottom. Miss Taylor is not an alcoholic, and, to my certain knowledge, she never drinks while working. When she does drink, on her own time, she can hold her liquor as well as anyone I've ever known, but that evening she was showing the effects of the sour mash by the end of the first half hour.

Elizabeth does not space out when she gets boxed, nor does she get sloppy or inarticulate. But she does grow more sentimental (perhaps a bit maudlin), and her speech slows up perceptibly. As the interview progressed, her pauses became more and more pronounced. It would have been a simple operation to cut out the silences and achieve a result which would have looked quite normal, but Elizabeth's "friend" couldn't resist the temptation to create a minor sensation. He released the film just as it had been shot, even making two shows out of it because of its increased length. There are times when you can depend on a reporter's complete honesty—when the subject appears in an unfavorable light.

Miss Taylor's entourage was a seventeenth-century royal court in miniature, including six or seven persons, among them a majordomo, a personal secretary, a hairdresser, and a photographer. They formed a tight protective circle around Liz; they had a great thing going, and they weren't about to lose it. At times I thought she was their prisoner. When it served their purposes, they helped to get her loaded. Like an efficient undercover agency, they filtered gossip and news through to their mistress as and when it suited them. Burton was aware of the cabal, but Liz was fiercely protective of her courtiers, and all his efforts to break it up ended in failure.

For Elizabeth's fortieth birthday, Richard threw a little party—well, three parties, really. Nothing like them had been seen in Budapest since Emperor Franz Josef's last Hungarian wing-ding before World War I. And it created more stir than the revolution of 1956. Guests came from the four corners of the earth, as did members of the press. Princess Grace, a paragon of informal and democratic charm, danced the polka, as did "Princess" Elizabeth. The three parties (including the Sunday brunch) were excellently and efficiently catered. Considering that Richard was stone-cold sober, he held up beautifully, as did I, who dislike most parties with a passion. But Jean was in Budapest for a brief visit, and all was right in heaven, even behind the Iron Curtain.

Naturally, it couldn't last. About this time, Richard's older brother died. He had been in a hospital in a semicomatose condition for months as a result of an accident, and his death was not unexpected. Indeed, under the circumstances, it was almost welcome. But Richard regarded this brother as a father figure, and he was deeply affected. He took a few days off to attend the funeral in Wales. When he returned, he had left the wagon behind somewhere in the Welsh countryside.

For a few days he kept himself under control. Then, one night, the British ambassador and Mrs. Derek Dodson invited us to dinner at their home. When I arrived, Richard and Elizabeth were already there, and Burton was reciting bits of Dylan Thomas for the edification of the Dodsons' teen-age daughter, who was deep into English poetry at school. Burton can read a poem better than anyone I've ever heard, and I've heard some of the best. As a Welshman, he practically worshiped

Thomas and knew every word that precocious genius had ever written. He now held his audience enthralled. And then, as dinner was announced, I saw him reach for his drink on the table beside him. My stomach dropped out.

Burton ate nothing at dinner, but continued to drink. The intimate party included the Swiss ambassador and his wife, and a young American attaché, with his wife. About halfway through the main course, Richard interrupted the conversation and directed his attention to the quite charming and pleasant wife of the Swiss ambassador.

"You remind me quite distinctly of a hungry vulture," he said.

That's what's known as a conversation stopper. The young American attaché bridled, but the Swiss ambassador, who looked like a very kindly English curate, tried to turn the other cheek and the conversation. Burton zeroed in on him. "You Swiss are a very bad lot," he said.

"Richard!"

It was his master's voice. Richard looked over at Liz, caught her steely-eyed gaze, and got up from the table.

"Excuse me," he said. "I had better go home."

And he did. The rest of the evening was very pleasant, indeed.

The next night, we were shooting in the streets of Budapest. It was close to midnight, and I had set up the last shot of the night. Nathalie Delon was standing by, and I sent an assistant after Burton. We waited quite a while, but finally he arrived. Taking Nathalie's arm, he said, "Let's go," and led her down the street, around the corner, and out of sight. I was sure it was a practical joke and expected him to turn around, laughing, at any moment. I waited five minutes before sending someone after him. The assistant came back, empty-handed. Richard, he reported, had shoved Nathalie into his Rolls, and driven off. I told my assistant to wrap it up for the night.

I canceled the next day's work and refused to answer the phone. In the afternoon I got an abject note of apology, asking me to believe that the Burton of the night before was not the real Burton. Perhaps he wasn't, and yet, perhaps he was.

That was the beginning of a long nightmare. Burton was often drunk when he arrived at the studio in the morning and always drunk when he left in the afternoon. I was lucky to get in three or four hours' work with him on any given day, and the quality was nowhere near his standard. As he himself once told me in a semisober moment, "I used to think I could act just as well when I was drunk as when I was sober. I've found out I can't." Of course he couldn't. Burton was a very bad drunk. I had to watch him carefully and get him off the set before he turned mean, or someone in the crew might have killed him. It could have been me.

But the leading ladies (Miss Lisi excepted) were still falling in love with him, and, when Elizabeth left Budapest, he was reciprocating their affections. One morning, while we were talking in his roulotte dressing room, he shook his head.

"Elizabeth called me from Rome at five o'clock this morning," he said, "and told me to 'get that woman out of my bed!'" He shook his head again. "How did she know?"

"You don't really know you're surrounded by agents?" I asked. "Why, you can't pick your nose without Liz finding out. You must know that."

Perhaps he did, but like Anthony Quinn with the gambler, he just wasn't going to accept it.

Somehow, we finished with Burton. On the morning he left Budapest, he walked out of the Intercontinental Hotel with his bodyguard and his manager pressed tight against each shoulder, propping him up. I felt as though I'd just emerged from under a suffocating blanket. I finished shooting in another week or two and flew to Rome for the final cutting. Then it was home and mother, at least for a couple of weeks. When I was ready to return to Italy for the dubbing, I got word that Alex Salkind wanted to see me in Geneva.

I met him at his hotel. Alex is a tiny, frightened-looking man, but he had obviously worked himself up for this meeting.

"The Germans insist on getting more sex and more violence, or they won't distribute the film," he said. "We're going to have to shoot some retakes. If you don't want to do them, I will have to hire somebody else."

He seemed relieved when he got it all out. I guess he had expected me to blow. To what purpose, I thought. I had played the sex and murder scenes obliquely, with only a slight bit of nudity to appease the distributors, and judging by the reactions we had gotten, they were quite funny that way. But indirection had no meaning for the Germans. Everything had to be explicit and overt. I told Salkind I would spare him the added expense. I wanted to keep at least some control over the new material.

So we wound up with a film which some viewers thought very amusing and some thought too explicit. Others weren't sure what they thought. If it had been possible, I would have added an explanatory card to the main title: "In films, compromise is a way of life."

A HIGH-RISK LIFE

The movies have been my life for more than a quarter of the life of the United States. A sobering thought, but growing old is no burden—growing useless is. I still spend most of my time looking ahead—even now there are a couple of films in me waiting to get out.

Reminiscence is a habit I am not anxious to acquire, but as I forced myself to look back over fifty-five years of work in the glamour capitol of the world, I found I had few regrets. If I had to do it all over again, I would, and I'd probably remake all my mistakes. Motion pictures have always been known as a high-risk investment, and a career in the movies is a high-risk life. The manufacture of films is the only business I know where no sensible father will encourage his daughter or son to follow in his footsteps. The risk of humiliating failure is too great, and even success brings heartbreak more often than not.

How can anyone explain its attraction or its requirements? Brains are not sufficient, though intelligence is necessary to excel; formal education is of minor importance, though knowledge makes things easier. Talent, backed up by self-discipline, is nearly all. And luck. Being in front of the right store at the right time, meeting the right person—yet I think that the role of chance is overplayed. The laws of chance bring opportunity to all—and more than once. But only those with talent can use it to long-lasting advantage.

At the moment, however, there are far fewer opportunities than when I was young. Feature production (for theaters) is a waning nova. I firmly believe that theatrical distribution is fast reaching an uneconomical, unviable level. There are too few blockbusters to keep the industry healthy. The "cathedrals" of our trade—the large theaters—have become auction marts and department stores. Even Radio City Music Hall nearly expired a few months ago, and could cease to function in the near future. Many neighborhood theaters are showing old films to keep alive.

I venture to say there wouldn't be a movie theater open a week from now if the sales of snacks were banned tomorrow.

And the quality of films has deteriorated. Most of the Oscar nominees of the last few years would have been dismissed as good second-raters in Hollywood's golden age. There are solid reasons for this. One is the law of averages. When we turned out 600 films each year, a 5 percent rate of superior films meant 30 pictures of better-than-average quality. But 5 percent of 180 films (not even that many are turned out by major picture-makers) means only 9 in the upper bracket. And if you figure that perhaps 5 percent of these select films are truly great, the ratio is one great film in two years in modern times. I don't believe we've achieved even that.

If it weren't for TV production, most studios would not exist today. Television is Hollywood's tragedy—and its hope for the future. In TV's vast spaces, talents wander in circles until they drop from exhaustion. Only the opportunists—and the slick, the trite, and the vulgar—can survive its stifling atmosphere. In a field where ad-men, sponsors, and their wives set the standards, little of quality can germinate.

Yet resurgence is at our doorstep. New, larger screens will make a private theater out of every home, with no pop-corn buckets, no Coca-Cola cups, no carelessly scattered wads of gum to wade through. When people finally realize, as they eventually must, that they have *never* had "free" TV, that they have paid for every program in increased prices on everything they buy, and that they have been furnishing the advertisers free billboards within their own homes, some form of pay TV will begin to get its share of the audience. That audience will be greater than ever, the financial return will be greater than ever, and the opportunities for filmmakers will be greater than ever.

It won't be the "old Hollywood" come back to life, but something quite new. However, it will be reminiscent of the old in its vitality, its genius, and the quality of its product. And the product, of course, *will* be the same—it will be movies.

As for me. . . . I have just read that Gadge Kazan thinks you should take chances, change careers, everything, so that you're constantly challenged. I agree. A couple of years ago I decided to take up a new career—teaching. So last January, I started my first regular stint at the University of Texas, at Austin—and I'm hooked. The students are wonderful, my fellow teachers are warm and friendly, and I'm having a ball. The school authorities have asked me back for another full year and I've accepted.

And the students seem to enjoy hearing it from someone who has spent a life-time in "the real world." Because I talk about more than techniques. I have spoken to my "kids" about the joys of creation, of rcognition, of world-wide camaraderie, with little conflict or jealousy, that only artists seem to share, and of "doing your thing" with love and understanding. But I have stressed much more the disappointments, the biting criticism, the minute probabilities of success, and the ten thousand to one chances for unhappy mediocrity or failure.

A young man confronts me. "It may be a hell of a life, as you suggest, sir," he argues politely. "Still, it's *living!*"

Well, yes. . . .

FILMOGRAPHY OF
EDWARD DMYTRYK

The Hawk, Independent (1935)
Television Spy, Paramount (1939)
Emergency Squad, Paramount (1939)
Golden Gloves, Paramount (1939)
Mystery Sea Raider, Paramount (1940)
Her First Romance, I. E. Chadwick (1940)
The Devil Commands, Columbia (1940)
Under Age, Columbia (1940)
Sweetheart of the Campus, Columbia (1941)
The Blonde from Singapore, Columbia (1941)
Secrets of the Lone Wolf, Columbia (1941)
Confessions of Boston Blackie, Columbia (1941)
Counter-Espionage, Columbia (1942)
Seven Miles from Alcatraz, RKO (1942)
Hitler's Children, RKO (1943)
The Falcon Strikes Back, RKO (1943)
Captive Wild Woman, Universal (1943)
Behind the Rising Sun, RKO (1943)
Tender Comrade, RKO (1943)
Murder, My Sweet, RKO (1944)
Back to Bataan, RKO (1945)
Cornered, RKO (1945)
Till the End of Time, RKO (1945)
So Well Remembered, RKO–Rank (1946)
Crossfire, RKO (1947)
The Hidden Room, English Independent (1948)
Give Us This Day, Eagle–Lion (1949)
Mutiny, King Brothers–United Artists (1951)
The Sniper, Kramer–Columbia (1951)
Eight Iron Men, Kramer–Columbia (1952)

The Juggler, Kramer–Columbia (1952)
The Caine Mutiny, Kramer–Columbia (1953)
Broken Lance, 20th Century–Fox (1954)
The End of the Affair, Columbia (1954)
Soldier of Fortune, 20th Century–Fox (1955)
The Left Hand of God, 20th Century–Fox (1955)
The Mountain, Paramount (1956)
Raintree County, MGM (1956)
The Young Lions, 20th Century–Fox (1957)
Warlock, 20th Century–Fox (1958)
The Blue Angel, 20th Century–Fox (1959)
A Walk on the Wild Side, Columbia (1961)
The Reluctant Saint, Columbia (1961)
The Carpetbaggers, Paramount (1963)
Where Love Has Gone, Paramount (1964)
Mirage, Universal (1965)
Alvarez Kelly, Columbia (1966)
Anzio, Columbia (1967)
Shalako, Cinerama (1968)
Bluebeard, Cinerama (1972)
The Human Factor, Bryanston (1975)

INDEX

Abie's Irish Rose, 9
Abel, Walter, 209, 268
Academy of Motion Picture Arts and Sciences
  accomplishments of, 12
  Oscar awards, 42, 148, 184, 186, 211,
    233, 249
Acquanetta, 55
Act of Anger, 286–287
Actors' Studio, 123, 209
Adler, Buddy, 189, 237
Adler, Luther, 71
AFTRA, 103
Agar, John, 75
Agents, 51, 52, 55–56
Agnew, Spiro, 100
Akins, Zoe, 40
Algren, Nelson, 244
Allen, Fred, 36
Allenberg, Bert, 52
Aller, Herb, 42
All the King's Men, 126, 141
Alvarez Kelly, 270–274
American Legion, 125, 148
American Society of Film Editors, 22
Amphitheatrof, Daniel, 207
Anhalt, Edna, 165, 166, 167, 220
Anhalt, Edward, 165, 166, 167, 220, 230
Antifascist Refugee Committee, 135
Anti-Semitism, 89, 92, 225
Anzio, 275–279
Appointment in Zaharain, 244
Arlen, Richard, 8, 63, 200, 237
Arthur, George, 27, 29, 32, 38, 69
Ashley, Elizabeth, 260, 261–262
Astaire, Fred, 191
Astor, Mary, 16
Audience Research Institute, 92

Aurthur, Robert Alan, 57, 233, 234, 238,
  239, 244
Awful Truth, The, 37
Ayres, Lew, 43, 261

Bacall, Lauren (Betty), 97, 178, 197
Back to Bataan, 63, 65–68
Baer, Parley, 221, 224
Baker, Carroll, 261, 262
Baker, Diane, 268
Balaban, Barney, 189, 257
Balsam, Martin, 261
Balzer (guard), 136, 140, 143
Banner, John, 243
Bardot, Brigitte, 283, 284
Barrett, Michael, 244
Barrett, William, 195
Barry, Don "Red," 237
Barry, Gene, 190
Barrymore, John, 42–43
Barrymore, Lionel, 145
Barzman, Ben, 65, 106, 119, 120
Bass, Saul, 247
Baxter, Anne, 246, 247
Beardless Warriors, The, 244
Beavers, Louise, 196
Beery, Wallace, 16
Behind the Rising Sun, 56
Behind the Silken Curtain (Crum), 94
Belli, Agostina, 290
Bennet, Hugh, 27
Berg–Allenberg Agency, 52
Bergerac, Jacques, 235
Bergman, Ingrid, 118
Bessie, Alvah, 64, 105–106, 127
Best Years of Our Lives, The, 78
Betz, Matthew, 9

Biberman, Herbert, 103, 104, 127, 144
Bigotry, 89, 92
Bikel, Theodore, 243
Birdman of Alcatraz, The, 128
Bissell, Whit, 237
Blacklist, 103–105, 118, 125, 145, 245
Blackman, Honor, 283, 284
Blankfort, Michael, 168, 173
Blasetti, Mara, 250
Blue Angel, The, 242–243
Bluebeard, 288–295
Bogart, Humphrey, 60, 97, 173, 178, 195, 197–198
Bondi, Beulah, 65
Boston Blackie, 53
Boyd, Stephen, 283, 284, 286–287
Boyer, Charles, 117
Brando, Christian, 229
Brando, Marlon, 23, 74, 76, 101, 191, 202, 207, 220–230
Brave One, The, 148
Brecht, Bertolt, 97–98
Brennan, George, 7
Brenner, Herb, 220
Brewer, Roy, 94
Brian, Mary, 8
Brick Foxhole, The (Brooks), 89
Briskin, Irving, 53
Britt, Mai, 229, 243
Broken Lance, 180–186, 189, 198, 200, 201
Bronson, Betty, 8
Bronson, Nat, 110–113, 118, 122, 124
Brooks, Richard, 89
Brown, Phil, 113, 118
Brynner, Yul, 270
Bulldog Drummond, 42–43
Burlesque, 19
Burton, Richard, 212, 289, 292, 293–295
Busch, Niven, 73

Cabinet of Doctor Caligari, The, 242–243
Cagney, James, 261
Cagney, Jeanne, 48
Caine Mutiny, The, 167, 171–179, 196, 209
California Institute of Technology, 10–11
Callaghan, Duke, 229
Cam Tong, 196
Capra, Frank, 10, 63
Captive Wild Woman, 55
Capucine, 246, 247
Carlson, Richard, 85

Carpetbaggers, The, 191, 256–257, 260–262, 263–265
Carradine, John, 28, 55
Carrol, Sue, 52–53
Carroll, Nancy, 19
Castle, Bill, 127
Celler, Emmanuel, 98
Chadwick, Ike, 52, 53
Chandler, "Happy," 214
Chandler, Raymond, 58, 60
Chaplin, Charlie, 14, 28
Chapman, Ben, 224, 227
Charade, 267
Cheirel, Micheline, 71
Christ in Concrete, 105–108, 115–125
Cinemascope, 181, 200
Claire, Ina, 20, 21
Clark, Colonel, 65, 66–67
Clark, Robert E., 93
Clark, Victor, 3
Clavell, James, 286
Clift, Montgomery, 101–102, 209–226
Clive, Colin, 43
Cobb, Lee J., 196
Coffee, Lenore, 187
Cohan, George M., 31
Cohn, Harry, 52, 144, 171, 172, 196
Colbert, Claudette, 40, 41
Cole, Lester, 127, 147
Colleano, Bonar, 117, 167
College Inn, 28
Collier, William, Sr., 45
Columbia Pictures, 53, 144, 171, 179, 181, 187, 245, 247, 270, 277, 279
Columbus, 285
Columbus, Christopher, 281–283
Comi, Paul, 237
Communists, 4, 64–65, 70–72, 83, 92, 116, 120, 126–127, 194, 290–291
    Dmytryk's break with, 126–127, 141–148, 224
    free speech and, 126–127, 141
    Un-American Activities Committee and, 94–103
    See also Hollywood Ten
Connery, Sean, 280, 283, 284
Connors, Mike, 265
Coogan, Jackie, 44
Cooley, Hallam (Hal), 52, 55–56
Cooper, Gary, 8, 96–97, 182, 235
Coppel, Alec and Myra, 110–112
Corby, Ellen, 71

Cornered, 68–72, 92, 126, 141
Covered Wagon, The, 7
Craig, James, 54
Crocollo, Carlo, 250
Cromwell, John, 16, 19
Crosland, Alan, 7
Crossfire, 88–93, 98, 114, 165, 208
Crum, Bartley, 94, 98, 141, 145, 169
Cruze, James, 7
Cukor, George, 16, 20, 31, 40, 43, 64
Cummings, Jack, 243
Curtiz, Michael, 103
Cushing, Peter, 188

Daily Worker, 165–166
Damon, Mark, 277
Dance of Life, The, 19
Darkness at Noon (Koestler), 70
Darvi, Bella, 74
Daves, Delmer, 38, 39
Davis, Bette, 264–265
de Concini, Ennio, 281, 282, 283, 285, 287, 288
De Felitta, Frank, 277
de Grunwald, Dmitri, 285
De Laurentiis, Dino, 274–279
Delon, Nathalie, 290, 294
De Mille, Cecil B., 7–8, 70, 93, 94, 103
Denning, Richard, 48
Dennis, Nick, 167
de Rais, Gilles, 287, 288
Devil Commands, The, 53
Diamond, 142
DiDonato, Pietro, 105, 106
Dietrich, Marlene, 18, 243
Directors
    advent of sound and, 16–19
    assistant, 35–36, 37–38
    contracts of, 51–52
    early success and, 30
    era of geniuses, 34
    See also specific individuals
Directors Guild, 94, 103
Dmytryk, Edward
    on accents, 116–117
    agent of, 52, 55–56
    on "attitude," 266
    awards won by, 89, 124, 137, 186, 255
    Communist affiliation of, 4, 64–65, 70–72, 83, 194
        break with, 126–127, 141–148, 224
    Un-American Activities Committee
        and, 94–103, 145, 146–148
    as a cutter, 18–26, 29–41, 42
    early film career of, 3–44
    Film Editors Guild and, 42
    films directed by. *See individual films*
    on future of films, 296–297
    IRS and, 144–145, 187
    lighting and, 90, 114, 121–122
    marriages of
        first, 27, 40, 63, 72, 79, 93, 105–109, 125–126, 144, 169
        second. *See* Dmytryk, Jean Porter
    on "method" acting, 123
    as "Mr. RKO," 88–93
    on Oscars, 42
    as premature antifascist, 63–65
    on the press, 100–102, 137
    as prisoner, 125, 127–143
        at Mill Point Prison Camp, 125, 131–143
    process techniques of, 87
    on screen credit, 51
    sketch artists and, 166–167
    on society, 194–195
    studio disintegration and, 189
    on stuntmen, 182–183
    on superstars, 191–192
    technical effects of, 60–62
    Un-American Activities Committee and, 89–103
    "using it," 45, 49–50
Dmytryk, Jean Porter, 196, 210, 211–212, 215
    Communist affiliation of Edward and, 106, 107, 110–112, 116, 120, 125, 127, 137, 140–143
    courtship of Edward and, 75, 77, 78, 79, 88, 93
    homes of, 187, 193, 194, 233, 256, 263, 265, 281, 286, 287
    on locations with Edward, 189, 199, 229, 238–242, 249, 279, 283, 284, 293
    marriage, 78, 108–109
    pregnancies and births, 115, 124, 148, 252–253
Dmytryk, Michael, 63, 169, 187, 263, 265
Dmytryk, Rebecca, 253, 286, 287
Dmytryk, Ricky, 124, 125, 187, 229
Dmytryk, Victoria, 187
Doctor Dolittle, 209
Doctor Zhivago (Pasternak), 72
Dodson, Derek, 293

Doran, D. A., 237, 242, 243, 244
Douglas, Kirk, 90, 168–171
Douglas, William, 181, 182, 183, 201–202
Doll, Dora, 221, 224
Dove, Billie, 7
Dozier, William, 69–70
Drake, Tom, 209, 237
Duck Soup, 31

Education for Death, 55
Egan, Ted, 13
Egyptian, The, 74
Eight Iron Men, 167–168
Eisenstein, Sergei, 97
Emergency Squad, 46–48
End of the Affair, The, 187–189, 209
English, Richard, 146, 147
Erickson, Leif, 268
Esquire, 106
Extra, The, 8

Fairbanks, Douglas, 28
Falcon series, 55, 58
Falk, Peter, 277, 279
Famous Artists Agency, 55–56, 247
Famous Players–Lasky studio, 3–7
Fante, John, 248, 249
Farewell, My Lovely, 58–62
Fast, Howard, 267, 268
FBI, 146, 166
Feldman, Charles, 144, 244–247
Ferrer, Jose, 173, 178
Fields, Peter Allen, 287
Film Daily, 279
Film Editors Guild, 41, 42
Film industry
  advent of sound and, 14–18
    actor's voice and, 15
    cutting rooms and, 17–18, 19–20
    directors and, 16, 19
    "live" theater actors and, 16
    microphones and, 17
    photography and, 17
  censorship and, 40
  cutting and, 21–26
  research and development by, 11–12
  retrospective look at, 22
  silent movies, 3–10
  unionization of, 42
First Grand Masterpiece Award, 124, 137
First National studio, 27
5000 Fingers of Dr. T., The, 171

"Flickers," 6
Flynn, Errol, 66
Fonda, Henry, 235, 236, 237
Fonda, Jane, 246–247
Fool of Venus, The, 43
Ford, Glenn, 226
Ford, John, 76, 254
Ford, Wally, 237
Fortune, 102
Francis, Bob, 173, 177
Frances, Madame, 29
Frankel, Benjamin, 214
Franklin, 218
Frankovich, Mike, 249
Franz, Arthur, 165, 167, 277
Franz, Eduard, 181, 182
Freeman, Y. Frank, 244
French, Valerie, 283, 284
Frings, Kurt, 289
Front Page, The, 258
Frost, David, 292–293
Fusco, Maria Pia, 287, 288

Gabani, Til, 204
Gable, Clark, 182, 189–193, 217, 244
Gann, Ernest, 189
Garbo, Greta, 16
Gardener, Cyril, 16, 20, 31
Garfield, John, 120
Garland, Judy, 97
Geiger, Rod, 105–108, 110, 116–120, 122, 124
Giannini, Giancarlo, 277
Gibbons, Cedric, 210
Gilbert, John, 15
Gish, Lillian, 4–5
Give Us This Day, 124, 137
Glen Glenn, 42
Golden, Doc, 55
Golden Gloves, 48–49, 184
Goldwyn, Samuel, 97, 207
Goodman, John, 199
Gone With the Wind, 209
Gordean, Jack, 144, 270
Gorshin, Frank, 236, 237
Gould, Elliot, 192
Grable, Betty, 44
Grace, Princess, 293
Graham, Gloria, 90
Graham, Sheilah, 189
Grand Ol' Opry, 138
Grant, Cary, 37, 245, 267

Granville, Bonita, 54, 55
Gray, Sally, 113
Greed, 242–243
Green, Harry, 196
Greene, Graham, 187
Griffith, D. W., 22
Griffith, Jim, 167, 280
Guns of Navarone, The, 275
Guy Named Joe, A, 188

Hall, Oakley, 231
Harder They Fall, The (Schulberg), 101
Harlow, Jean, 260
Harrison, Doane, 27
Harvey, Laurence, 113, 246, 247, 249
Hathaway, Henry, 31–33, 74, 181
Hawk, The, 41–42
Hawkins, Jack, 283, 284
Hayes, Alfred, 195
Hayes, Helen, 246
Hayes, John Michael, 260, 263–264
Hayward, Susan, 190, 264–265
Heatherton, Joey, 265, 290
Hecht, Ben, 69, 101, 245–246
Heisler, Stu, 27, 259
Hell's Angels, 259
Henri's Restaurant, 28–29
Henry, Bill, 45
Hepburn, Katherine, 191, 201
Hickey, Donna Lee, 173
High Noon, 165
Hitchcock, Alfred, 167
Hitler's Children, 55, 56
Hoffman, Dustin, 192
Hogan, James, 50
Hold 'Em, Navy!, 43, 261
Holden, William, 270–273
Holiday, 196
Holliman, Earl, 181, 277
Hollywood Committee for the Arts, Sciences
    and Professions, 64
Hollywood Reporter, 102
Hollywood Ten, 72, 103, 104, 106, 108,
    109, 126–144, 166
Holt, Tim, 55
Homosexuality, 134, 138, 139, 234
Hopkins, Miriam, 264
Hopper, Hedda, 93
House of Strangers, The, 180, 186
House Un-American Activities Committee,
    93–103, 145, 146–147
Howard, John, 43

Howard, Trevor, 85, 87
Howe, James Wong, 64, 197, 210
Hudson, Rock, 211
Hughes, Howard, 95, 183–184, 257–260
Hunt, J. Roy, 90–91, 114, 197
Hunter, Tom, 277
Hurley, Harold, 44, 46, 50
Huston, John, 103, 277
Hyer, Martha, 261

IATSE, 94
If I Had a Million, 31
Ince, Thomas, 23

Jacobs, Mike, 101, 246
Jaffe, 254, 255
James, Harry C., 3
Jannings, Emil, 243
Jarrico, Paul, 81, 83
Johansson, Ingemar, 246
Johnson, Van, 173, 177, 178, 187–188, 189
Jones, Dickie, 42
Jones, Quincy, 269
Joseph of Cupertino, Saint, 248–249
Jubal Troop, 96
Judgment at Nuremburg, 223, 249
Juggler, The, 168–171
Jurado, Katy, 180–181, 184
Jurgens, Kurt, 243

Kaiser, Kay, 43
Kalmus, Herbert and Natalie, 197
Kaplan, Harry, 199
Karloff, Boris, 53, 195
Karp, Jack, 244
Kashfi, Anna, 202, 207, 229
Katya, 105, 107, 122
Katz, Charles, 95
Katz, Sam, 165
Kaufman, Millard, 208–209, 213–218
Kaye, Danny, 85, 97
Kazan, Elia, 227, 297
Keech, Judge, 127
Keeler, Ruby, 53
Kelley, DeForest, 209, 237
Kelly, Paul, 90
Kennedy, Arthur, 277
Kennedy, George, 268
Kenney, Robert, 95
Kerr, Deborah, 187, 188
Khan, Meboob, 242
Kid Galahad, 48

Kiley, Richard, 165, 166, 167
King, Henry, 43, 238
King, Lou, 43, 45–46, 50
King brothers, 148
Knopf, Eddie, 27–28
Knox, Alexander, 283, 284
Koerner, Charles, 58–59
Koestler, Arthur, 70
Kramer, Stanley, 148, 165–179 *passim,* 181, 223, 225
Kruger, Otto, 59

Ladd, Alan, 52, 256, 261
Lahr, Bert, 40
L'Amour, Louis, 280
Lancaster, Burt, 167
Landis, Carole, 49
Lane, Yancey, 42
Lang, Fritz, 243
Lang, Hope, 221
Lansbury, Angela, 148
Lardner, Ring, Jr., 100, 127, 145, 147
Larson, John, 238
Lasky, Jesse, 10
Laughton, Charles, 7–8, 24–26
Laurel and Hardy, 35, 37
Lavery, Emmet, 56
Lawson, John Howard, 71, 72, 99, 108, 126–127
LeBaron, Bill, 49
Left Hand of God, The, 195–197, 199
Lemmon, Jack, 266
Levene, Sam, 90
Levine, Joe, 257, 260, 261, 262
Lewis, David, 209, 217
Lewis, Jarma, 209
Lewis, Jerry, 249
Lewton, Val, 73
Lichtman, Al, 219
Life, 269
Lighting, 90, 114, 121–122
Lincoln Brigade, 64
Lisi, Verna, 290, 295
Lloyd, Euan, 280, 283
Lickridge, Ross, Jr., 208
Lok Wan Tho, 239
Lombard, Carole, 193
Lone Wolf films, 53
Lorentz, Pare, 54
Loring, Jane, 19
Love Affair, 38, 117
Love Is a Many-Splendored Thing, 238

Lovering, Otho, 27
Loy, Myrna, 16
Lubitsch, Ernst, 25
Luraschi, Luigi, 238
Lyles, A. C., 199, 202

M, 243
MacArthur, Charles, 69
MacArthur, Douglas, 65, 66, 266
McCarey, Leo, 24, 25, 31, 34–39, 117, 217
McCarey, Ray, 75
McCarey, Tom, 34
McCarthy, Kevin, 268
McDaniel, Hattie, 196
MacDonald, Joe, 185, 227, 229, 236
MacDougall, Randy, 199, 200
McGrath, J. Howard, 142
McGuire, Dorothy, 73, 75, 78
MacMurray, Fred, 173, 177, 178
Macomber, Elizabeth, 238
McPherson, Virginia, 102
Madison, Guy, 74–75, 77–78
Magnificent Ambersons, The, 62
Malone, Dorothy, 235–236
Maltz, Albert, 72, 108, 109, 147–148
  as prisoner, 127–143 *passim*
Maltz, Margaret, 141
Man About a Dog (Coppel), 110–113
Mander, Miles, 59
Mangano, Silvana, 275
Mann, Thomas, 103
Mannix, Eddie, 216–217
March, Frederick, 20
Margolis, Ben, 95
Marquand, Christian, 229
Marshall, E. G., 181, 184, 196, 197, 200, 205
Marshall, Herbert, 40, 41
Martin, Dean, 101, 102, 221, 223
Marushka, 111–112
Marvin, Lee, 167–168, 178, 209, 211
Mastroianni, Marcello, 282, 285
Matheson, Richard, 244
Matthau, Walter, 268–269
Mayer, Louis B., 96, 145
Mazurki, Mike, 56, 59
MCA, 101, 102
Melford, Frank, 7
Men, The, 225
Menjou, Adolphe, 93, 97, 165–166
Menzies, William Cameron, 64
Metty, Russ, 57, 114

MGM studio, 15, 75, 145, 148, 179, 186, 188, 189, 191, 208, 209, 210, 216, 217
Michaels, Dolores, 237
Milestone, Lewis, 64, 95, 96, 257–259
Million Dollar Legs, 44
Mill Point Prison Camp, 125, 131–143
Mills, John, 85, 87, 88, 188
Mirage, 267–269
Misfits, The, 191, 244
Mitchum, Robert, 60, 75–76, 85, 90, 276–279
Monroe, Marilyn, 57
Montalban, Ricardo, 250
Montevecchi, Liliane, 221
Montgomery, Robert, 60, 93
Moore, Joanne, 246
Moorehead, Agnes, 196, 197, 209
Mother Massetti's restaurant, 39, 65
Motion Picture Industry Council, 145
Mountain, The, 196, 198–207, 222, 232
Mountain Is Young, The, 238–242, 243–244
Movie industry. *See* Film industry
Muir, Florabelle, 4
Murder, My Sweet, 62, 89
Murnau, Franz, 62, 243
Murphy, George, 228
Murphy, Richard, 180, 186
Musmanno, Justice Michael, 282–283, 285
Mutiny, 148
Mystery Sea Raider, 49
Mystery Writers of America, 89

Naish, J. Carrol, 48
Name, Age, and Occupation, 54
Nathan, George Jean, 22
National Catholic Theater Conference Drama Award, 255
Negri, Pola, 8
Nelson, Ossie and Harriet, 53
Network, 273
Neuman, Kurt, 43, 50
Next Voice You Hear, The, 211
New Masses, The, 72
Newton, Robert, 113
Nichols, Dudley, 76
Nichols, George, Jr., 19, 28
Nichols, George, Sr., 19
Nixon, Richard M., 96, 99, 100

O'Brian, Hugh, 181
Obsession, 113–114, 116, 118

Ochs, Adolf, 8
O'Connor, Donald, 44
O'Curran, Charlie, 77
Odets, Clifford, 135, 136, 142, 245
Old Ironsides, 9
O'Neal, Charles (Blackie), 54
O'Neal, Patrick, 271, 272
Only Saps Work, 20
Orgasm, 262
Ornitz, Sam, 127
Oscar awards, 42, 148, 184, 186, 211, 223, 249
Othello, 118

Pacino, Al, 192
Padovani, Lea, 118, 122–123, 250
Page, Robert, 48
Painters' Union, 94
Paisan, 105
Panavision, 200, 213
Paramount Pictures studio, 37, 42, 44, 48, 52, 53, 69, 179
    Dmytryk as cutter at, 20, 25, 27, 29, 35, 40, 41
    Dmytryk as director at, 199, 207, 222, 231, 237, 243–245, 256, 257, 260, 263, 265
    early Hollywood and, 3, 5, 13–15
Paris–Presse Cup, 124
Parks, Larry, 95, 100, 146
Parsons, Louella, 40, 102
Pasadena Community Playhouse, 48, 49
Pasternak, Boris, 72
Patrick, Nigel, 209
Patterson, Floyd, 246
Paxton, John, 58, 70, 79, 89
Peck, Gregory, 267–269
Penn, John, 105, 106
People's Educational Center, 64
Peppard, George, 191, 192, 261
Peron, Evita, 71
Peter Pan, 8
Peters, Jean, 181, 183–184
Petracca, Joe, 248, 249
Phantom President, The, 31
Piaf, Edith, 83
Planer, Franz, 196–197, 199, 204, 259, 277
Pogany, Gabor, 291
Pomeroy, Roy, 8
Porter, Jean. *See* Dmytryk, Jean Porter
Powell, Dick, 59–62, 68, 71, 243

Powell, William, 16
Power, Tyrone, 270

Quinn, Anthony, 45, 47, 65, 66, 67, 235, 236

Rackin, Marty, 256–257, 260, 261, 264
RADA (Royal Academy of Dramatic Art), 123
Radford, Admiral, 173
Rainer, Louise, 116, 117–118
Raintree County, 101, 208–219
Randall, Tony, 101–102
Rank, J. Arthur, 79, 80–81, 86, 87, 113, 118–119, 124, 125, 144
Rathvon, N. Peter, 54, 89, 103, 119
Reagan, Ronald, 228
Reluctant Saint, The, 248–255, 275
Rennie, Michael, 190
Rich, Robert, 148
   See also Trumbo, Dalton
Richards, C. Pennington "Penny," 113, 114, 121–122, 250
Riis, Irving, 55, 79
Ritt, Marty, 275
Rivkin, Allen, 76
RKO, 19, 38, 54, 55, 58, 59, 69, 73, 79, 103, 165, 245
   "Mr. RKO," 88–93
Robb, Don, 238
Robbins, Harold, 257, 263
Robert, Stanley, 172, 173
Roberts, Theodore, 7
Roberts, Walter, 223
Robeson, Paul, 109
Robinson, Edward G., 180, 261
Rock, Patricia, 85
Rogers, Ginger, 56–57
Rome, Open City, 105
Roosevelt, Franklin D., 71
Rose, David, 187
Ross, Katherine, 260–261
Rossellini, Roberto, 105
Rossen, Robert, 126
Rota, Nina, 254
ROTC, 4
Rottuno, Giuseppe "Peppino," 277
Royal Family of Broadway, The, 20, 26, 31
Ruggles of Red Gap, 24–26, 34, 35
Runyon, Damon, 101
Rush, Barbara, 221
Ryan, Robert, 48, 54, 56, 90, 277

Sabin, Jack, 273
Sahai, Bagwan, 240
Saint, Eva Marie, 209, 211
Saint of the Satellites, The, 248
Salkind, Alexander, 287–290, 295
Salkind, Ilya, 287, 289
Salt to the Devil, 125
Santoni, Reni, 277
Saturday Evening Post, 146, 147
Schary, Dore, 73–76, 89, 90, 92, 97, 99, 103, 189, 208, 209, 211, 217, 218
Schell, Carl, 222
Schell, Maximilian, 222–223, 226, 228, 229–230, 249, 250
Schreiber, Lou, 237
Schubert, Karin, 290
Schulberg, B. P., 13, 37
Schulberg, Budd, 101, 246
Schwab brothers, 27
Scott, Adrian, 58, 59, 69–72, 79, 89, 92, 165
   Communism and, 70, 71–72, 93, 98, 100, 103, 127
Scott, Martha, 85–86
Selznick, David O., 73–76, 97, 207, 209
Seven Miles from Alcatraz, 54
Shalako, 280–281, 283–285
Shankar, Ravi, 240
Shaw, Irwin, 219, 220
Shaw, Lieutenant Commander, 174, 176, 177
Shea, Billy, 27
Sherman, Vincent, 264
Shirley, Anne, 59
Shore, Dinah, 253
Shurlock, 245
Siegel, Sol, 50, 179, 180, 186, 217, 218, 270
Silent movies, 3–10
Silver Spurs award, 186
Simon's cafeteria, 29
Since You Went Away, 74
Six of a Kind, 31
Skelley, Hal, 19
Skouras, Spyros, 189, 231
Slezak, Walter, 71
Sloan, John, 249, 250
Sniper, The, 165–166
Soldier of Fortune, 189–193, 273
Sorell, 94
So Well Remembered, 62, 79–88, 89
SPCA, 182–183
Spicer, Bart, 286
Stanwyck, Barbara, 246, 247

Stewart, Jimmy, 191
Stone, Leroy (Roy), 23, 27, 30–31, 34, 42
Stone, Peter, 267, 268
Stripling, 100
Strode, Woody, 283
Stuntmen, 182–183
Sturges, Preston, 259
Sunrise, 62, 243
Supreme Court, 98, 108, 125, 127
Surtees, Bob, 211
Sutherland, Edward, 16, 19
Sutton, John, 43
Suyin, Han, 238, 239
Sweetheart of the Campus, 54

Tamiroff, Akim, 250
Taradash, Dan, 272
Taurog, Norman, 31, 32
Taylor, Elizabeth, 209–218, 292–295
Taylor, Robert, 96
Taylor, Rod, 209
Taylor, Vaughn, 237
Teahouse of the August Moon, 226
Technicolor, 197
Television Spy, 45–46, 47
Temple, Shirley, 75
Ten Commandments, 7, 8
Tender Comrade, 56–58
They Dream of Home, 72–73
Thieman, K. E., 133–142 *passim*
This Gun for Hire, 53
Thomas, J. Parnell, 93, 96, 99, 100, 102, 147
Tierney, Gene, 196
Till the End of Time, 73–78
Time, 100
Todd, Mike, 218
Tolo, Marilu, 290
Toomey, Regis, 237
Townes, Harry, 200
Tracy, Spencer, 74, 179–185, 188, 189, 191, 193, 198–207, 223, 225, 266
Trevor, Claire, 59, 200
Trezona, Charlie, 59, 200
Troyat, Henri, 198
Truman, Harry S, 94, 169
Turnbull, Hector, 10–11, 13
Trumbo, Dalton, 56, 100, 108, 126, 127, 148
Tully, Tom, 261
20th Century–Fox, 74, 179, 184, 189, 200, 222, 229, 231, 242, 243

Tyler, Walter, 263

United Artists, 165
Universal studio, 55, 261, 265, 267

Van Eyck, Peter, 283, 284
Variety, 46, 48, 193, 230–231
Vendetta, 259
Villiers, Sir Edward, 80
Virginian, The, 266
VistaVision, 200, 213
von Sternberg, Joseph, 8, 18, 243
von Stroheim, Erich, 9, 19, 88

Wagner, Robert, 181, 182, 200, 204
Wagner Labor Relations Act, 42
Walk on the Wild Side, 244–247, 248
Walsh, Joey, 277
Walsh, Raoul, 7
Walters, Representative, 147
Wanamaker, Sam, 118–120, 122–123
Wanderer of the Wasteland, The, 9
Warlock, 231–237
Warner Brothers studio, 12, 27
Waterbury, Ruth, 255
Watts, Bill, 81–83
Wayne, John, 65–68, 93, 191, 254
Wayne, Naunton, 113
Weatherwax, Paul, 9
Wedding March, The, 9, 19
Weismuller, Johnny, 68
Welch, Raquel, 290, 291
Welles, Orson, 17, 30, 43, 54, 62, 118, 119, 165
Wellman, William "Wild Bill," 7, 14
West, Mae, 24
Weston, Jack, 268
Wexley, John, 70, 71–72
Where Love Has Gone, 263–265
White Tower, The, 81, 199
Widmark, Richard, 181, 182, 184, 223, 235–236, 271–273
Wilcoxon, Henry, 49
Wilde, Harry, 114
Wilder, Billy, 57
Wilding, Michael, 211, 218
Williams, Bill, 75, 84, 87, 88, 181
Willkie, Wendell, 94
Winchell, Walter, 137
Windsor, Duke of, 88
Windsor, Marie, 165
Wings, 14

Wood, Sam, 93
Woodcraft Rangers, 3
Wouk, Herman, 171–172
Wray, Fay, 9
Writers Guild, 73, 94, 246
Writers' Mobilization, 64
Wyler, William, 28, 78

Yordan, Philip, 186

Young, Freddie, 84
Young, Loretta, 260
Young, Robert, 90, 92
Young Lions, The, 101, 219–231, 233, 243

Zanuck, Darryl, 74, 179–180, 184–186,
   195, 196, 284
Zaza, 40–41, 43, 189
Zimbalist, 218